The Great Masters of Modern Painting

History of Art

Title-page illustration:

Henri Matisse
Cateau-Cambrésis (Nord) 1869-Nice 1951
The Rumanian Blouse, 1940
Oils on canvas 36″ × 28″
Musée National d'Art Moderne, Paris

Cover illustration:

Marc Chagall
Vitebsk 1887
To My Wife, 1933-1934
Oils on canvas 51″ × 76″
Musée National d'Art Moderne, Paris

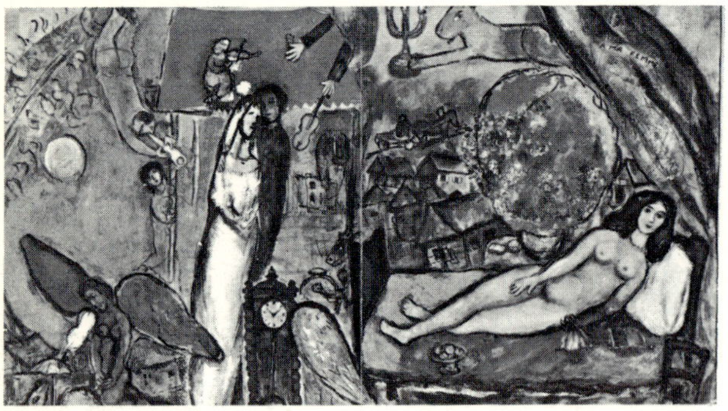

Impressionism
Post-Impressionism
The Renaissance I
The Renaissance II
The Renaissance III
The XVIIth Century I
The XVIIth Century II
The XVIIIth Century
Cubism
Romanticism
American Painting
Futurism and Dadaism
Gothic Painting I
Gothic Painting II
Romanesque Painting
Expressionism
Greek and Etruscan Painting
Surrealism
Egyptian Painting and the Ancient East
Great Masters of Modern Painting
Roman and Palaeochristian Painting
Abstract Painting
Prehistoric Painting
Byzantine and Russian Painting
Chinese Painting
Japanese Painting
Islamic and Indian Painting

The Great Masters of Modern Painting

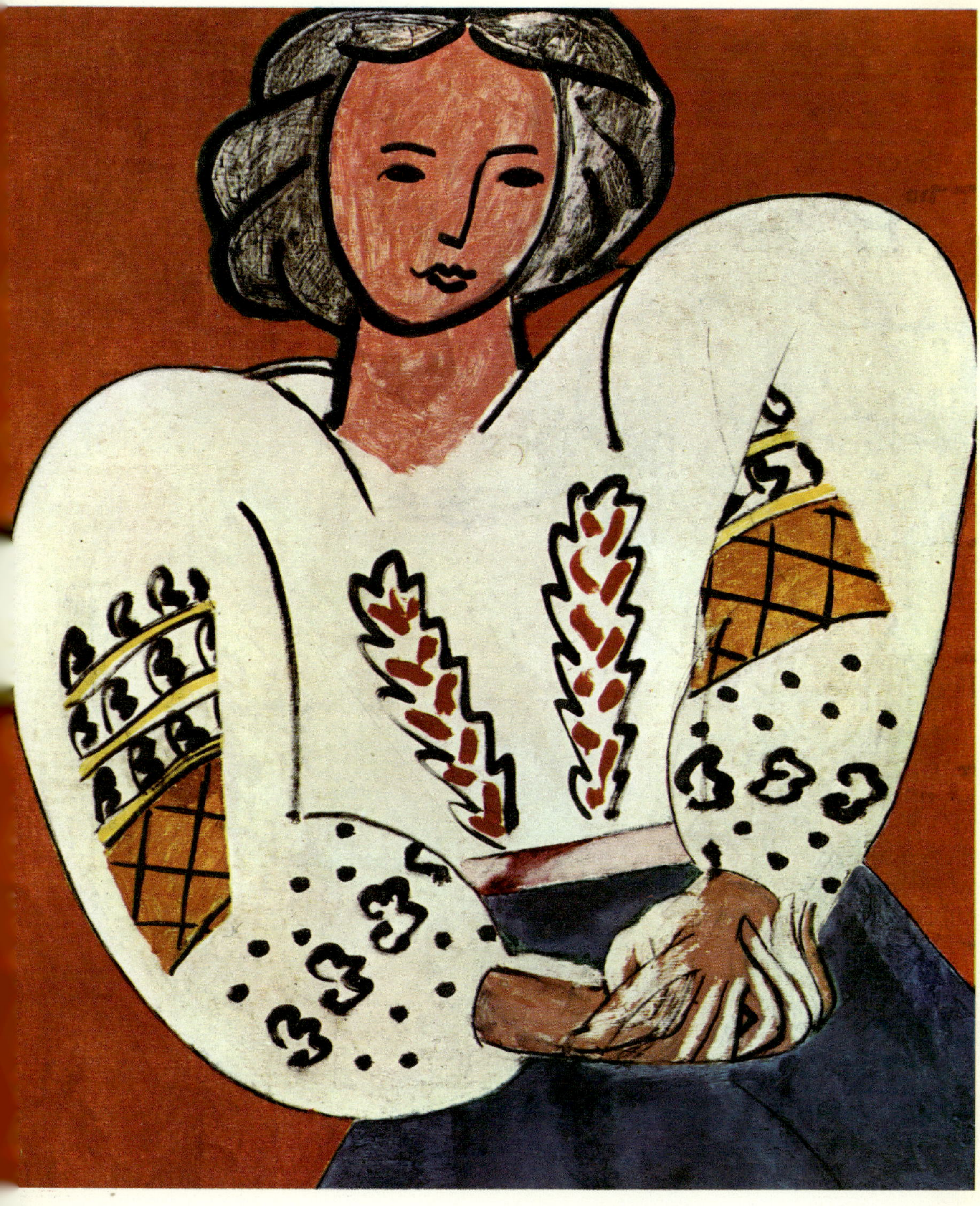

rges Charensol **Heron Books, London**

Series edited by Claude Schæffner
Artistic adviser: Jean-Clarence Lambert
Illustrations chosen by Hélène Schæffner
Assistant: Martine Caputo

Translated from the French
by Pamela Marwood

The colour illustrations in the first part were provided by:
André Held, Lausanne: Cover, pages 3, 6, 14, 15, 22 above, 23, 27, 28, 34, 35, 36, 37, 38-39, 43, 46, 51, 52, 65, 67, 68, 69, 71 above right, below left and right, 74 below, 75, 83 below, 84, 85, 87, 91 above, 93 and 94;
Giraudon, Paris: pages 10, 13, 25, 26, 33, 40, 44-45, 49, 50, 53, 55, 56, 57, 58, 61 above and below left, 62, 64, 71 above left, 72, 74 above, 76, 79, 80, 83 above, 88, 91 below and 92;
Garanger, Paris: pages 18, 21 and 61 below right;
Bayeler, Basle; pages 17 and 22 below.

The black-and-white illustrations in the Dictionary were provided by:
Giraudon, Paris: pages 150, 152 left, 153, 154, 156 right, 158, 160, 161, 162, 163, 164, 165, 166, 167, 168, 171, 172, 177, 178, 180, 181, 183, 186, 190, 192, 194, 195, 197 and 200;
Roger Viollet, Paris: pages 148, 152 right, 170, 173, 174 right, 184, 188, 189, 191, 196 and 198;
Harlingue-Viollet, Paris: pages 155 and 174 left;
Laure Albin-Guillot (Roger Viollet, Paris): page 156 left;
Cartier-Bresson (Magnum): page 169;
Desoye, Ed. Lanchere, Bourg-la-Reine: page 179.

Contents

7 Introduction

9 The Great Masters of Modern Painting

97 Evidence and Documents

107 Chronology

114 Museums

139 Principal Exhibitions

145 Dictionary

203 Bibliography

204 List of Illustrations

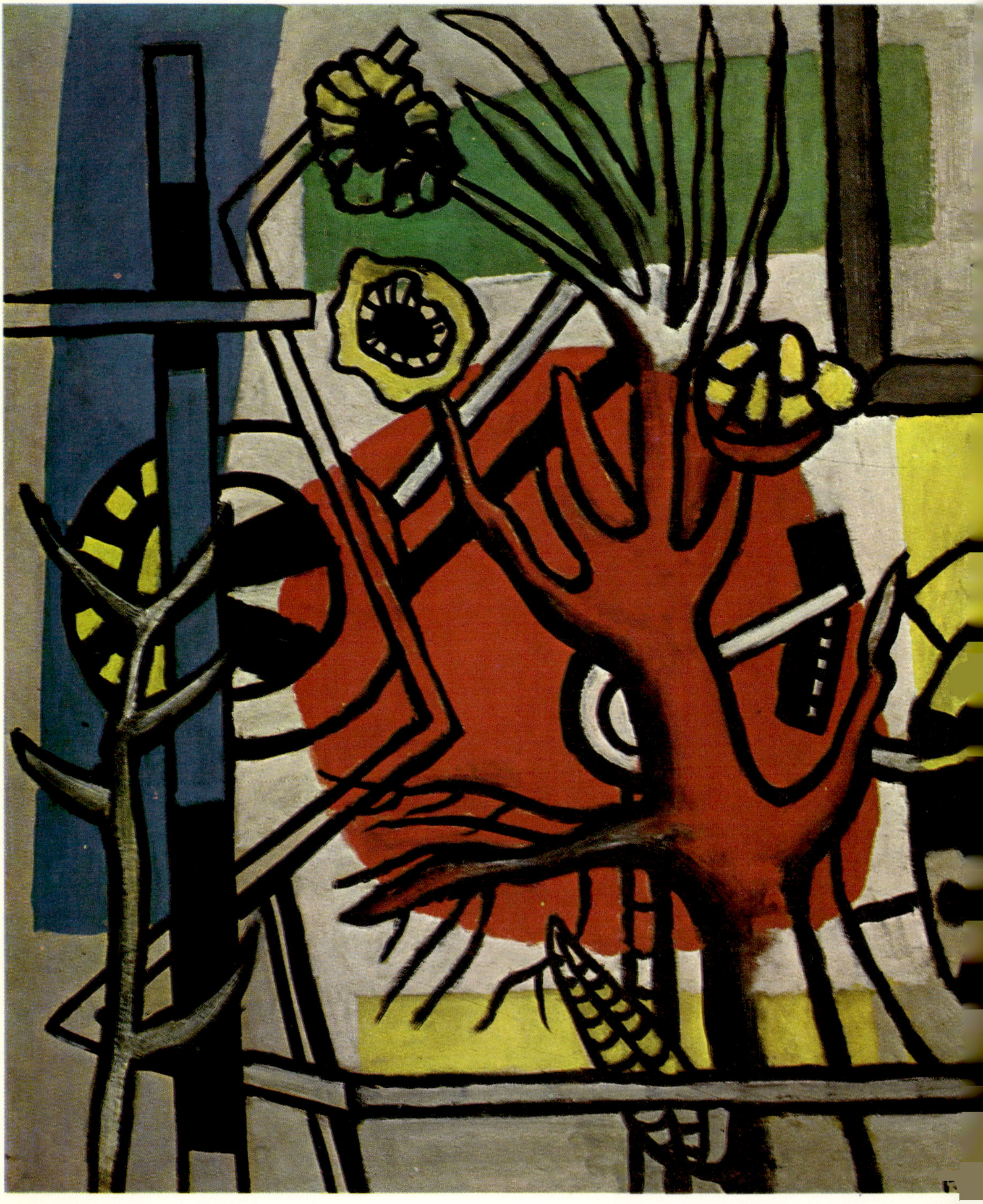

Fernand Léger
Argentan, Orne, 1881–Gif-sur-Yvette 1955
Tree against a Red Background, 1954
Oils on canvas 26″ × 21″
Sonia Henie Collection, Oslo

Introduction

It is often said that the great periods in art are those which attain unity of expression; and that this unity derives from a harmony between the various art forms: the musician, the poet, the architect, the painter and the playwright existing within one and the same movement of thought, and works of art in each category reflecting works in other fields. Examples thus relate collectively and individually to neighbouring disciplines, as they do to the people for whom they are intended.

Such an interrelationship is often held to be lacking in the painting of our own time—let us say, from the beginning of the 20th century; it tends to look as though the ties that unite painting with other means of artistic communication have become insignificant. The artist is reproached today with seeking originality at any price, of inventing for himself a vocabulary of which he alone knows the true meaning, and of evading all imitation, whether of nature or art: he now wishes to paint neither the face of the world nor the faces of people, and desires to be close neither to the old masters nor to artists who are his contemporaries.

We may be disturbed by the short-sightedness of such criticisms of present-day art. But we should also be grateful: nothing is more dangerous than general acquiescence, the consensus of praise which accompanies the careers of certain artists. And those who see in the art of the last fifty years nothing but disorder, wilful eclecticism, and a refusal to develop from traditional ideas, would be astonished if shown what discordances have been expressed by some of the painters whom they regard as being in line with unity of expression. . . .

Here, as elsewhere, in art criticism as in literary criticism, generations follow and resemble each other: within each one there are always some for whom truth and splendour are the prerogative of the dead; particularly the national dead, interred with the highest ceremonial. These individuals extol the struggle of the dead against destiny, heap anathema on those who failed to recognise the genius of their contemporaries; and, satisfied with thus having "defended" heroic art, the art of mixing colours, they turn back to the living. And to the living they turn a different face: contemporary painting and the plastic arts in general, they say, have not conquered minds and hearts; they have no place in the city except by gate-crashing, against the citizen's consent. . . .

Witness for the past, judge for the present: there is the paradox. Artistic judgement cannot claim to spring from eternal justice, inspired by immutable values. Criticism itself forms part of the history of art, and it furthers artistic creation by identifying new values. Besides, the best and most lucid art criticism (such as is practised by Georges Charensol) is essentially actual, modern*; it evolves within a moving present.*

At least, this is how the best of modern criticism manifests itself. It knows the museums, but does not wait for an art gallery to become a museum before making its pick, latching on to something just beginning, something which is going to exist for the future. The true critic is the true contemporary, who looks with hope and for whom everything is new. "As for criticism as such," wrote Baudelaire just over a hundred years ago, "I hope the philosophers will understand what I am trying to say: that criticism, if it is to be fair and justify its existence, must be partial, impassioned, political—that is to say, formed from a point of view which is exclusive, but a point of view which also reveals the widest horizon."

And Zola: "When the masses do not understand, they laugh. A complete education is necessary before it is possible to accept genius."

Art criticism which gets genius accepted can become confusingly involved with the battle for art. But there is no such thing as Art per se*—contrary to a woolly conviction which is at the basis of many judgements. There is only actual, material art. And for every critic art will mean something different.*

It is only through the art of the present that we are able to understand the art of the past. That which is no more can be understood only in terms of that which is. The present is father to the past, and criticism to the history of art (Bernard Groethuysen).

Can anything be added to these laws of artistic understanding? When Georges Charensol quotes Guillaume Apollinaire, Blaise Cendrars, Mac Orlan, Max Jacob and several other important writers in his descriptions of Picasso, Léger, Van Dongen, Modigliani, Utrillo and Derain, he is naming that fraternity which allows the reader to enter the painters' world, not by a side-track, but by a parallel path. Things connected by time, common experiences, and the same struggle cannot be separated. Reality*—which people accuse artists of having rejected (the accusation dates from the mid-19th century, but continues to be popular)—is experienced in a disjointed, piecemeal, and immediate fashion as much by poets and novelists as by painters.*

Writers, however, have words which hardly change, even if they can be rearranged. The vocabulary of modern painting on the other hand is accessible only through a general effort of understanding. Today's painting is collectively and individually related, like that of all the great periods; related to problems and to agonies, to the experiences of ordinary living people. The latter must either learn to look *at writers at the same time as they look at painters, or else give up trying to know the truth about their times. Everything in art which spans the centuries possesses a significance, everything speaks of man, his passions, his dreams, his deaths, his renewals. Art is also a story, the most profoundly expressive there has ever been. What man dreams is his portrait, Hegel said. What man desires is his art. But it is not necessarily true that those who desire are contemporary with the art of their time. . . .*

Gilbert Sigaux

At the root of all creative work there is a subtle interplay between the artist and his time. The stronger his personality, the less he feels the influence of the period and the more he himself affects his own times. Without Cézanne or Picasso, our world would not be the same. For this reason, while not denying the importance of movements or neglecting groups or schools, the history of art is essentially a record of individual achievements. When no master stands out, movement in the arts is merely anarchy and disorganised experiment.

Trying to select a few strong personalities from contemporary art presents a major difficulty: time has not yet made its choice between artists who, seen close to, appear to be of equal stature. One must therefore fall back on personal taste, not evading the fact that all choice involves an arbitrary factor.

We are well aware of the criticisms which might be levelled at this work, its selectivity for one thing. It may also be reproached for missing out Les Nabis*; but these were heirs to movements that belonged in the last century, whereas Matisse, though contemporary with Bonnard and Vuillard, points the way for Fauvism*; the first great liberating force of our own century's art.

The 20th century is so rich in material that we have had to leave out certain important personalities if we were not to reduce the texts devoted to those we have concentrated on to mere notes. This has led, for example, to a choice of Derain rather than Vlaminck, Léger rather than La Fresnaye, Dufy rather than Segonzac, Matisse rather than Marquet and Jacques Villon rather than Juan Gris.

The absence of certain pioneers of French Abstract Art, particularly Delaunay, is no more justifiable.

We can only plead guilty to these omissions.

The Series Editor

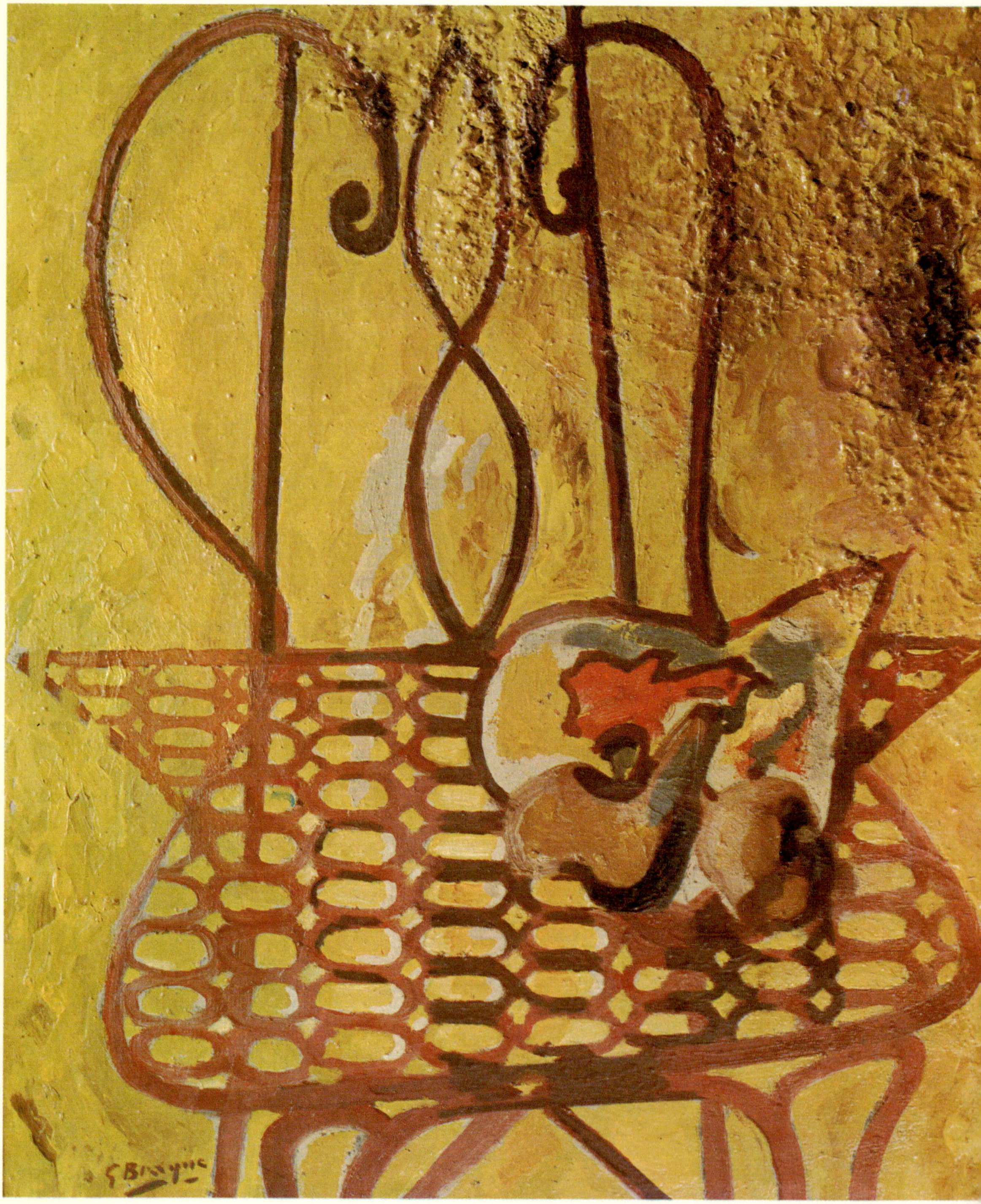

Georges Braque
Argenteuil 1882-Paris 1963
The Chair, 1948
Oils on canvas 24″ × 20″
Musée National d'Art Moderne, Paris

Matisse

Henri Matisse heralds the painters of the generation which came after him, whilst he himself belongs to that of Bonnard and Vuillard. Two years older than Georges Rouault, whom he knew in the studio of Gustave Moreau*, he was born on 31 December 1869, in his grandfather's house in the rue du Chêne-Arnaud, Le Cateau, in the Cambrésis region. His father was a seedsman in Bohain, and it was in this little town that he spent his childhood.

At the age of twelve, he entered the Lycée at Saint-Quentin, the birthplace of Quentin de la Tour. But it was a far cry to this serious boy from the portraitist of fragile 18th-century beauties.

He was an excellent pupil, and in 1887 he went to study at the Faculty of Law in Paris, passed his first examination to allow him to practise law, and then entered the office of Maître Théophile Duconseil, attorney at Saint-Quentin, as a clerk. He stayed there four years, apparently content with his lot and the prospect of becoming an attorney himself one day; since his family was well-to-do, he could hope that his father would eventually buy him a practice. In many ways he was obviously different from the rebels who, both before and after him, constitute the majority of those who create "living art". In later life, bearded, very dignified, looking thoughtful behind his spectacles, he could have been mistaken for a provincial schoolmaster.

He affords an example, quite rare among painters, of a late vocation. Admittedly Paul Cézanne planned to become a banker, but that was in obedience to his father. No such pressures were involved with Matisse, who calmly accepted the future offered to him.

However, he fell ill and went to convalesce with one of his uncles. He became bored, and chanced to read a treatise on painting. To fill in the time he decided, with characteristic application, to put into practice the technique he found described. When he returned to Saint-Quentin, he went to the Museum and, on Sundays, amused himself by daubing a few little landscapes. He came to enjoy this occupation, and enrolled at the art school founded by La Tour in his native town. There again, the dominant trait in his character showed itself: in fact, although it was still only a hobby for him, he assiduously got up at the crack of dawn and from 7 to 8 a.m., before the attorney's office opened, studied with a M. Croisé, pupil of the very academic Bonnat.

As he progressed, and became familiar with the masters represented in the museums at Arras, Cambrai and Lille, he warmed to the art whose secrets he was slowly discovering. It may seem surprising that he did not at this stage go to try his luck in Paris, especially since his father, probably because he saw the experiment as futureless, raised little objection. The reason lay in the boy's pride and inability to face a failure. His state of mind in 1892 when he finally prepared to leave for Paris was revealed in a message he sent when Le Cateau-Cambrésis inaugurated a Matisse Museum in November 1952: "Despite the certainty," he said, "that I was doing the right thing, I was seized with fright, because I knew I could not go back. So I buried my head in the

An asterisk placed after a word refers to the dictionary at the end of the book, where the word is the subject of an article or reference.

Henri Matisse
Luxe, Calme et Volupté, 1904
Oils on canvas 83″ × 55″
Private collection, Paris

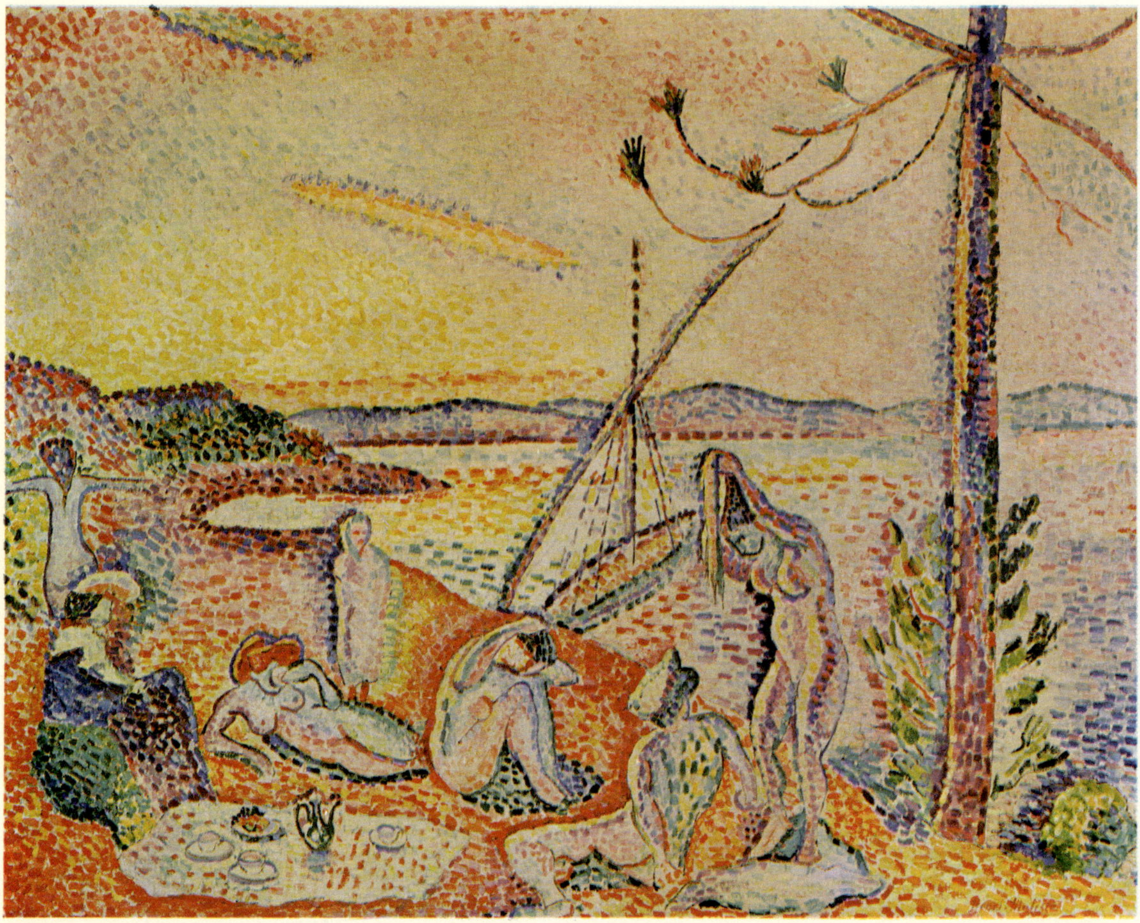

work." These early days foreshadowed the pattern of Matisse's entire life: invariably, having pondered, he bent his will and set his mind. . . .

Armed with a letter of recommendation to Bouguereau, the academician, he presented himself at the Académie Julian *, where Bouguereau was teaching. Chance was on his side since this academy had already seen the birth of an *avant-garde* movement founded on Gauguin's principles, namely Les Nabis. In fact Sérusier, the master of the group, was no longer "massier" (student in charge of the funds) at the Julian, and Bonnard, Vuillard and Maurice Denis had already deserted the old house. But their passage had left deep traces. Besides, Matisse, in his eagerness to learn, enrolled at the same time with another school, the Ecole des Arts Décoratifs, where he formed a lifelong friendship with Albert Marquet.

From there the two friends went on to the Ecole Nationale des Beaux-Arts and entered the studio of Gustave Moreau. It is impossible to overstress what an excellent teacher Moreau was. While not all the hundreds of pupils who received his instruction

Henri Matisse
Interior with Aubergines
Oils on canvas
Grenoble Museum

became masters, that Matisse, Rouault, Desvallières, Camoin *, Manguin *, and Guérin should have been in his studio at the same time testifies to the liberalism of an instructor who, not content with merely teaching these young men techniques, was primarily concerned to open their minds and help them to sort out their own personalities.

Perhaps Matisse may have been wrong to have taken so literally one of his more debatable precepts: "In art, the more basic the method, the more evident the sensitivity." It none the less follows that he owed much to Gustave Moreau, who told his father, when he came to ask whether his son was making a mistake, "I am not at all worried, he is one of my best pupils."

This judgement is amply substantiated by a still-life dated 1895, which, although showing none of the originality Matisse manifested later, has a rare solidity and sobriety. His copy of Raphael's *Baldessare Castiglione* displays the same serious

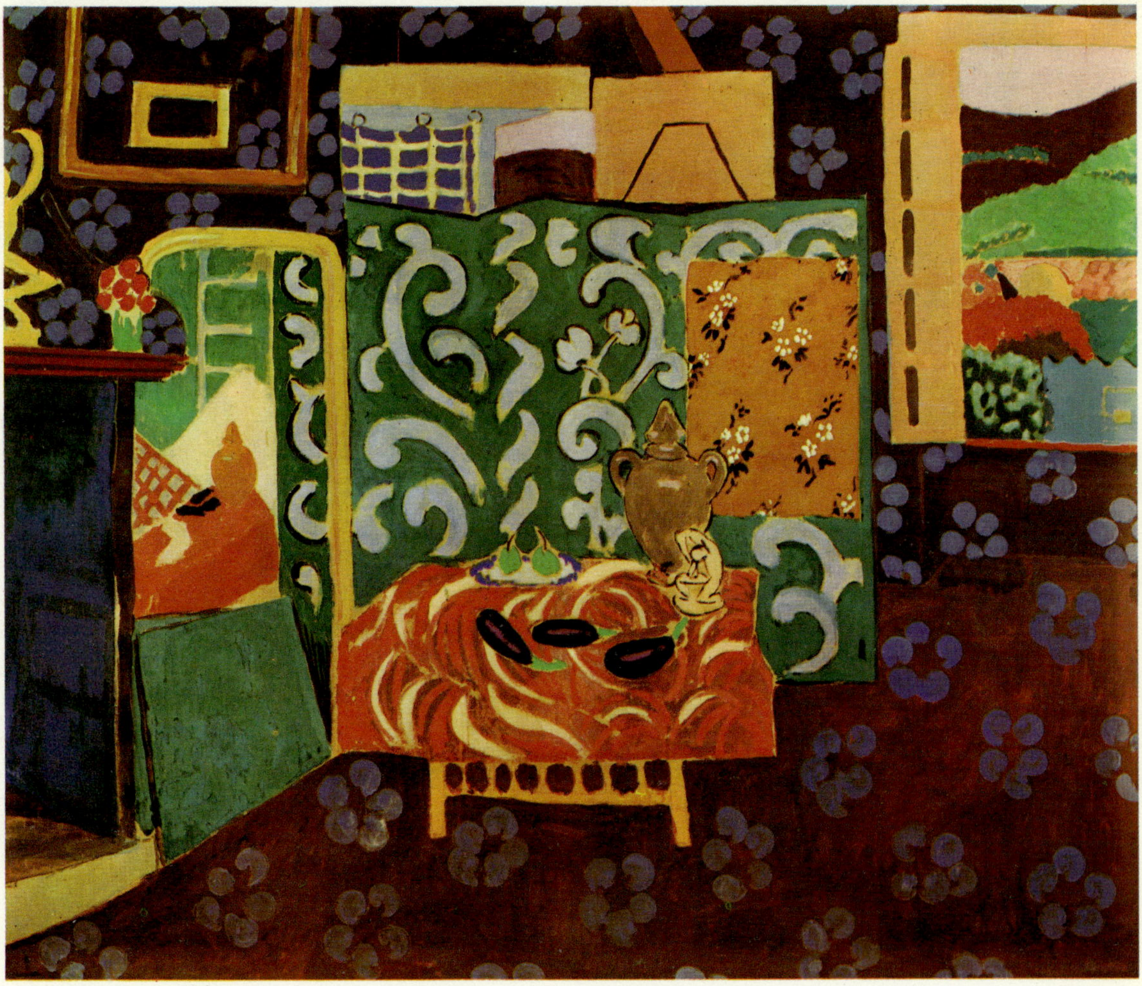

Henri Matisse
Woman Reading against a Black Background, 1939
Oils on canvas 36″ × 29″
Musée National d'Art Moderne, Paris

Henri Matisse
Odalisque with Blue Armchair, 1925
Oils on canvas 19″ × 15″
Bayeler Gallery, Basle

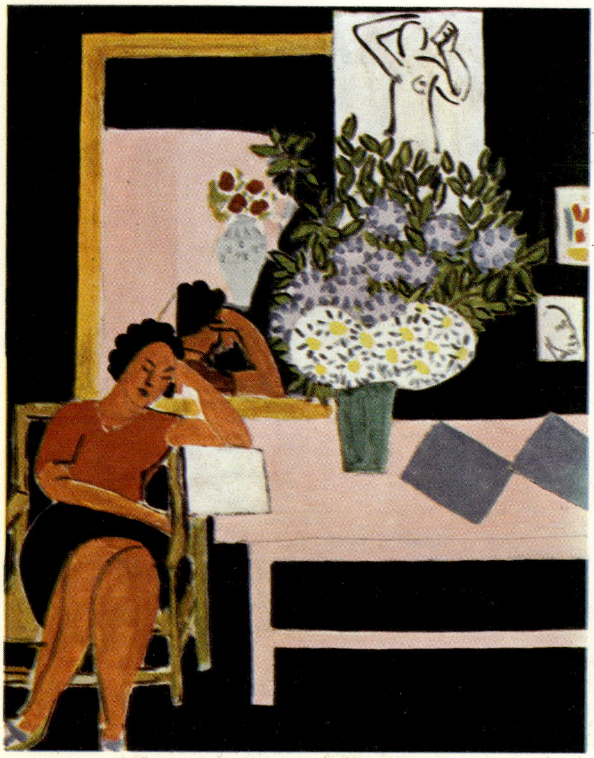

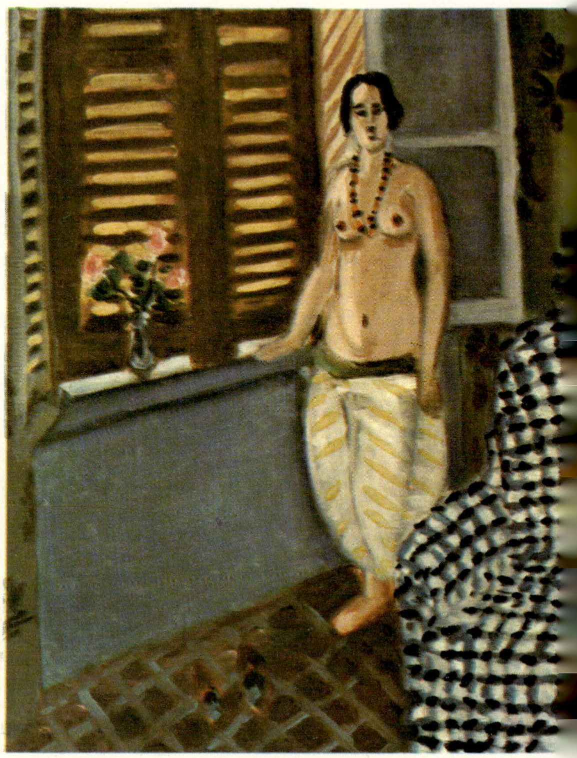

qualities. He worked daily in the Louvre and made many copies of Poussin, Philippe de Champaigne and Chardin. As an artist who later deliberately sacrificed form for colour, it is interesting that he gravitated towards the most solid masters. Nineteen of these copies are known, including Chardin's *Ray*, now in the Le Cateau Museum, which was bought by the State for the considerable sum of 1,000 gold francs.

"I spent my days in the museum and, on my walks afterwards, I recognised certain delights comparable to those I had felt in painting. I studied masters just as, in literature, one studies authors before choosing one or another," he said in some notes published by M. Raymond Escholier*.

At the end of one rather long life class at the studio, Marquet led him away saying, "Let's get away. Let's go and draw buses." Gustave Moreau saw nothing incongruous in that, for he advised his pupils not to be satisfied with going to the museum, but to go down the street as well. The two young men accordingly amassed sketches, sometimes in Paris, sometimes from the windows of the studio at 19 quai Saint-Michel which was inhabited for a long time by them both.

At this period, his art remained very traditional and it was only at the insistence of John Russel, Van Gogh's friend, and the painter Wéry whom he met in Brittany, that he started to take an interest in the Impressionists. After that he rapidly became familiar

Henri Matisse
Corn Poppies, 1953
Gouache cut out and pasted 32″ × 135″
Matisse Family

with all that they had contributed, and bought a little Cézanne from Ambroise Vollard.

This revelation coincided for him with that of Southern Europe. Coming from the North, he had never seen the Mediterranean until 1898, when he made his first visit to Corsica. He was so captivated that he settled in Nice for the last thirty-seven years of his life.

From his early journeys in the Midi he brought back Impressionist landscapes, and several years elapsed before he took a new step, this time towards Divisionism*. At Collioure in 1905, he painted his two versions of *Luxe, Calme et Volupté*, one now in the Musée d'Art Moderne, Paris, the other in Copenhagen Museum. One of these great compositions used to belong to Paul Signac, the theorist of Neo-Impressionism, who had converted Matisse to Seurat's ideas while he was staying with him in Saint-Tropez.

He had already discovered the virtues of pure colour in the *Blue Standing Nude* and *Carmelina*, but these were experiments he kept to himself: he was thirty-five and still seemed totally undecided. Born, as he was, into a bourgeois setting, trained by academic painters, and having visited the Louvre daily, he very naturally hesitated before joining the movements which were then brewing in Montmartre and Montparnasse. It is hard to see a clear way along the irregular course of Matisse's development at that time—all the more so since he did not concentrate solely on painting but also on sculpture, and attended evening classes for modelling in the rue Etienne-Marcel, in a Ville de Paris School.

His doubts were such, and his material existence so difficult, that he considered becoming a drawing teacher or a printer. In 1900, to earn a little money, he worked with Marquet on the decoration of the Grand-Palais. However, he broke with academic circles, and exhibited for the last time at the Salon de la Nationale in 1899; he left the Ecole des Beaux-Arts for Carrière's Studio, where he came to know Derain and went painting with him to Collioure.

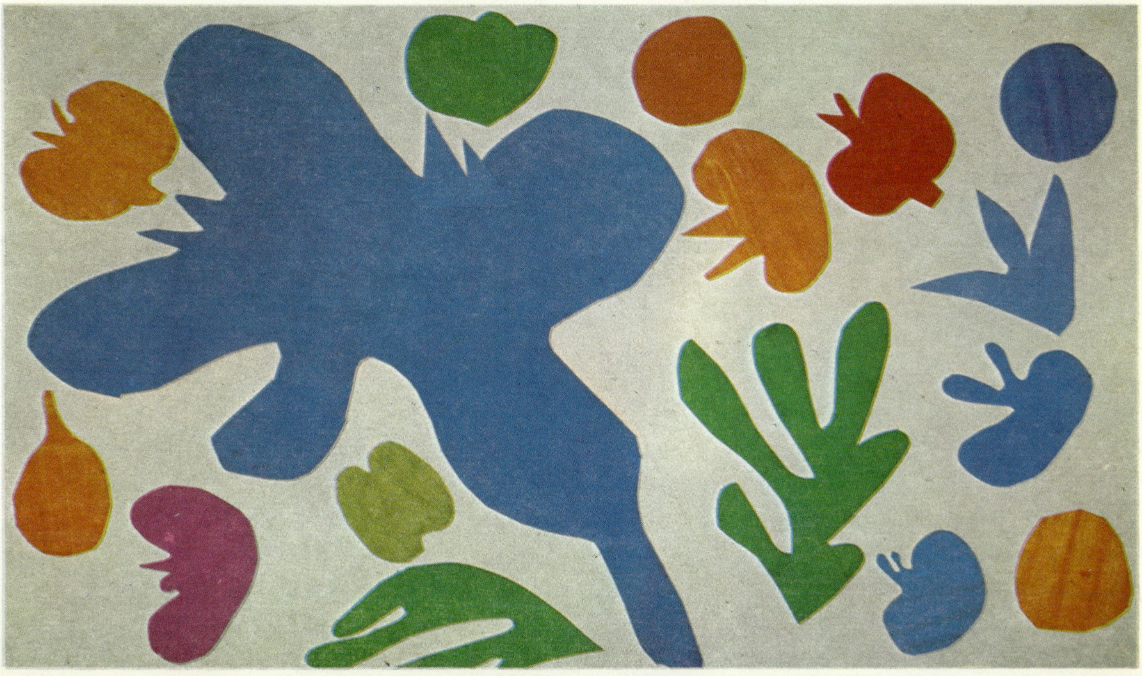

Georges Rouault
Paris 1871-1958
Clown, 1904
Oils on paper 29″ × 18″
Bayeler Gallery, Basle

After he had exhibited in independent salons, admirers occasionally approached him. He began to accept the publicity, which both pleased and worried him. From his window he painted views of Notre-Dame in pure colours and exhibited in the *cage aux fauves* (" wild beasts' cage ") in the 1905 Salon d'Automne. The *Woman in a Hat* was strongly reminiscent of some experiments attempted by Derain when they worked side by side in the little port of Roussillon, which is one of the main centres of modern painting, for, after the Fauves, the Cubists* also went to Collioure to make their mark.

The years of apprenticeship had come to an end. Matisse had assimilated the important experiences recently offered to young painters by the retrospective exhibitions of Cézanne, Gauguin, Seurat and Van Gogh. He had worked out a personal style, expressed in *The Joy of Life* in the Barnes Collection. In his vivacious colouring and supple line he was opposed to the Cubists, who were then coming to prominence; these manifested little sympathy with him, although Matisse did not remain indifferent to their concern for " constructivism ", as his great schematic compositions, *The Moroccans* and *The Piano Lesson*, witness.

There is, however, no doubt that from 1906 onwards he was essentially interested in the coloured line, as expressed in *The Dance* and *The Concert*, acquired by the Russian collector Shchukin and now to be seen in the Pushkin Museum in Moscow; he used a light texture, colours that were both fluid and bright, and chose very simple subjects. Although a Northerner, he became a great lyricist as soon as he had a brush in his hand. Elegant nudes, women in interiors, still-lifes, windows open on to the Mediterranean were all opportunities to express his delight in painting. His brush caressed the flesh of the women he painted with a delicacy quite different from the sensuality of Renoir or Van Dongen.

From 1919, Matisse was at last in control of the firm technique he had succeeded in working out through numerous experiments and innumerable influences. During the next ten years a series of masterpieces appeared, including *Slave-girl in Red Culottes*, which confirmed their creator as one of the masters of French art.

Many of these pictures were painted at Nice, where he lived from 1917 until his death on 4 November 1954, at first in various hotels, then in the old Senate Palace, lastly at the Regina. Not far from his last residence, and from the Cimiez cemetery where he is buried, a very important collection of his work has been assembled in the villa of Les Arènes, comprising about twenty canvases, about a hundred drawings, engravings and gouaches, the plans for the Dominican chapel he carried out between 1947 and 1950 at Vence, and also certain personal objects which can be recognised in his compositions.

His life on the Côte d'Azur was punctuated by numerous visits to Italy, Spain and North Africa; his last journey, to Tahiti, enabled him to go round the world.

His prestige was immense, and his influence no less. In 1907 he had opened an academy to which numerous foreign artists, mostly Northerners, thronged, who were to disseminate his teaching throughout the world. He held an exhibition in Moscow in 1907 and one in New York in 1913. In response to the innumerable invitations he

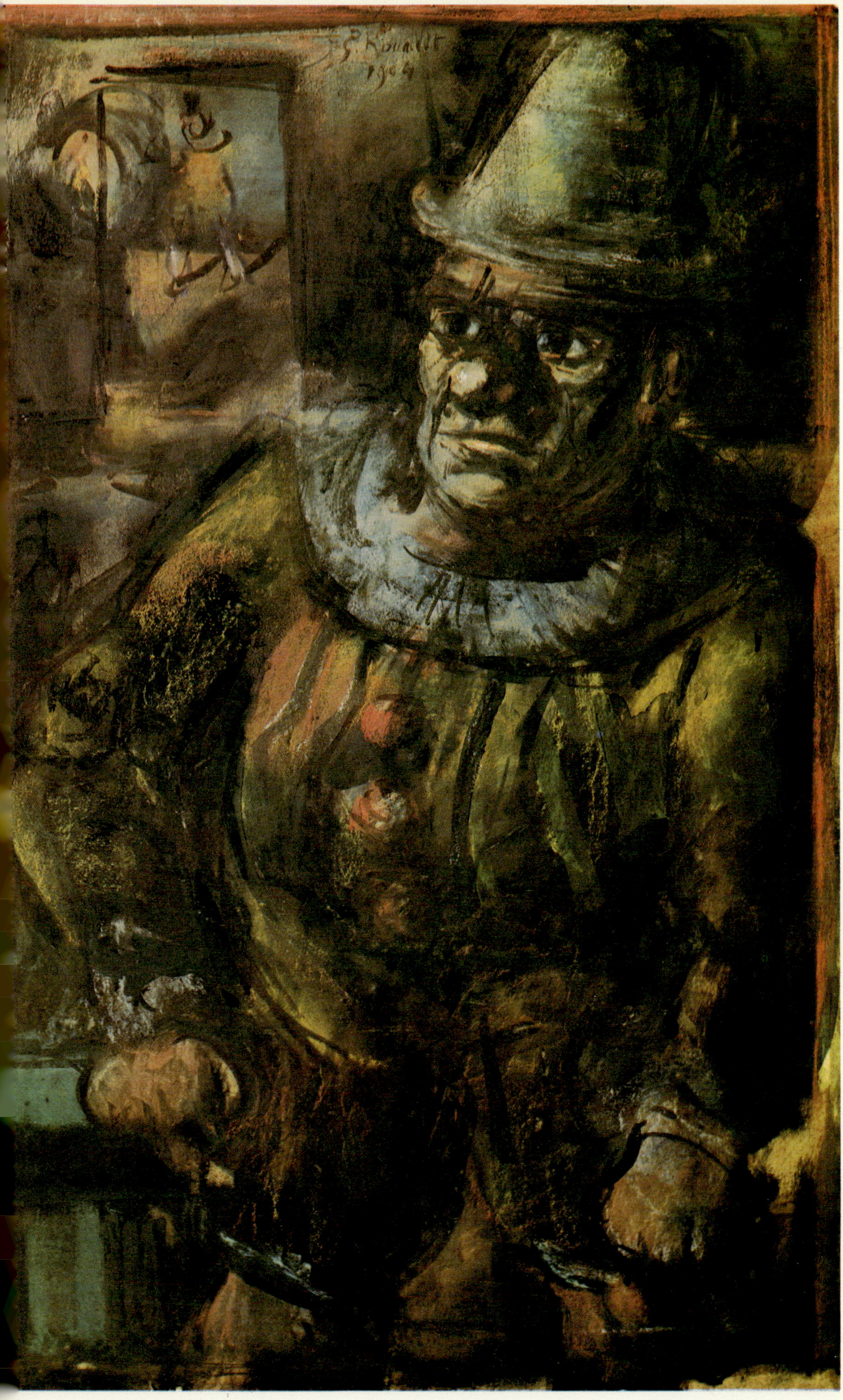

Georges Rouault
At the Mirror, 1906
Water-colour on hardboard 28″ × 21″
Musée National d'Art Moderne, Paris

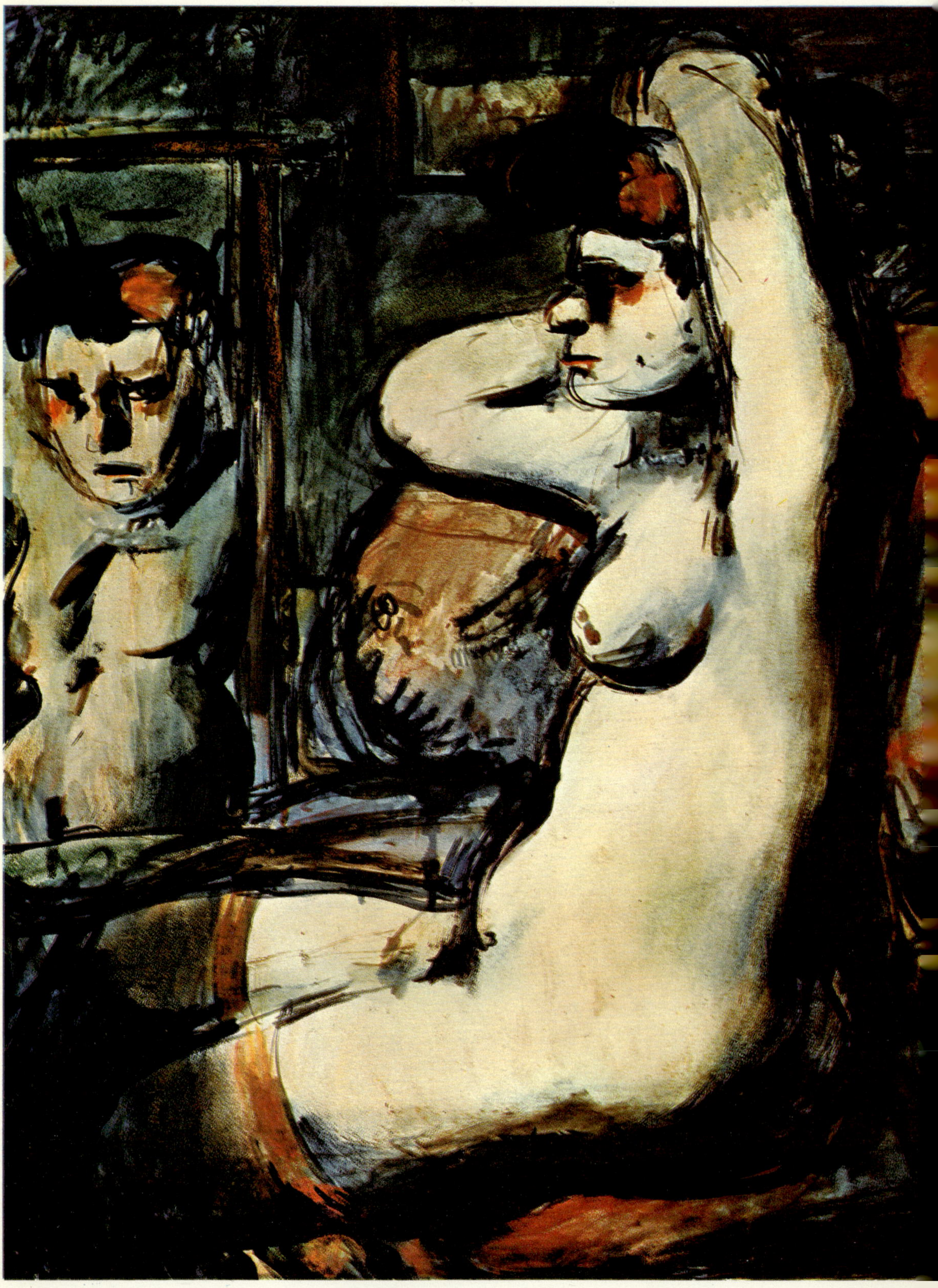

received, he sketched décors for the Ballets Russes*, illustrated books, and took an interest in tapestry, ceramics and stained glass.

His creativity was brutally interrupted in 1941 by illness, and he never got over the serious operation he underwent at Lyons during the war. Unable to leave his bed, he drew without pause, and his line was firmer than ever. But, being such a whole-hearted lover of colour, he suffered from not being able to paint. Returning to a process he had once used for the first version of *The Dance* (Ville de Paris Museum), he substituted for the subtle strokes he had once been able to apply to canvas, papers brightly coated with gouache which he cut up on his bed. All his life he had resisted the lure of decoration, but now he yielded to it with a joy which illumined his last years.

Rouault

The striking thing about Rouault is the strange contradiction between his shy character and middle-class way of life, and his work, which is full of mysticism and revolt. Perhaps he put into his painting all that he regretted not being in life, which was uncompromising but peaceable, while his work is as poignant a cry as any from Daumier or Goya. He cannot be said to have been a revolutionary spirit. While he took a pessimistic view of the world he lived in, he expected everything from the next; profoundly religious, he never doubted the infinite mercy of the Creator, to whom he prayed every day.

Born into modest circumstances, he believed in the value of tradition, and at the Ecole des Beaux-Arts he wisely enrolled in the studio of Delaunay*. Competing for the Prix de Rome, and holding his first exhibition at the Salon des Artistes Français, he seemed set for the smoothest of academic careers. The incomprehension of the painting "establishment", and not his own wishes, threw Rouault on to the side of the Fauves, and it was to the Indépendants, for the Salon d'Automne*, that he sent the canvases rejected by those members of the Institute he would have liked to respect and admire.

Rouault's crisis was played out between 1898, the year of the death of Gustave Moreau, who until then had encouraged, helped and sustained him, and 1903, when he finally accepted his fate as a great solitary pursuing his work on the fringe of contemporary movements, entirely absorbed in transferring his inner drama on to canvas.

It is only necessary to consider the subjects he treated during these five years to measure his terrible mental confusion. All the rejects of society, he gathered and magnified. Monsters, prostitutes and clowns—far from condemning them he felt drawn towards them, as, standing on the edge of a gulf, one is drawn to throw oneself down. Rouault's blank silence when these years were mentioned to him was no less eloquent than the works themselves, and no one can ever know the depths of the crisis he went through.

He assured me that he did not know the shady places; his most terrible evocations of prowling women he painted back at home in Versailles after skirting an

Georges Rouault
The Holy Face, 1933
Oils on canvas 36″ × 26″
Musée National d'Art Moderne, Paris

ill-famed street: a shadow perceived, a vague silhouette, an uncertain light were sufficient to rouse within him a world of sensations he could only rid himself of by putting them on canvas. Far from being a realist, Rouault was a visionary. He dreamed of resembling, of mixing with the people whose violent nudity he painted: "Folk to-the-manner-born on every street . . . you who, in winter, travel quietly towards the sun, the green meadow in spring, or to the ocean sea, I have always envied you, attached to the pictorial soil as the peasant is to his field. . . ."

Unaware, perhaps, of the evident rapport between his art and his life, he never liked to talk about himself. When he did so, it was in the form of parables, in writing of unusual style, or in his memoirs about his friends Gustave Moreau, J.-K. Huysmans* and Léon Bloy*.

He was born in Belleville, in a cellar, on 27 May 1871, while the guns of Versailles were wiping out the last survivors of the Commune. The tragic circumstances of this birth made a deep mark on him. A puny child, he learned the craft of painter-glazier, and his employer set him to work on the restoration of the windows in Saint-Séverin. At the end of his life he returned to stained glass, being always attracted by artisans' techniques: ceramics, enamel, tapestry and engraving.

The outlines which frame his shapes, the violent impact of colours contrasting with the black underlining and reinforcing them, evoke the methods used by Romanesque and Gothic glaziers; but he was inspired far more by their spirit than by their technique.

His early years not only afforded him the chance to learn an admirable trade, but brought him into contact with the common people of Paris, and this familiarity with the realities of life was to be his salvation when he found himself thrust into an academic milieu.

He had the luck to enter the Ecole des Beaux-Arts just when Gustave Moreau took over from Elie Delaunay, and, in his studio, he encountered Matisse, Marquet and Desvallières. He prepared for the entry competition by attending evening classes at the Ecole des Arts Décoratifs, and his technique was firm enough to win him the Prix Chenevard in 1894 for his *Jesus Among the Doctors*.

His works of that period were academic only in appearance: the Prix de Rome jury knew what they were about when they stubbornly refused Rouault the entry to the Villa Medici which might perhaps have changed his life. In *Samson Turning the Mill*, in particular, there are some superb and remarkable sections, which promised that he would soon break free from scholarly restraint. Gustave Moreau in helping him said: "I am the bridge over which you will pass."

His master's death in 1898 was, for Rouault, a tragedy which, even at the end of his life, he still spoke of with terror. His mother having had to go back to Algeria, all his emotional ties were cut simultaneously, and for a time he thought of entering the priesthood. He even seems to have stopped painting, abandoning himself to grief. The few landscapes we have from that period are as black as those which Van Gogh painted in Holland when he, too, was going through a terrible period of mental crisis.

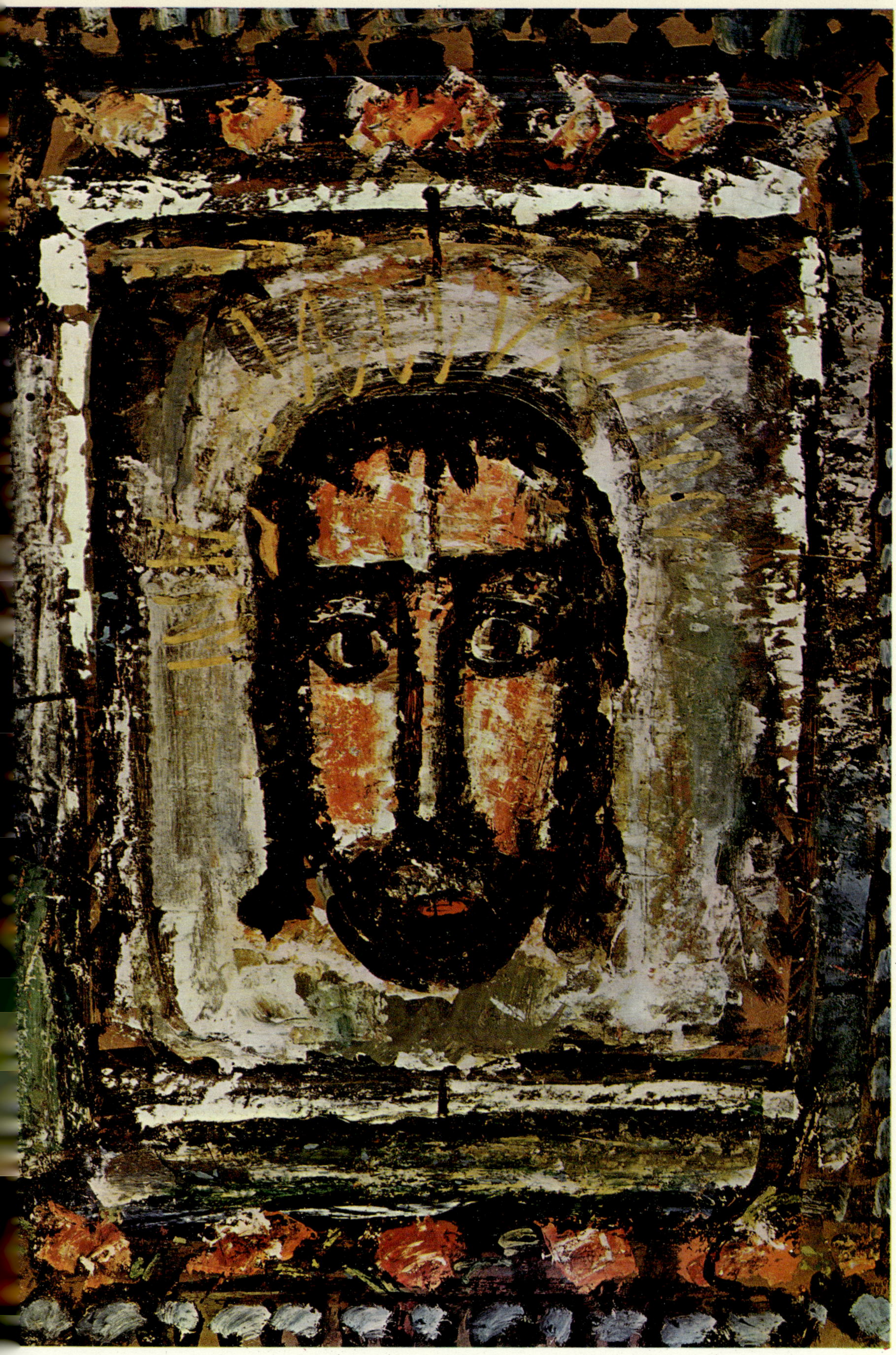

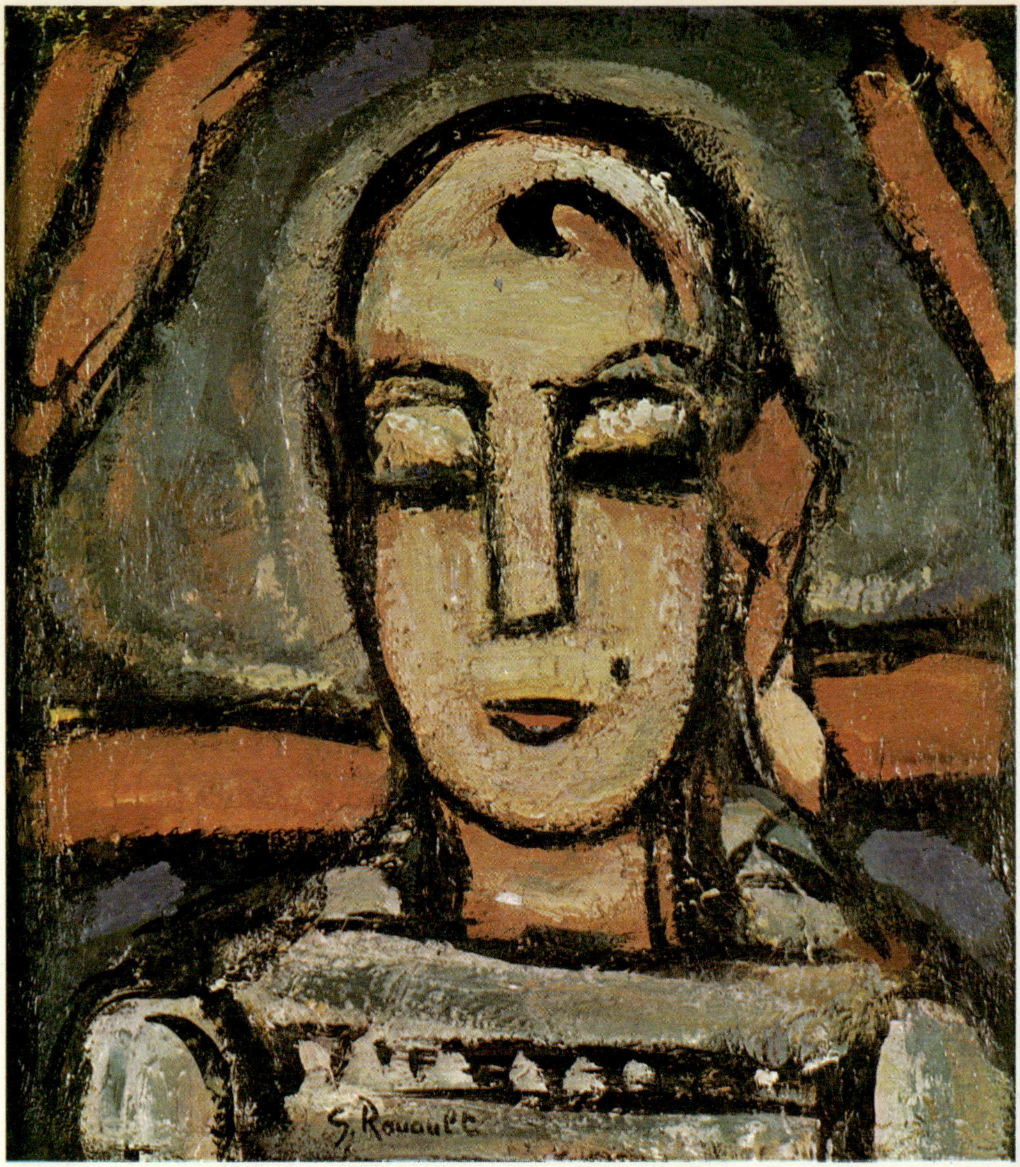
G. Rouault

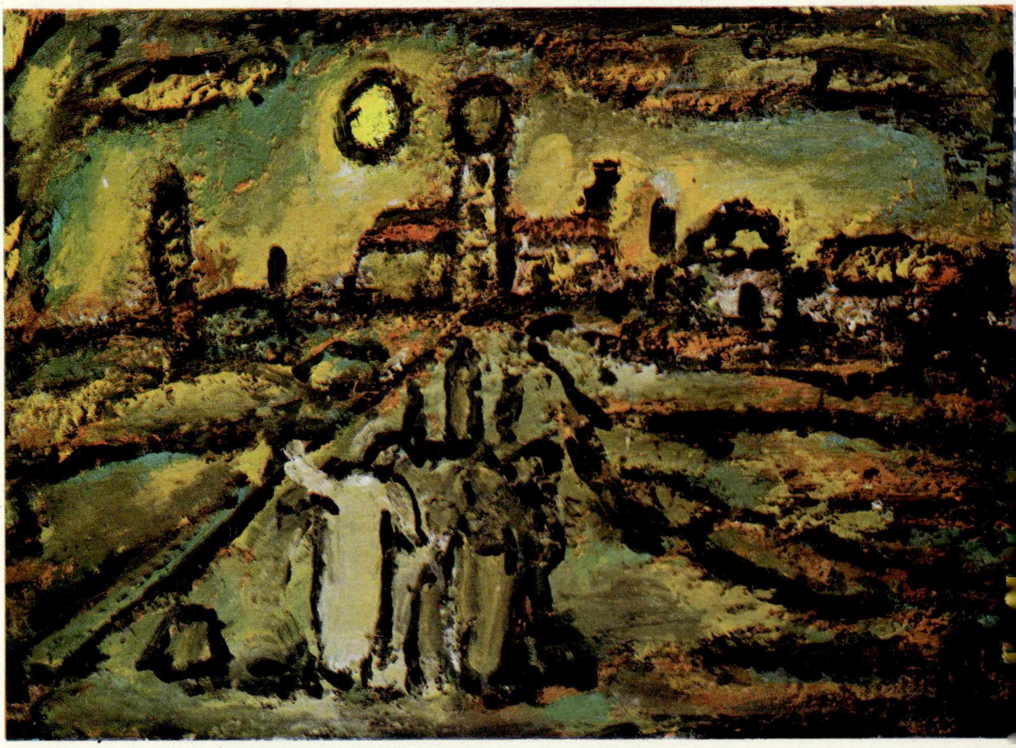

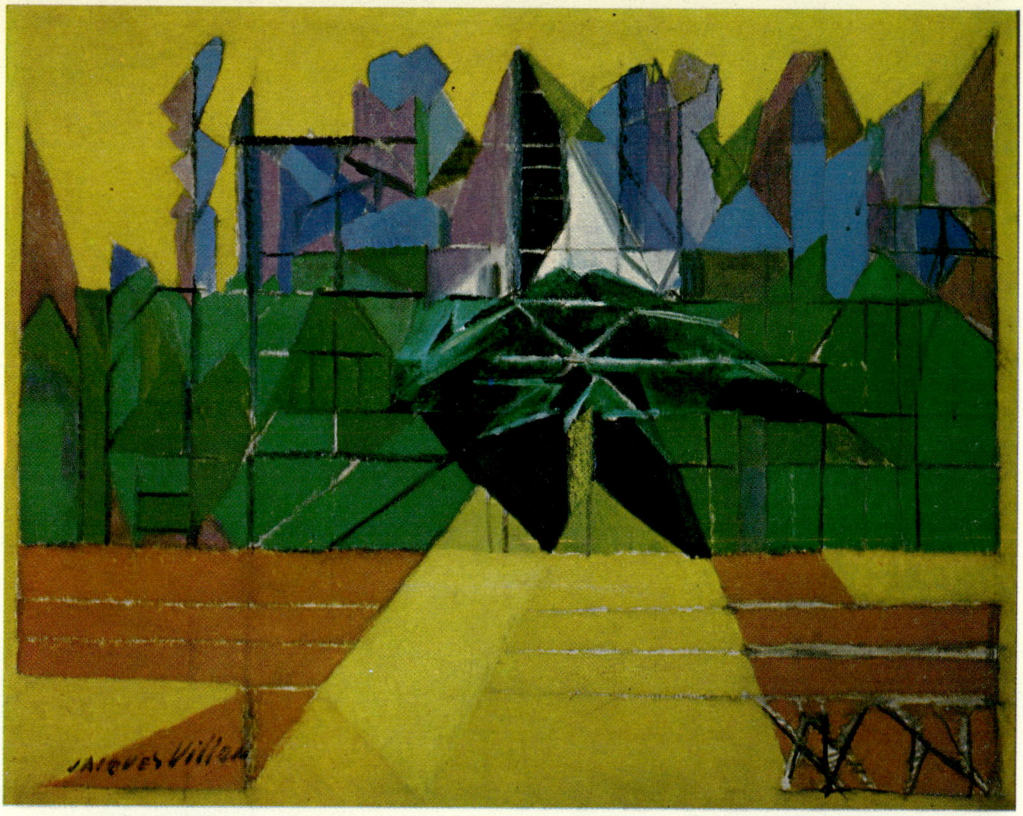

He frequented a studio on the boulevard Rochechouart, where the whores of the district came to rest and get warm in winter. From this human dross he composed some of his most striking works. These were ink paintings on paper, for he had not enough money to buy canvas and oils. Here the human animal, unaware of being observed, displays itself in all its nakedness. One has only to compare these forms, violently streaked with red and blue, with the caricatures produced by his studio comrades to realise the difference between genius and talent.

Excluded from the Ecole des Beaux-Arts, and from the official Salon, he finally renounced, after a long inner struggle, the academic career he had dreamed of. He was later to write: "This instinctive movement, this touch on the tiller which I gave, came from neither the influence of Lautrec, nor that of Degas, but from a more urgent inner need, from a sharper and more penetrating eye."

His meeting with Ambroise Vollard was perhaps as important an event for him as was his friendship with Gustave Moreau. It matters little whether this dealer understood Rouault or not, nor that they had basic disagreements. The important point is that the painter was engaged to illustrate the sequel Vollard wished to produce to Alfred Jarry's *Ubu*, and so was able to live shielded from want for twenty years. A modest livelihood, no doubt, but at least he was not reduced to seeking buyers for paintings nobody wanted.

Rouault assured me that Vollard never entered the studio that he provided for him in his own house in the rue Martignac, where the artist could devote himself to the experiments which resulted in the works in his last style, heavily textured, assiduously revised and worked over—different from the rough, spontaneous sketches of his youth.

He produced hundreds of canvases like this, many of which were designs for the *Miserere* engravings. A great number remained unfinished. Three hundred were burnt by the artist when he gained possession of them on Vollard's death; the artist's family gave the others to the Musée d'Art Moderne in 1963.

◀
Georges Rouault
Biblical Landscape, 1956
Oils on canvas 19″ × 25″
Bayeler Gallery, Basle

◀ ▲
Georges Rouault
Pierrot
Oils on hardboard 14″ × 12″
Sonia Henie Collection, Oslo

▲
Jacques Villon
Damville, Eure 1875-Paris 1963
The Cedar, 1948
Oils on canvas 26″ × 32″
Sonia Henie Collection, Oslo

Georges Rouault died on 13 January 1958, after devoting his last years to finishing a certain number of these pictures, many of which had religious themes, and publishing his *Miserere*, a monumental series of etchings which he had been working on for thirty years.

Rouault's technique underwent a triple evolution: classic in his early years, it then developed an extraordinary spontaneity, while he preferred ink to oils, or pigment generously diluted with benzene. Then he devoted himself to exploring materials. Never satisfied, he piled on layers of colour, ceaselessly enriching an ever denser impasto. No other body of work, however, possesses greater unity than his. Its origin is mysterious and it remains without a progeny, as befits all creations of genius.

Villon

Jacques Villon was born on 31 July 1875, in Damville, Normandy, where his father was a notary. It would be interesting to know what that man of law thought of his four children, who all became *avant-garde* painters or sculptors. The most daring among them was Raymond Duchamp-Villon*, whose striking bust of Baudelaire is in the Musée National d'Art Moderne. His sister, Suzanne Duchamp, who married the painter Jean Crotti, was, with Jacques Villon, one of the founders of the "Section d'Or"*. Their brother, Marcel Duchamp*, became famous in New York by *not* painting. . . . Apart from a few youthful pictures, almost all that we know of his are his famous "ready-mades".

Gaston Duchamp, who later took the name of Jacques Villon, was educated at Rouen. At the age of nineteen, he enrolled in the Faculty of Law in Paris. He quickly left and went back to Rouen. In 1895, he returned to Paris, where his brother Raymond was studying medicine, and joined Cormon's studio. Since he had to live, he contributed to *Le Courrier français*, *L'Assiette au Beurre*, *Le Rire*, and *Le Chat noir*, designed posters, and began to practise the craft of engraver learnt from his grandfather, to whom the Duchamp family's artistic vocation must be attributed.

He lived in Montmartre, sketching types observed in street or café, accumulating rapid drawings, washes and water-colours, seeing life through the eyes of his great precursors, such as Lautrec and Bottini*; any observant art-lover, however, should have been able to guess through the influences and techniques that this young unknown had a great future in front of him.

Fame kept him waiting a long time: Raymond Duchamp-Villon, who had abandoned medicine for sculpture, had his studio at Neuilly, which was a novelty in an era when official art had its base on the Plaine Monceau, and the *avant-garde* at Montmartre. Hoping to be near his brother, Jacques Villon in 1905 hired a studio at Puteaux, where was born one of the most active of those movements which, at the beginning of the century, prepared the way for the arrival of Abstract Art*.

His subtle and cultivated mind was never satisfied with the summary theories which inspired the early Cubists. He sought an order in geometry. The "Section d'Or",

Jacques Villon
Portrait of the Engraver J.-P. Dubray, 1933
Oils on canvas
Musée Fabre, Montpellier

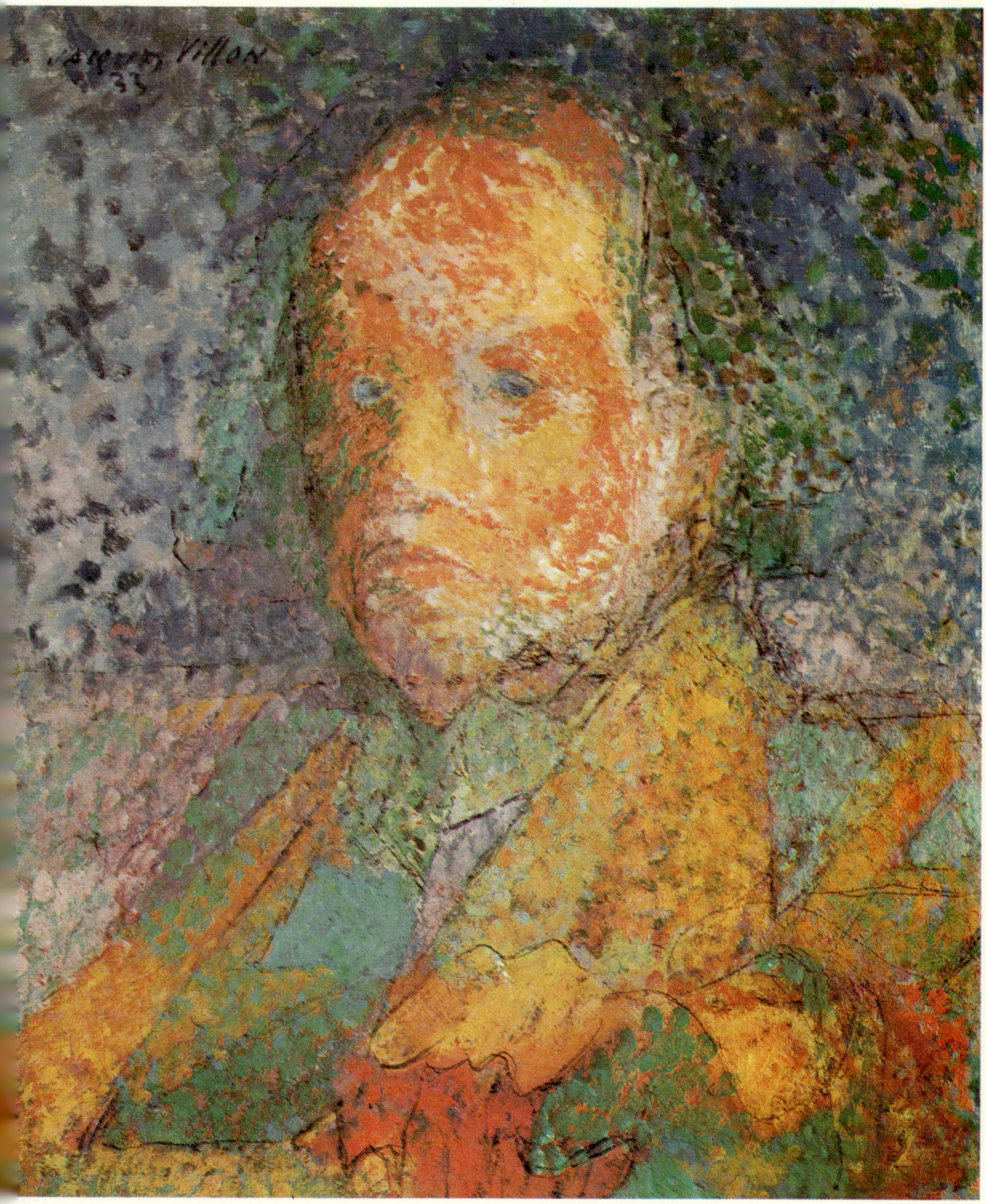

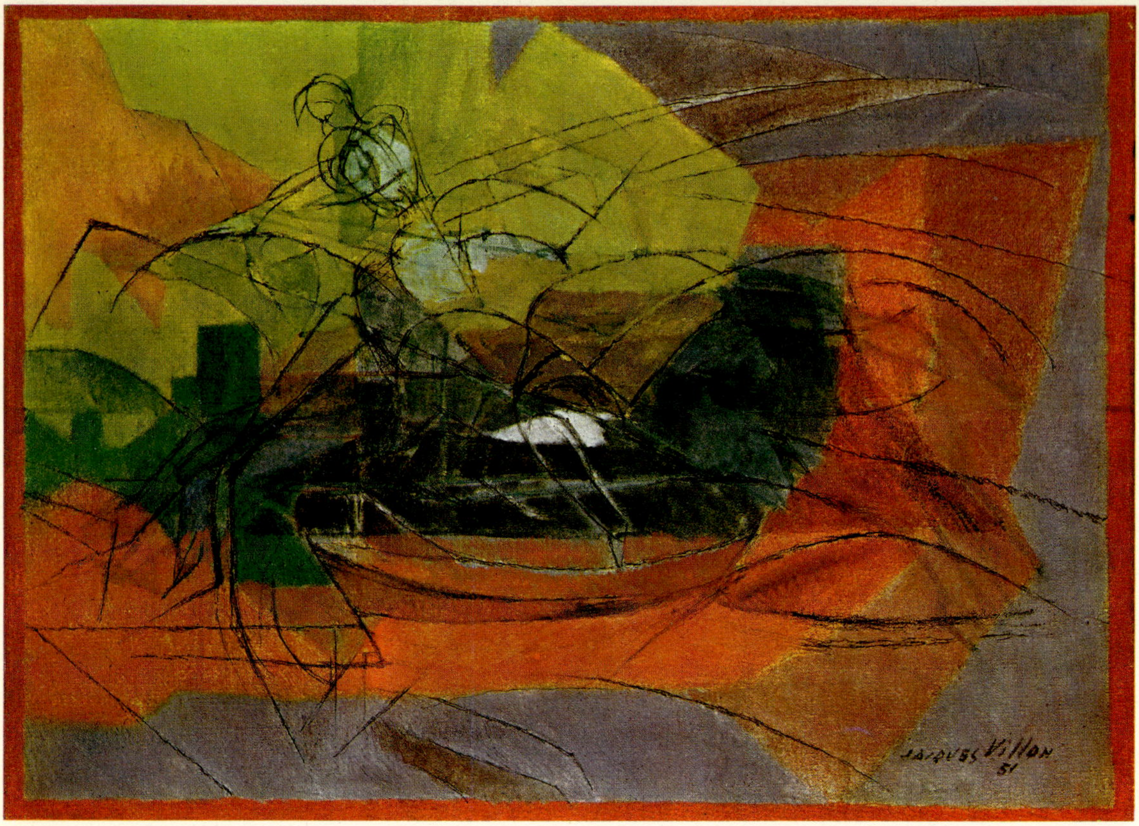

which he promoted, was intended to further deep exploration into the realm of shapes and ideas. Thus the "Puteaux School" came into being, holding its friendly gatherings on Sunday evenings in Jacques Villon's garden. His neighbour, the painter Kupka*, was one of his first associates. Gleizes*, who lived quite near, at Courbevoie, was seen there too, and also Metzinger*, La Fresnaye*, Picabia, Villon's two brothers and his sister, as well as some poets.

It was Apollinaire* who, in 1912, mounted an exhibition embracing the work of all these innovators. But they found hardly any purchasers. Moreover, Villon grew tired of contributing to satirical journals. He wanted to live by engraving. When he returned from the first world war, the Louvre engraving department and the Bernheim Gallery commissioned reproductions of works by Cézanne, Renoir, and so forth, from him, and these colour etchings are masterpieces both of fidelity and of subtle transmutation.

The earliest painting we have of his dates from 1900; it is a portrait of Raymond Duchamp, fairly traditional in appearance, but treated in violent shades which pre-echo Fauvism. In 1909 he painted a *Portrait of the Artist* in a decidedly Fauve style, at a time when this movement had been swept aside by Cubism. His attempts during the years leading up to the war bear comparison with those of Robert Delaunay and Fernand Léger. Villon, however—subtle and refined—is as different as possible from those two men, who both moved towards a simplification of problems.

The first works which might be called Abstract came in 1912 to 1913 (*The Acrobat*, *Soldiers on the March*). Here again, he worked ahead of his time: his experiments of that period have been compared to the art of Mondrian; but he preceded the Dutchman by several years, and remained sensitive even after yielding to the excitement of geometry.

This "sensitive geometry" occupied him for a long while. In the 1930s we see him obsessed with a play of shapes boxed one inside another and related to architecture,

Jacques Villon
Equestrienne, 1951
Oils on canvas 21″ × 29″
Musée des Beaux-Arts, Lyons

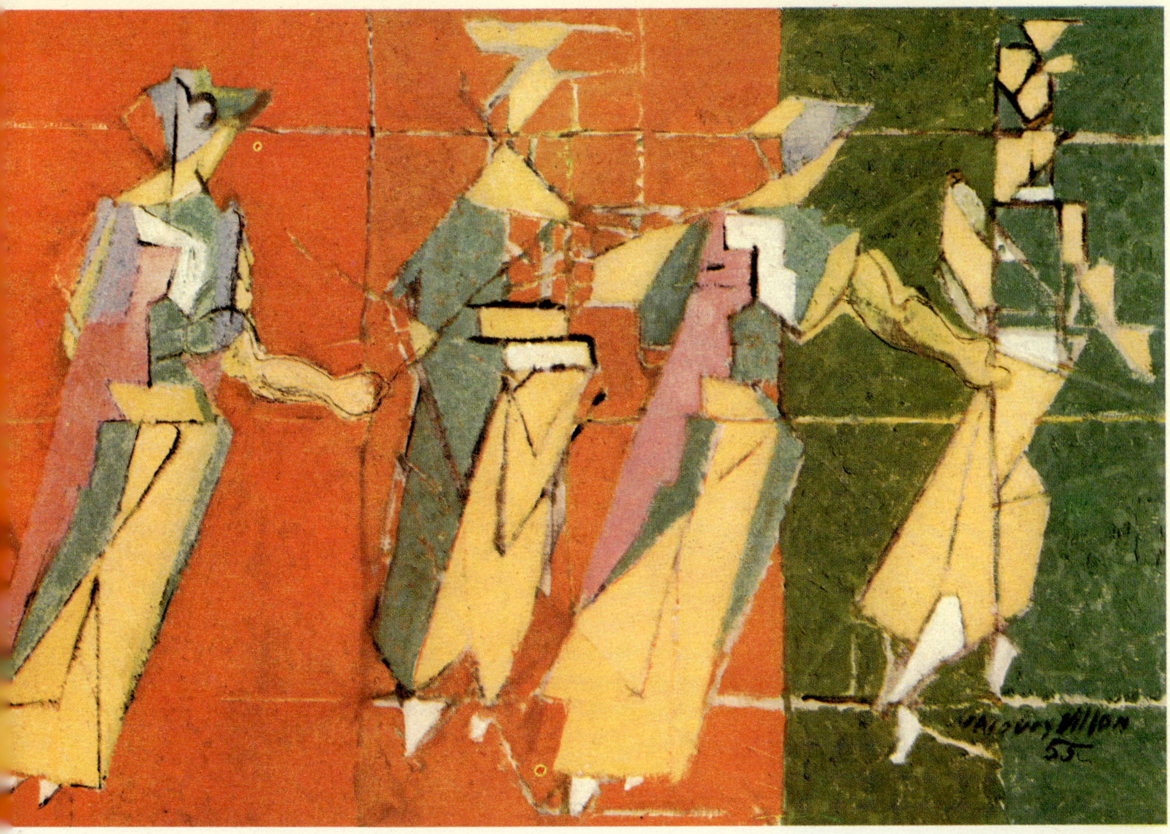

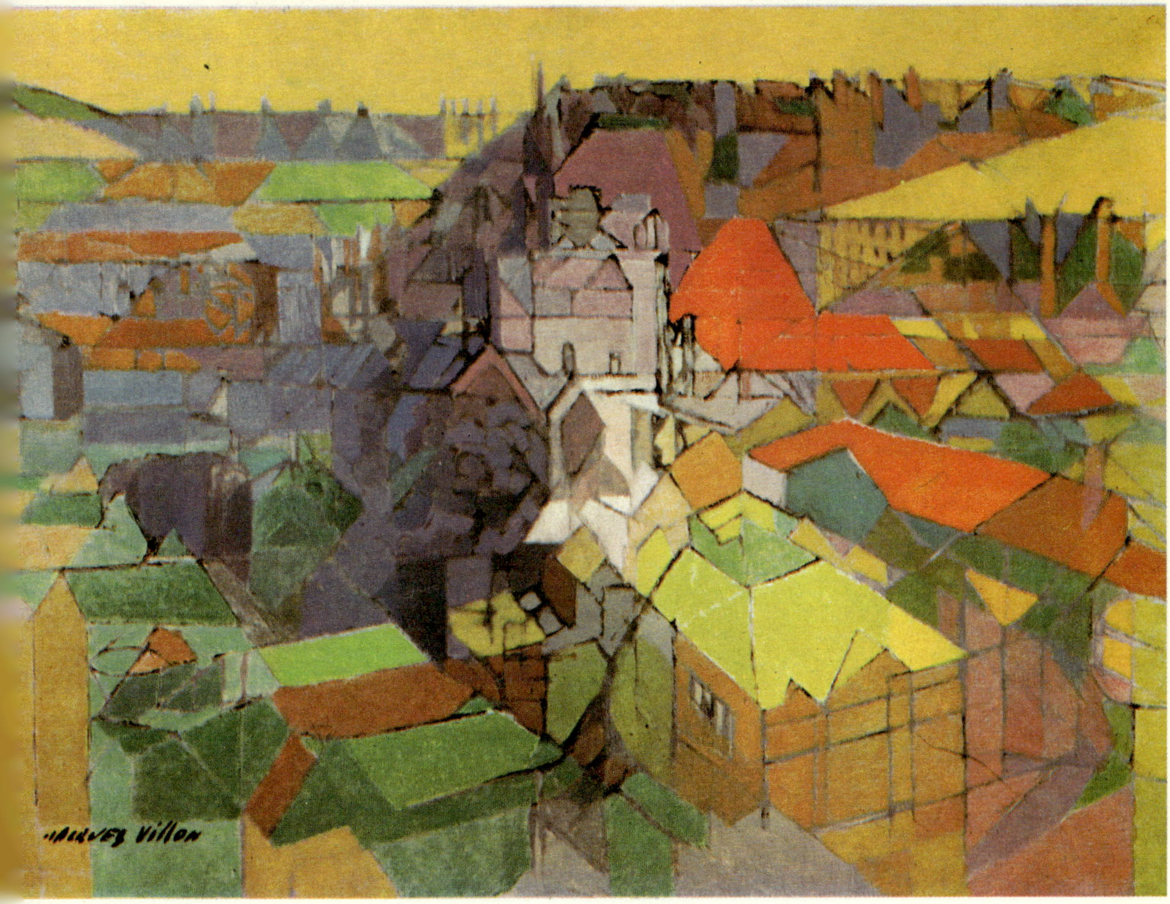

▲
Jacques Villon
The Little Town, 1944
Oils on canvas 29″ × 40″
Sonia Henie Collection, Oslo

▲▲
Jacques Villon
Athenian Women, 1955
Oils on canvas 21″ × 32″
Sonia Henie Collection, Oslo

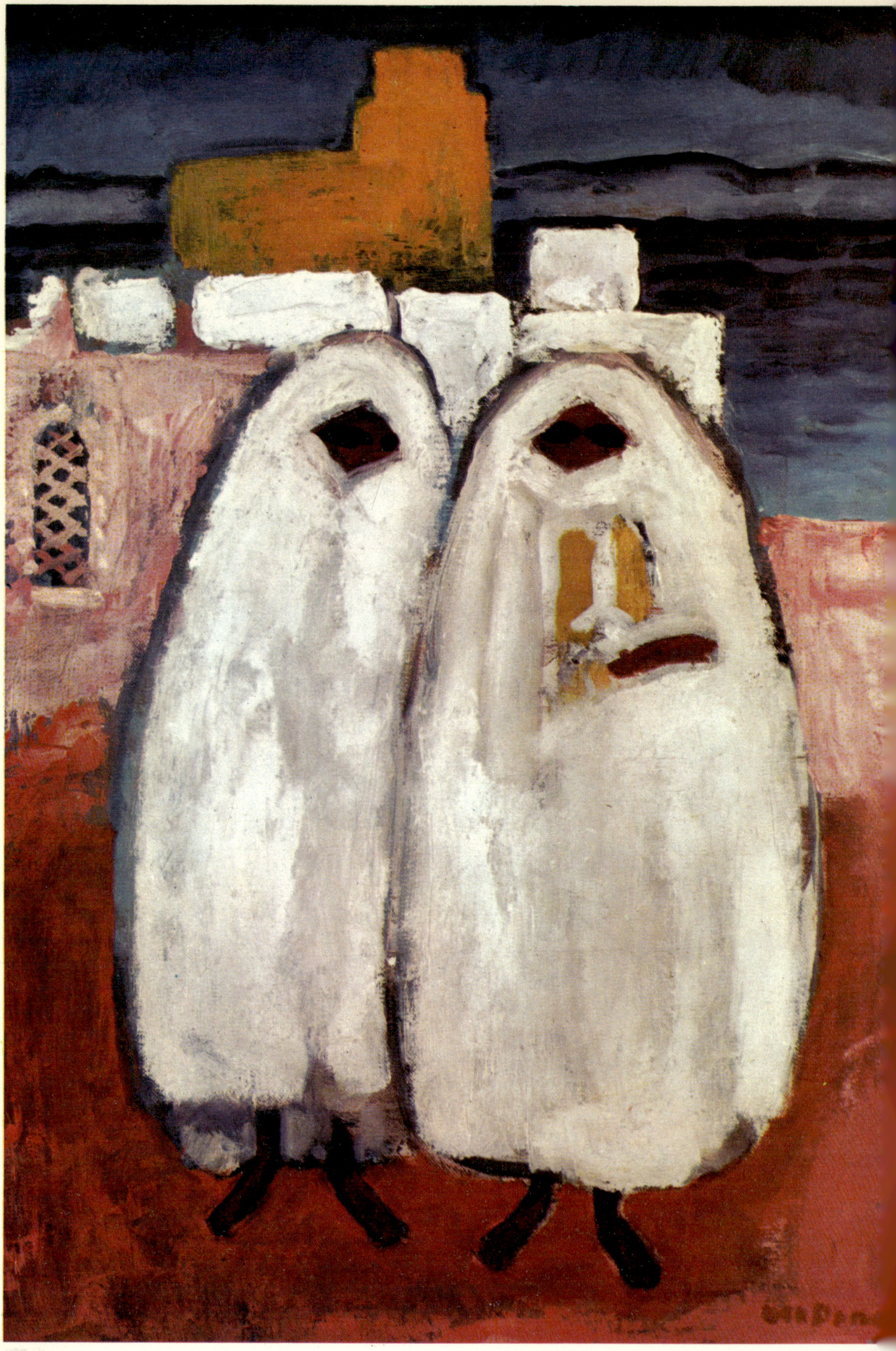

Kees Van Dongen
Delfshaven 1877-Monte Carlo 1968
Moroccan Women at Cap Spartel, 1910
Oils on canvas 22″ × 15″
In the artist's possession

innovations all the more unexpected because his temperament would seem to have inclined him towards the study of light: "I was the Cubist Impressionist," he said, "and I think I have remained so. Perhaps less Cubist, less Impressionist, more I don't know what and I'm still searching."

The manifestations of this strange, free spirit were often puzzling. The modest-sized canvases he sent to the Salon d'Automne did not pass unnoticed, but he organised no controversial exhibitions in the major galleries. Known in his capacity as an innovator, esteemed by all, receiving friends of quality at his Puteaux Studio, Jacques Villon was none the less unrecognised.

Then, during the second world war, poets and painters discovered him; Bazaine* and Estève*, for instance, acknowledged him as a master and dealers did not remain indifferent: his exhibitions at the Galerie de France in 1942, and at Carré's in 1944, number among the artistic events of occupied France. Overnight this quiet septuagenarian became a celebrity.

We see him, at this time, making a move to return to figurative art as though, feeling more sure of himself with the arrival of success, he gave up hyper-schematic experiments. In *The Bridge at Beaugency* and *The Three Estates: Castle, Church and Countryside*, he succeeded in capturing the light of the Loire Valley.

With the exception of a brief incursion in about 1947 into the realm of dynamic forms (*Machine Shop, Din*), we can recognise in him a sensitivity that has been sharpened rather than weakened by age. The real world is recognisable through the fine network of lines and colours with which he clothed it. He remained faithful to this basic palette of yellow, green and pink bordering sometimes on mauve which makes his canvases distinct among thousands.

His exhibition in 1951 at the Musée National d'Art Moderne was a triumph. It did not, however, mark a final accolade, rather a further stage in his development. At the age of eighty-six, he returned with astonishing vitality to his own Normandy. There, on the banks of the Seine, he rediscovered the secret of the quiet greys which give charm to his native soil. One of his last canvases, *Cranes near Rouen*, shows a perfectly coherent industrial landscape, both delicately and powerfully conveyed.

By the time he died, on 9 June 1963, he had become the doyen of French painting. Modest and forbearing, he never betrayed his convictions and always kept his sense of proportion. The somewhat crystalline figures in his painting belonged to Impressionism, while at the same time Abstract artists regarded him as one of their masters. Jacques Villon was one of the purest painters of our time, and the semi-obscurity in which he lived for so long protected him from specious publicity and unhelpful privileges alike.

Van Dongen

Just as Blaise Cendrars* replied to the question: "What is the first qualification for a novelist?" with: "Lying", so Van Dongen cheerfully replied to the question as to what was the first qualification for a painter, with "Artificiality". His taste for paradox stood much in his way, as did his refusal to let himself be regimented and the attraction which festivals, entertainments and places where he could show off held for him. For a long time no one would take him seriously. Even after he became famous, he rarely showed in galleries or salons, content to display his recent works in his studio in the rue Juliette-Lambert, the scene of some memorable soirées.

An inveterate humorist, he took a secret delight in visiting the famous of this world for whom, not so long before, he had been no more than a tramp on a Rotterdam quayside. His joker's temperament led him to assume the appearance of a worldly painter, letting innocents take him for someone like Sargent, or Jean-Gabriel Domergue*, although at no time did he cease to be an out-and-out Fauve.

Those who, in following the fashion, posed for him from 1920 onwards, whether they were academics, politicians, demi-mondaines, or theatre and cinema stars, ran the risk of seeing themselves held up to the light, for Van Dongen's numberless portraits always aimed at exposing the sitter. If he had in front of him a beautiful girl who was proud of her body, he painted her nude; if another excelled in obtaining rich presents from the men around her, we see her covered with excessively flashing jewels; his brush reduced the aged Anatole France* to a softened-down humanist, the Comtesse de Noailles* to a poetess trying to increase her stature by the glitter of her lyricism, Boni de Castellane* to a fop, and Rappoport to a drawing-room fellow traveller.

This uncompromising lucidity obliged him never to allow himself to be fooled, and always to dominate the world which surrounded him so as not to be crushed by it. Such an attitude could have been a weakness in a less gifted painter. Yet, of all his contemporaries, Van Dongen was probably the most natural artist; he handled colour as a bird sings, if we can risk applying such a simile to a man who was prevented by the embittering effect of a poor childhood from trusting his natural ability. Even when this ability revealed itself, it seems there always remained an underlying determination not to be taken in by appearances, but to find out what lay behind the most brilliant façade.

Van Dongen therefore rejected both the *avant-garde* and the academic, and this rejection made him an unclassifiable master who spent a long time winning a place in the top flight, which today no one would dream of disputing.

All artists are profoundly affected by their childhood and adolescence, and it is difficult to understand certain subsequent choices without knowing their personal backgrounds or the difficulties surrounding their débuts.

Cornelis Theodorus Marie Van Dongen (known as Kees) was born in Delfshaven, Holland, on 26 January 1877. He broke with his family early on and left the school where he should have been studying industrial design. He chose to live in Rotterdam, in whose hot streets it seems likely that he began to draw as a means of livelihood, being more interested in sailors and prostitutes than in machines.

He worked at all sorts of jobs until one day in 1897, when, the story runs, he got himself hired as a guide on an excursion train taking Dutch tourists to Paris for the 14 July celebrations. The train returned to Rotterdam without him, but his life in Paris was even more difficult, because he couldn't speak French. Being strong and tall, he earned a few sous nightly as a market-porter in Les Halles. Then he discovered the night-clubs, where he did numerous sketches, offering them to interested customers at 5 francs apiece.

Since buyers were rare, he adopted the occupation already practised at that time by Villon, Galanis* and many other future stars of the Paris school; he took some drawings to *L'Assiette au Beurre* and other humorous journals in Montmartre. Finally, he went to live in the Bateau-Lavoir*, in the Place Ravignan. Since he had no money to pay models, he borrowed those of his comrades, and Fernande Oliver*, Picasso's mistress, posed several times for portraits or nudes of convincing authority.

In his early exhibitions at Druet's in 1903 and at Vollard's in 1904, he had not yet broken with Impressionism, and in an introduction to the latter exhibition Félix Fénéon* spoke of an atmosphere effectively poised between light and shade, making the transition in clear, delicate tones of grey. Already at this stage his views of Paris contrasted, in their firmness, with those he did in Normandy and in Holland when he had a chance to go back to his country.

His development was rapid, and in 1905 he exhibited in the "*cage aux fauves*" at the Salon d'Automne. He was a Fauve by nature, without accepting the label. He joined neither this group nor the Cubists, among whom he had many friends, and he was perhaps the only master of contemporary painting who remained unresponsive to Cézanne's influence.

At first a landscape artist, he soon came to prefer circus or music-hall scenes, and portraits of actresses; he returned to landscape in the course of his travels, a visit to Egypt particularly impressing him. He relied on his own imagination, rejecting no extremity, always laughing up his sleeve and composing his palette preferably of greens, blues and bright reds.

Germain Bazin* commented with justice that "Van Dongen's painting is hot-house painting, his colour is in a state of saturation, incandescent; it has the same brilliance as exotic plants and artificially bred flowers. . . . He inflames colour to the point of aggravation, when it causes a nervous irritation in our senses. And if it seems surprising that such an assembly of crude colours can result in anything but a discord, the cause must be sought in the same reason which makes a succession of dissonances in the music of Ravel* or Stravinsky* result in consonant harmony."

Another paradox among all those which constituted this astonishing personality was a sadistic ability to conciliate his models by exhibiting their defects or vices. When, just after the first world war, he decided to make a bid for success, he managed to find enough masochists to assure him of a comfortable living. Even with the most beautiful women, he emphasised their painted eyes, lacquered nails, sparkling jewels and sequinned gowns, reserving for their skin those shades of green so dear to him: as a fashionable painter, he could permit himself the most outrageous liberties, and he freely executed portraits which criticism took for caricatures but which we see today as masterpieces of insight.

He was to be found at Cannes, at Deauville, at the Lido. He appeared to belong to the artificial high society life that he led rather than to the world of painters, but in fact, silent and withdrawn, he was less an observer than a seer.

He was never more surprising than when, between two fancy-dress balls, or two portraits of great ladies, perhaps, he went to stay for a few weeks in Versailles or Venice and came back with a series of landscapes of a spontaneity and accuracy which could disarm the most determined prejudice.

Van Dongen died in Monte Carlo on 28 May 1968. Can we say that the wild man had, by then, grown wise? His superabundant productivity from between the wars was followed by a semi-retirement, a certain lassitude, as though the deep pessimism always latent in him had, at the end of his life, risen to the surface.

Dufy

No one was more truly of his time than Raoul Dufy; but no one rejected its violence with more elegance. As to its fashions, he created rather than followed them. He missed nothing happening around him, and knew well how to skim off the cream of life. Independent in his art as in his behaviour, he escaped convenient classification and developed like a luxuriant plant.

Dufy was a son of that same Norman soil which, since Boudin and Monet, has given so much to contemporary art with Braque, Villon, Léger and Friesz*. He was born on 3 June 1877 into a musical family in Le Havre. All his life he responded to the charm of music, and often returned to it in paintings of orchestras and still-lifes with instruments and scores.

He had eight brothers and sisters, and life was not always easy; he had to break off his studies prematurely, and to go to work for an import business. In the evenings he used to escape from the uninspiring work and attend lessons at the Académie Municipale des Beaux-Arts. There he met Othon Friesz, and the friendship they formed was to play a decisive role in their careers. Had they not come to depend on each other, or to share enthusiasms in the course of their long conversations, they might never have found the courage to involve themselves deeply in painting.

Another man who exercised some influence on them was Charles Lhullier, the director of the Ecole des Beaux-Arts in Le Havre, who had a gift for developing the budding personalities of his students. He obtained a grant for Friesz, then aged twenty, which enabled him to go to Paris. Dufy still hesitated, and it was not until 1900 that, armed with a similar grant, he was able to go and enrol in Léon Bonnat's studio, where Friesz was waiting for him. The two friends settled in Montmartre.

In 1904, during a visit to Le Havre, he painted *Yacht Dressed with Flags*, which provided a foretaste of Fauvist boldness. He liked to revisit his family and always remained close to his brothers, who were talented violinists. In 1905, at the Salon d'Automne, he discovered the full brilliance of the Fauvist movement to which he subscribed, if still timidly, but encouraged by Friesz. Dufy never liked exaggeration, but

Kees Van Dongen
The Amazon, *c.* 1922
Oils on canvas
Private collection, Paris

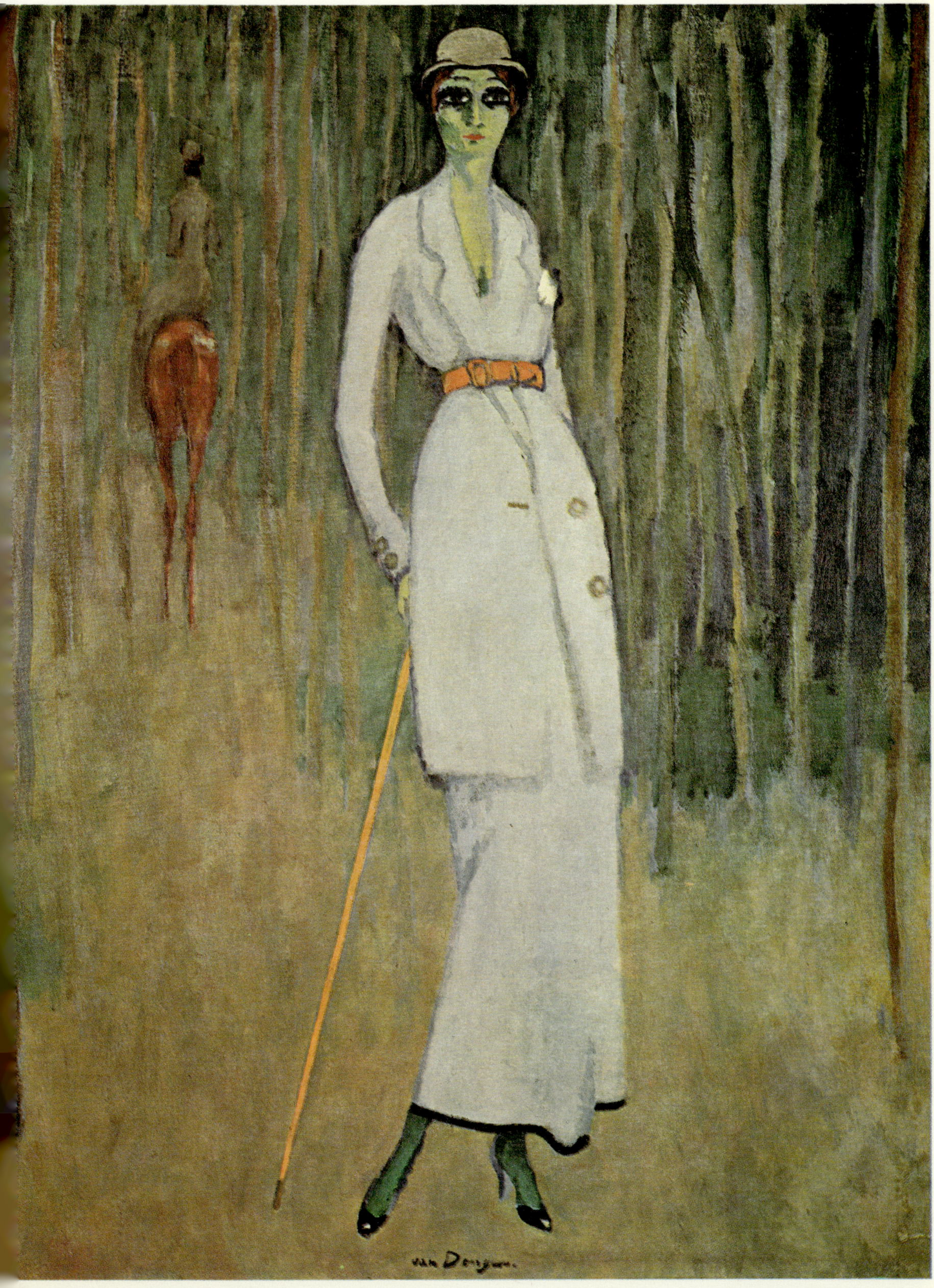

Kees Van Dongen
Fernande, 1903
Oils on canvas 22″ × 18″
In the artist's possession

Kees Van Dongen
Back View of Seated Woman, 1905
Oils on canvas 22″ × 18″
In the artist's possession

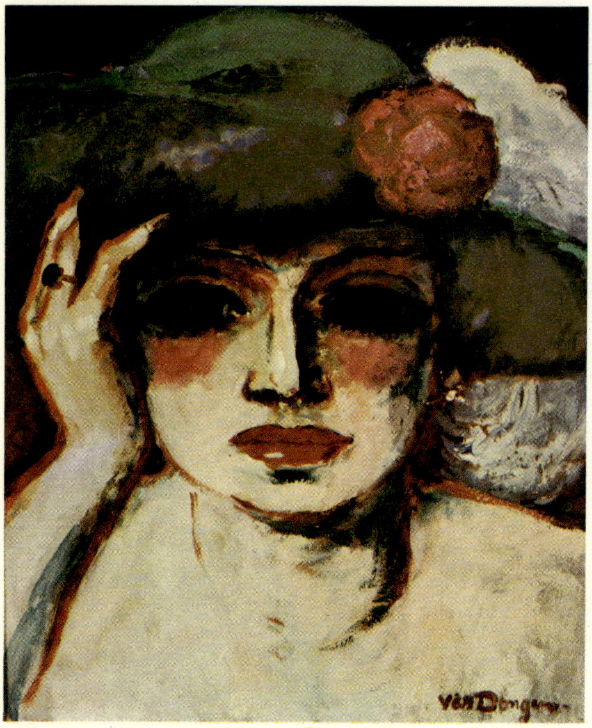

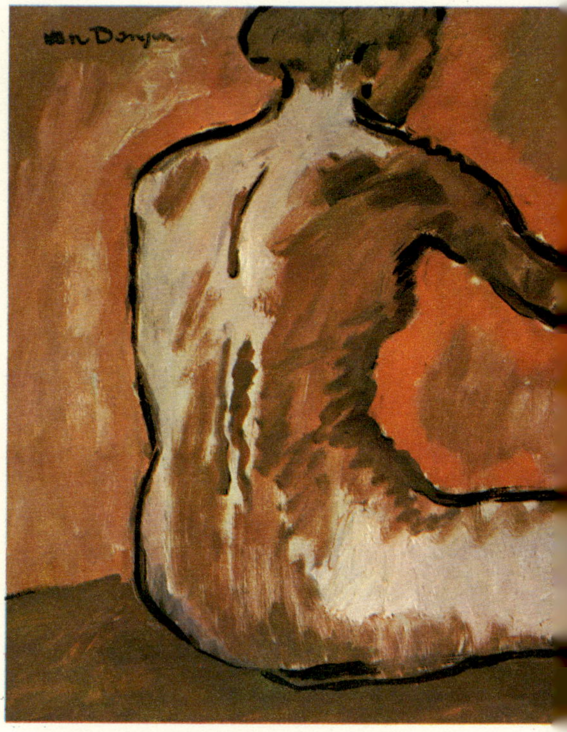

he was in love with colour and could not resist painting pictures like *Street Decked with Flags*. He made friends with Albert Marquet, who took him to Trouville, then with Braque, currently in the midst of his Cézanne period, and they painted side by side at L'Estaque.

By 1908 he had already clearly thrown off all influences and evolved a style which owed nothing to anyone but himself and expressing an intense love of life. He relished life in all its forms, always letting himself be drawn to three constantly repeated major themes which recalled his youth: the yachts are those he watched, from high up in Sainte-Adresse, leaving the port of Le Havre and heading for the open sea; the horses are those that galloped free in the Normandy meadows, or that he observed on the Deauville race-track; and the musicians are those he knew through his father and brothers.

Life was hard for young artists in the years just before the first world war. Dealers were rare, and buyers even rarer. Like Villon, he relied on engraving for his livelihood. He illustrated the books of his poet friends, and his insatiable curiosity led him to discover medieval woodcuts. Xylography was a technique almost abandoned when he reinstated it in 1910 with Apollinaire's *Bestiary*. He spent that year as a boarder at the Fondation Bonjean at Orgeville (a large mansion placed at the disposal of artists); afterwards he moved to Guelma, a picturesque impasse, where he occupied lodgings, which, by the end of his life, had become a veritable Dufy museum.

(page 36 above)
Raoul Dufy
The Riders under the Trees, 1931
First version of the portrait of J. B. Auguste Kessler and his family on horseback
Musée National d'Art Moderne, Paris

(page 36 below)
Raoul Dufy
Le Havre 1877-Forcalquier (Lower Alps) 1953
Indian Woman, 1928
Oils on canvas 18″ × 22″
Galerie Louis Carré, Paris

Kees Van Dongen
Nude with Garter, 1910
Oils on canvas 32″ × 52″
In the artist's possession

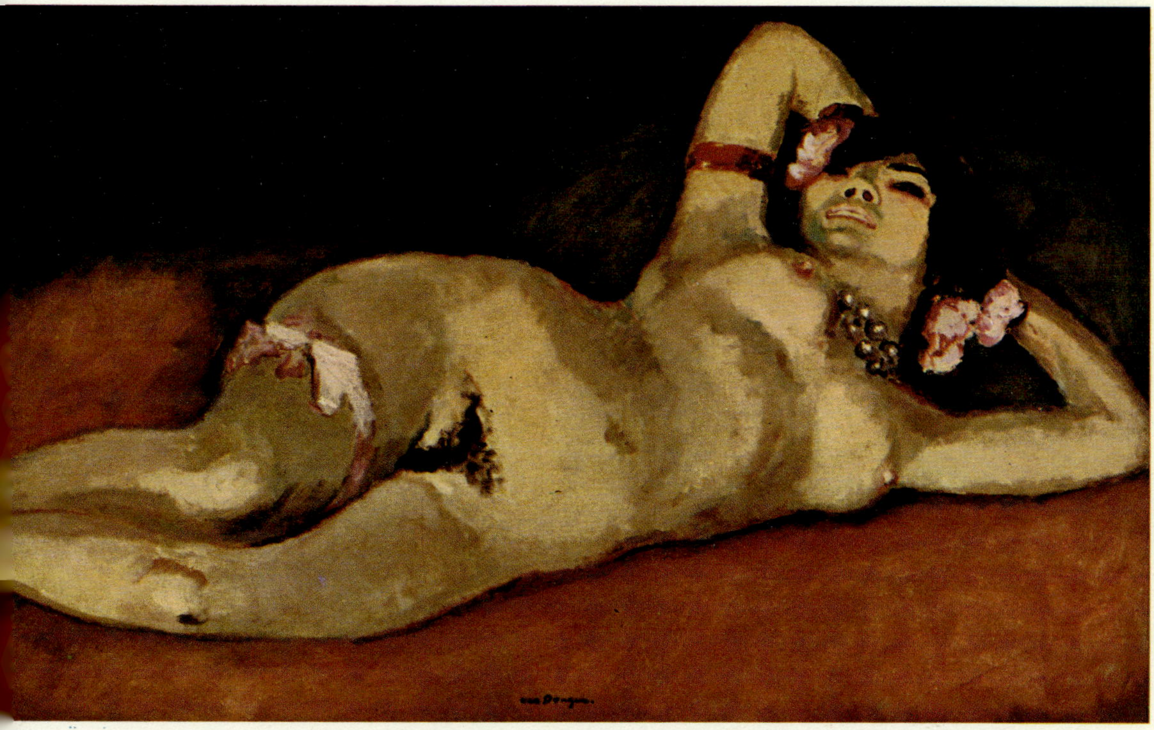

He pursued parallel experiments in the fields of both painting and decorative art; interested in new techniques and materials, he found, in Paul Poiret*, a businessman determined to exploit all the latest fashions, and designed wall-papers and fabrics for him. There was no conflict of interest between his work on crafts and his painting; he passed effortlessly from one field to the other. On his canvases and his fabrics he traced marvellously supple and sensitive designs, then filled them in with coloured areas deliberately not following the boundaries of the drawing. This unusually free art enchanted a fabrics firm in Lyons, which guaranteed a sale for his designs and thus enabled him to devote himself to private experiments in his pictures.

He was captivated by Provence, which he had visited before the war, and he moved to Vence in 1919. There he followed his inspiration without restraint. The word freedom keeps cropping up in any discussion of Dufy. No difficulty hampered him, and he made light of all pitfalls. His drawing is unusually evocative; in a few lines, sketchy in appearance but extraordinarily perceptive, he can present the essence of any subject he chooses. That he was also a great colourist is displayed as certainly in his water-colours as in his oil-paintings.

His *Boaters on the Marne* (1923) is among this period's most dynamic compositions, displaying the most uninhibited line and colour, at the same time lively and subtle. A journey to Italy helped him to acquire even more facility. His series of Sicilian landscapes of 1922 show him in command of a style resembling no one else's,

(page 37 above)
Raoul Dufy
Concert in Orange, 1948
Oils on canvas 24″ × 29″
Louis Carré Collection, Paris

(page 37 below)
Raoul Dufy
Studio with Two Models, 1930
Oils on canvas 32″ × 39″
Mabille Collection, Brussels

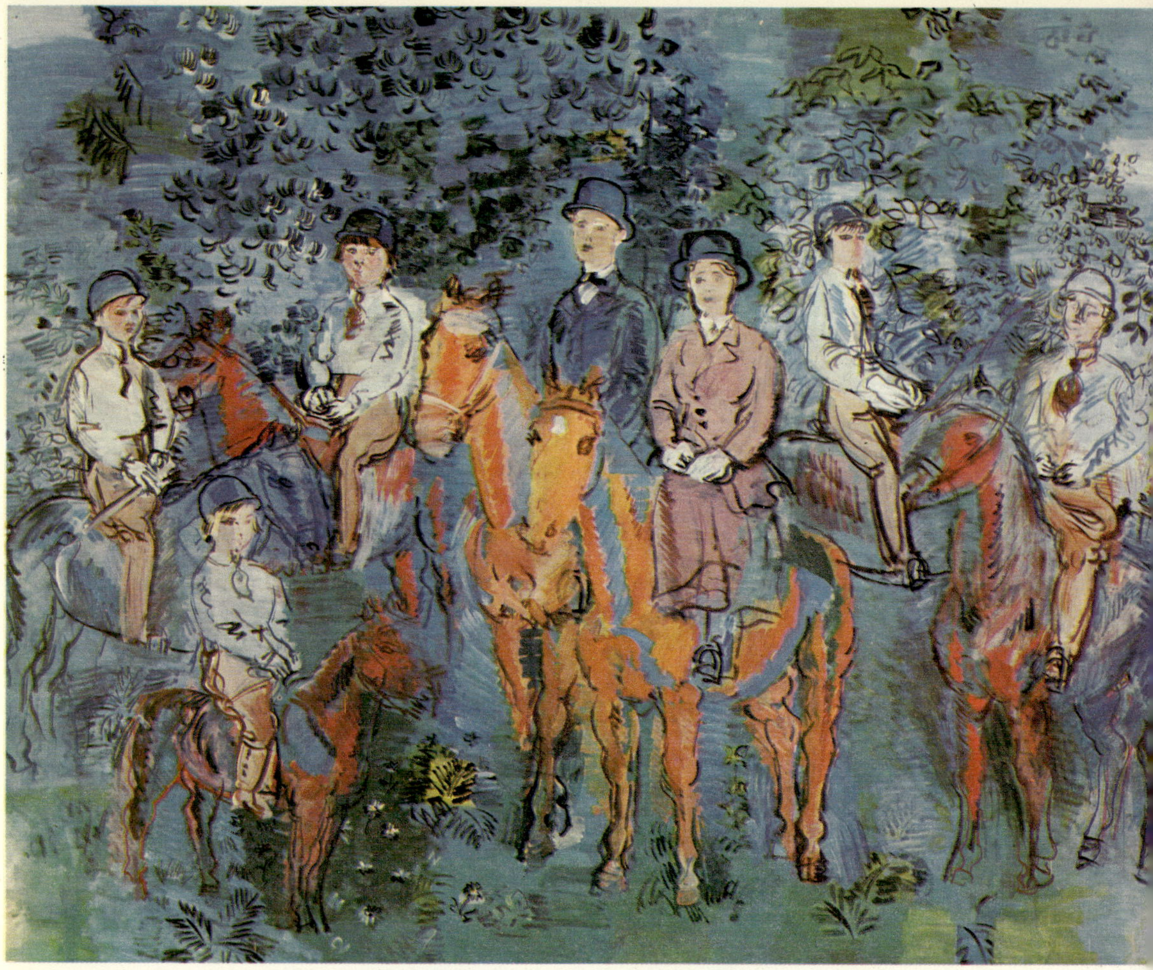

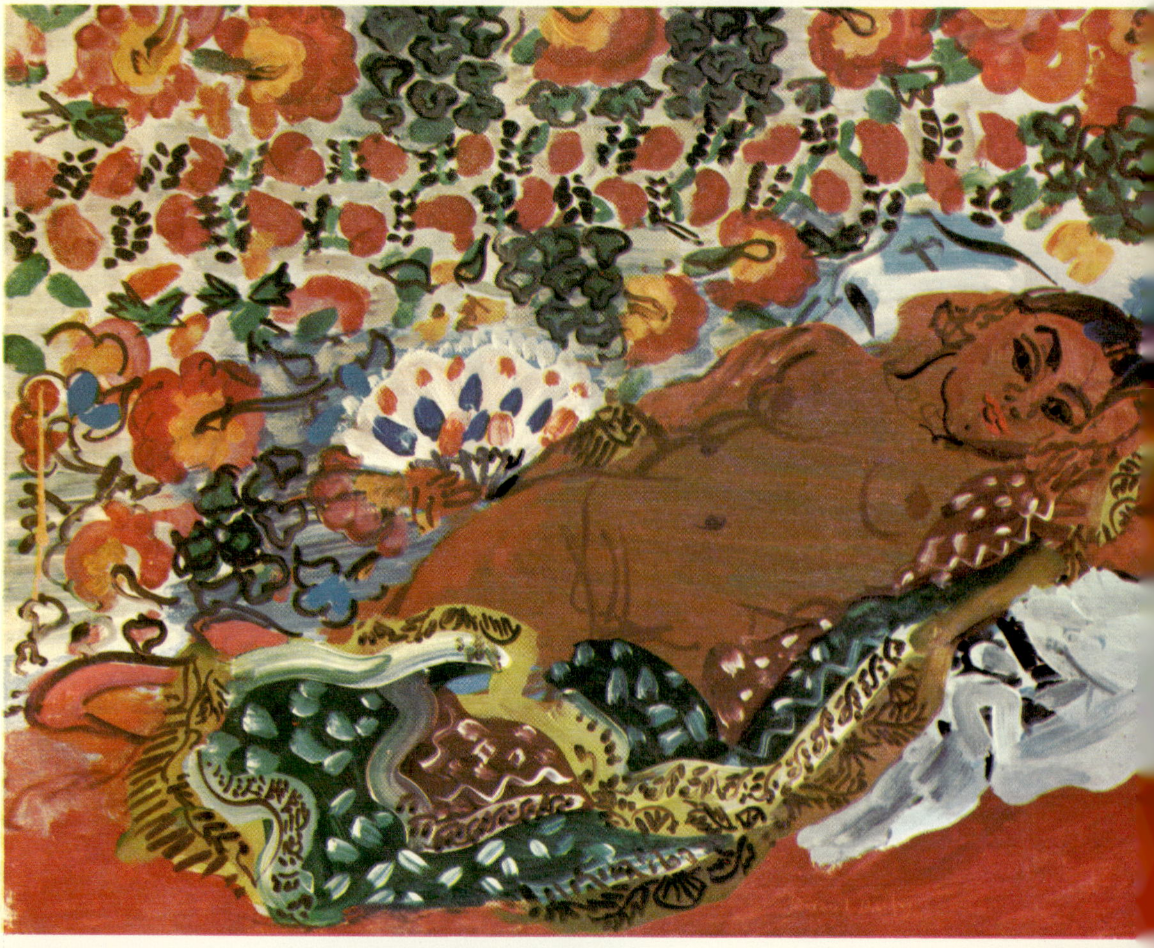

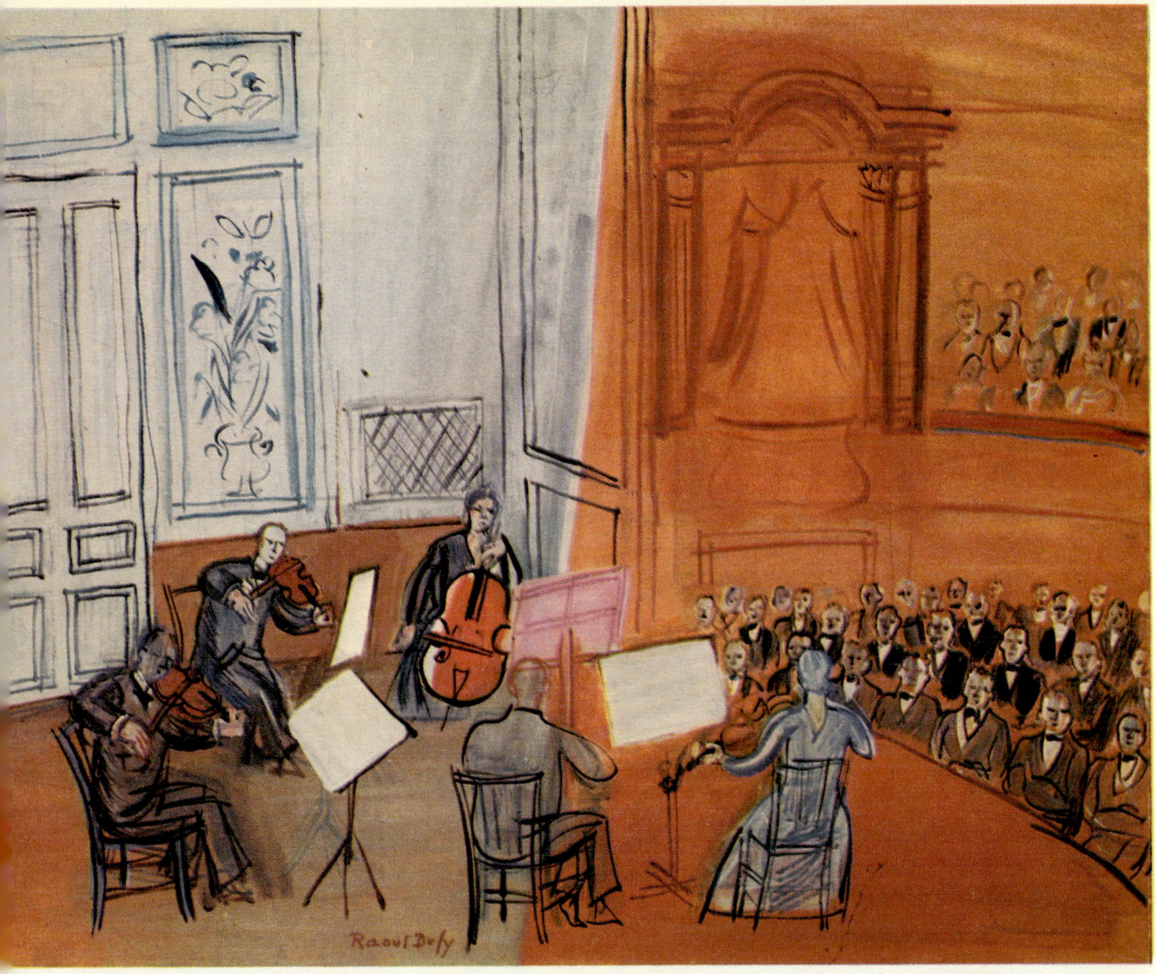
Raoul Dufy

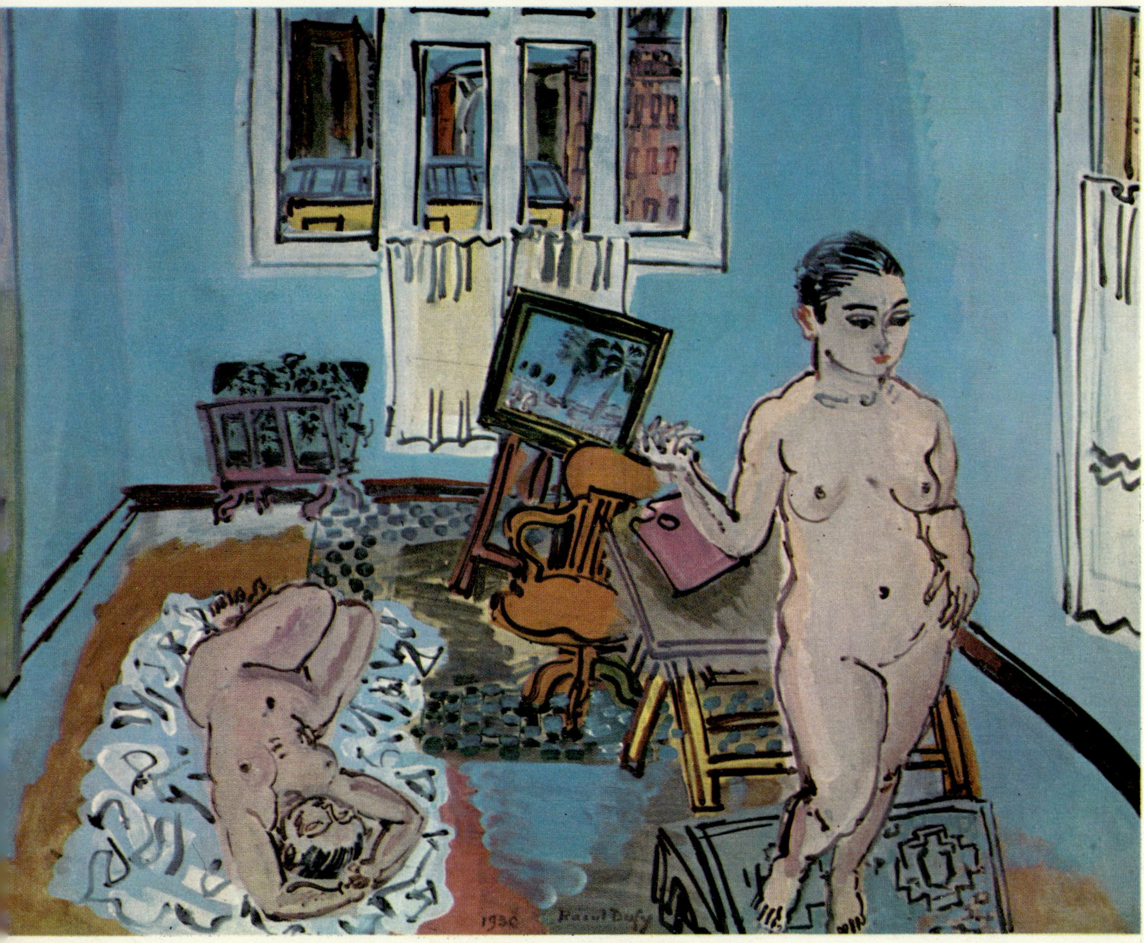
1930 Raoul Dufy

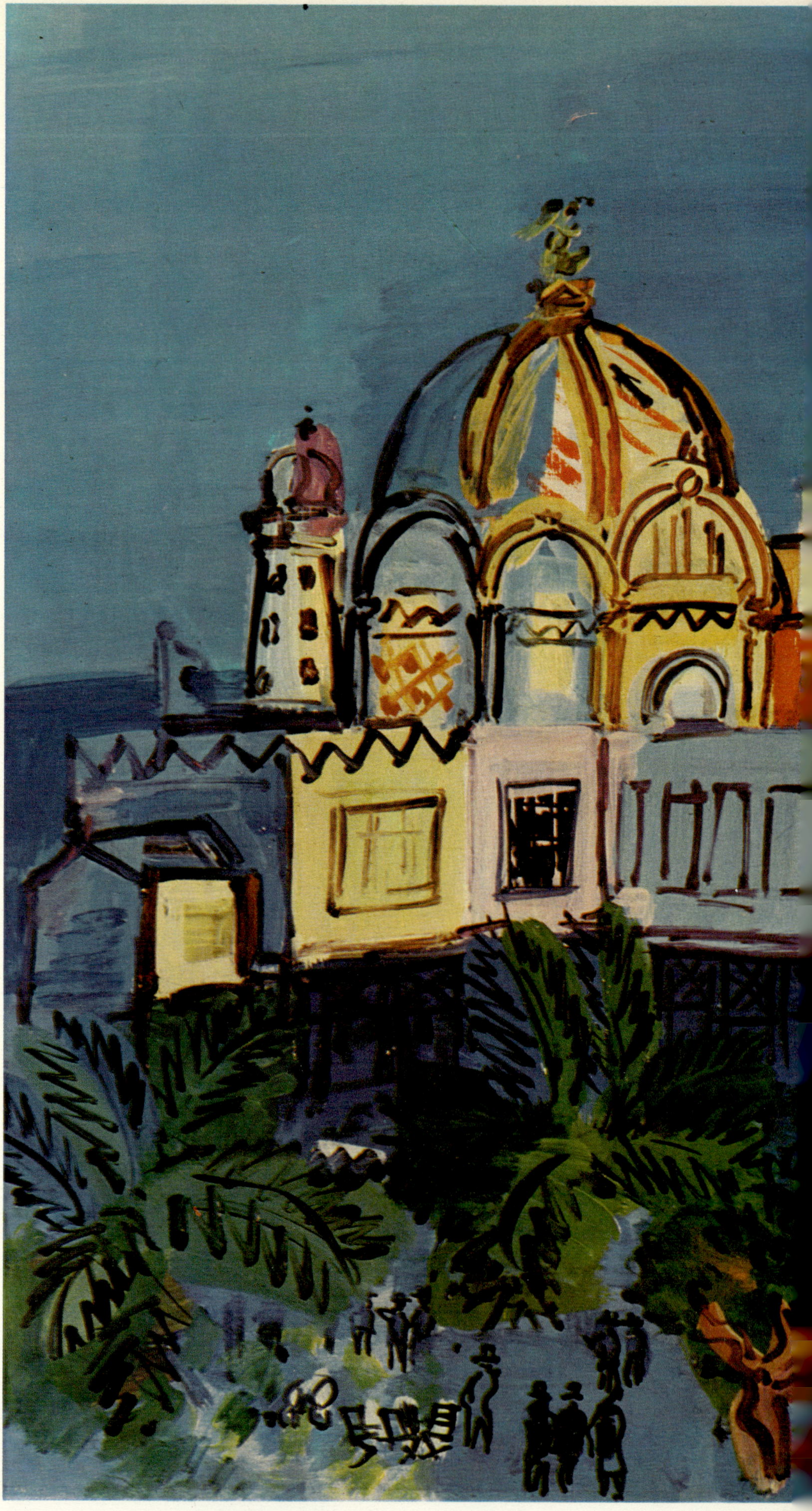

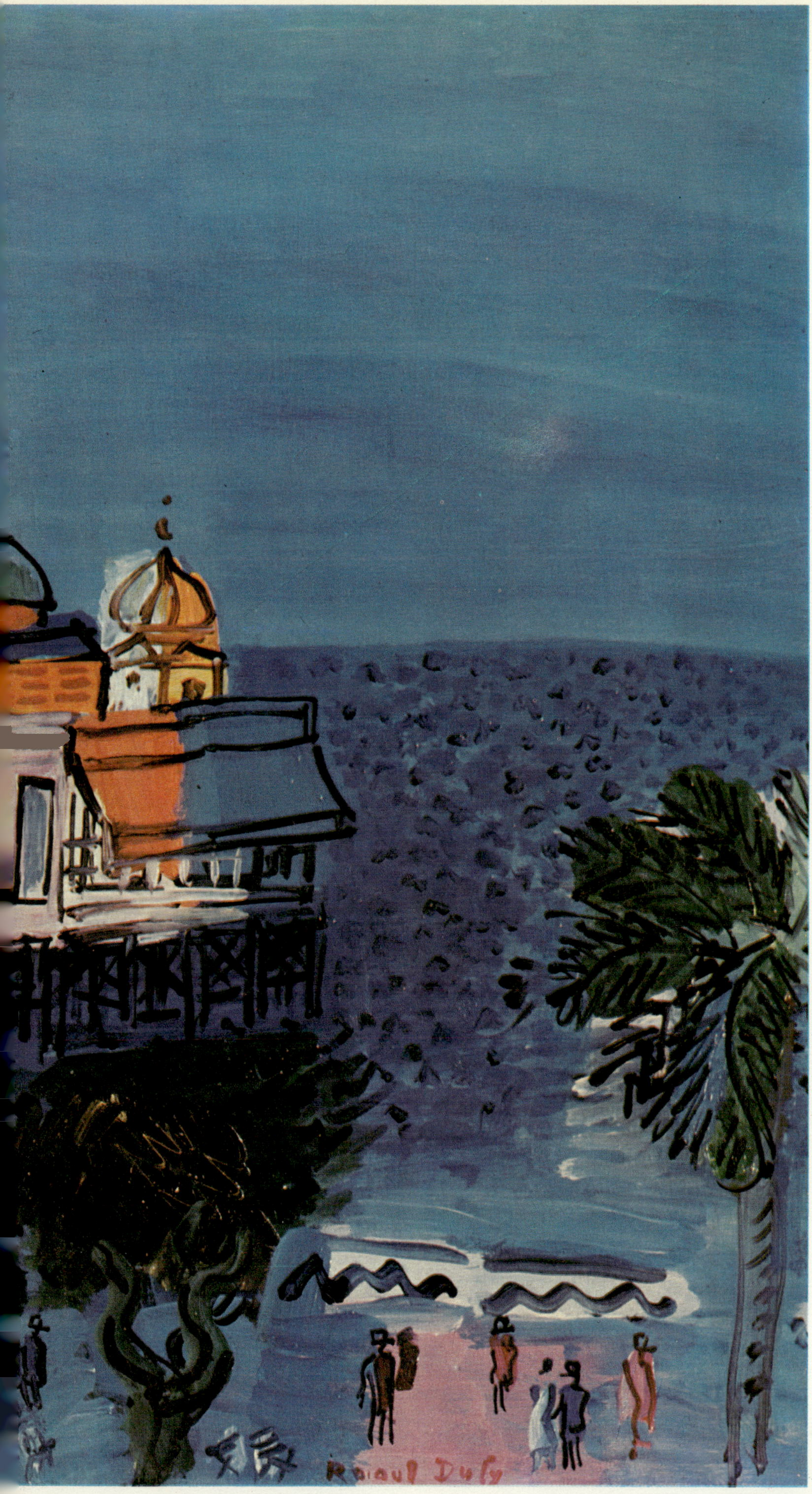
Raoul Dufy

(pages 38-39)
Raoul Dufy
The Casino at Nice, 1928
Oils on canvas 18″ × 22″
Bayeler Gallery, Basle

André Derain
Chatou 1880-Garches 1954
Woman in a Shawl, 1908
Oils on canvas
Private collection, Paris

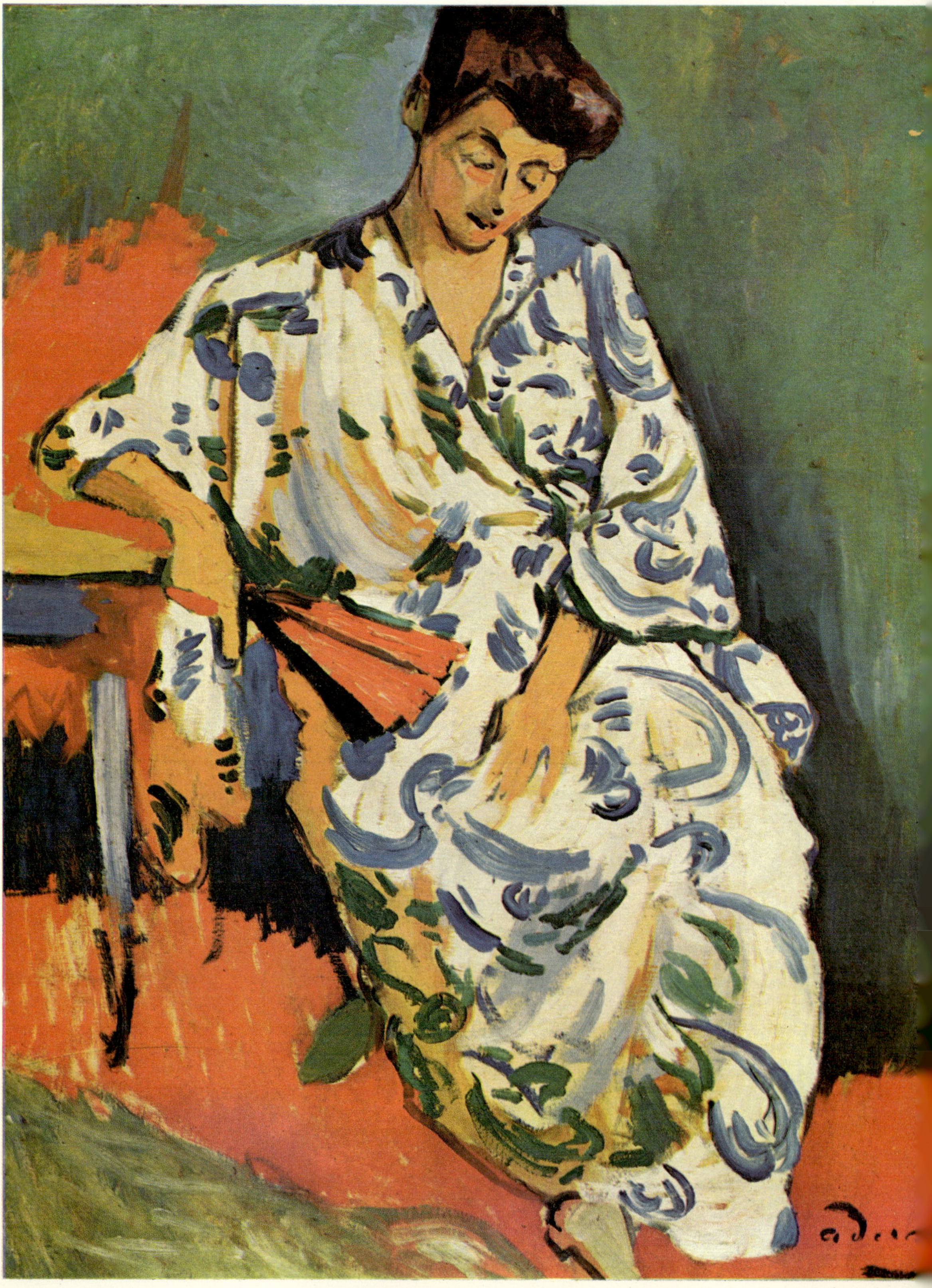

but whose charm is inescapable. Even more than Picasso or Léger, Dufy is, of all contemporary painters, without doubt the one who has most profoundly influenced everyday design.

He never gave up experimenting. After concentrating for a long time on fabrics and after designing some tapestry cartoons for Beauvais, he worked with the potter Artigas* on ceramics, a form in which his natural abilities produced marvellous results. Meanwhile, he had also started on lithography and was tackling large-scale decoration, first on the occasion of the 1925 Exhibition, then in the dining-room of a Dr Viard with a stunning *Itinerary from Paris to the Sea.* Finally, in 1937, for the EDF pavilion at the International Exhibition, he executed an immense composition measuring 197 ft by 32 ft 10 in entitled *La Fée Electricité*, imaginatively but accurately tracing the history of electricity. He carried out this major work simultaneously with a decoration for the bar at the Palais de Chaillot and a design depicting naturalists and explorers for the monkey-house in the Botanical Gardens in Paris, but since 1963 decorating the Museum library.

From among his abundant output of easel paintings he always made a point of keeping the best. In his studio at Guelma and the adjoining apartment he kept characteristic works from all his phases. No stage of his development was absent from this personal collection, which began when he was still studying with Lhullier in Le Havre. An exhibition mounted early in 1963 in the Louvre's Mollien gallery gave the public an idea of it before it was distributed among the museums in Paris, Le Havre and Nice to which Mme Dufy had bequeathed it.

The man was no less charming than the painter. His good humour was unquenched either by the difficulties of his youth or by the sufferings of his old age.

After leading a wandering life between 1940 and 1944 he was attacked by rheumatics, which hampered his work. He then went to the United States. During a two-year stay he held exhibitions, designed a production of *L'Invitation au Château* by Anouilh*, and underwent a course of cortisone treatment which improved his rheumatism but provoked heart trouble.

He returned to work in his Paris studio, and then visited Venice, where he won the International Grand Prix and had a studio built at Forcalquier, in the Upper Alps. He was barely installed before he died, on 23 March 1953.

Right up to the end his friends found him affable and smiling. His last canvases proved that he had lost none of his faculty of imagination, his vitality or his youthfulness. He had the face of a young man; his conversation was as brilliant as ever, his enthusiasm for work as great.

The diversity of his work in no way detracts from its unity. But, as he said to Pierre Courthion: "When one wins success for something or other, one must quickly turn one's back and throw oneself into a new adventure." His curiosity always drove him to seek new sights: he went to England to attend Henley Regatta, to Spain to paint the ramparts of Avila, to Italy, where he composed *Homage to Claude Lorrain* on the theme of the fountains of Rome, to Morocco, and many other places.

André Derain
Mountain Landscape, 1908
Oils on canvas 27″ × 18″
Fernande Graindorge Collection

In comparison with other artists, who profess inordinate ambitions, Raoul Dufy was at one time considered a minor master. This was one of the errors which contemporaries sometimes make. In reality, having embraced all genres—landscapes, still-lifes, portraits, nudes, compositions—his work can, with the passage of time, be appreciated as one of the most vast and most personal to have been produced in the 20th century.

Derain

Although Derain's meeting with Vlaminck* was fortunate for Vlaminck, it cannot be said so confidently that the reverse was true. Their subsequent quarrel in 1914 was the consequence of a deep-seated incompatibility between Vlaminck's romanticism and Derain's classicism. Derain had quickly tired of the solutions offered by his comrades, and reacted by immersing himself in intellectual theorising and the study of past masters. This produced a conflict which he never managed to surmount. He might, perhaps, have escaped if he had not, for more than ten years, strayed from the path which, with his liking for order, he should have followed. If he had instead come to grips with the movements which, early in the century, were revolutionising the concepts of painting, he might perhaps have become the key figure which André Salmon* saw him as, playing an essential role reserved for him alone in the story of contemporary art.

If today André Derain appears anachronistic, this is because he was caught between that subjection to reality which was accepted by painters who were close to him, such as Vlaminck and Segonzac*, and the great formal boldness of the Cubists and their descendants, the Abstract painters. In trying to impose an order on the disorder of his period, he met with failure, but a failure more glorious than many a success. It is hard, however, not to be puzzled by a painter who was sometimes wildly ambitious, but who under different circumstances was satisfied with superficial success.

Probably his character was not strong enough to sustain his reactionary urge; it was characteristic of him to swim against the current, but he did not pursue this with a consistent enough conviction. There is this conflict in Derain: he was a giant whose natural strength was curbed by the gentleness of his bearing and behaviour.

Melancholy? Doubt? Pride? While he was alive it was difficult to form an opinion on a man who shrouded himself in deliberate misanthropy. Today his work survives; its nobility is touching, and through it, as through Picasso's, run the recognisable currents of the century. But, instead of Picasso's spontaneous outpouring, an over-prolonged reflectiveness chills Derain's work: "As for my painting," he told Gaston Diehl, "I think about it too long and too hard. I look at it too much. I see my form. My form will be the death of me. I am trying to immobilise my will between two recognised forms. So it is complete disaster."

Derain was born on 10 June 1880. He was intelligent, and wanted to be an engineer. But soon a lack of keenness began to show and he pursued his studies half-heartedly. At the Collège Chaptal he made the acquaintance of a colleague, Linaret,

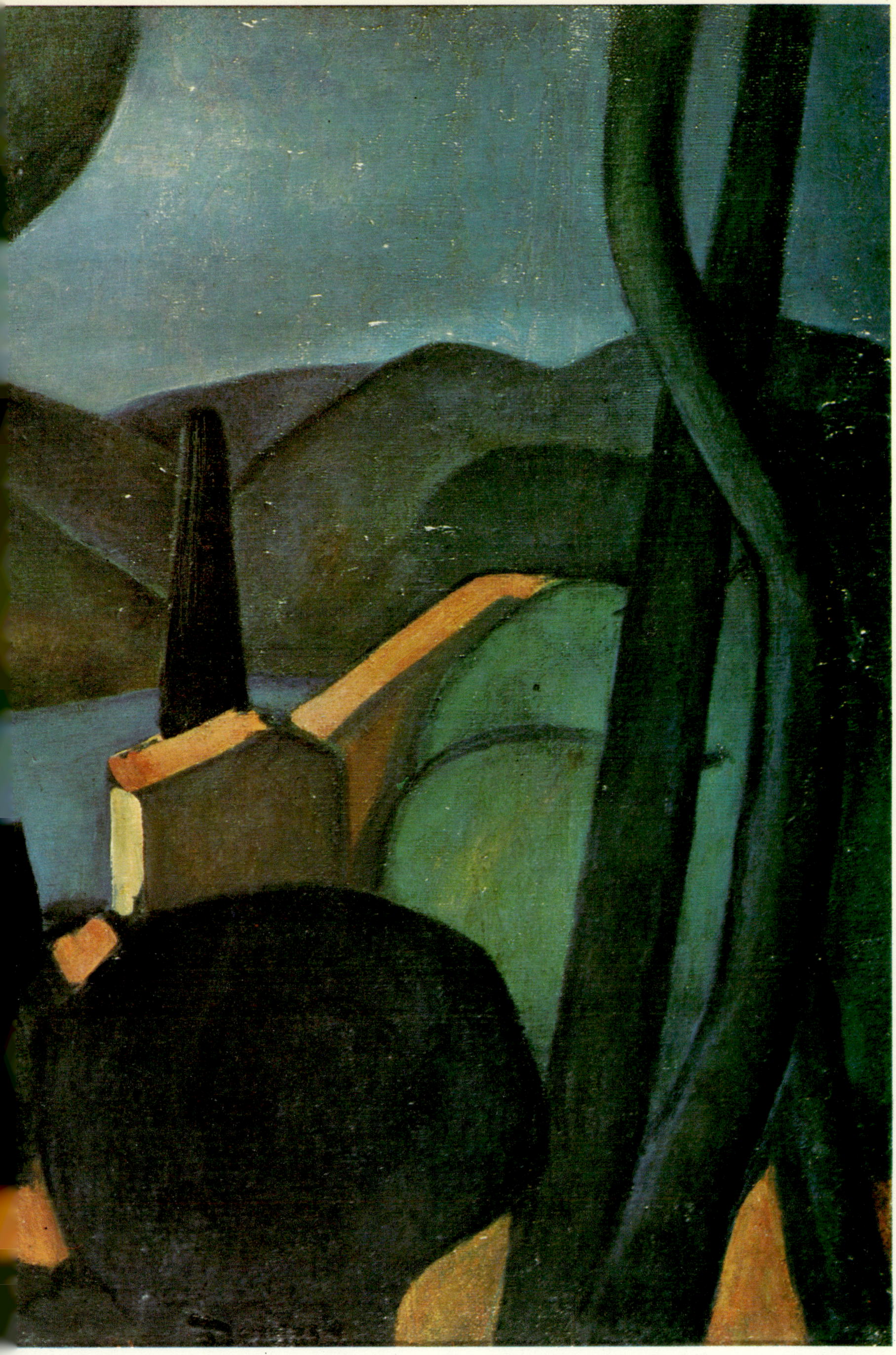

André Derain
L'Estaque, 1905
Oils on canvas
Private collection, Paris

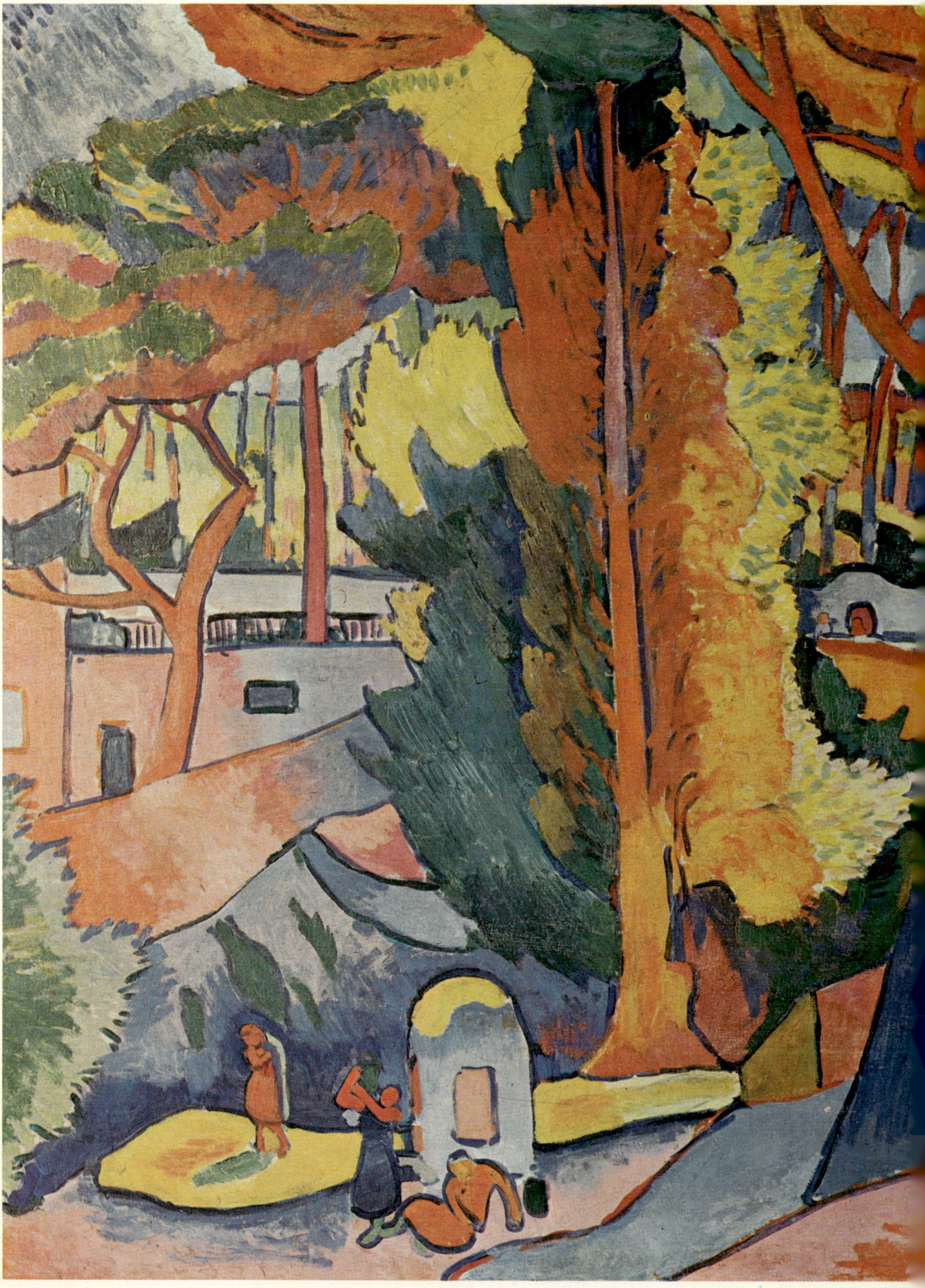

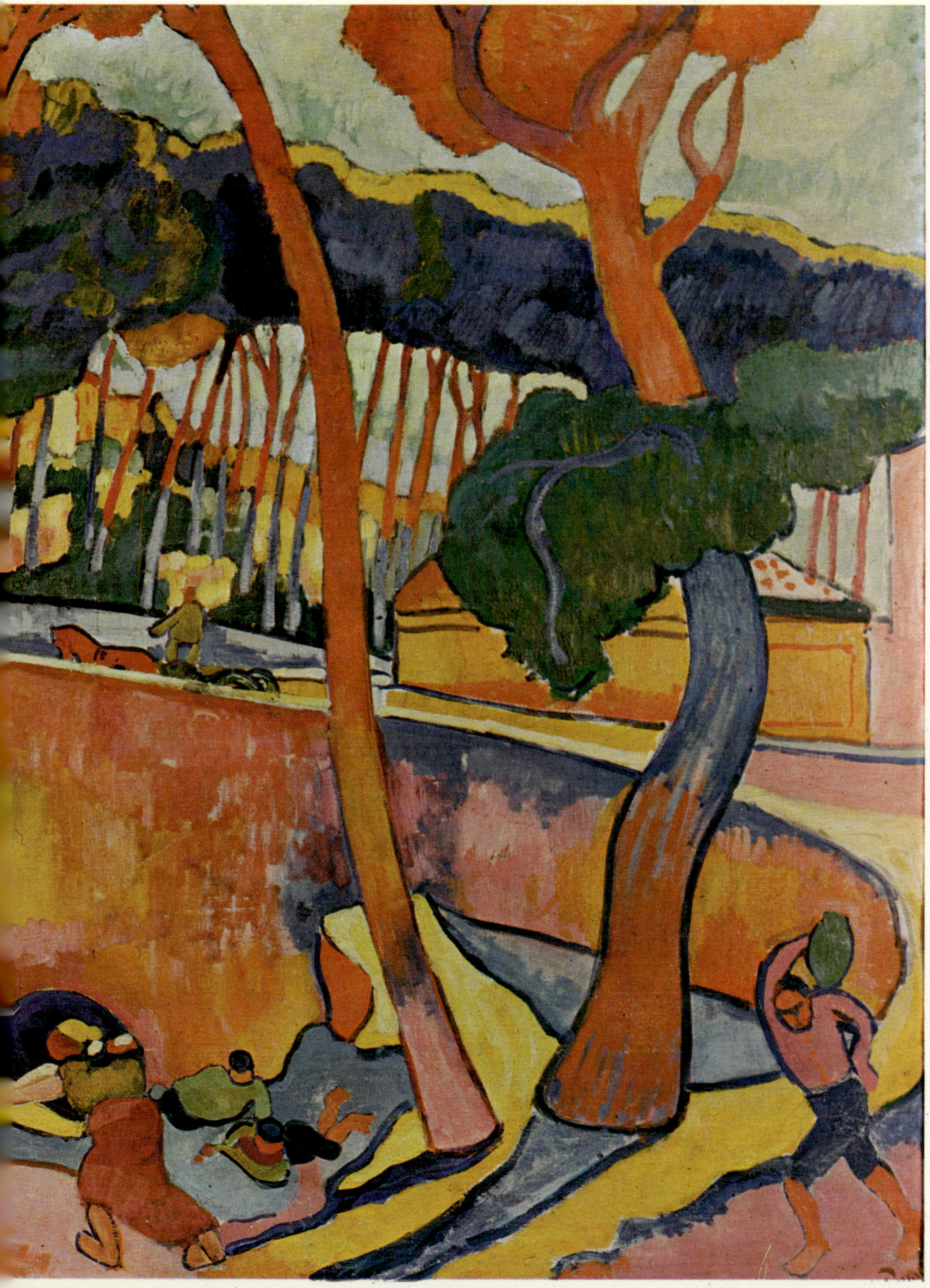

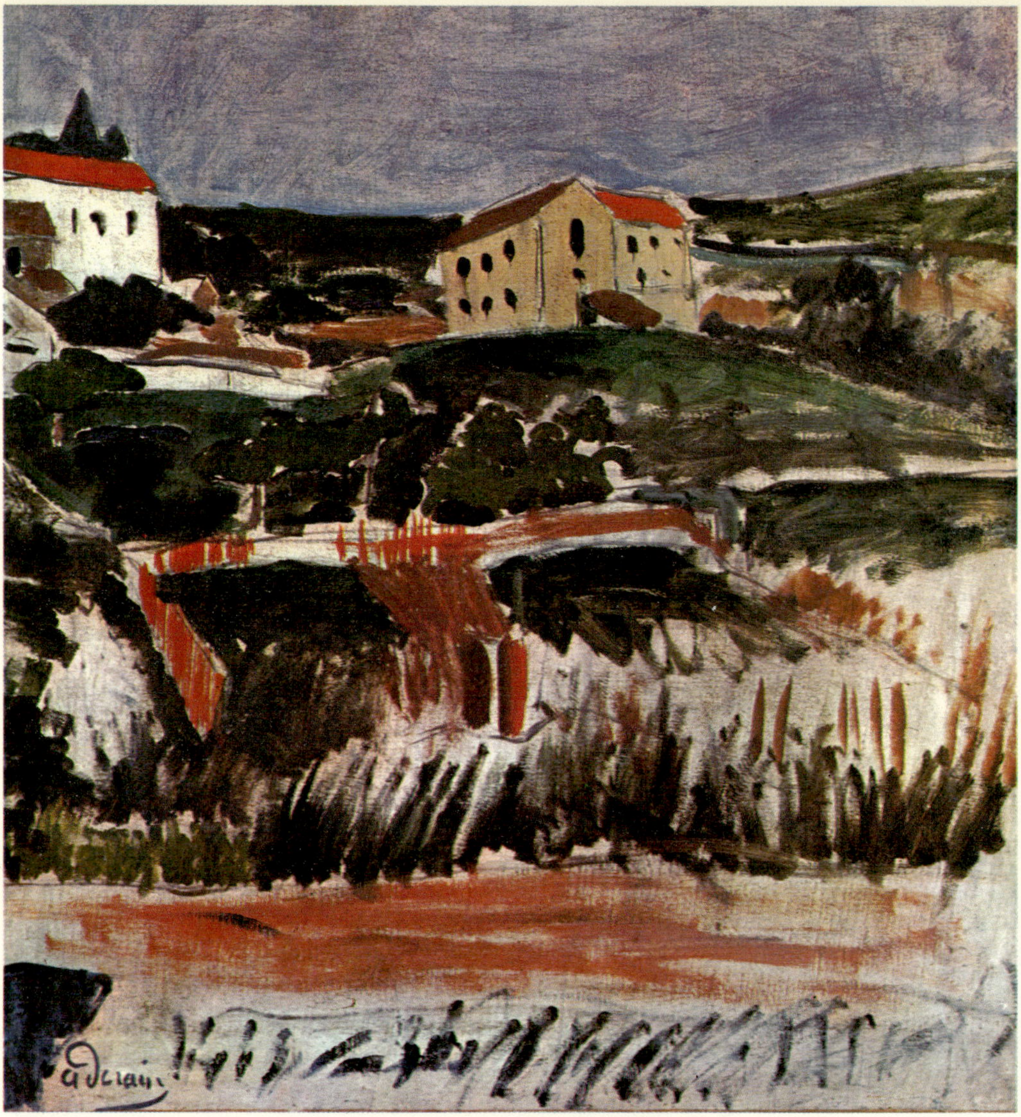

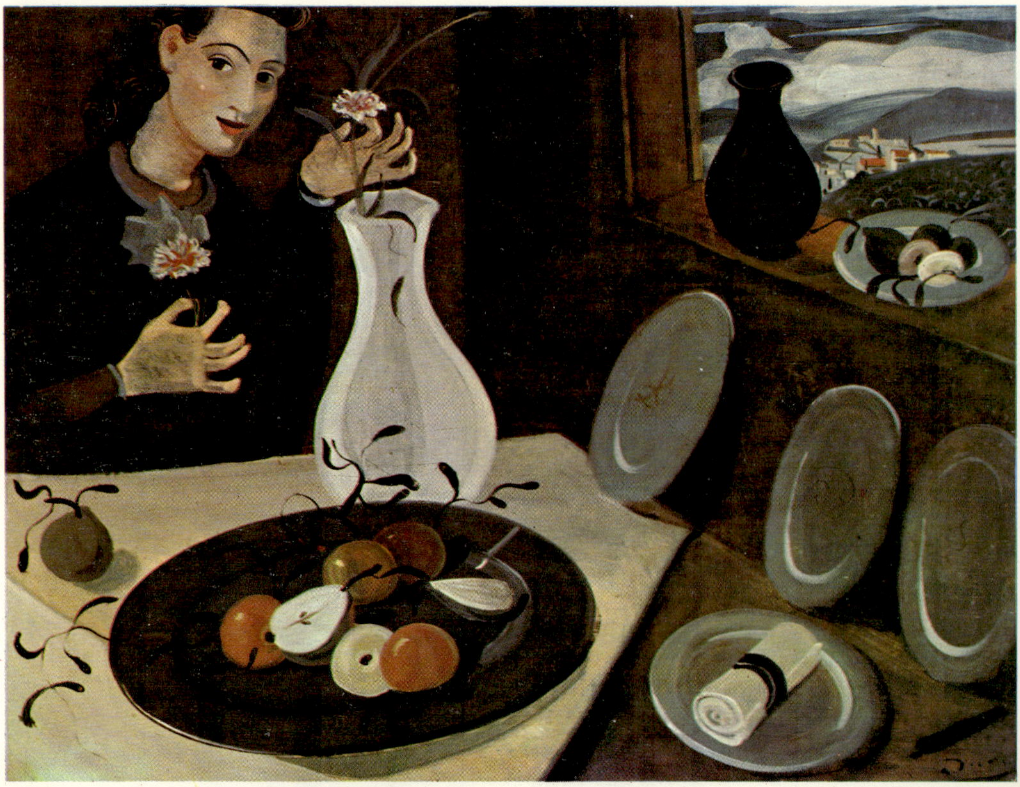

◂ André Derain
Villeneuve-Loubet (Fauve period), 1905
Oils on canvas 28″ × 24″
Pierre Lévy Collection, Paris

André Derain
Still-life with Young Woman
Oils on canvas 45″ × 34″
Georges Daelmans Collection, Brussels
▾

who loved painting, and whom he found making bold copies in the Louvre. He began to paint too. But it seems that, as soon as he got to know Vlaminck, painting became nothing more to him than a pretext for idling.

He met Matisse at the Académie Carrière, which they both attended, but this was far less decisive for him than that other meeting which is described by Apollinaire: "In 1900, in the early autumn, a young man living on the Ile de la Grenouillère was painting the bridge at Chatou. He painted fast, using pure colours, and his dazzlingly coloured canvas was nearly finished when, hearing a cough behind him, the young artist, who was called Maurice de Vlaminck, turned round quickly and saw a tall young man examining his work with interest. They began to discuss painting. Maurice de Vlaminck knew the work of the Impressionists—Manet, Money, Sisley, Cézanne—of which Derain was still ignorant. They also discussed Van Gogh and Gauguin. Vlaminck was living in Rueil and Derain in Chatou. They saw each other again every day, and their enthusiasm for the new things in painting went on increasing. Vlaminck, always on the lookout for aesthetic curiosities in second-hand shops during his rounds of the villages along the Seine, had bought wooden sculptures, masks, and fetishes carved by Negro artists of French Africa. . . . Maurice de Vlaminck's taste for Negro sculpture and André Derain's meditation on these bizarre objects, at a time when the Impressionists had at last delivered painting from its academic chains, were to have a decisive influence on the course of French Art."

Derain's encounter with Vlaminck opened his eyes not only, as Apollinaire said, in the direction of Impressionism, Gauguin and Van Gogh, but also towards the Neo-Impressionists; Derain was attracted by the divisionist touch, and, while his comrade used pure colours as his impulse led him, he already used them himself in a more systematic way. He certainly applied this technique in a different manner from Seurat or Signac; he never thought of obeying the rules of optical contrast and rejected none of the violence which was firmly excluded from the canvases of his elders. Today, however, when we compare the landscapes painted side by side by Derain and Vlaminck, we already find in the former an attempt to organise his pictures which the latter manifested only later.

Behind the strident glare of Derain's yellows and reds, there is the same desire to compress form which he had observed in old masters. In 1903 we find him quartered between the Louvre and the rue Laffitte; in fact, this year is the date of his first important work, a copy of *Christ Carrying the Cross* by Ghirlandaio, which marks a definite break from Impressionism.

His going into the army separated him from the Louvre and obliged him to work from nature; the total freedom with which he interpreted it in the *View of Le Pecq* (1904) heralded the revolution that was to shake the Salon d'Automne in 1905.

His Fauve work, although less exciting than Vlaminck's, displays an impressive mastery. He exploited to the full the opportunities offered by pure colour.

In the spring of 1905, after his military service, he went to Collioure with Matisse. It was there, in L'Estaque, and in London (which he visited with Vlaminck in

1906, and revisited alone in 1907 and 1910), that he painted his most characteristic Fauve canvases.

His reaction against his early experiments was more rapid, perhaps, than that of any of his comrades. In 1908 he began to withdraw into lofty solitude, and firmly refused to show his work. His Jansenism suited the technique of wood engraving, and he illustrated *L'Enchanteur pourrissant* by his friend Apollinaire. The latter wrote: "After these juvenile phases, Derain has turned to soberness and proportion. From his efforts have come works whose grandeur borders sometimes on the religious, and in which some people have claimed to see traces of archaism."

After mastering colour, he set out to conquer form. Like all young painters of the time, he was moved by the grace of Cézanne and, with a sudden brutal change, browns and ochres replaced the hot colours he had systematically employed on his palette. Some of his still-lifes anticipate Cubism. *The Last Supper* (1907) reveals a deliberate attempt at composition, an ambition not noticeable in any of his contemporaries.

The limitations of painting in his day were so apparent to him that he went to the past for his models. He studied the Middle Ages with such enthusiasm that the style he imposed on compositions such as *The Drinkers*, *The Two Sisters* and *Saturday* has been termed "Gothic".

The first world war had a profound effect on him. It seems to have brought a certain serenity into his troubled mind. Firmly rejecting the hieraticism of the Giottesques, he turned to more classic forms. Feeling disorder paramount everywhere, he sought his lessons from the painters of Pompeii, the Renaissance Italians, Caravaggio, Corot and others besides; this prompted certain malicious commentators to call his work an anthology.

In fact, André Derain's aspirations towards an art of serenity and equilibrium were fulfilled less by his compositions than by certain of his portraits and still-lifes. But even his more abortive attempts are exciting, particularly when he refrains from bridling his lively sensitivity.

He was also capable of descending from his ivory tower. He engraved an astonishing series of coloured wood-cuts for Rabelais and painted décors for the Ballets Russes; he loved racehorses and beautiful women.

A sense of disenchantment, however, weighed on his work and on his daily life. Perhaps he was aware of not having attained the ambitious goal towards which he had reached all his life. There came a time when he no longer worked except spasmodically, forsaking in his studio some advanced works on which he had been engaged and others which he left only as sketches.

He lived at Chambourcy in a house surrounded by a high-walled park until his accidental death on 10 September 1954, after which a whole series of models was discovered; cast in bronze, they revealed Derain as a sculptor obsessed by the human face.

Surely no one can be unmoved by the pathos of this potentially great career.

Fernand Léger
The Tug-Boat, 1920
Oils on canvas
Municipal Museum, Grenoble

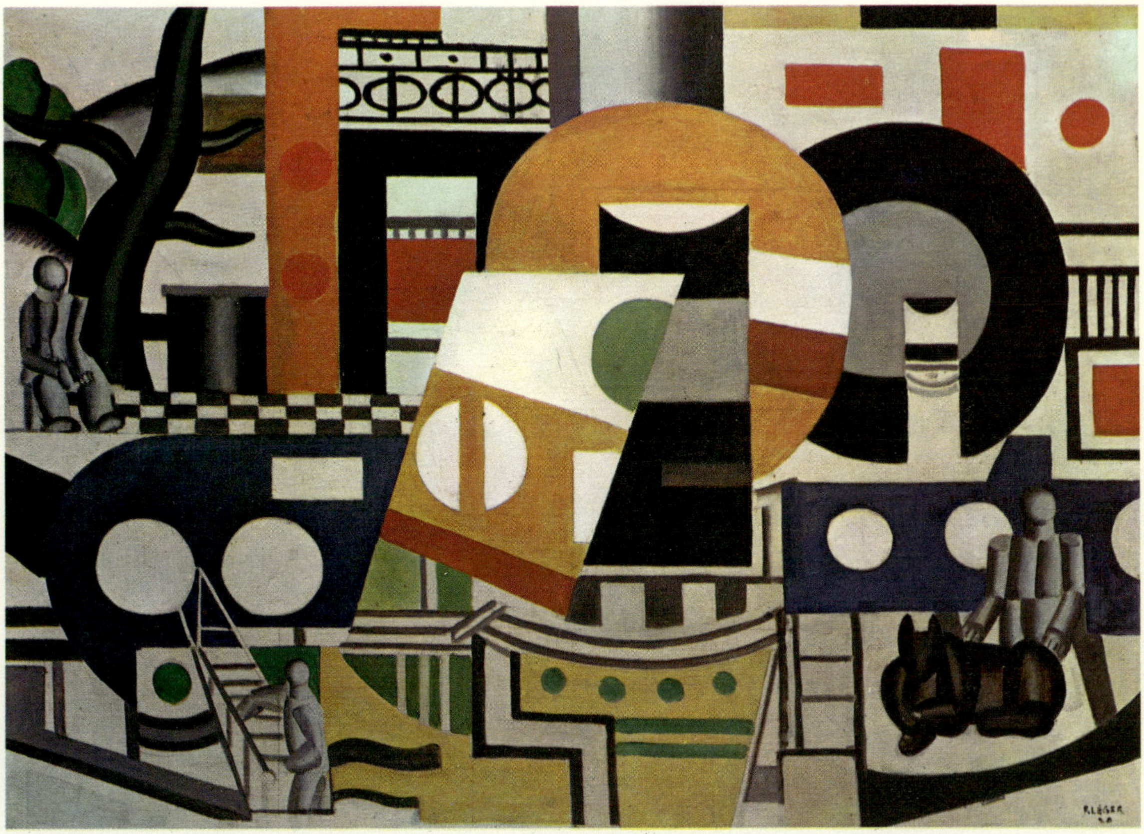

Léger

No painting is more serious, or lacking in a sense of humour, than that of Fernand Léger. While Picasso's work is one immense improvisation, Léger, on the contrary, aimed to be a planner. He held firm ethical and social convictions which, with a clumsiness which his persistence should have conquered, he attempted to infuse into his pictures, mosaics, stained glass and coloured sculptures; he widely overstepped the boundaries of painting, and his influence on contemporary decorative art was immense. There is no doubt that he was the instigator of the movement which changed the whole look of street posters introduced between the wars by people like Cassandre and Anne Carlu.

He was born in Argentan (Orne) on 4 February 1881. His father was a rough man who died suddenly when his son was very young. He was brought up by his mother and his uncle, and chose architecture as a profession. This initial inclination left such a mark on him that it is debatable whether, in choosing painting, he did not miss his vocation. His interest in architecture in later life, when he carried out numerous mural décors and collaborated with architects, surely indicates that he sometimes regretted

Fernand Léger
Three Musicians
Oils on canvas
Munich Museum

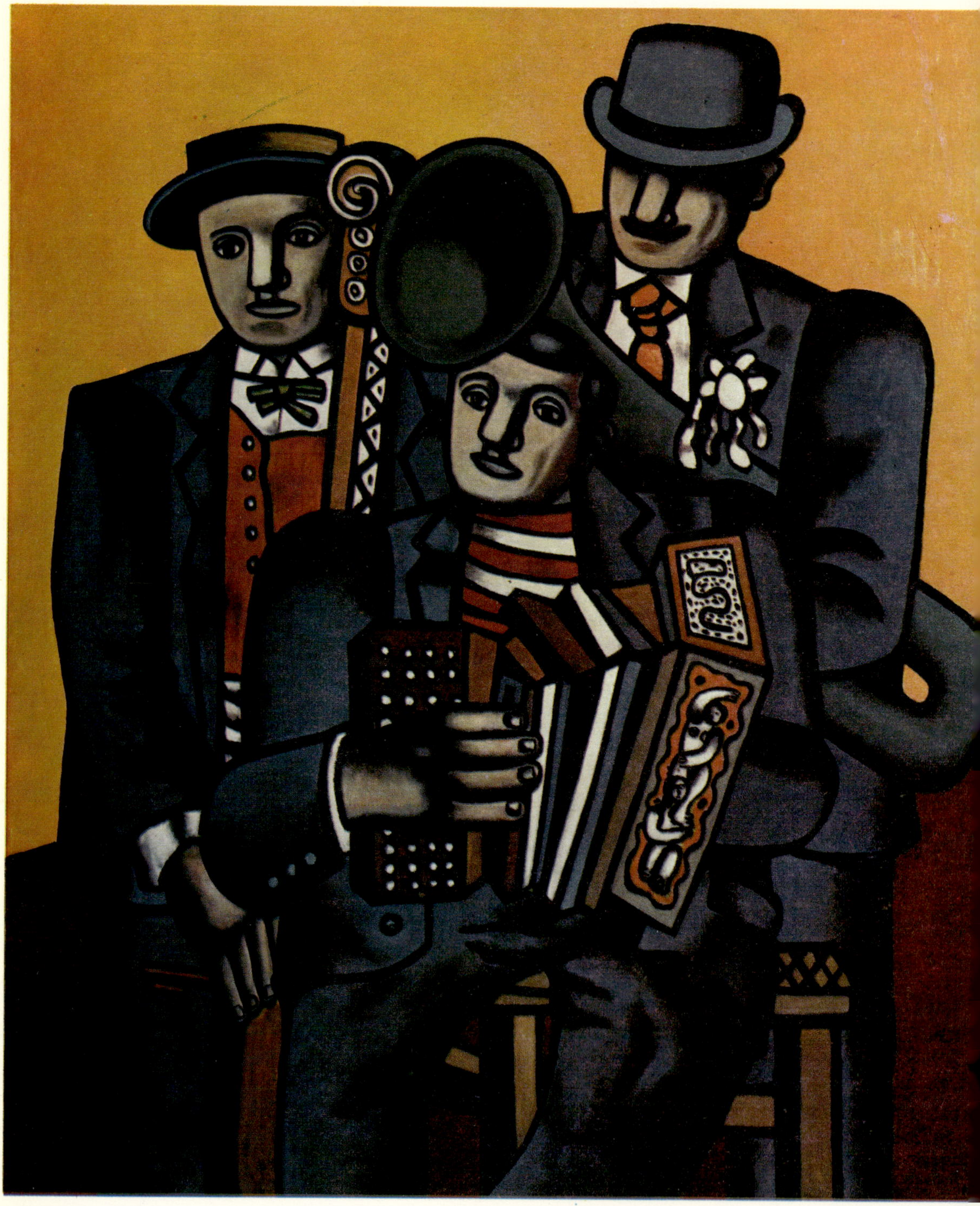

Fernand Léger
Still-life with Three Fruits, 1954
Oils on canvas 20″ × 26″
Sonia Henie Collection, Oslo

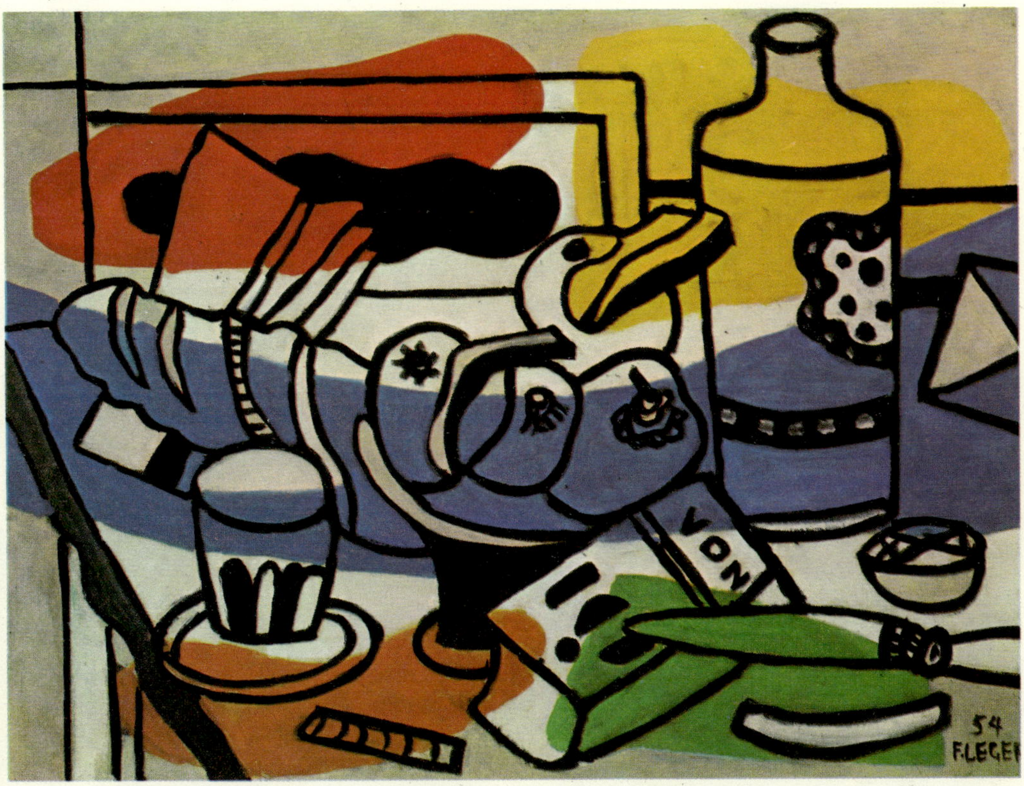

leaving the profession which he practised in Caen and Paris before doing his military service.

When he came out of the army, he experienced such hardship that he fell ill. His uncle, who, according to Pierre Descargues, had been saying: "He has really got to feel the worst pinch before he will understand that he can't make his living that way," relented and sent him to Corsica for the winter.

So, this man from Normandy discovered the beauties of the Mediterranean. He was so struck by this first visit that he went back to Corsica twice. At the time he practised a fairly ineffectual Impressionism, as is shown in *My Mother's Garden* (1905). Portraits of himself and his uncle from the same date are far more individual.

He entered the Ecole des Arts Décoratifs, but failed to get into the Ecole des Beaux-Arts. Nevertheless, he frequented the studios of Gérôme* and Gabriel Ferrier*. But these academic painters had far less influence on him than did Cézanne, whom he discovered at the famous 1907 retrospective exhibition.

In these traditional studies, however, he acquired a technical ability which enabled him, when he wished, to respect nature scrupulously. But already at that time he felt a need to break away from obsolete disciplines and accept new ones. Cézanne's theories, which claimed to reduce everything "to cylinder, cone or sphere", he took

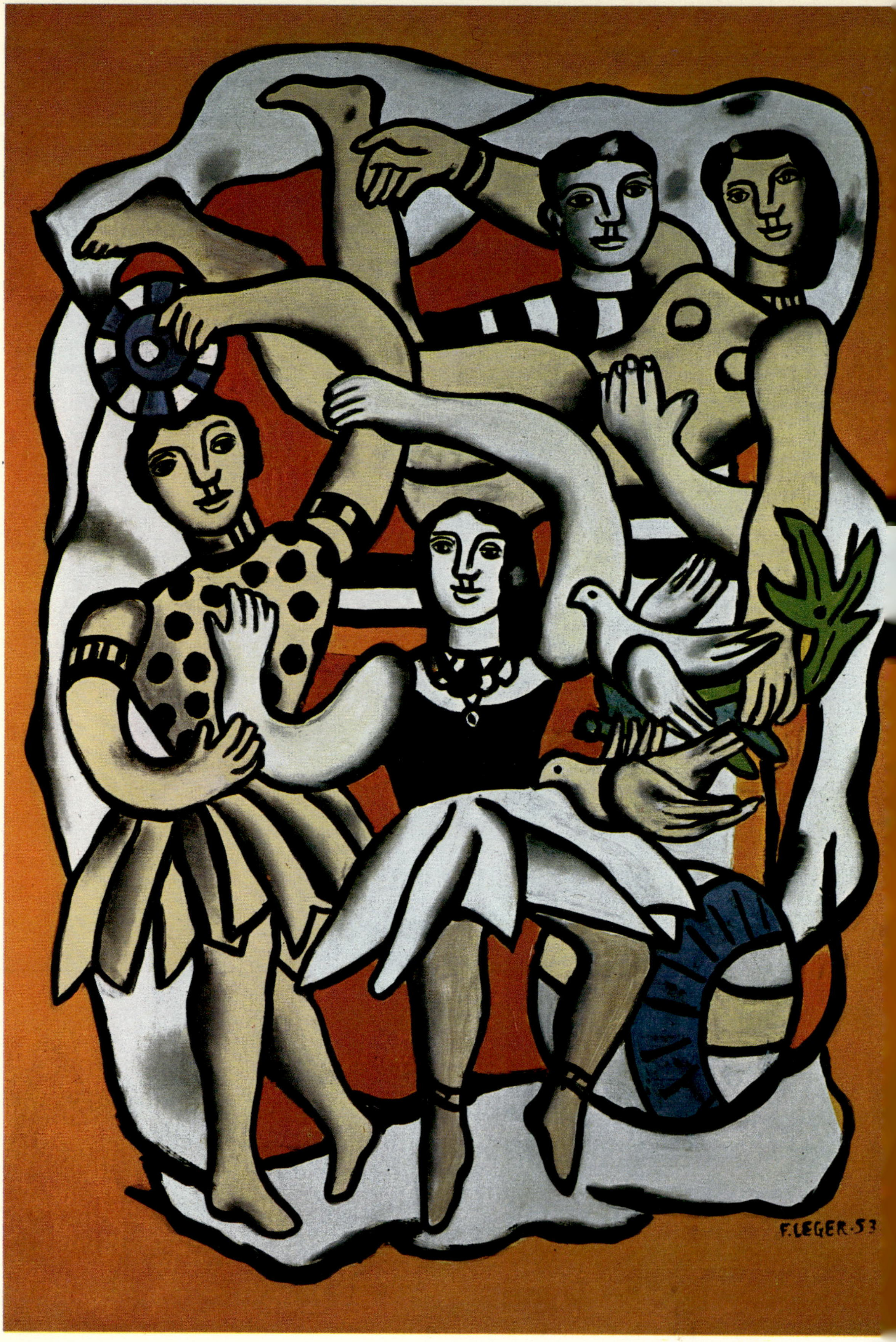

Fernand Léger
Dancers with Birds, 1953
Oils on canvas 52″ × 35″
Sonia Henie Collection, Oslo

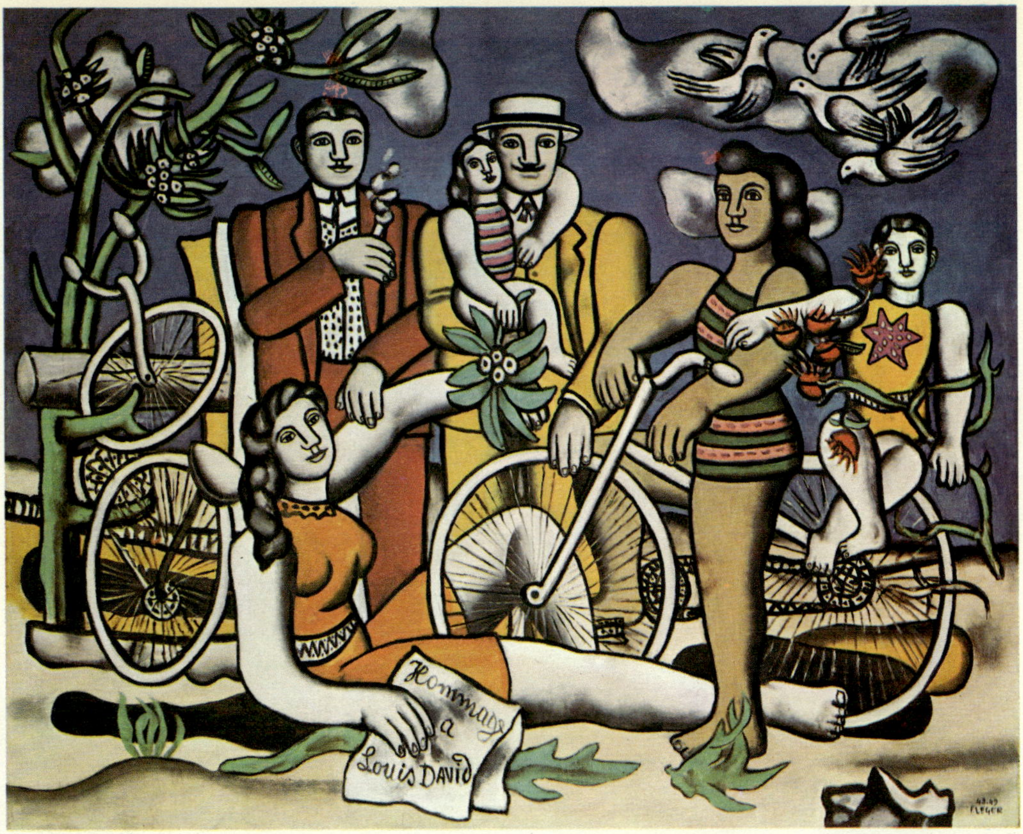

literally to such an extent that certain compositions of connecting white, yellow, blue and red cylinders were maliciously described as "Tubist". He said later: "I have spent three years ridding myself of Cézanne's influence. I was so strongly hooked that I have had to go completely abstract."

It is regrettable that he destroyed most of his works of this period, for *Nudes in the Forest*, shown at the Indépendants in 1911, was the end-product of a series of experiments of which we have only one example, *Woman Sewing*, a portrait of his mother constructed of large, abrupt areas, comparable with certain works by La Fresnaye and Segonzac, who were to develop entirely differently.

He was at that time very near to the sculptors Laurens*, Lipchitz* and Archipenko*, who had neighbouring studios in La Ruche. *The Wedding* likewise recalls, literally if not in mood, certain compositions of the young Russian, Marc Chagall, who had just settled into what were in effect the remains of the 1900 exhibition transported to the confines of Montparnasse and Montrouge. These studios were described by Blaise Cendrars in the following verse:

La Ruche
Stairs, doors, stairs
And his door opens like a newspaper
Covered with visiting cards
Then it closes.
Disorder, one is in utter disorder.
Some photographs of Léger. . . .

Through Archipenko he learned that in Montmartre those who were shortly to be named the Cubists were pursuing experiments parallel to his own. He took an interest in their attempts without joining the group, although a few of his canvases were

Fernand Léger
The Leisures (Homage to Louis David), 1948-1949
Oils on canvas 61″ × 73″
Musée National d'Art Moderne, Paris

acquired by the dealer Henry Kahnweiler*, who already had Braque and Picasso under contract. In 1911, he exhibited in company with Delaunay, Gleizes and Metzinger.

The Roofs of Paris and *Paris from My Window* (both 1912) are the works which mark the break from his "contrasts of forms", though later he was to return to the attempts he made at this time to apply a geometrical treatment to reality. The violent colours he used distinguish his canvases from those of first-generation Cubists, who stayed loyal to browns and greys: "Colour," Léger said, "has been a necessary tonic for me. There again, Delaunay and I were far away from others. They painted in monochrome, we in polychrome." No painter was nearer Fernand Léger than Robert Delaunay, the champion of Orphism*.

In 1914, however: "The war was an enormous event for me. It was during the war that I planted my feet on the ground. I left Paris in the middle of the Abstract style. Without any transition I found myself on a level with the French people; the reverse of genius, my new comrades were miners, navvies, wood- or metal-workers. At the same time I was dazzled by the breach of a 75 open in broad sunlight—magic of the light on the white metal. When I had grasped this reality, the object stayed with me." He had discovered the beauty of tools and machines: "Beauty is everywhere, in the order of your saucepans against your white kitchen wall. . . . In our day and age a work of art has to stand comparison with all sorts of manufactured articles. . . . I wish the whole world of engineers, labourers and businessmen could realise the beauty they are fabricating and in which they live."

Returning to civilian life, he launched into a very important work, *The Town*, in which he attempted to incorporate the ideas he had acquired during those terrible years. He painted from then on in flat tones, never reluctant to use bold colours. He frequented the Effort Moderne Gallery in the rue de la Baume, where he met the painter Ozenfant* and the architect who became famous as Le Corbusier*. He contributed to their magazine, *L'Esprit Moderne*, which covered all the original movements. This was the period of the "objects in space".

In his large studio in the rue Notre-Dame-des-Champs, he reacted violently against certain deteriorations of style, and exercised his activity in all fields: he painted décors for the Opéra, the Swedish Ballet at the Théâtre des Champs-Elysées (*Skating Rink*, *La Création du Monde*) and for Marcel L'Herbier's film, *L'Inhumaine*. Enthusiastic about the cinema, he himself composed *Ballet Mécanique*. He conceived vast mural compositions for the 1925 and 1937 exhibitions. After the war he decorated the great hall of the U.N. in New York and conceived the mosaic which occupies the façade of the church at Assy. He founded L'Académie Moderne, attended by young painters from all over the world. With his pupils he undertook large collective works in ceramics, tapestries and fabrics.

Anxious to reconcile art and everyday life, he moved close to tangible reality and refused to consider artistic creation as a gratuitous function. His long stay in the United States during the second world war had a considerable influence on him. He established a contact with the outside world as deep as that which the first war imposed on him.

Pablo Picasso
Málaga 1881
Three Dutch Women, 1905
Oils on canvas
Musée National d'Art Moderne, Paris

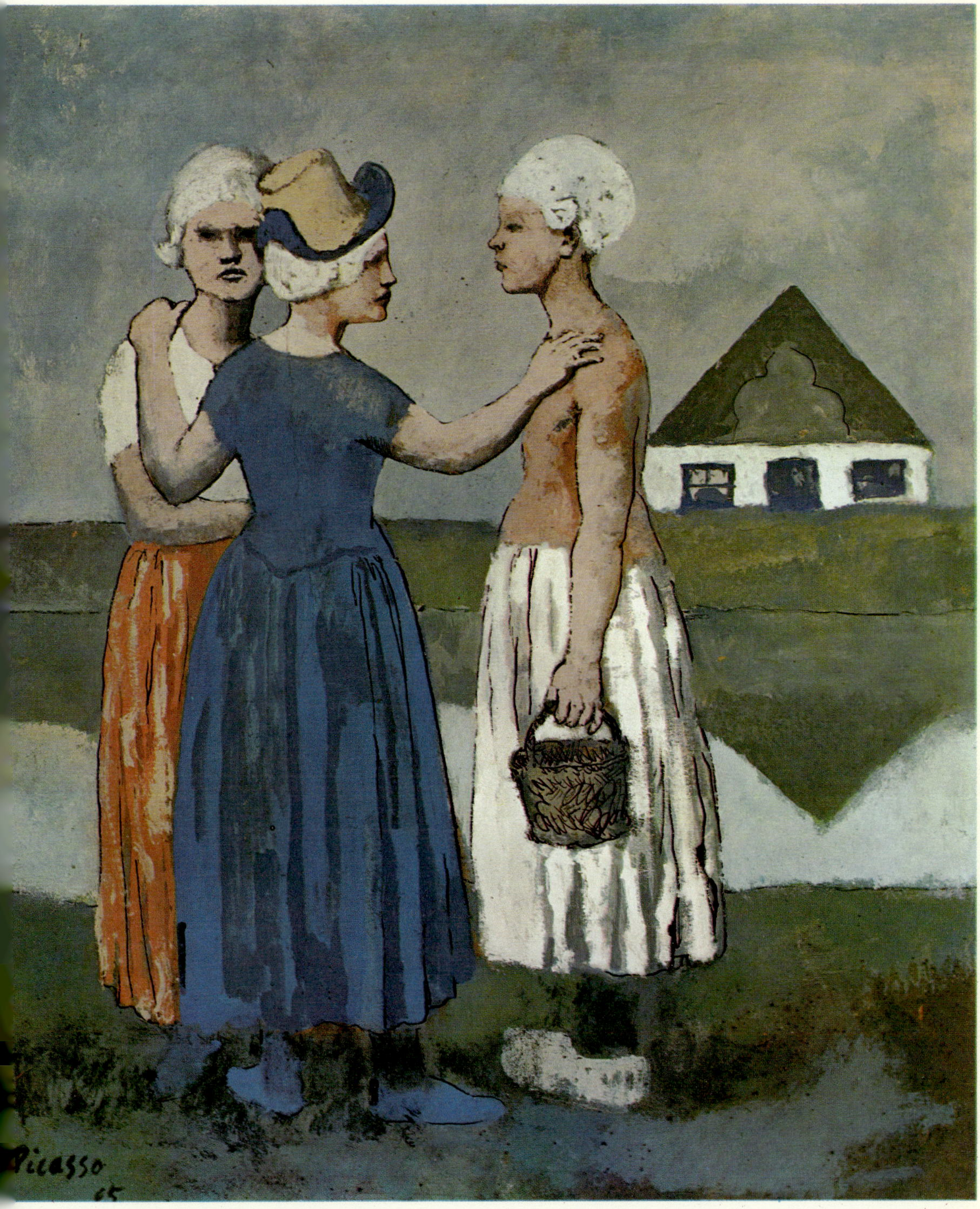

Pablo Picasso
Head and Shoulders of a Woman, 1907
Oils on canvas
National Gallery, Prague

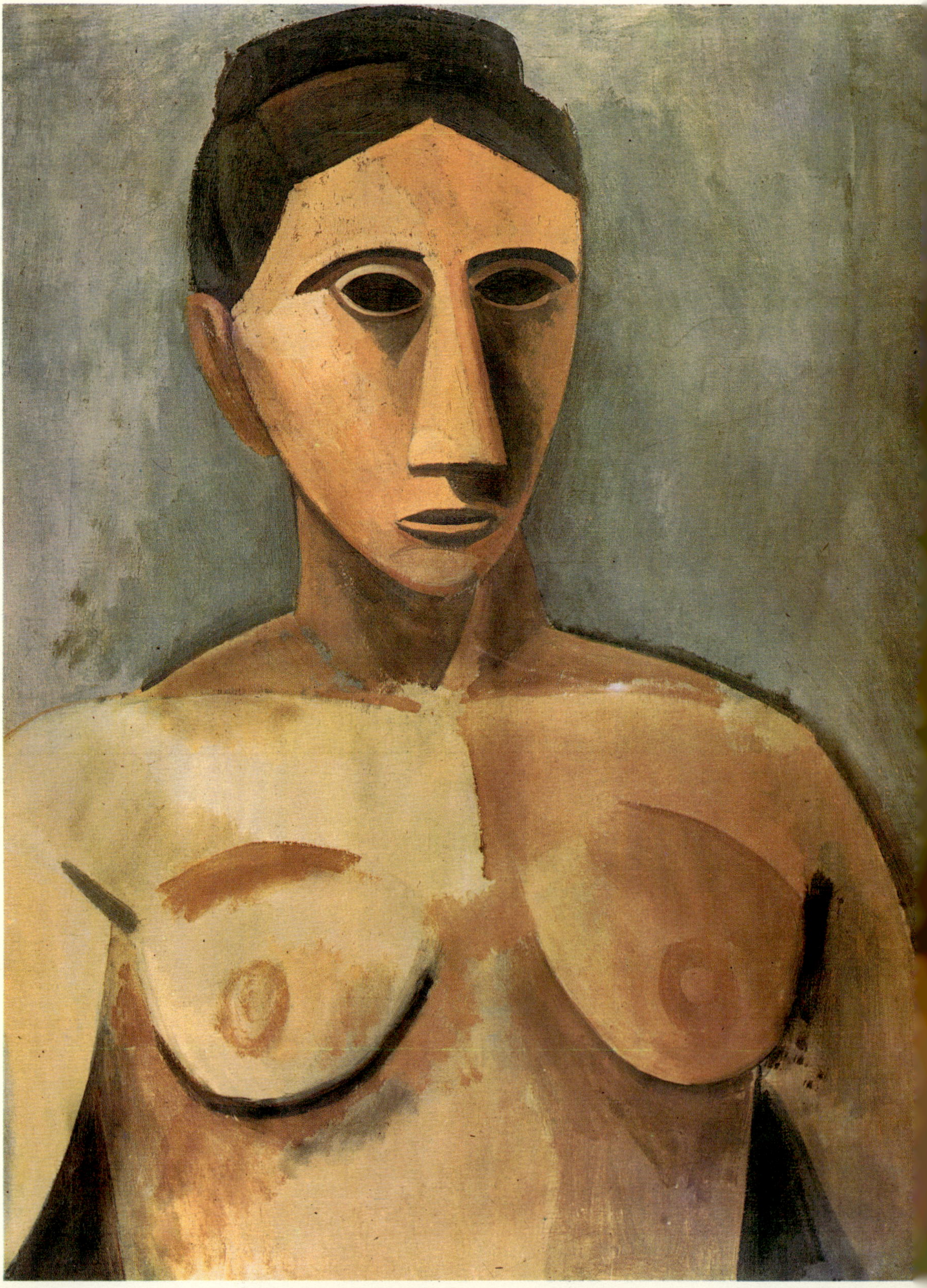

Pablo Picasso
Newspaper, Glass and Packet of Cigarettes
Oils on canvas
Private collection, Paris

The social ideas he took back to France inspired him to *The Divers*, *The Acrobats*, *The Cyclists*, *The Great Parade* and the *Homage to David*, of which he said: "I have tried to mark a return to simplicity by a direct style, comprehensible to everyone, without subtlety." Fernand Léger did not adhere to social realism, but in the last years of his life he practised a style of painting far removed from the abstractions of his youth.

That his art, which could be dismissed as summary, possesses an incontestable shock value can be verified at Biot, where his widow has built an important museum preserving the essence of his work, and was evident in the retrospective exhibition organised by the Musée des Arts Décoratifs shortly after his sudden death in Gif-sur-Yvette on 18 April 1955.

Picasso

André Rouveyre [1] applied the expression "leading contemporary" to André Gide, but Picasso deserves it equally; he, like Gide, has exercised a decisive influence. He too has loved to perplex people, and behave unpredictably with the intention of surprising and reassuring in turn. Basically, there is in Picasso that love of invention which made André Salmon call him "the animinator"; he himself said to Jean Cocteau*: "I don't seek—I find."

On the other hand, Picasso enjoys a sense of fun. The sparkle in his Andalusian eyes and his sarcastic laugh make it quite clear that he takes himself less seriously than we do. He paints because it amuses him, and one can assume that he has not been displeased to graduate from the rank of struggling painter to that of a genius enjoying a fame more far-reaching than that of the Renaissance masters. All the legend that surrounds him cannot disguise his endowment of genius.

Yet whimsicality falls far short of explaining him. He harbours deep passions, and during the Spanish Civil War it was impossible not to be overwhelmed by *Guernica*,

[1] André Rouveyre (b. 1879), French writer and draughtsman.

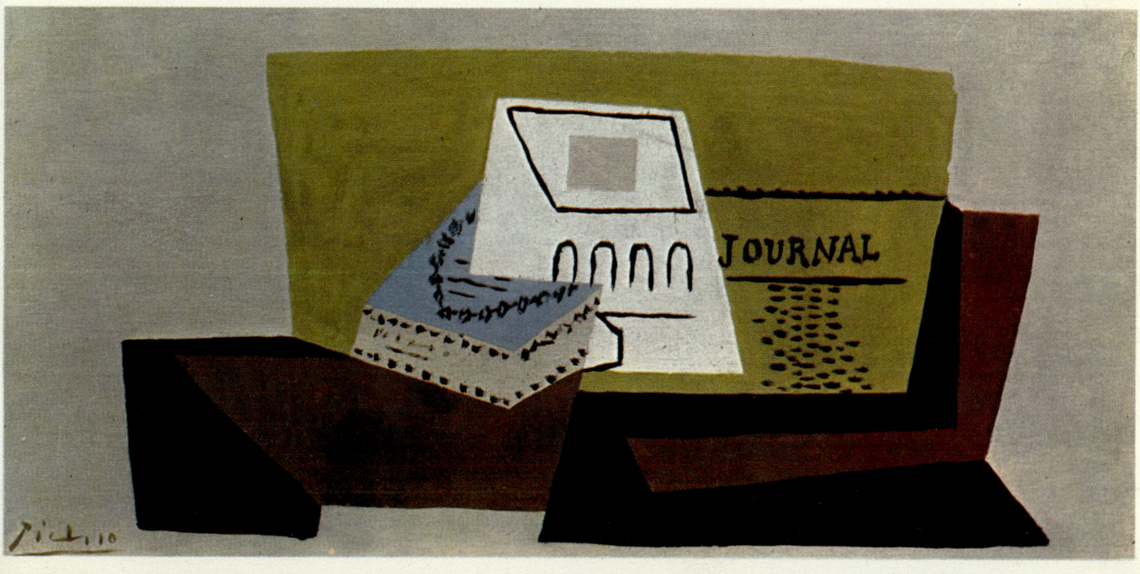

Pablo Picasso
Women on the Banks of the Seine, 1950
Oils on canvas 39″ × 79″
Kunstmuseum, Basle
▼

Pablo Picasso
Spring
Oils on canvas
Private collection, Paris
▼▼

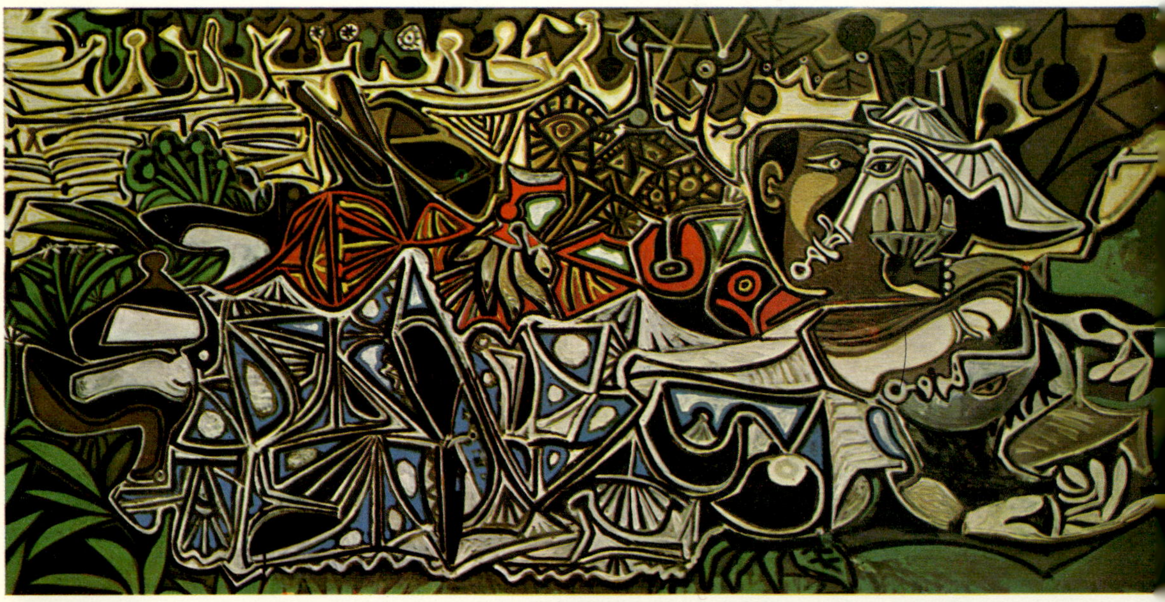

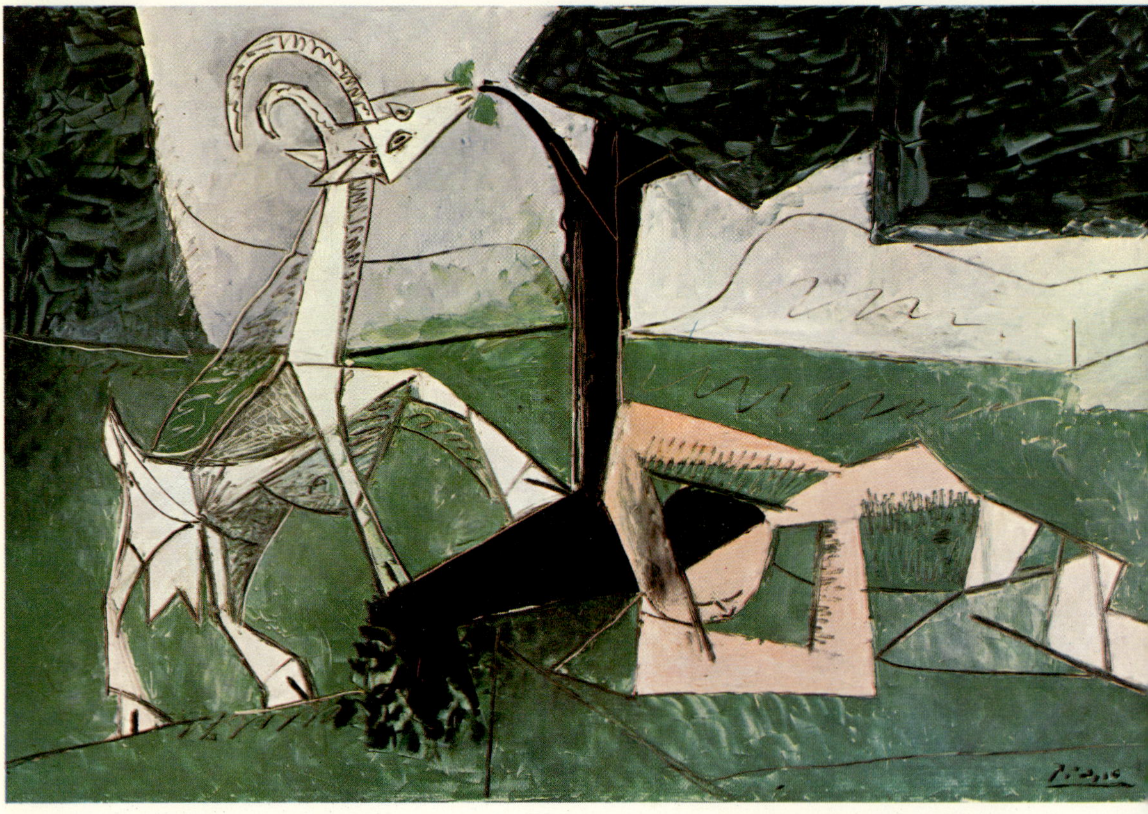

the large monochrome composition he painted for the 1937 Paris International Exhibition.

One of the main factors which help to elucidate his baffling work is his race. He was born in Málaga in 1881, of a father with mixed Andalusian and Castillian blood and a mother—whose name he assumed—whose family came from Italy and possibly had distant Jewish ancestors.

Then followed a long stay in Barcelona at a time of intense political, intellectual and artistic ferment. These formative years in the Catalonian capital, where his father taught drawing, is another key to his personality. Ultimately, he visited Paris several times between 1900 and 1904, when he settled finally in Montmartre.

If there is any such thing as a "Paris School", it is due entirely to him. Before him, certainly, there was Jongkind, Pissarro and Van Gogh, but after him came thousands of painters from Spain, Russia, Poland and Holland. In Montmartre he associated with two poets, Apollinaire and Max Jacob*, two inspired magicians with words and ideas who were to contribute not a little to that break with all traditions which Cubism represents.

This creation of a "surreal", this attempt to construct a subjective reality more true than the objective reality, sprang from conversations between this circle of painters and poets and also the mathematician Princet*. These theories particularly inspired the "second-generation" Cubists, Gleizes, Metzinger and Juan Gris. Out of fashion today, they are unknown to the Abstract painters who, far from considering doing "constructive" work, live on Picasso like fleas in a lion's mane. Innumerable generations may follow, but there will never be enough of them to exploit all the seams he has mined, leaving them behind without bothering to exhaust them.

Up to 1915, Picasso's blue, pink, green, Cubist and Expressionist* periods can be exactly dated, but afterwards his works in their extreme complexity convey his various states of mind in the hour he painted them. One may well say "in the hour", for in the course of one day he can realise compositions as different in inspiration as style. Claude Roy* has published a series of majestic drawings which are sketches for his great compositions, *War and Peace*, in the Vallauris Chapel. These drawings have a realism which is categorically rejected by the compositions themselves. But make no mistake: however adventurous they may be, these experiments rely on a technique of consistent quality, and on drawing which sometimes approaches that of Ingres.

The rapidity of his variations cannot be attributed to the versatility of his wit: Picasso is a man for whom the external world has great importance, and it is impossible to pass in silence over either his political attitudes or his love-life.

Although these are fields of which art critics usually steer carefully clear, it is impossible to observe such a discretion in the presence of a painter who, more than any other, has put himself into his work. Not that he often painted his own portrait or the trappings of his private life. But he put his life into his painting and it is difficult not to share the opinion of his official biographer, Jaime Sabartès*, when he says: "Never did his creative ability show itself with more power than during the throes of his amorous

Georges Braque
The Port of Estaque, 1906
Oils on canvas
Musée National d'Art Moderne, Paris

experiences. It is enough to mention the dates of his works; they always coincide with periods of elation, periods whose starting and finishing points can be easily fixed; during each of his adventures there is the same ascending then descending curve, and the same parallel creative activity. At each new experience we witness the progress of his art, the appearance of a new shape, a new language, an individual mode of expression which could well be given the name of a woman instead of identified by the name of a colour or a geometrical shape."

Picasso's work certainly cannot be considered *en bloc*; it is possible, in fact imperative, to select. He can sometimes show mere virtuosity or impishness (as was demonstrated in the Paris Exhibition celebrating his eighty-fifth birthday). The influence he has had on the course of painting could be judged severely, considering that he imposed on it the concept of originality at all costs on which art has been feeding for the last half-century.

Picasso's importance in our world, however, seems to me no less important than that of Einstein*, and, in the same way that the latter's theories are at the basis of nuclear fission, it may be suggested that Picasso's activity has led to the fission of Western painting.

Braque

Had Georges Braque lived in the last century, he might have been like Corot or Monet, but who could regret that he has been a man of our own time, sensitive to prevailing influences, particularly those which revolutionised painting during his youth? In 1913, Apollinaire wrote: "We are heading towards an entirely new art form; it will be to painting as we have known it until now, what music is to literature." Whereas art had always hitherto developed by *evo*lution, it was in fact to the Cubist *revo*lution that Braque put his name. He did not accomplish the break with reality without hesitation: "I had learned to paint from nature, and when I became convinced that I must free myself from models, it was not at all easy." It is paradoxical that this grave and moderate young man should have played a principal role in the enterprise which was to lead painting to total abstraction.

Just as Fauvism sprang from the meeting between Vlaminck and Derain, the collision of two such widely different personalities as Braque and Picasso generated the spark which was to produce Cubism. Their early conversations in 1908 and their joint visits to the Midi resulted in the large still-lifes of 1913, so alike that it is impossible to tell who painted which.

Small, dark and mischievous, always on the look-out for new things, Picasso exercised an extraordinary hold over his big, calm, attentive friend. Braque had learned to paint by watching the workmen employed by his father, a painter-decorator, first at Argenteuil, where he was born on 13 May 1882, then in Le Havre, where the family business was installed when he was eight. He was slightly younger than two other artists

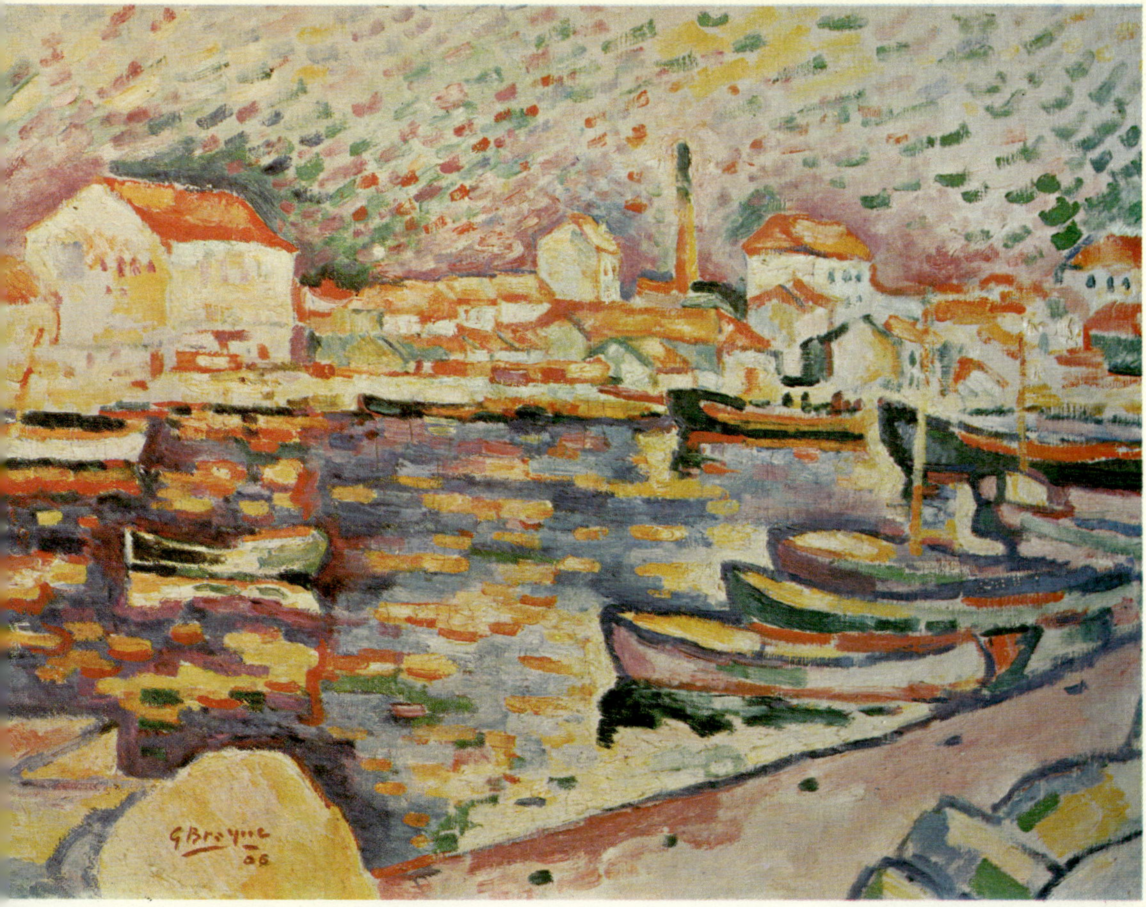

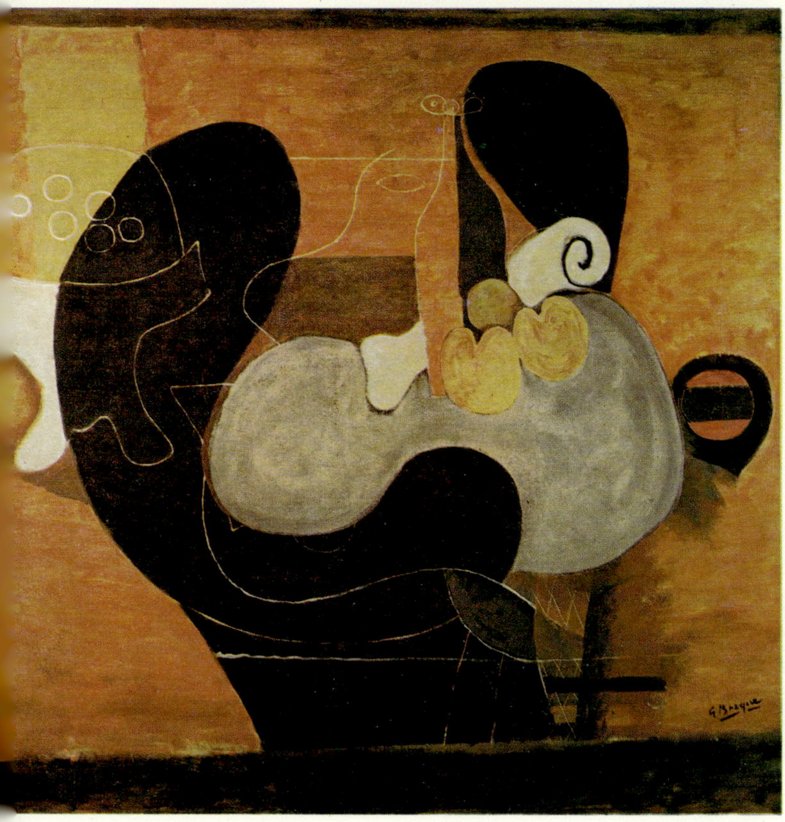

Georges Braque
Still-life, 1932
Oils on canvas
Musée National d'Art Moderne, Paris

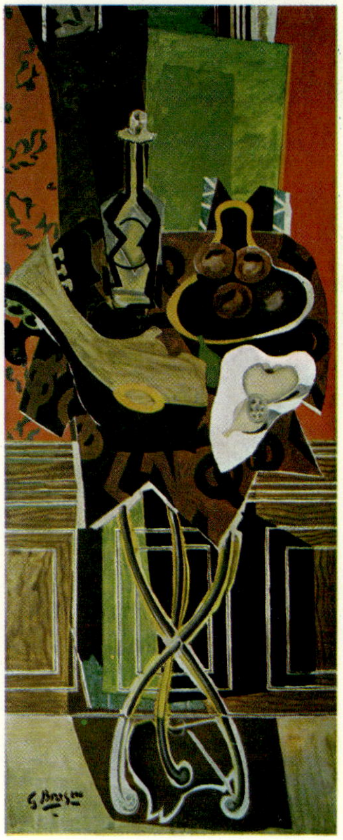

Georges Braque
The Round Table
Oils on canvas
Musée National d'Art Moderne, Paris

Georges Braque
The Carafe, 1941
Oils on canvas 13″ × 22″
Musée National d'Art Moderne, Paris
▼

Georges Braque
The Weeding Machine, 1961-1963
Oils on canvas 47″ × 69″
Louvre, Paris
▼▼

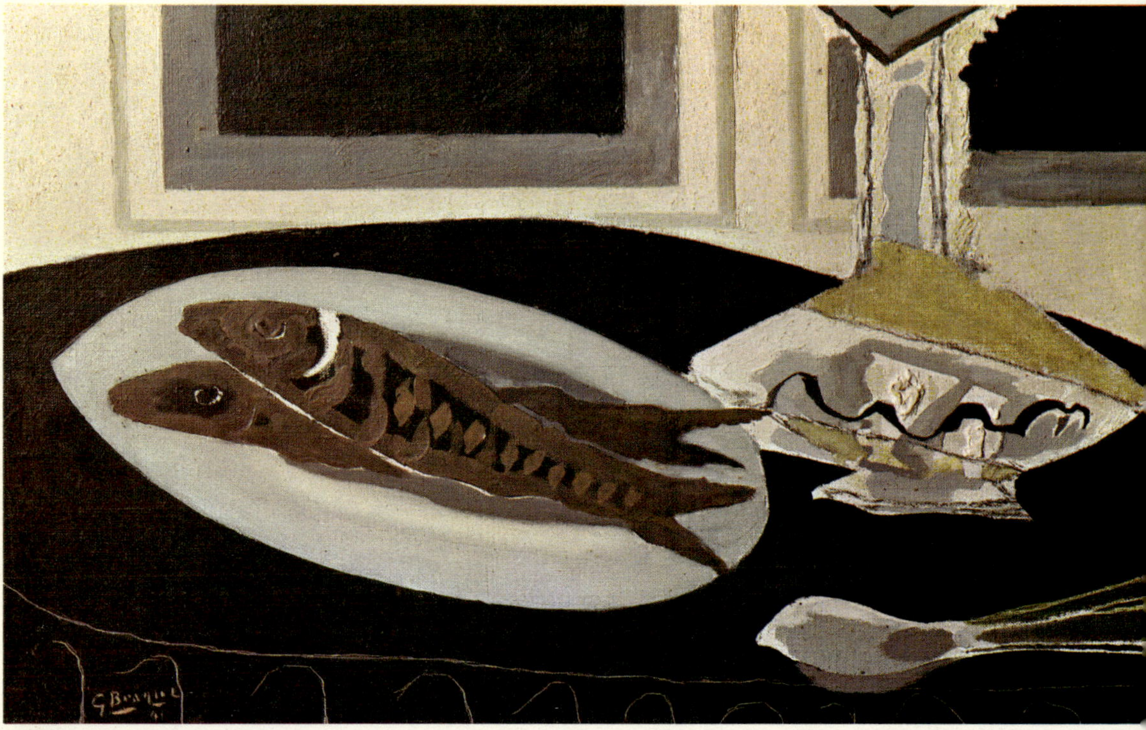

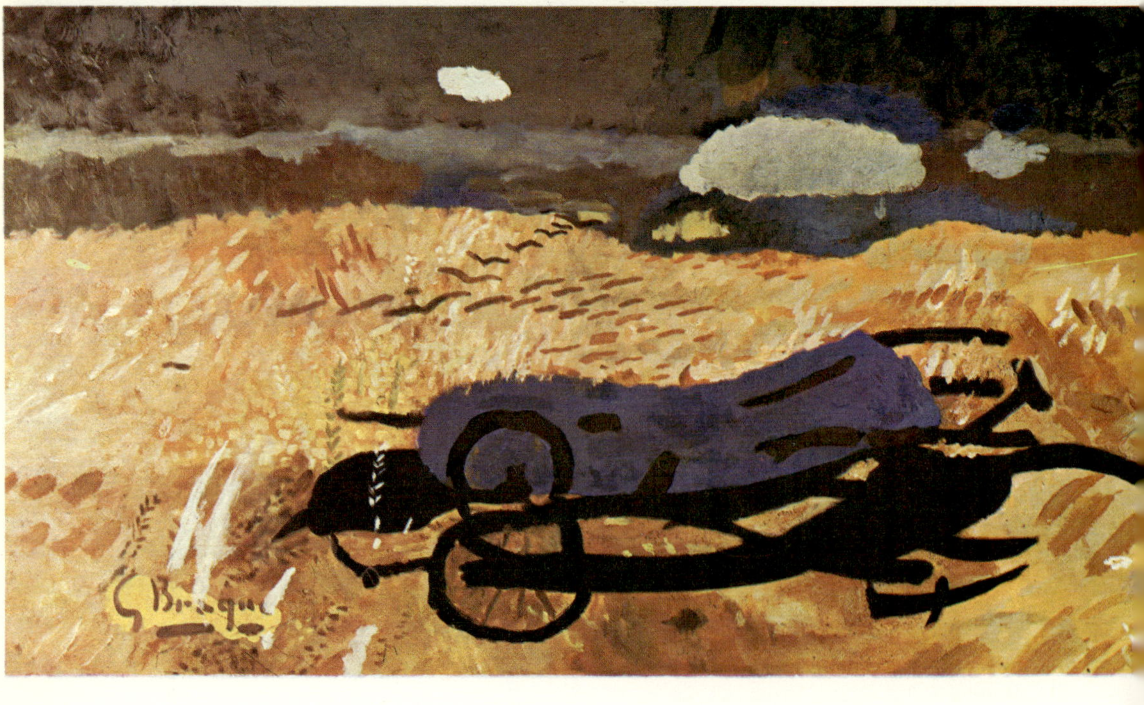

from Le Havre, Dufy and Friesz. He came to know Dufy when taking music lessons with one of his brothers; later, in Paris, Friesz introduced him to the Fauves.

In his adolescence he prepared to succeed his father. He attended evening classes at the Ecole des Beaux-Arts in Le Havre, and when seventeen he entered a decorating workshop to be trained in brush-handling for imitating wood or marble. His painting always retained a reflection of these early years.

He went to Paris to finish his apprenticeship, and while he was working with a decorator—a friend of his father—Dufy and Friesz entered the Ecole des Beaux-Arts where he himself enrolled after he had done his military service. He attended the Académie Humbert, and went to live in Montmartre. In 1903, Braque's painting was modest, but not without quality. He destroyed most of his early attempts, however, just as he later disowned his Fauve period which was, all the same, a decisive episode which opened the doors of adventure for him. In 1906, he exhibited a few still tentative essays at the Indépendants, and it was only in the course of a visit to Antwerp with Othon Friesz that he freed himself entirely from Impressionism.

Unlike the authentic Fauves, however, he did not sacrifice form to colour. His Fauvism was less affirmed than theirs, and his drawing already showed that suppleness which was to become characteristic of him.

Cézanne's retrospective exhibition at the 1907 Salon d'Automne was an event which had a decisive effect on the course of painting; it is there, far more than in Negro art, that the origin of Cubism can be seen; none of the young *avant-garde* painters was more impressed than Braque, and the new school's first masterpiece was not Picasso's *Demoiselles d'Avignon* but the *Nude* which Braque began to paint late in 1907. It marked the finish of Fauvism.

It was, moreover, Braque's canvases which prompted Matisse and Vauxcelles to utter the word "cube". From 1908, in his Estaque landscapes, he seems to have taken literally Cézanne's remark about needing to reduce nature to geometric forms. Perhaps this need for discipline should be seen as a desire to combat his own uncertainty. Not until later did he acquire sufficient mastery to follow his instinct towards the supple harmonies which make his mature still-lifes so enchanting.

At this time he painted the *Houses at l'Estaque*, reminiscent of the *Grandes Baigneuses* which marks the end of Cézanne's formal experiments.

Braque was baffled by Picasso at first, but drew closer to him. He seems to have been spellbound by such an amazing magician. Although he was at La Roche-Guyon, and Picasso at Horta de San Juan, they brought back astonishingly similar works from these very different places, and this sealed their friendship: "We saw each other every day and talked. During those years Picasso and I said things which nobody will ever say again, no one would understand, and which gave us so many joys. It was rather like being roped together on a mountain; we both worked a great deal."

The two friends spent the summer together at Céret in 1911, and at Sorgues in 1912. Their still-lifes were at this time so similar that it is easy to think they collaborated on the same canvas. This phenomenon is all the more surprising because everything else

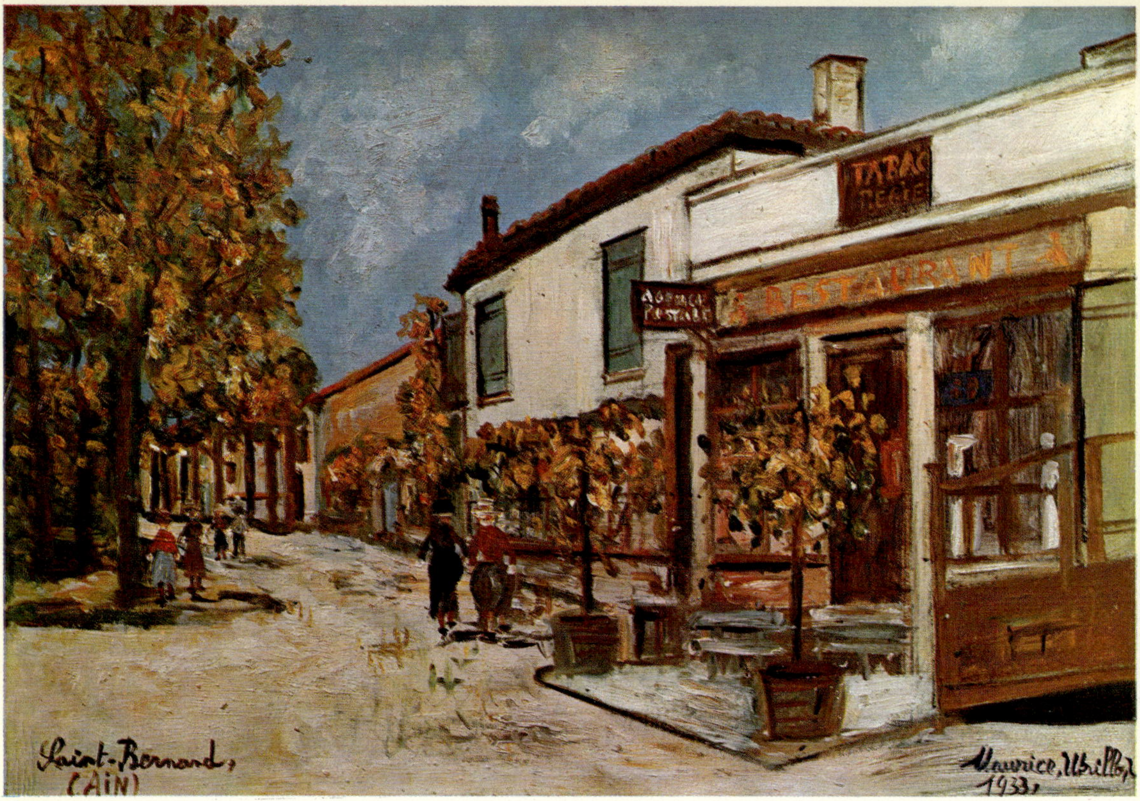

in their temperaments was in contrast; like Vlaminck and Derain, however, their close relationship did not survive the war.

For a long time Braque felt some conflict between his wish for discipline and his liking for decoration inherited from his early training. He sometimes reproduced wood or painted papers. Then he, or Picasso, discovered that instead of imitating these materials it was better to use them. So they stuck pieces of tapestry or wrapping-paper on to their canvases. They also saw clearly what decorative use could be made of typographical characters, and there again, rather than reproduce them, they preferred to borrow them from newspapers; whence, from 1912, came numerous *papiers collés* (collages), in which a pipe, a guitar, or a tobacco pouch were painted or drawn on a background of printed papers.

Braque always had an artisan side which led him to take an interest in all sorts of different techniques. The Church at Varangeville, beside which he is buried, has some large stained-glass windows by him, and he conceived some mosaics in great cubes of white, black or blue stone. He designed fabrics, tapestries, jewellery and bronzes, particularly a large horse's head in 1943. He was attracted by mythology, and interpreted it as equally well in his etchings for Hesiod's *Theogony* as in his large plaques of black-coated plaster deeply incised with subtle arabesques. He went so far as to construct invented shapes from pebbles picked up on the Normandy beaches.

In the field of painting, 1914 was a crucial date, this time for Braque: he broke with Picasso and his influence and the advanced theories of the Bateau-Lavoir and the Stein* clique.

When he was demobilised after being seriously wounded and returned to Paris, he wrestled with his doubts for some time. But from 1918 he was content to become the heir of Chardin, the master of subtle harmonies.

After having been a great revolutionary with a decisive influence on the course of

Maurice Utrillo
Montmartre 1883-Le Vésinet 1955
The Artist's House in the Country, 1933
Oils on canvas
Musée Fabre, Montpellier

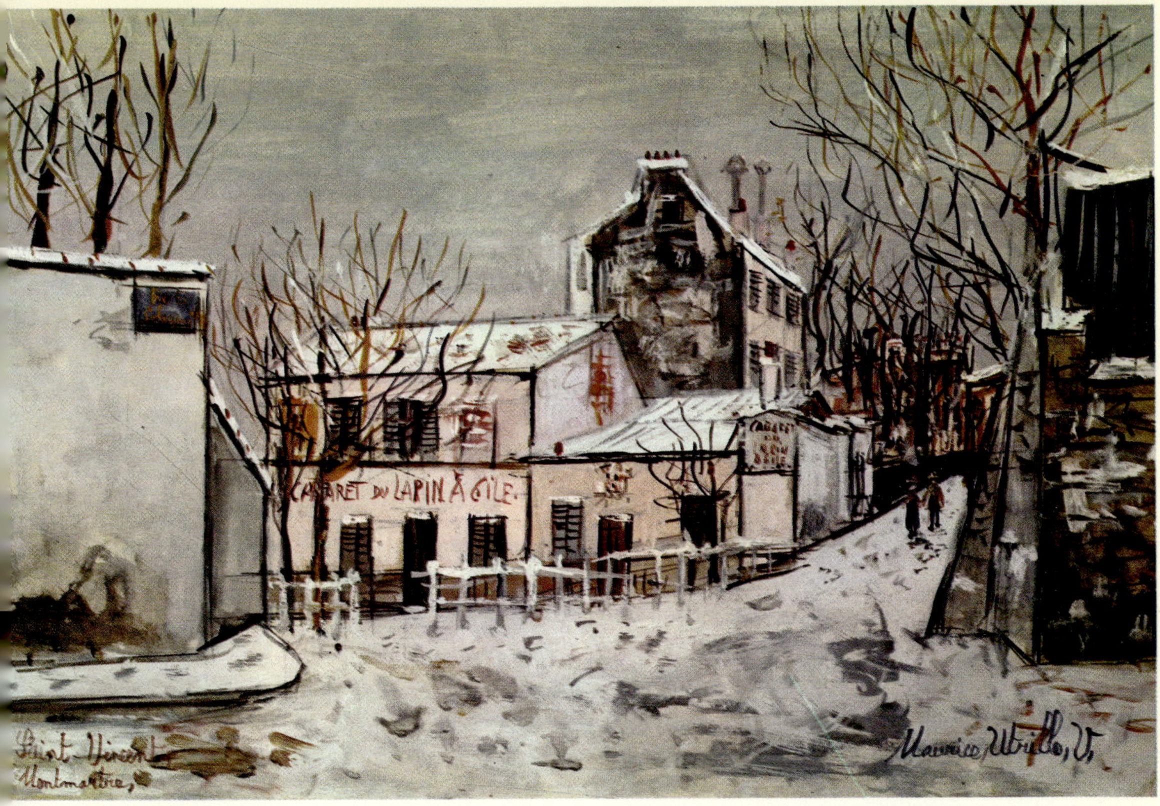

painting, as soon as he came into full possession of his powers he could abandon himself to the joy of painting. Like Cézanne, he did not need a great number of items to compose his still-lifes, and he no longer felt obliged to analyse and dissect their shapes. On a mock-marble mantelpiece, he arranged a guitar, some pears and some grapes, and was able to express the relationships which sprang from the proximity of these items, they obviously being mere starting points.

To define our feelings on studying his mature compositions we must turn to those tactile values dear to Berenson*. Landscapes now became rare; figures, on the other hand, had an ambitious classicism, and it is possibly with the *Canephorus* series that he reached his peak. For a long time he would use only greys and browns relieved by thin greens. Then, in about 1929, yellows and reds appeared, bursting out in *Still-life with Mandolin* in 1938.

The objects he painted are perfectly recognisable and their distortions progressively less arbitrary. He never ceased observing the little world around him, for he scarcely went out of his studio except to his house in Varangeville. He painted interiors: a sitting room, a kitchen—still like Chardin—women playing cards. But, he said, "objects don't exist for me unless there is a harmonious relationship between them, also between them and me".

In his sixties, in spite of ill-health, he undertook a task which possibly exceeded his physical strength: all his life he had been interested in "space" and he now attempted its visual embodiment in a series of canvases known as the *Studios*, which are mainly dominated by birds. He returned in his old age to the ambitions of his youth and throughout his subsequent work the bird seemed to him the appropriate symbol to express what he wanted to tell us. His ceiling in the Louvre, however, is not entirely convincing, and the great inspiration which sustained him through thirty years was visiting him only rarely by the time he died on 31 August 1963.

Maurice Utrillo
Rue Saint-Vincent, Montmartre, 1930
Gouache 20″ × 14″
Private collection, Geneva

Utrillo

If the name of Van Gogh frequently recurs in these pages this is because both his life and his work gave him an extraordinary prestige among his contemporary artists. There are particularly striking similarities between his way of life and that of Maurice Utrillo.

Both suffered from a mental disability which alarmed those around them. Theo, the brother of Vincent Van Gogh, was a picture dealer; Suzanne Valadon, Maurice Utrillo's mother, was a painter. Both these two, faced with deciding the future of the people they loved, came to the same conclusion within twenty years of each other: they put paint brushes into their hands, not in the hope that they would produce work of any value, but simply to give them some diversion. And a miracle happened: between 1885 and 1890, Van Gogh painted some prodigious masterpieces, and an almost identical phenomenon occurred with Maurice Utrillo.

In discussing Utrillo, it is hard to distinguish myth from reality. The setting in which his drama—for want of a better word—unfolds has been described by Carco*, Dorgelès*, Salmon, Mac Orlan* and Warnod. But the essentials have never been told, for I believe no one truly knew the man himself—awkward, childish and taciturn, or, under the influence of alcohol, excited and delirious; a man whose mentality was that of a child of fourteen who refused to live in the world of adults, a person with whom all contact was impossible. He had no friends, and his drinking companions were never more than drinking companions. Painting was a refuge for him against a hostile world, an outlet for the expression of his strange state of mind.

He chose landscape to express his impenetrable inner world; landscape, gay or bitter, animated or serene. Roland Dorgelès, in his introduction to the extensive 1959 exhibition in the Charpentier gallery, wrote: "Utrillo is not a person, he is a body of work. His entire existence is contained within the frames of his pictures. When he paints a Paris street he is painting his own portrait."

Utrillo's genius is one of those mysteries to be met with at every step when we try to clarify the elusive phenomenon of artistic creation. Why are we excited by the transformation he wrought on the humble postcards which inspired him? Why did the great poets who supported the young *avant-garde* artists as well as the up-and-coming painters who gathered before 1914 in the Lapin-Agile* think only of avoiding this unbearable soak, without paying any attention to the canvases he offered them for 5 francs each?

The years he spent in cells and police stations produced his highest masterpieces. The person who has gone furthest towards understanding this perplexing individual is assuredly Adolphe Tabarant. In a book published in 1926, he tells us practically all we know for certain about Utrillo's obscure life. He informs us that his father was one Boissy, "an incorrigible Bohemian, seriously affected by alcoholism". He played no part in his son's life.

In complete contrast, Utrillo's mother, Suzanne Valadon, looked after him as well as her careless nature allowed. The history of this little girl from Limousin is

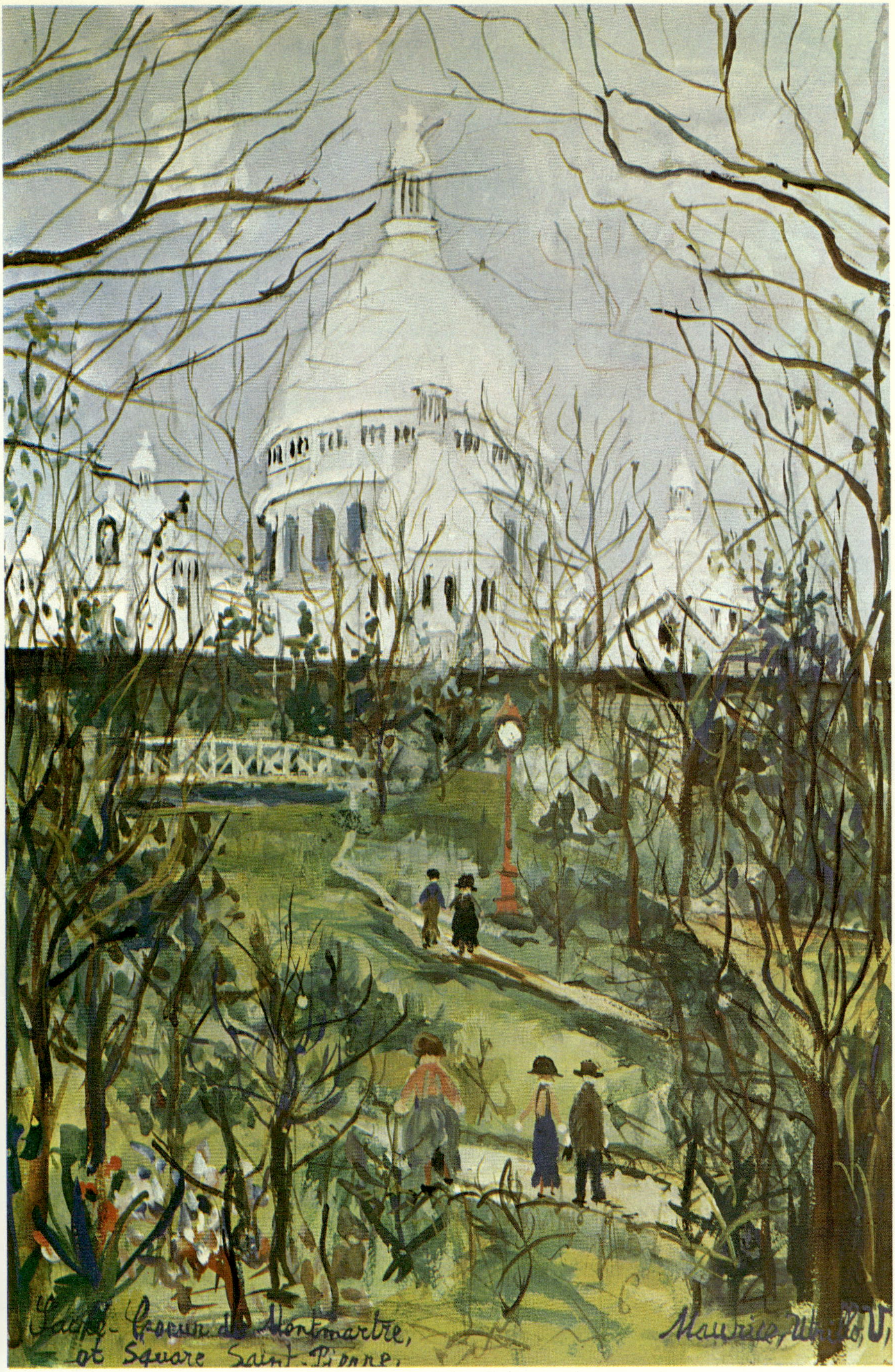

Maurice Utrillo
Sacré-Cœur, 1948
Gouache 19″ × 13″
Museum of Art and History, Geneva

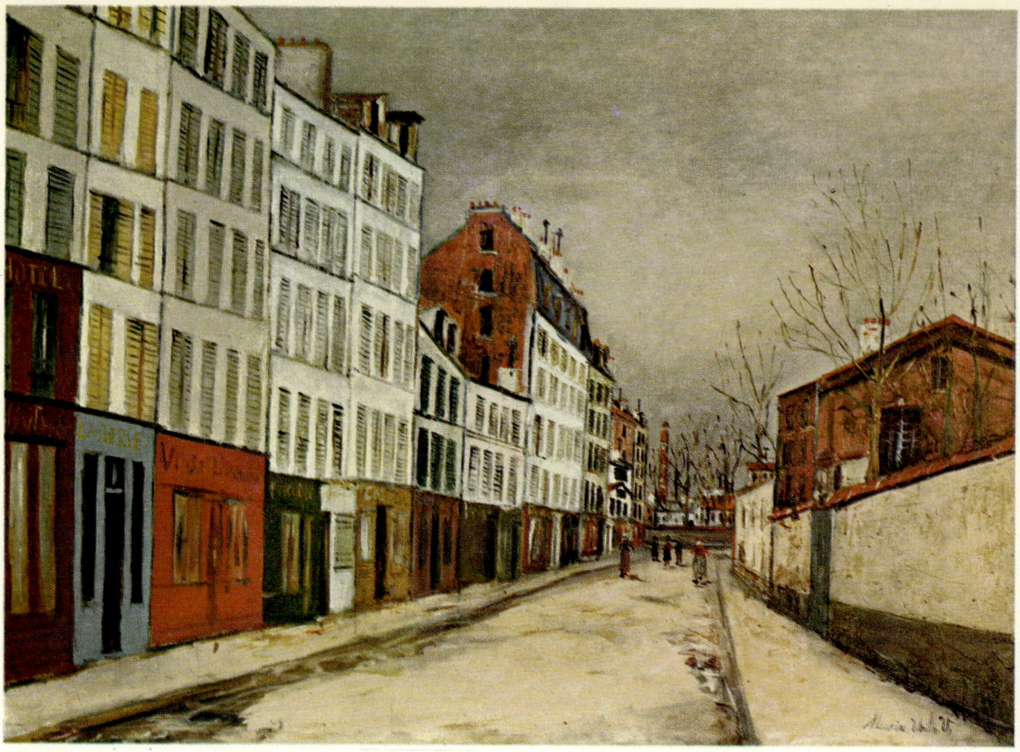

picturesque, eventful and like something from Balzac. How did she become a circus acrobat? How, after an accident, did she become the favourite model of Puvis de Chavannes? "I posed," she said, "for *The Sacred Wood*, not only the women, but the young fellows too. Puvis would ask me to give a pose, a movement, or a gesture."

The young Marie (Suzanne's real name) hung around the studios and bistros in Montmartre, and on 26 December 1883 she gave birth to a son; he did not take the name Utrillo until 1891. At that time she posed for Renoir and came to know Degas, who showed an interest in her firm and vigorous drawings and pinned one of them on the wall of his studio.

Then she conformed. A well-to-do businessman, Paul Mousis, married her and helped her to bring up her child, but would not adopt him. The man who did do this, perhaps a little out of bravado, was the Catalan poet, friend of Picasso, Miguel Utrillo, who, soon after registering his act of adoption, returned to Barcelona.

During the 1890s, M. and Mme Mousis lived in Montmagny, a Paris suburb, before moving to the famous house at 12 rue Cortot, Montmartre. At this time Suzanne Valadon was not yet the great painter we love, but she was drawing continually, and her portraits depicting *My Son Aged Seven* or her old mother reveal her authority.

Maurice was a thoughtful, shy, withdrawn child, unstable and subject to terrible tantrums. His mother had little time to attend to him, and he was left in the hands of the feeble grandmother.

His stepfather arranged for his education and enrolled him at the Lycée Rollin. The boy failed utterly, and since he began to drink whenever he was idle, his mother persuaded him to draw and paint. Rather than this enforced occupation, however, he preferred long walks in the Paris suburbs, the melancholy there appealing to him as much as the picturesqueness of the Butte. Later, when he went alone or with Modigliani to Montmartre or Montparnasse in the evenings, he always did the journey on foot, except for frequent stops at bistros en route. At the age of seventeen he took his first cure for alcoholism at Sainte-Anne.

Maurice Utrillo
Rue des Poissonniers, 1930
Oils on canvas 37″ × 45″
Private collection, Paris

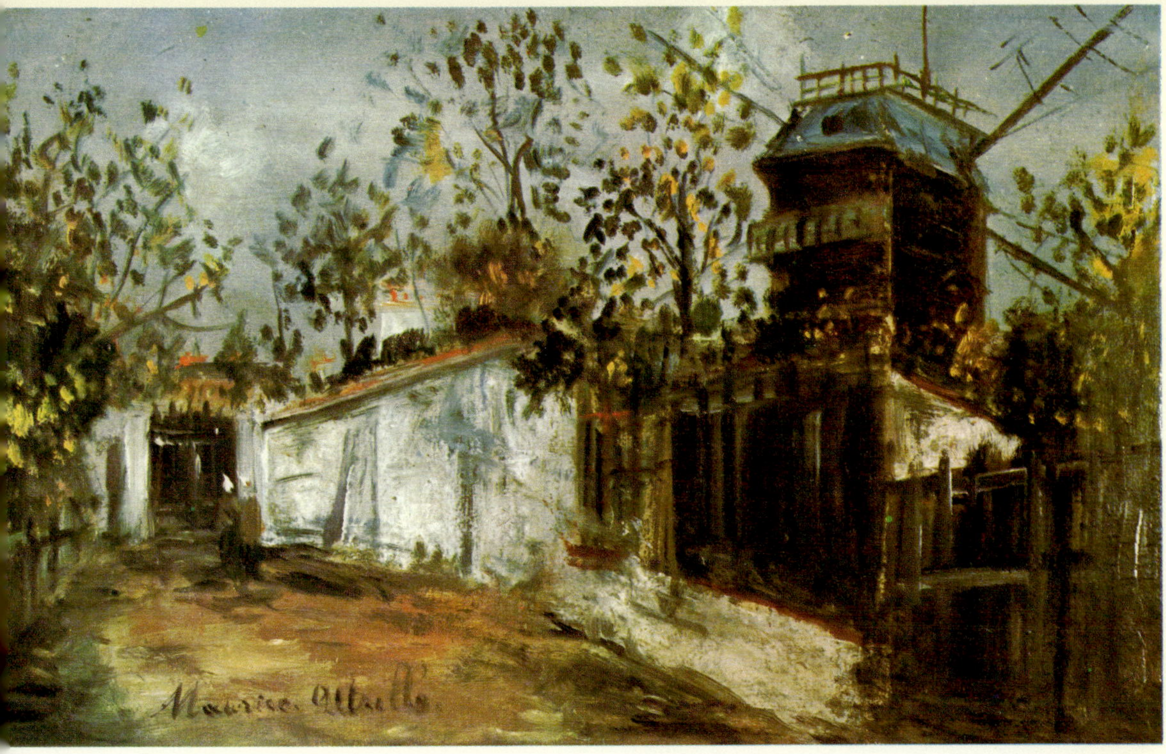

Led by his mother into the way of painting, Utrillo soon saw there a means of procuring some income, which decided him to go to the rue Laffite and see how artists like Sisley and Pissarro contrived to interpret the Ile-de-France landscapes before which he set up his own easel.

Pont Saint-Michel, painted at this time and signed M. U. Valadon, owes all to the Impressionists; soon, however, his methods became different from theirs, and his impasto recalls that of Van Gogh. This first period, from 1903 to 1908, is still fairly impersonal and there are plenty of canvases hastily dashed off like classroom detention work.

After Utrillo had worked at Pierrefitte, Montmagny and the Butte Pinson, he seemed to have come to his senses, so his mother said he could come back to Montmartre, where he had spent his childhood and which he still missed.

In 1905 a dealer, Clovis Sagot, became interested in his pictures. But Maurice preferred to offer the landscapes he painted so rapidly to the wine-sellers who would pay him in kind. "Painting, drinking," said Tabarant. "Painting in order to drink; painting with the bottle within reach of his hand. A skinful every day, and every day a masterpiece."

The word masterpiece is not excessive. The "white period", which preceded the war, is nearly all admirable. Here we are in the presence of an art that owes nothing to anyone. Utrillo was past the time when, undecided about his vocation, he asked: "Do you think that one day people will speak of me as they do of Sisley?" His art is instinctive; it moves us not only by what it reveals of the man, but because the harmonies it creates are themselves admirably right. There is never the slightest dissonance, the least error in the blending of the whites and greys with a delicacy all the more impressive when we know under what conditions these canvases were painted.

There have been frequent attempts to classify Utrillo's successive styles. In fact he used very different techniques simultaneously. The colour and substance interpreted his current state of mind.

Maurice Utrillo
Le Moulin de la Galette, 1913-1915
Oils on canvas 11″ × 18″
Private collection, Villeret

Amedeo Modigliani ▸
Leghorn 1884-Paris 1920
Madame Zborowska with Clasped Hands, c. 1917
Oils on canvas
Private collection, Roubaix

Amedeo Modigliani ▸▸
Man from Nice, 1919
Oils on canvas 36″ × 24″
Masurel Collection, Paris

Much insistence has been laid on the tragic character of his landscapes, but they are all far from expressing morbid emotions. Some are serene and joyful. But it is certainly true that they are most moving when they convey his distress. These Montmartre streets, suburban corners and country churches seem to be channels through which he could express what he was powerless to translate into words.

The human element is almost entirely absent from these self-revealing works. There are sometimes passers-by in the streets, but they are only extras with exaggerated, caricatural shapes. They could be eliminated without modifying the composition. It is not they, but the white walls and monotonous perspectives which speak to us in muted voices.

It is astonishing how often Maurice Utrillo painted from simple postcards. He needed something to go on, however modest. I was able to compare one finished canvas with the little photograph on which it was based. The fidelity was apparently total, but from a stock print he had succeeded in evolving a completely individual poetry. Indeed, however uneven, all his enormous output bears his mark and none of his work could be attributed to any other hand than his.

We have to thank Edmond Jaloux* for a description of the little room in the rue Cortot whence so many masterpieces came: "He could hardly see his way about, because he often needed half-light to get into the mood. His canvas was covered with a geometrical design traced with minute patience and almost exaggerated clarity. It was the drawing of a schoolboy—a schoolboy genius. This preliminary drawing complete, he placed to hand a choice of colours which were to cover his picture. Here a blue, there one of those clear shell-pinks, a dense, full green or a red of spilled blood, and he would never change any of these tones; the picture was entirely done, composed in his head, and he had only to carry it out, coming back to it twenty times to add whatever it needed until it looked to him complete."

Evidently Jaloux saw Utrillo on one of his good days. On others he would escape from the family house. Then, drunk since morning, spending his days in the bistro and his nights in the police station, he still found time to work so much that one of his first dealers, Libaude, wrote to him: "You are bringing me a picture every two days. That is much too much." And Libaude was well aware that besides these canvases, plenty of others were in the hands of Montmartre wine-sellers.

When he was thrown out of bars he wandered round the streets, causing such a rumpus that the police often had to intervene. Also, when, the next day, he installed himself on the street corner to paint, he was subjected to a hail of jokes, even insults and blows. He received so much attention from the urchins that he had to give up working in that way. It was then that his mother got him the picture postcards, which enabled him to paint so many village churches that he had never had a chance to see.

He did travel, however. Before the war he visited Brittany and Corsica; from there he brought back canvases of a luminous intensity which expressed his joy in living, but they were situated between two spells of confinement in nursing homes, in 1912 and 1914; the subsequent years were without doubt the most terrible he knew.

Amedeo Modigliani ▸
Landscape
Oils on canvas 18″ × 22″
Mme Netter's collection, Paris

Amedeo Modigliani ▸▸
Little Girl in Blue
Oils on canvas 29″ × 46″
Mme Netter's collection, Paris

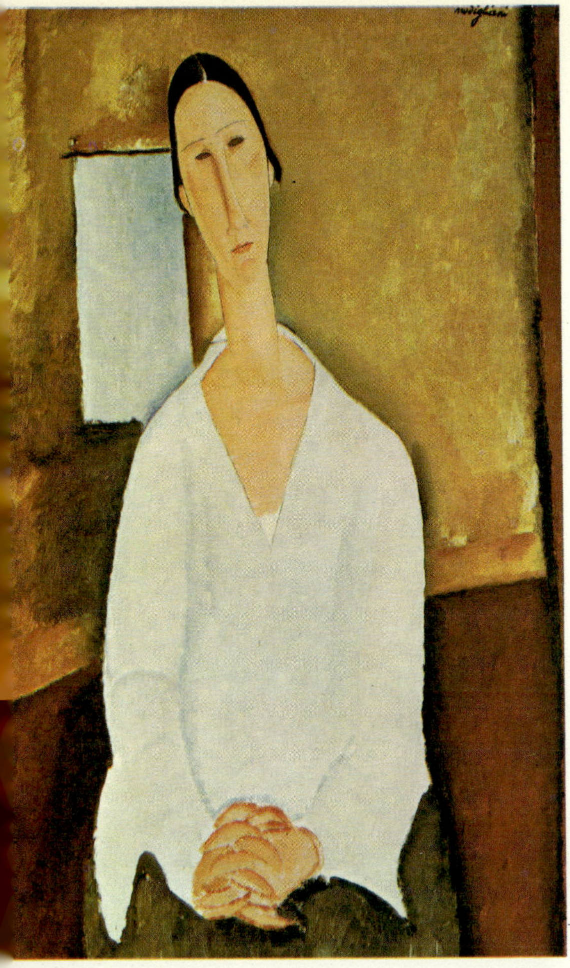

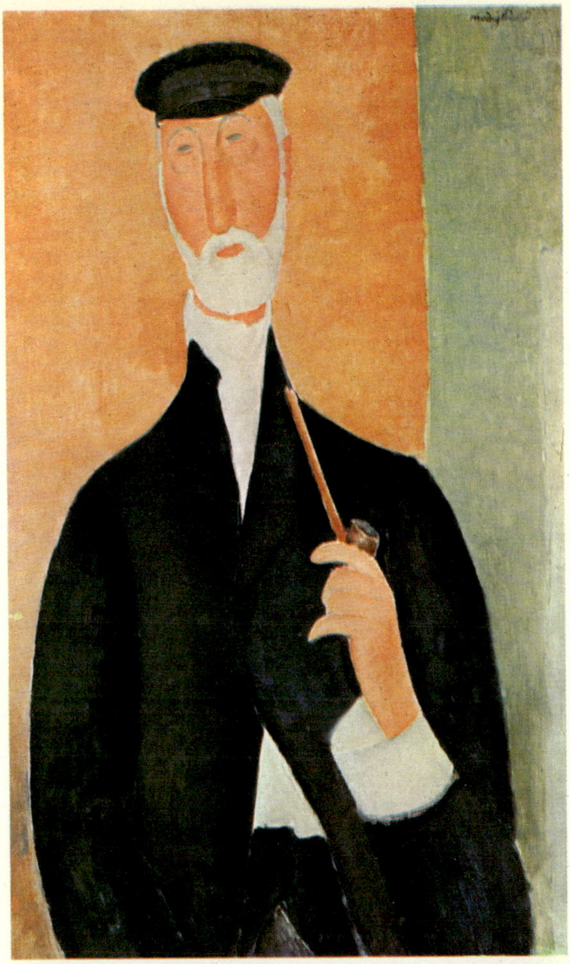

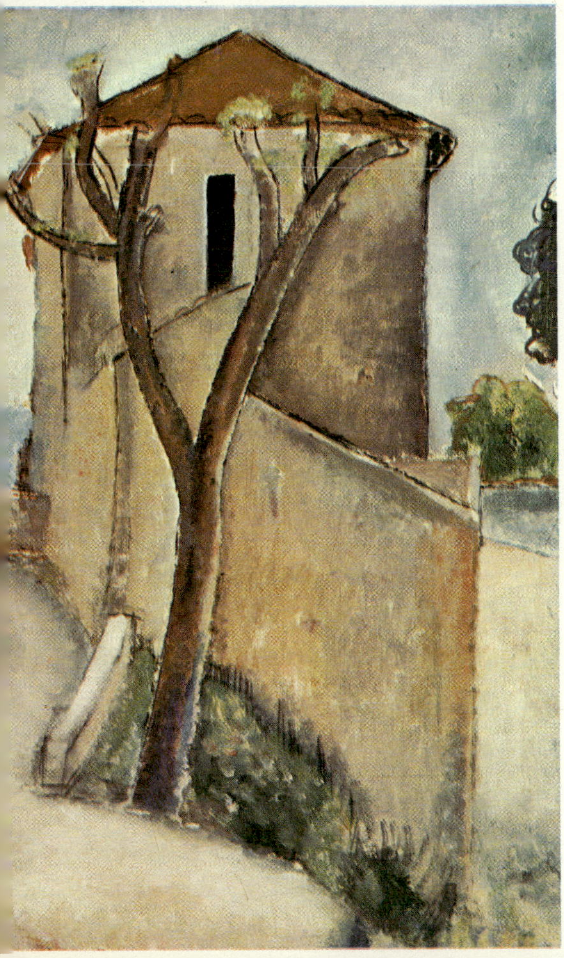

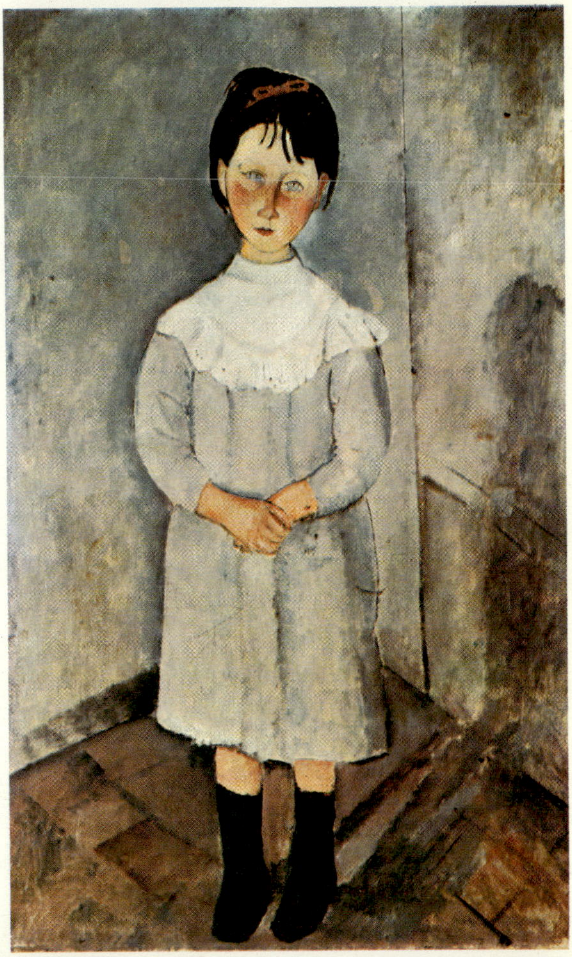

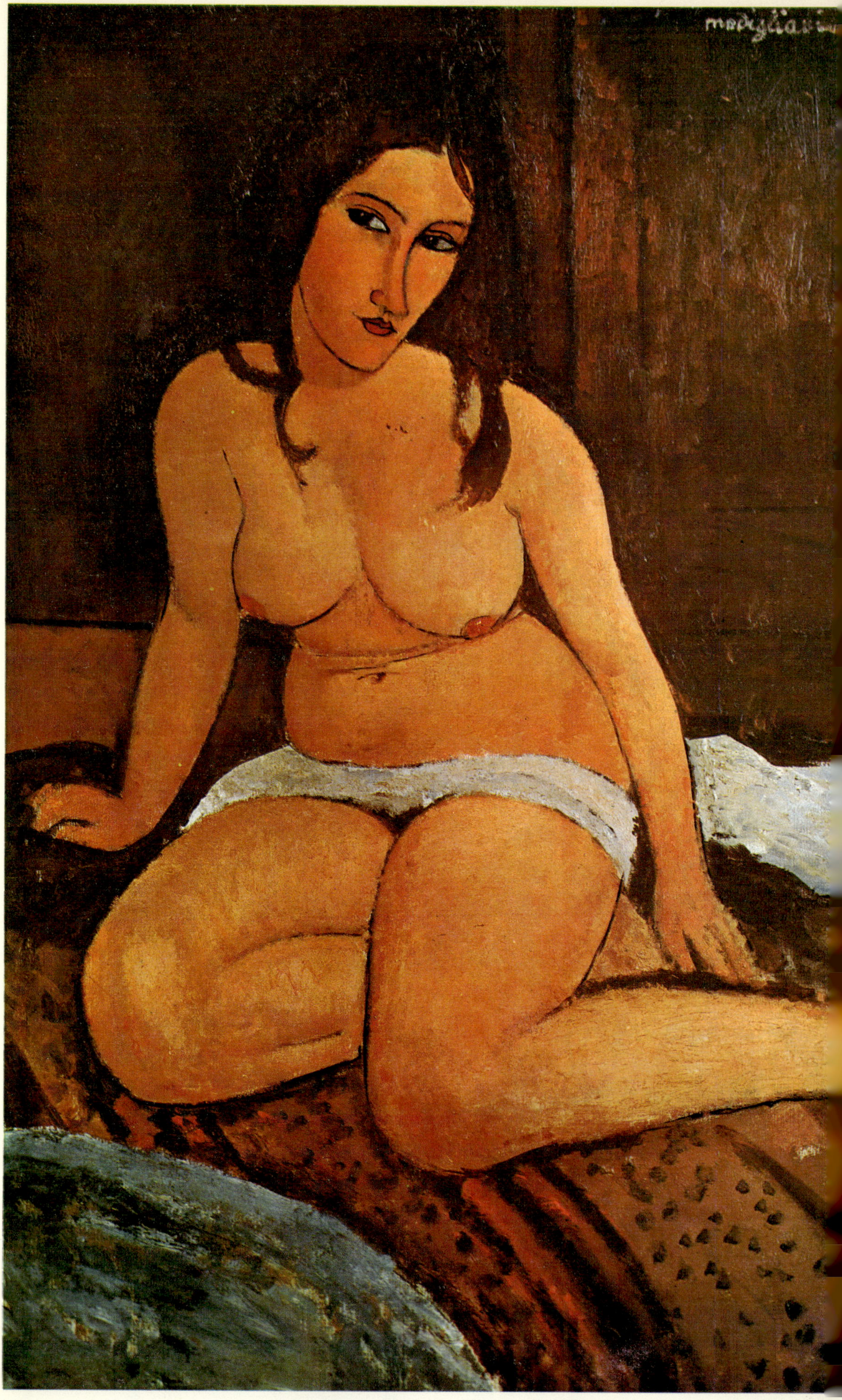
modigliani

Amedeo Modigliani
Seated Nude
Oils on canvas
National Museum, Antwerp

Suzanne Valadon and Marcel Mousis separated, and she married the painter André Utter*; scenes of such violence broke out between her husband and her son, who were about the same age, that she was driven to buy a dilapidated chateau at Saint-Bernard in the Beaujolais region. For four or five years, Maurice did not leave there, except for brief walks under close supervision.

He was now as far from the white period as from the sombre, heavily built architecture which excited him for a time. His forms were more linear, his colours sharper. This still enormous output contains further astonishing successes.

His mother was growing old and, however carefree she was by nature, she was not careless about her son's future; in 1935 she ensured that he would have someone to look after him by marrying him to one of her friends, Lucie Valore. From then on, the painter's life was uneventful. Instead of wine, he had painting. The mysticism which for so long he had expressed only in painting churches and cathedrals, took more precise form. He used to withdraw to pray in the oratory he had built beside his villa in Le Vésinet. He died in Dax on 5 November 1955.

Modigliani

Amedeo Modigliani was born in Leghorn on 12 July 1884, into a family which was rich because his grandfather—following an old Jewish tradition—was banker to the Pope. His mother was French and lived for a long time in Marseilles.

He was a frail child, having to interrupt his schooling to nurse a chest ailment of which he was never cured. Like so many other contemporary masters, he began to draw to occupy his free time, but soon displayed such gifts that his parents arranged for him to have lessons from a Leghorn landscape artist, Micheli. But he was already attracted by portraiture more than landscape, and he began to build up a small clientèle among the townspeople.

In 1902 he stayed in Florence; he enrolled in the Fine Arts School, and met Ardengo Soffici, who became one of the first initiates of the Futurist* group, when the turn-of-the-century artistic ferment reached Italy.

When he went home, he rejoined his brother, who was to become a leader of the extreme left, but his health obliged him to travel south. He went to Rome, then to Venice, where he took the entrance examination for the Fine Arts Academy, and won several prizes. He is probably the only 20th-century artist to have assimilated the lessons of the Quattrocento masters. More, however, than the Venetian or Roman Renaissance painters, it was the Florentines who helped to mould his personality. Without exaggerating the influence on him of painters earlier than Raphael, it is incontestable that Modigliani is linked to his country's most ancient pictorial tradition. If he had remained in Italy he might have come near to pastiches of Florentine Virgins. But he went to France in 1906, the year when Cézanne died, and his great lesson began to be understood.

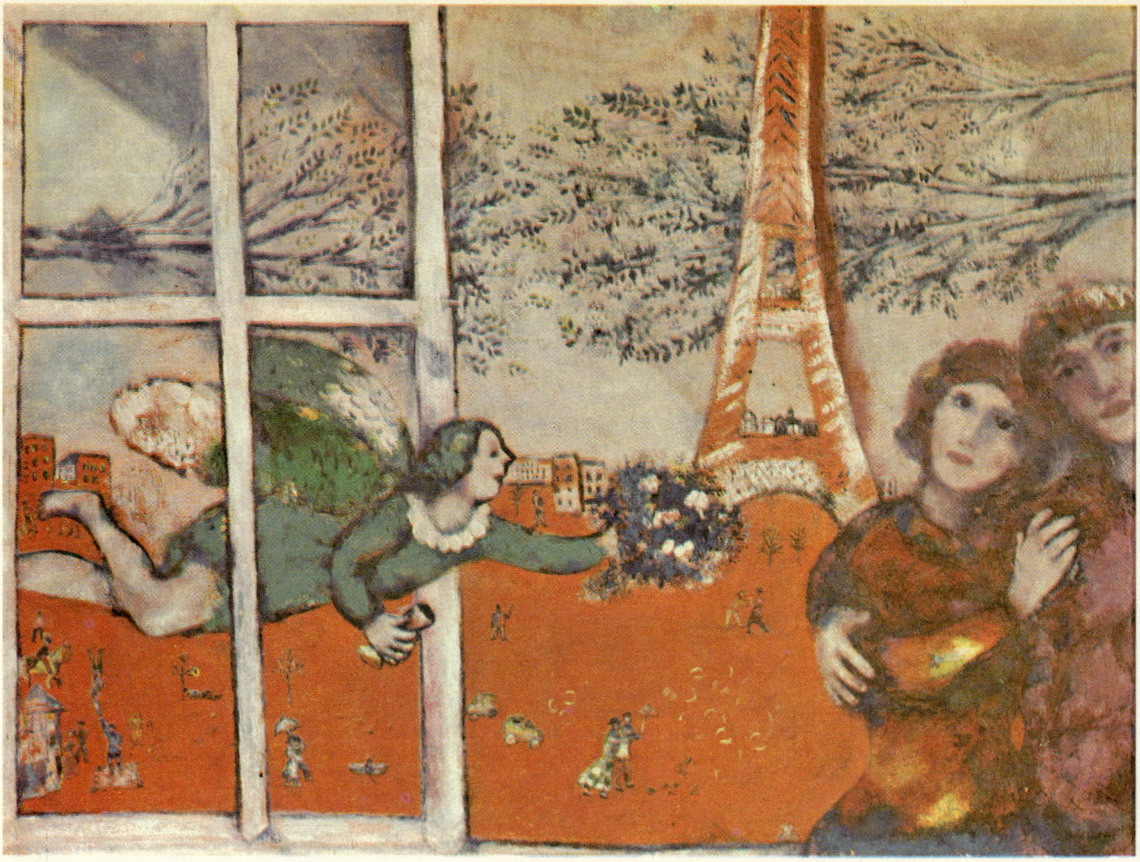

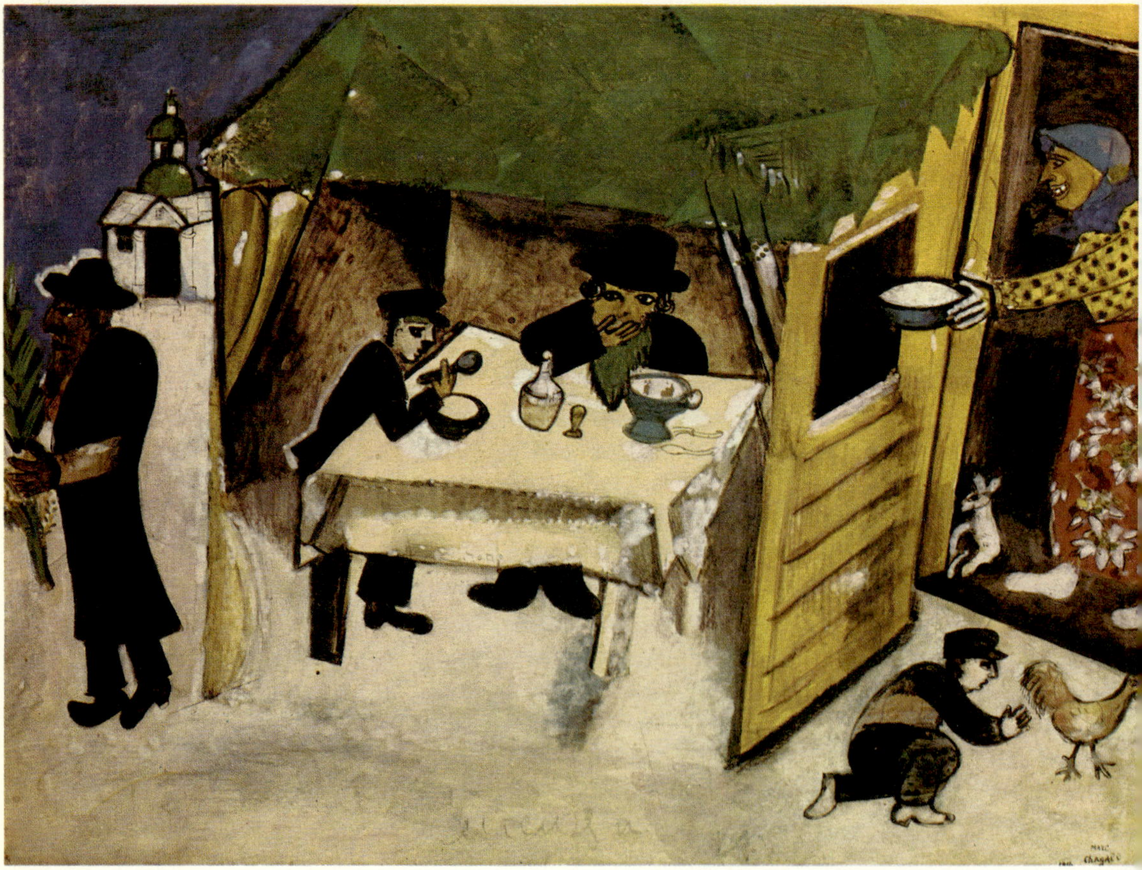

▲
Marc Chagall
The Feast of Tabernacles, 1907-1918
Gouache on paper 13″ × 16″
Dr h.c. J. B. Belmont, Binningen

▲▲
Marc Chagall
The Married Couple with the Eiffel Tower, 1928
Oils on canvas
Private collection, Paris

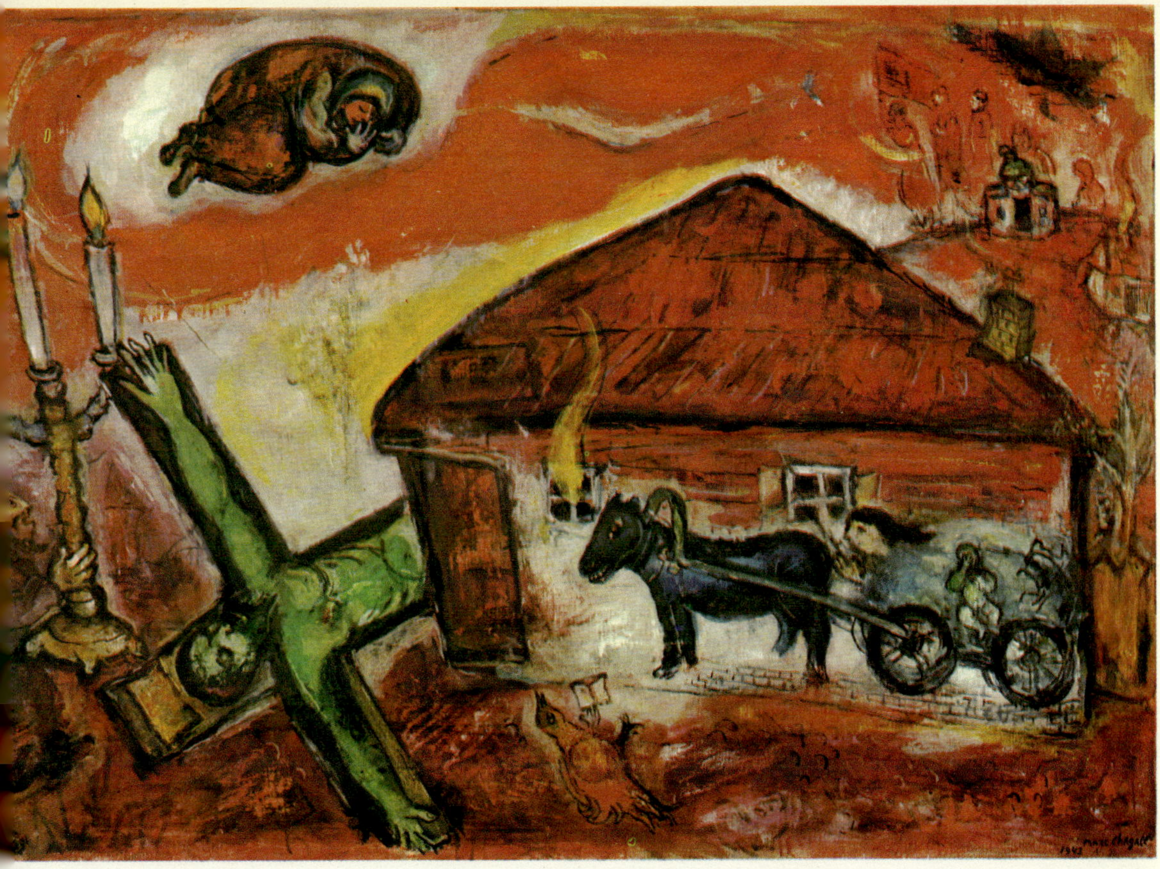

Modigliani's first portraits evoke early Cézannes in their ruggedness and rich impasto, but immediately afterwards, in 1908, *The Jew* suggests the influence of contemporary French painters: Lautrec, Pascin*, Rouault, Picasso—his early Parisian works are an anthology of currently fashionable styles. All of these influences, rapidly assimilated, nevertheless helped him to express his own personality, which manifests itself in *The Beggar Woman*, drawn already with the great style of his mature works.

During his first stay in Paris, Modigliani lived in Montmartre, where he led a vagrant and impoverished existence. The allowance he drew from his family was all the more inadequate because he already needed alcohol to stimulate him to paint.

These early works already contain the tone of strangeness and melancholy which later became so deeply moving. Nevertheless, it is hard to reproach connoisseurs for not having noticed a genius in them which was not yet evident. Dr Alexandre alone had an inkling of his still obscured future. One of the earliest portraits Modigliani did of him is a superb piece showing the young doctor in a firm stance, hand on hip. This first patron, and the most disinterested of all those he ever met, persuaded him to exhibit at the Indépendants, and in 1908 he submitted five canvases, including *The Jew*.

Another friend who had a profound influence on him was the Rumanian sculptor Brancusi*, who gave him a corner of his studio where he could begin carving directly in fragile limestone. If he had not destroyed most of his sculptures we should see how he was, at the beginning, less a painter than a sculptor.

In both his sculpture and his painting he was interested in scarcely anything but women. On his busts he imposed a degree of stylisation which apparently owed less to Renaissance portraitists than to the Negro masks just discovered by *avant-garde* French painters. The necks elongated like the shafts of columns, the triangular noses and the

Marc Chagall
Obsession, 1943
Oils on canvas 30″ × 43″
In the artist's possession

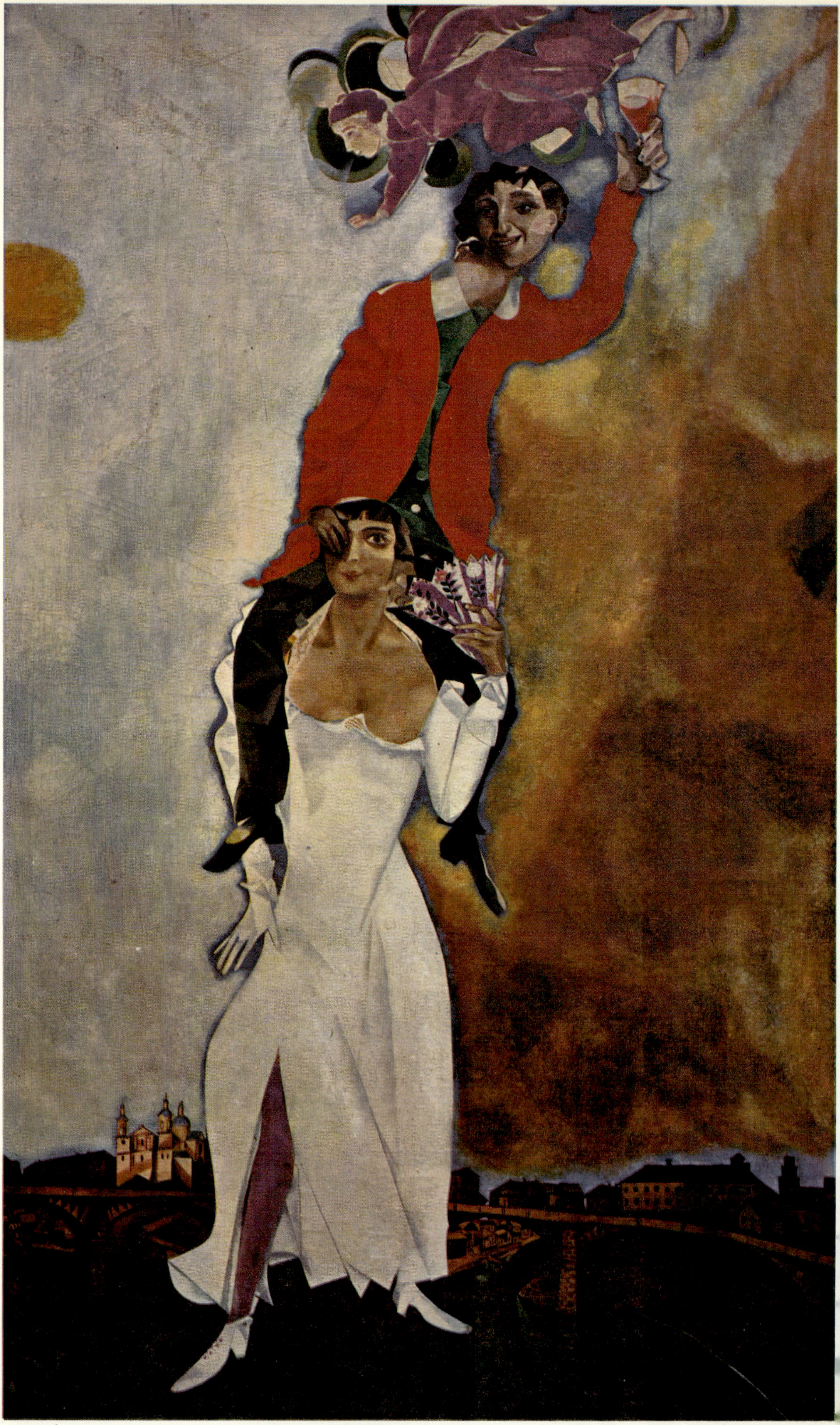

Marc Chagall
Double Portrait with a Glass of Wine, 1917
Oils on canvas 92″ × 54″
Musée National d'Art Moderne, Paris

empty eyes are all to be found in his painting after he had, with a wrench, rejected the idea of being a sculptor. He was at that time obsessed by the subject of the Cariatyd and used it in drawing, water-colour and oil painting, but his statue in the New York Museum of Modern Art bears witness that he never succeeded in attaining in stone that haunting ambition for monumentality.

In 1909, undermined by sickness and his abuse of alcohol and sedatives, he decided to go back to Leghorn. Perhaps he hoped, in returning to his sources, to find the confidence which was eluding him in Paris. He dreamed of setting up a studio in the Carrara quarries, where he could measure himself against the finest marble, instead of stone occasionally acquired from a demolition yard; but he was so dissatisfied with his attempts of that period that he abandoned nearly all of them.

Returning to Paris in 1910, he took back scarcely anything except a picture in the style of Cézanne, *Leghorn Peasant*, which he exhibited at the Indépendants. He left Montmartre and the friends in the Bateau-Lavoir who had influenced him—in particular Picasso and Van Dongen—and chose Montparnasse. From his settling in the city Falguière dates the affirmation of a personality which, during the following four or five years, was to make itself felt as one of the most original of our time.

Modigliani found his first dealer in the person of a young Polish poet, Zborowski, to whom Soutine, Utrillo and Kisling owed so much. Modigliani's canvases sold at a very low figure, but he worked fast: in the last five years of his life he produced about 400 oil paintings and thousands of water-colours, not counting drawings he dispersed carelessly on paper napkins in restaurants where he sketched portraits of his friends with staggering virtuosity.

The anxiety his work expresses lay in his life, where drink and women held a disproportionate place. Installed in the basement of the Chéron gallery, he used to paint with a litre of alcohol within reach of his grasp, and he had a taste for hashish, given him by the English poetess Beatrice Hastings.

With all his debauchery, it is a wonder he found time to paint his large, supple, beautifully proportioned nudes and the portraits which constitute an enormously interesting gallery of contemporaries. Among those of whom he has left unforgettable images are the poets Max Jacob, Jean Cocteau, Pierre Reverdy* and Blaise Cendrars, the painters Picasso, Vlaminck, Kisling, Diego Rivera* and Soutine, his dealers Zborowski and Paul Guillaume*, friends, mistresses, and many impressions of Jeanne Hébuterne.

Before the people he liked, Modigliani was most himself. When he did not know his sitter very well, he used graceful but artificial elongations. On the other hand, when he was intent on observing a person whose features he already knew in detail, his love of painting carried him away and all deliberate stylisations vanished.

He analysed the features of these sitters, ignoring their surroundings, roughly indicating their clothes and hands, but really interested only in their faces, preferring to accentuate the melancholy in them. In the same way his nudes were simply bodies. The poses he required of his models were always the same, usually stretched out in a position similar to that imposed on the women they painted by the masters of the Fontainebleau school, Rosso and Primaticcio, from Italy like himself. He never bores us, however; his personality is so strong that it can always be felt through the subject he treats.

In his later years, when sickness and over-indulgence should have weakened him, he was still in full possession of his powers, disdaining methods, dominating fashions.

In 1917, when his affair with Beatrice Hastings was at its most tempestuous, he met, at the Rotonde, a very young student from the Ecole des Arts Décoratifs, belonging to the middle-class Hébuterne family. She was immediately conquered by the extraordinary prestige surrounding Modigliani, for, though he lived in some poverty, his genius went unchallenged in a society he dominated by his culture, his disdain and his genius.

Jeanne Hébuterne became his favourite model while still living with her parents, who disapproved of her connection with an older man who was drunk every evening and consumed by tuberculosis. She became pregnant and departed with her mother to Nice, where her daughter was born towards the end of 1918.

When they came back to Paris, Modigliani and Jeanne installed themselves in a studio in the rue de la Grande-Chaumière. The painter continued his nightly sprees, sometimes in the company of Utrillo, who alone was capable of handling him in the innumerable cafés they stopped at.

One morning, Modigliani was so ill that the doctor ordered his immediate removal to the Hôpital de la Charité. There he died on 25 January 1920. The following day the sculptor Lipchitz, the doctor Barrieu and the art critic Florent Fels made a striking death mask of his wasted features.

As his friends left the cemetery to which they had escorted his body, they received tragic news: Jeanne Hébuterne, pregnant again, had thrown herself from a window in her parents' home.

Chagall

Except for a short period in the 1930s when, imbued with the climate of the Ile de France, he serenely expressed his joy in living, Chagall's whole work is one vast Apocalypse, though not devoid of either a zest for life or an unusual humour. All his work is dominated by his childhood. There has surely been no artist in the history of painting who has drawn so heavily on memories of childhood and youth all through his life.

In order to interpret his racial and family background, however, he had to get away from the Russian town of Vitebsk, where he was born on 7 July 1887. He himself described the beginnings of his vocation in his autobiography *My Life*: for him painting originally represented the opportunity to escape from the ghetto, his father's shop, and over-rigid traditions.

Marc Chagall
War, 1943
Oils on canvas 41″ × 30″
Musée National d'Art Moderne, Paris

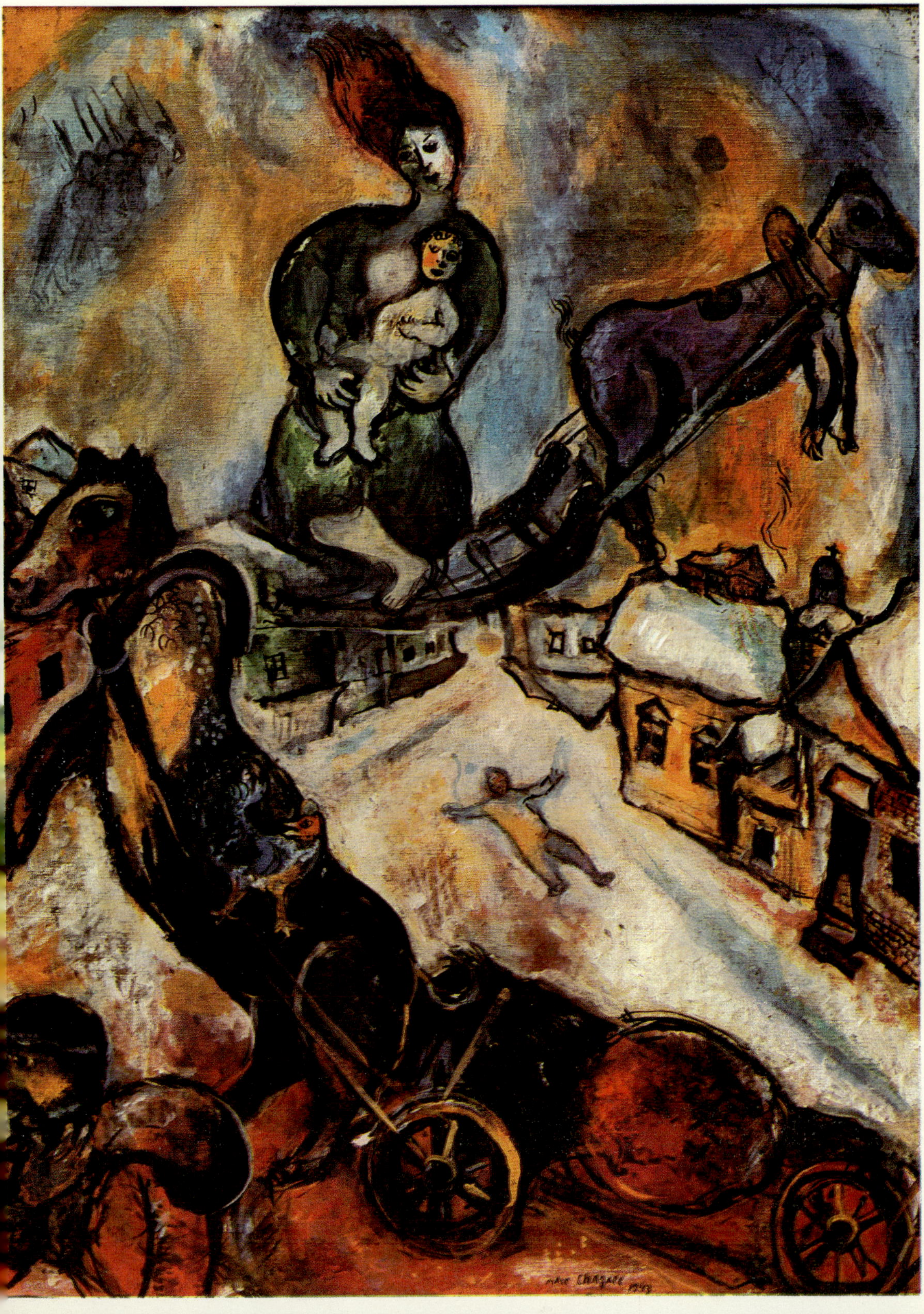

Marcel Gromaire
Noyelles-sur-Sambre (Nord) 1892
The Lines of the Hand, 1935
Oils on canvas 39″ × 32″
Musée National d'Art Moderne, Paris

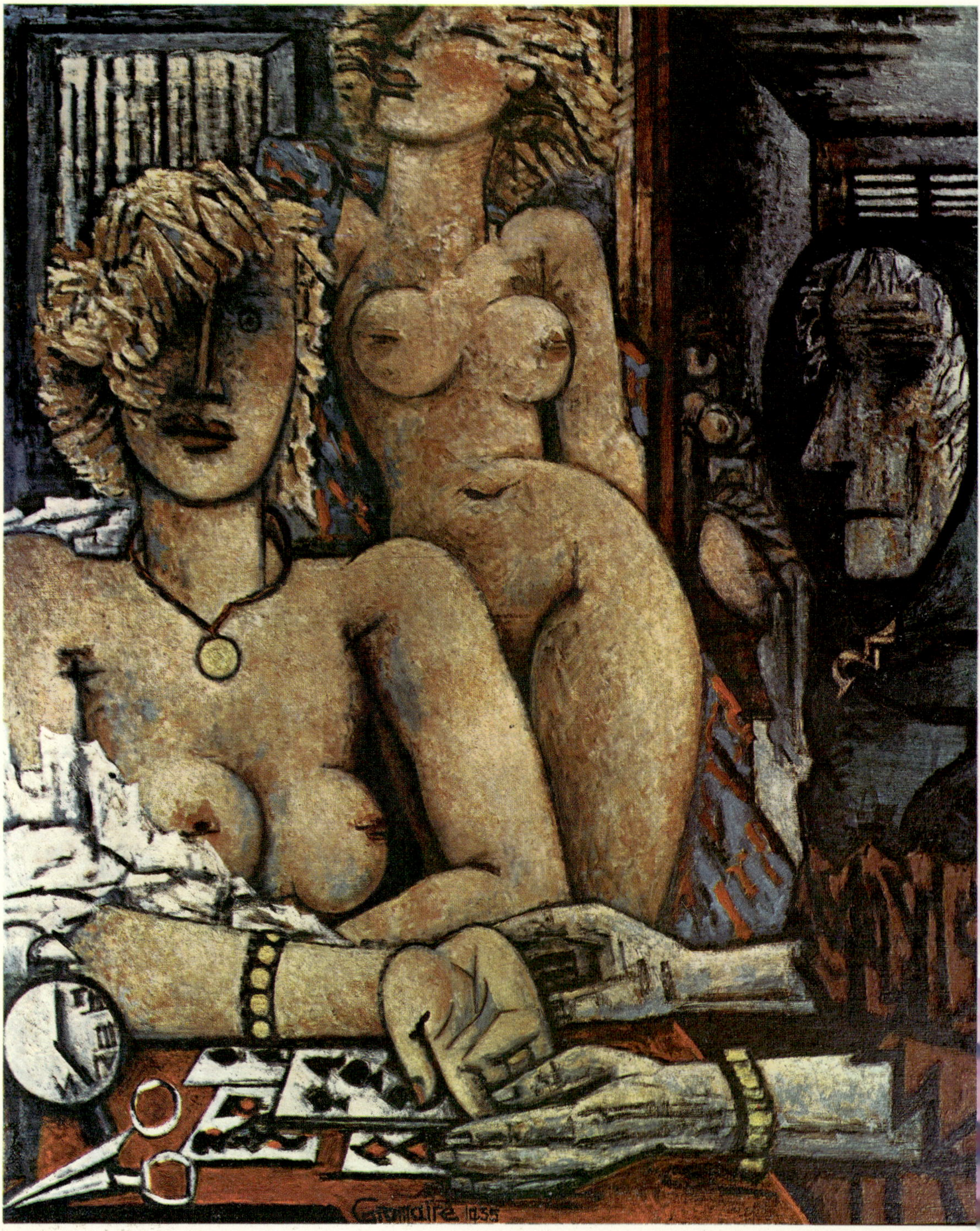

His early pictures were carried out under difficult conditions; for instance, he was obliged to use a canvas of rough sacking which the paint did not succeed in covering; when he entered the Art School in his native town at the age of twenty he could not afford to buy the most indispensable material.

The colours he used were browns, reflecting the drab surroundings in which he lived. Only after the passage of time did his imagination endow this dismal world with strange poetic colours. Already he was becoming drawn to the subjects to which he was to remain faithful: his first *Motherhood* dates from 1908; two years later he painted *The Holy Family*, then a more realistic *Birth.*

Marc Chagall's luck changed the day Vinaver, a deputy at the Duma, sent him to St Petersburg, where he enrolled at the Imperial College for the Promotion of the Arts. Then he met Léon Bakst, future designer of the Ballets Russes, who was a famous painter and knew the West. Bakst showed him reproductions of Gauguin, Cézanne and Van Gogh, whose influence can be seen in *The Little Room.* This picture indicates in its vivacious colouring that Chagall would soon break free from the sinister atmosphere still weighing on him in that extraordinary composition entitled *The Dead Man*: we are in a street in Vitebsk where, according to tradition, a corpse is on view surrounded by candles; a woman raises her arms; a sweeper pursues his task, but a fiddler is perched on the roof of a cobbler's shop with a boot for a sign. The painter's whole world is already present in this extremely early work.

He then painted his first nude. Bella, his fiancée, agreed to pose for him, but the reactions of her relatives were such that he effaced the offending canvas and painted a realistic but fantastic *Burial* on top. *The Wedding* and the strange *Sabbath* date from 1909, the year before the young painter went to Paris: Vitebsk, he said, held the roots of his art; Paris was the water they needed.

His discovery of Paris stirred him profoundly. *The Studio*, painted after he had visited a Van Gogh exhibition at Bernheim's, shows that within a few months he had shaken off everything that had hampered him in Russia. In many of his canvases he echoed the experiments of the Orphists, Fauves and Cubists who worked alongside him.

The work in which his personality really emerged, and where he drew on childhood sources, rejecting superficial influences, is *Me and the Village*. There exist both a preliminary gouache sketch and the great composition itself, which was exhibited at the Indépendants in 1911 and now belongs to the New York Museum of Modern Art: the painter is there, face to face with the cow which the milkmaid is milking, in front of the village with its bulbous cupolas and the isbas with their pointed roofs planted in the ground: "Sharing," he said, "in the technical revolution of art in France, I returned in thought to my own country," and added: "Why should I paint guitars like Picasso? There were no guitars in Vitebsk, but there were pendulum clocks, so I paint pendulum clocks."

During the years 1910-1914, Chagall gained control of his individual technique, discovered the value of light, and learned the virtue of bright colours: "No one at that time was in a better position than I was to get an idea of the insurmountable difference

Marcel Gromaire
The Reaper, 1924
Oils on canvas
Girardin Collection, Paris

Marcel Gromaire
The Card Party, 1928
Oils on canvas 32″ × 39″
Pierre Lévy Collection, Troyes

separating French painting from that of other countries." His compositions *Dedicated to my Fiancée* and *To Russia, to Donkeys and Others* bear witness to both his attachment to his country and his interest in the experiments of his friends, the painters Delaunay and Gleizes, and the poets Canudo and Cendrars.

The names of these last figure beside those of Apollinaire and the German writer Walden * in a large, strange canvas dating from 1911 to 1912, which shows a man and a woman forming a single body against an astrological background.

He was brought up in a strictly Orthodox Jewish society, but *Calvary*, of 1912, shows that he was already obsessed with Christianity, and, about 1938, this inspired him to several *Crucifixions*. But always—particularly in *The Cattle Merchant*—memories of his Jewish childhood in Russia were dominant. Paris hardly appears at all, except in a landscape where he outlined the Eiffel Tower and the Grande Roue.

A few weeks before the first world war began, he left Paris to attend his first large exhibition, organised by Walden in Berlin. From there he went to Vitebsk to get married. Having left Paris for eight weeks, he remained exiled for eight years.

The Hens, *The Mother at the Oven* and *The Smolensk Gazette* show that his return to his country was a return to his sources. He reverted to his monochrome palette and his careful observation of daily life in his town. He was much nearer to reality than when he dreamed of it in Paris in *The Musician* or *Self-Portrait with Seven Fingers*.

The formidable events he witnessed at that time—the war and the Bolshevik Revolution—left only slight traces on his work. Not until twenty years after the world-changing events of 1917 did he paint his great composition *The Revolution*.

He was appointed Commissar of Fine Arts in Vitebsk and Director of the Academy there, but was supplanted in 1919 by the Abstract artist Malevitch. He then went to live in Moscow, where he did décors for the Jewish Art Theatre. But Socialist Realism was already gaining ground in the USSR, and so he went to Kaunas, where an exhibition of his works was organised. From there he moved on to Berlin, and at last, in 1922, back to Paris.

He lived first in Montparnasse, not far from that La Ruche where, eight years before, he had abandoned all his canvases; then in Boulogne. The French light impressed him so vividly that he painted flowers and landscapes of utterly French inspiration. In *Ida at the Window*, *Double Portrait* and *Bella with a Pink* it is possible to think he had forgotten his own country. His inspiration came from Brittany landscapes, Paris locations and the people around him. The years following his return to France were among his most productive.

While he was staying in Berlin, he received a letter from Blaise Cendrars telling him that Ambroise Vollard was thinking of pursuing his activities as a publisher, which gave us the masterpieces illustrated by Bonnard, Maillol* and Maurice Denis; Rouault was already working on the *Miserere* for him; he was preparing to commission *The Georgics* from Segonzac and *The Unknown Masterpiece* from Picasso.

Chagall arrived, and Vollard invited him to choose for himself the text he would like to illustrate; several years later he undertook his series of etchings for *Dead Souls* by

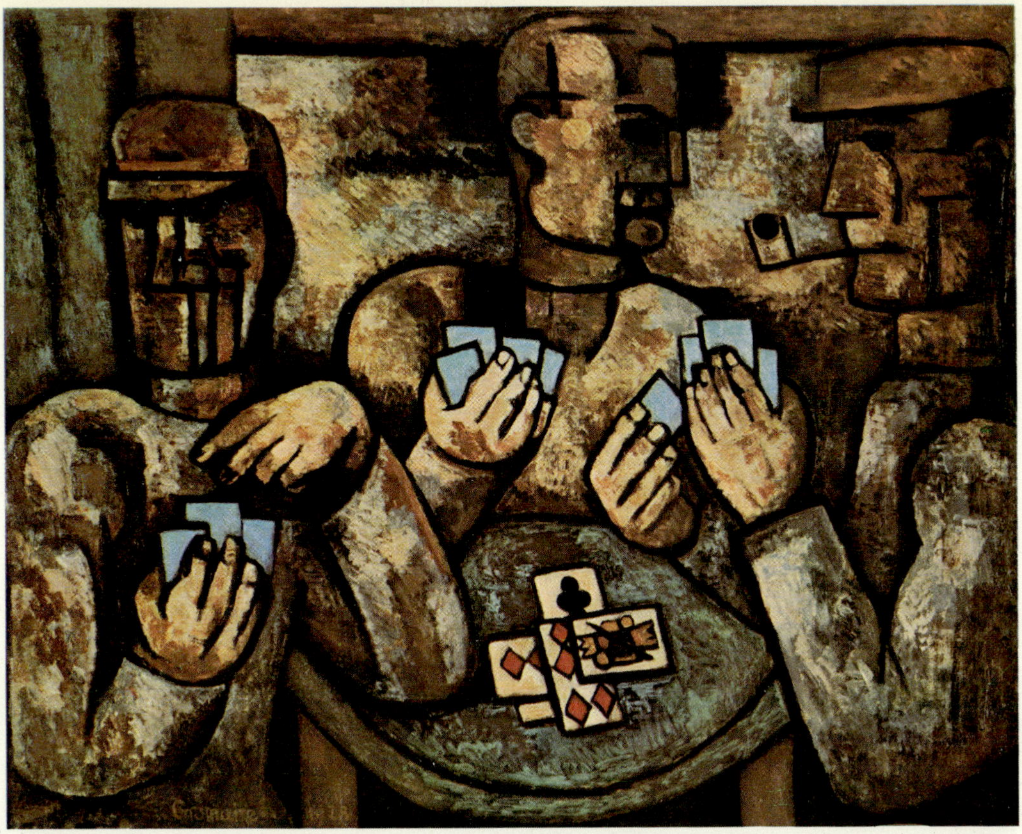

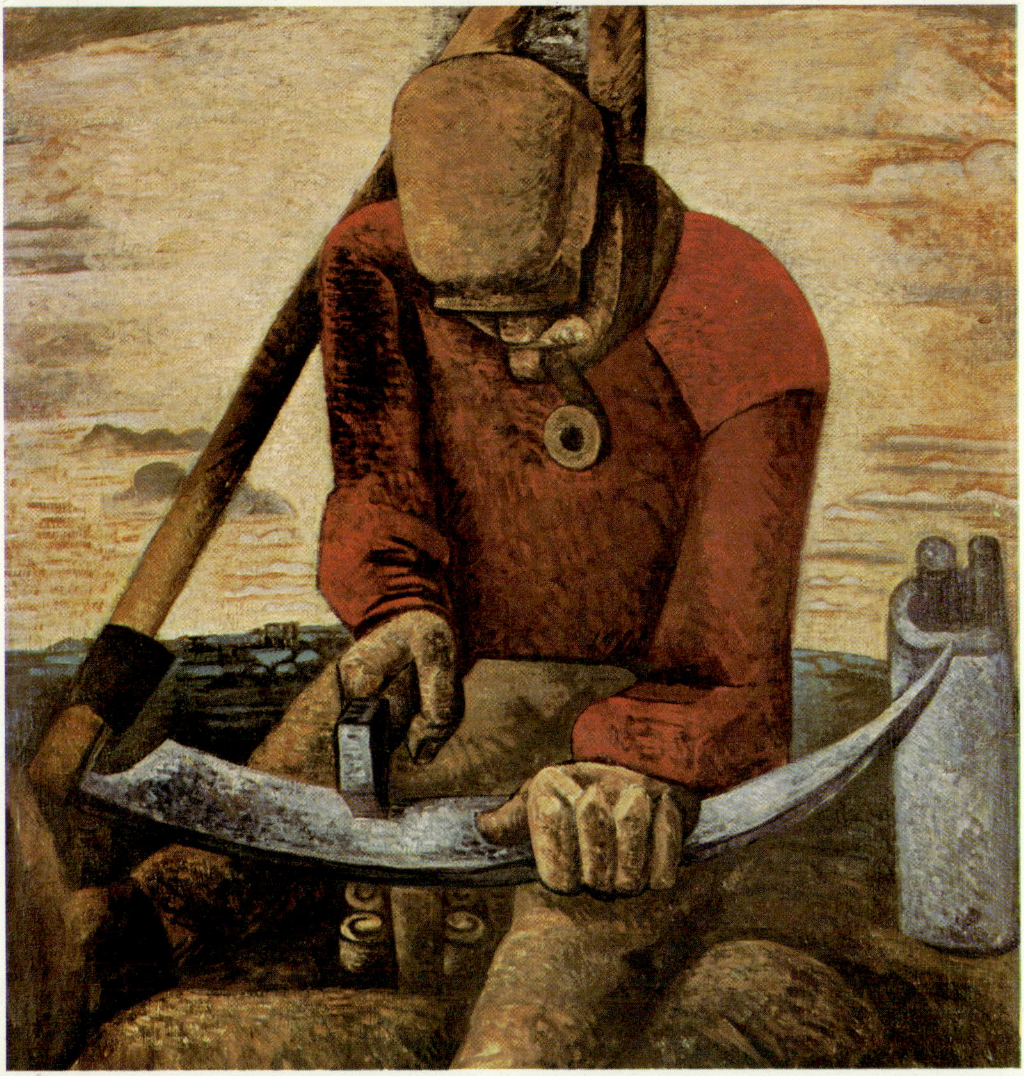

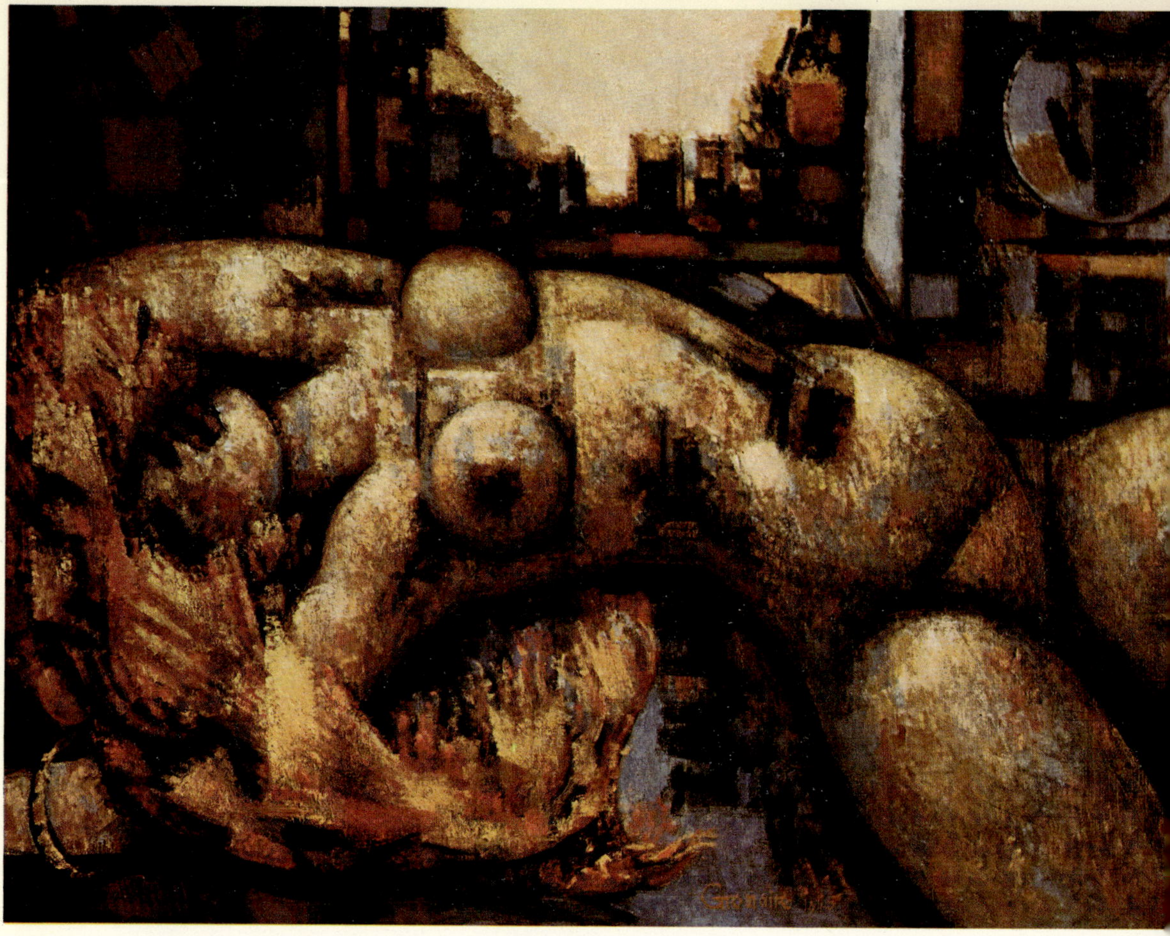

Gogol*, of all Russian writers the one nearest to him in his blend of realism and fantasy.

He had scarcely finished the 118 plates for *Dead Souls* when Vollard commissioned another set of illustrations from him, to La Fontaine's *Fables*; it seemed to give Chagall's imagination an open opportunity and inspired him to a dazzling series of gouaches.

After returning from a stay in Palestine in 1931 he undertook to illustrate the Bible, and produced 105 etchings which appeared much later, after Vollard's death in 1939.

Perhaps his involvement with Gogol and the Old Testament are related to a return in his imagination, noticeable in his painting of that time, to the town of his childhood, flying animals and imaginary circuses.

The terrible events which shook Europe during the 1930s brought him back to dramatic compositions: *The White Crucifixion* and *The Martyrdom*, dating from 1940, are among the most impressive.

In 1941 he went to the United States, but was far from finding serenity there. Although the new country gave him a sympathetic welcome and commissioned décors for brilliant ballets from him, he never felt at home. He refused to learn the language, and it was there that his wife Bella died.

His stay in the United States, extended until 1946, had no influence at all on his art. Totally indifferent to the country's charms, he appeased his nostalgia by placing the Eiffel Tower and the Place de la Concorde in his pictures.

After spending several months round about Paris, he settled in Vence with his

Marcel Gromaire
Woman with Red Hair
Oils on canvas 32″ × 39″
Musée National d'Art Moderne, Paris

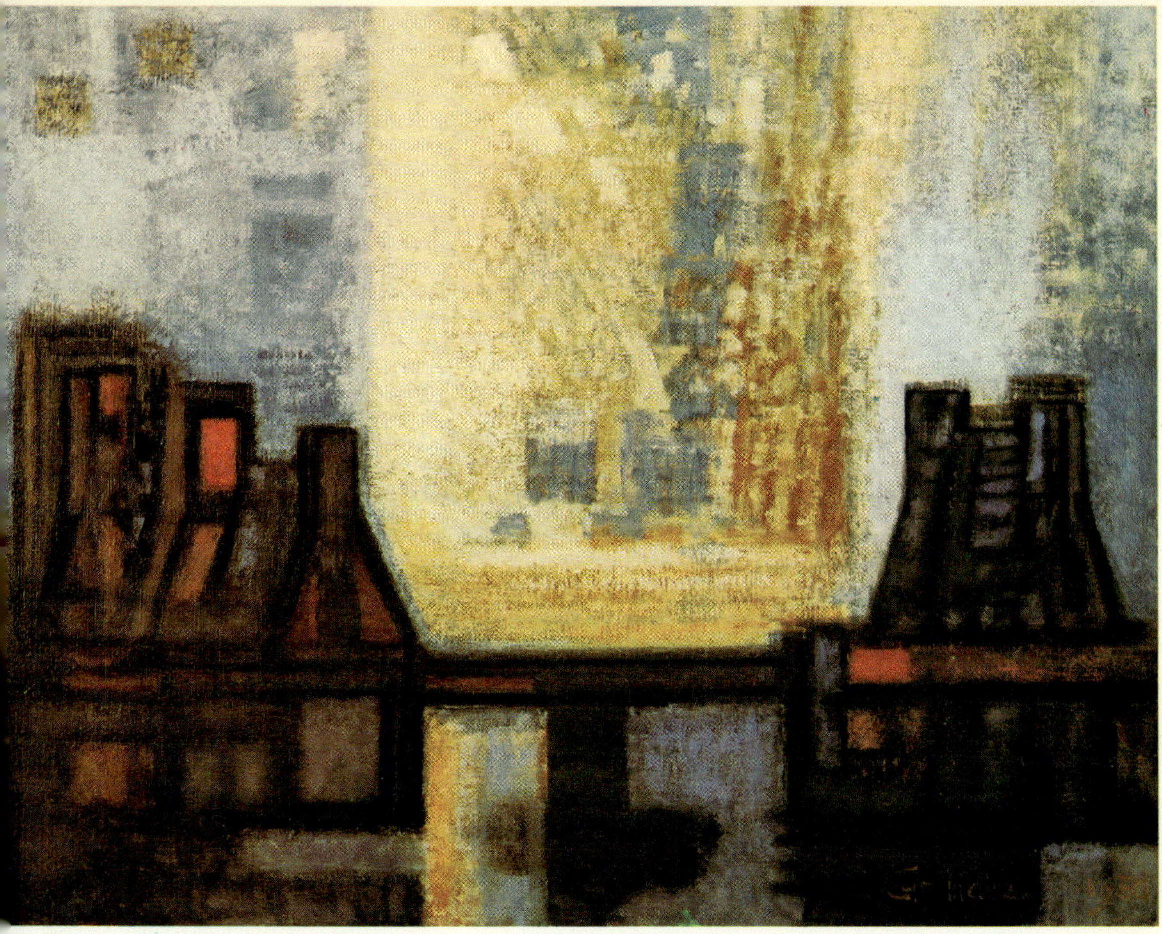

second wife, who organised his work. On renewing contact with France, he recovered all his genius, both in the works inspired by Paris and in his biblical series. *The White Window*, *Large Nude with a Basket*, *Around Vence*, *The Cyclists* and *The Almond Trees* reveal the same youthfulness he showed when he first arrived in Paris at the age of twenty. In possession of an admirably sure technique, he could now trust himself to all sorts of bold experiments and indulge in a sensuality which he had for a long time suppressed.

Simultaneously with his engravings, he attempted other media: ceramics, sculpture and, above all, stained glass. He worked for Assy Church and Metz Cathedral, and his set of windows for the Jerusalem synagogue were exhibited in the Tuileries Gardens before their departure for Israel.

During two years, 1959-1961, Chagall shuttled between Vence, his flat on the Ile Saint-Louis, the studio of Charles Marcq in Rheims, and the glass-works in Saint-Just-sur-Loire, where he chose the range of glass specially made for these great windows.

Far from being content to supply models to the glass-workers, he made them himself; they are not in any way interpretations of his paintings, although the inspiration is identical. Faithful to the Jewish religion's embargo on representing the human face, he had recourse to his familiar beasts: cock, fish, donkey and sheep; also to flowers, trees and many liturgical themes: tablets of the Law, Hebrew characters, flaming suns—an entire heraldry transformed and heightened by the light piercing through the shapes as it moves round. These windows, animated by a cosmic intensity, together with the great compositions for the ceilings of the Paris Opéra and the New York Metropolitan Opera House (1966) are the crowning glory of his work.

Marcel Gromaire
Houses near a Lake, 1951
Oils on canvas 21″ × 26″
Jacques L'Huillier Collection, Geneva

Chaim Soutine ▸
Smilovitch 1894-Paris 1943
Pageboy, *c.* 1927
Oils on canvas 37″ × 32″
Musée National d'Art Moderne, Paris

Chaim Soutine ▸▸
Portrait of a Woman
Oils on canvas 26″ × 21″
Bayeler Gallery, Basle

Gromaire

Marcel Gromaire reacts strongly against the theories of art for art's sake which are having a fresh vogue today. He believes that a painter, without renouncing his creative ambitions, should reflect his times.

Nature is the great reservoir from which Gromaire derives his inspiration, though he does not hesitate to venture far beyond it; for he is no realist; it has even been possible to compare him to certain Expressionists such as Rouault who, like him, favoured smouldering colours, and especially to Flemish artists such as Permeke, and (going further back) Brueghel. Gromaire was born on 24 July 1892 at Noyelles-sur-Sambre. Physically and intellectually, in his seriousness and his vigour, he is typically Flemish. He has their liking for solitude, their refusal to compromise, their desire for complete self-expression, and their obstinacy, which does not preclude a love of life in all its forms.

His work is serious but not at all severe, and is often humanised by a sense of pleasure. He painted the streets of Montmartre, the fairground lotteries and the flea-market, but what excited him more than people's pastimes was their work. His first finished pictures, dating from 1913 and 1914, are *Peasant with a Black Cap* and *The Brewers*. In 1921, at his first exhibition, he showed *The Peasant Meal* with echoes of Louis Le Nain, and *Man in a Blue Smock*. After that came *Carriage on the Métro*, *Man with Bread* and *The Bargewoman*, all of these works representing fresh triumphs by the painter over both his technique and the world.

His interest in drawing became evident at a very early age. His father attached no great importance to those attempts and made him enrol at the Faculty of Law in Paris; he had to overcome much resistance before he could attend the Ranson* and Colarossi academies. At first he worked with a Cubist, Le Fauconnier*, who taught him the seriousness of art. Then he travelled. Coming from the North, he was particularly attracted to Germany, England, Belgium and Holland.

He went to do his military service in 1913. Then war broke out and for six years he never touched his brushes. At the front, and on his hospital bed after he was wounded in 1916, he had time to reflect. When he returned to Paris he was twenty-seven; tough experiences had matured him. He had acquired the certainty that the career he had embarked on before the war was the right one. From now on nothing would deflect him.

He offers an example, unique in contemporary painting, of a master whose work is entirely homogeneous, and this is because, for one thing, long reflection preceded his actual start, and, for another, he arrived at a time when it was at last possible to digest the lesson of Cézanne.

When Cézanne jotted down his thoughts on art in a letter to Emile Bernard*, he was far from suspecting that they would be extensively developed and systematised.

Marcel Gromaire arrived armed with strong convictions, at a time when the most clear-sighted minds began to perceive the dangers of experiments springing from

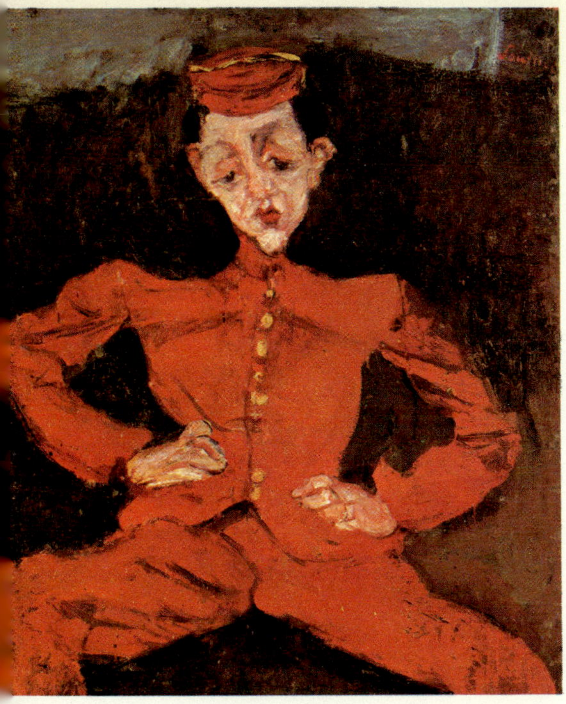 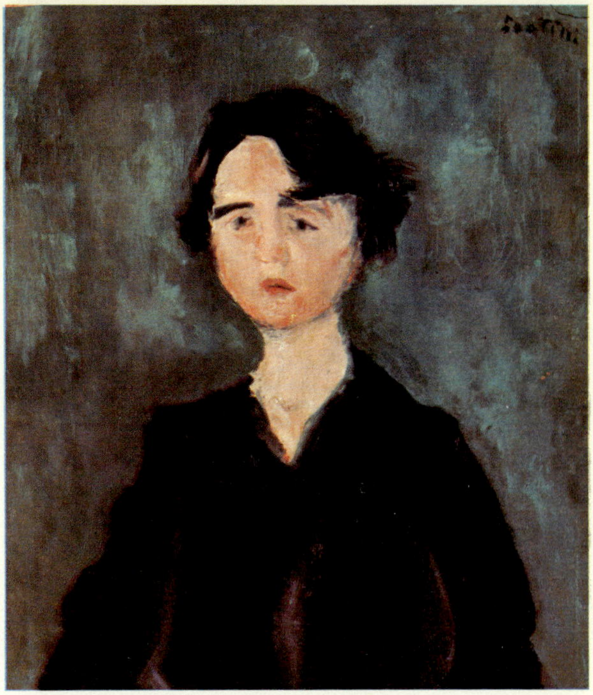

Cubism. He advanced against the tide with the obstinacy which is a trait in his character. But the lesson was too sophisticated to be easily grasped at once. Although he taught for a long time at the Ecole Nationale des Arts Décoratifs, he has not exercised on today's art the influence which could have established him in the mainstream of artistic development.

His work is there, however, reminding us that an artist is not set apart, but must remain in contact with the world. He interpreted it at first in drastically simplified forms. Then his drawing became suppler and his palette brighter. The basic ochres and browns were relieved by reds and blues, giving them an emphasis of effective power. Examples are *The Beer Drinkers*, *War*, a long-gestated composition, not painted until 1925 after he had carried it inside him since his long spell in the trenches, and *The Flemish Reaper*, a man in a red smock, steadying his scythe with the left hand, while his right grasps the hammer that sharpens the blade. Subsequently Gromaire painted more complex works; none of them demonstrates so vividly as this last one the harmony between man and soil and the tool which enables him to master it.

The schematic character of his early works is less marked. He painted the nude, and its vibrant sensuality is nowhere better expressed than in the picture called *The Lines of the Hand*, which holds an echo of the two canvases by Goya, *Young Women* and *Old Women*, which he must have seen in Lille Museum when he was young. What freedom there is in Gromaire's nudes—on the balcony, or with the map of the world, or in the *Fair Nude on a Black Background*! For him the female body is an inexhaustible subject; it has inspired him to hundreds of admirably accurate, well-observed drawings.

Each of his canvases is preceded by twenty or thirty pen sketches. His successes owe nothing to improvisation. But this premeditated art is never cold; serious, certainly, but always sensitive and alive.

He knows how to keep in touch with life, even in his most elaborate compositions. He is one of the rare modern painters who are not afraid to tackle allegory. In 1919, when he took up his neglected brushes again, he composed *Haymaking Allegory*, with a beautiful recumbent nude in the foreground. In *The Face of the Sea*, a woman's body stands in front of a lighthouse and a forest of masts, and he

Chaim Soutine
The Pastrycook, 1922
Oils on canvas
Private collection, Paris

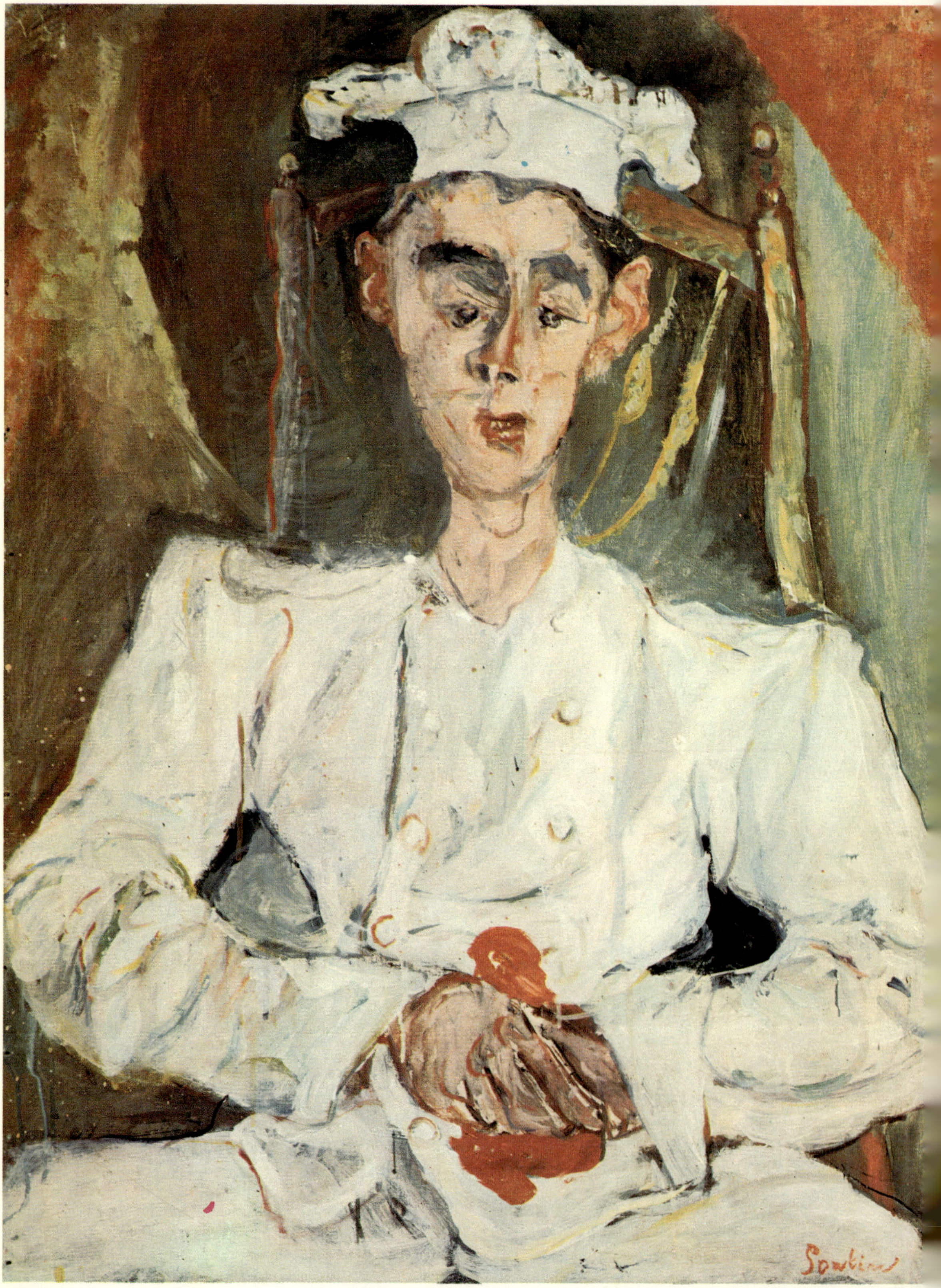

treated further classic themes in *The Three Ages*, *The Labours of the Soil*, and his murals, particularly those in the meeting hall of the Palais de la Découverte.

Not one of his canvases is devoid of significance; he constantly succeeds in going beyond anecdote, transcending the subject. *Out of Work*, dating from 1936, poignantly interprets the social unrest of that troubled period. Life is not even excluded from his still-lifes with their powerful undertones. In all his canvases, Gromaire is trying to say something, and this in no way conflicts with his deliberate construction and firm pictorial organisation.

He is also a great portraitist, and, as a landscape painter, he brought an arresting series of pictures back from New York; struck by the city, he has expressed its visual beauty, but has not disguised the disturbing nature of its mechanised civilisation.

He has expressed himself no less extensively in etchings, and he is one of the revivers of the art of tapestry, but it is probably in water-colours that he has shown the greatest freedom. Far from being regarded as mere sketches, these are, for him, actual pictures, as strictly composed as his oil paintings. They are originally very elaborate line-drawings of shapes. Then he adds colour, often brighter colour than when he is working in oils, but no less deep.

So much for this monumental work, which surely will defy time.

Soutine

Soutine is an artist who has introduced into present-day painting a whole world of trouble, obscurity and tragedy, with tortured shapes springing from a soil never lit by the midday sun. Like Van Gogh, however, he loved Arles, also Vence and Cagnes, yielding to the fascination that the Mediterranean coast has always exercised over people from the North.

Soutine has given us some remarkable images of these luminous landscapes; locked within himself, he remained insensitive to the art and nature of France. He follows in the lineage of the Flemish James Ensor*, the Norwegian Edvard Munch, the Russian Max Weber*, the German Emil Nolde and, above all, the great Austrian Oskar Kokoschka*. It is more than probable that, had circumstances not led him to Paris, he would have been easily integrated into the "Sturm" group in Berlin run by Herwarth Walden.

Art like Soutine's, maintained constantly in a state of frenzy, would be fatiguing did he not possess a profound sense of form, colour and texture, over and above the terrible intensity with which he expressed all that tormented him.

His sincerity is his most appealing quality. Surrounded by dealers and eager art-lovers, he never for a moment yielded to the temptation to work to commission. Successes or failures, his canvases are gestures towards something he lacked and would never possess. Like those of Van Gogh, Rouault and Modigliani, each one of his canvases is a drama, a confession, a protest against the human condition.

Chaim Soutine
Leaning Tree, 1922
Oils on canvas 26″ × 32″
Private collection, Paris
▼

Chaim Soutine ▶
The Red Flight of Steps at Cagnes
Oils on canvas 23″ × 19″
G. Waechter Collection, Geneva

Chaim Soutine was always a misfit. It is difficult to visualise what the life of this tenth child of a poor Jewish tailor must have been like; the poverty of the ghetto in Smilovitch, Lithuania, where he was born in 1894, seems to have marked him incurably.

At the end of his life, although rich and surrounded with care and affection, he was still obsessed with the thought of dying in the workhouse. The remembrance of the first thirty years of his life weighed on him so heavily that he could not rid his mind of the terror that he would one day perhaps relapse into poverty if the connoisseurs withdrew their favours, and find himself back at the stage when his father sent him to Minsk because he could not afford to feed him.

When we used to meet him in Montparnasse, hugging the walls and hiding his face between his hat and his coat collar, it never occurred to us to ask him about himself; so all that is known of his youth are a few anecdotes:

To teach him to retouch prints, the Minsk photographer who engaged him made him take a course in drawing. Taking a liking to painting, he saw there the sole outlet from a future which had seemed predetermined. Soon after entering the School of Fine Arts in Wilno, he met a doctor who admired his talent and gave him the means to go to Paris. In 1913, together with his friend Kremegne, he enrolled at the Cormon Studio where Van Gogh had worked before him; Van Gogh and Rembrandt were his real masters.

It is impossible to know what he learned there because his earliest preserved canvases date from 1916, by which time he had long ceased to work in any academy whatsoever. *The Forks* and *Still-life with Pipe* show him as timid, painting the kippers of his meagre repast with earthy colours he seems to have brought from his native country.

They must be examined closely for their pictorial qualities to be recognised; in appearance they resemble the thousand still-lifes painters of that time produced under the influence of Cézanne or Derain, but they herald that involvement with poverty displayed thirty years later by artists like Bernard Buffet.

On his arrival in Paris he lived in La Ruche, the community already inhabited by Chagall, Léger and Cendrars. He became friends with Modigliani, both of them poor and sick. They both had the good fortune to be supported by the poet-dealer Léopold Zborowski.

Soutine was a taciturn man with whom it was impossible to establish a conversation. No one, anyway, would have dreamed of drawing him out of the silence and poverty about which he seemed so complacent. Immediately after the first world war, Zborowski sent him to Céret, hoping that contact with nature in the South would brighten his palette. The shock he received stimulated him, and, to cut a long story short, he painted 200 canvases.

Half of them, the finest, were bought at one go by Barnes, the American founder of the Merion Museum. Overnight Soutine passed from penury to opulence without changing anything in his behaviour. He bought new clothes, but they very soon looked exactly like his shabby old cast-offs.

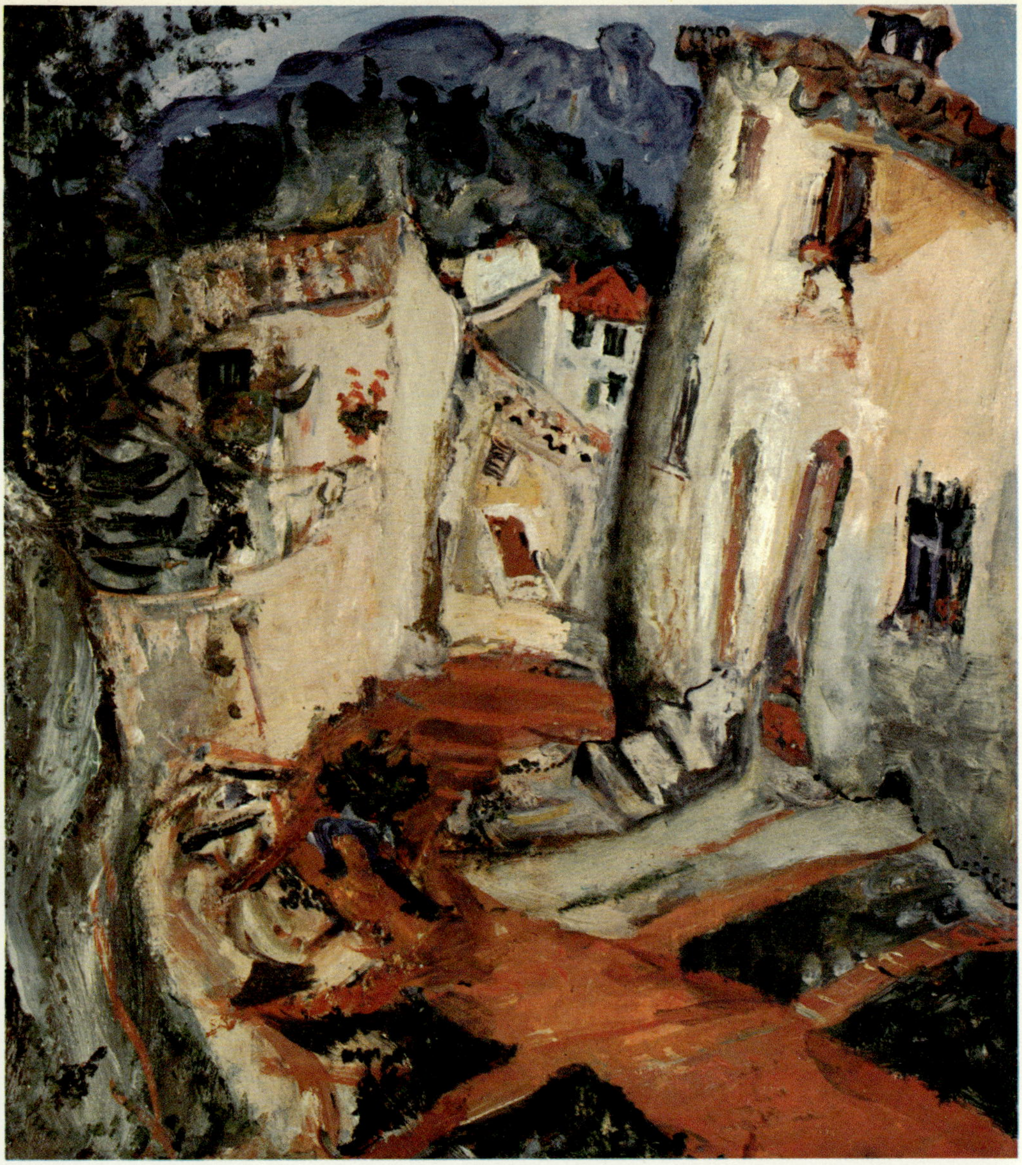

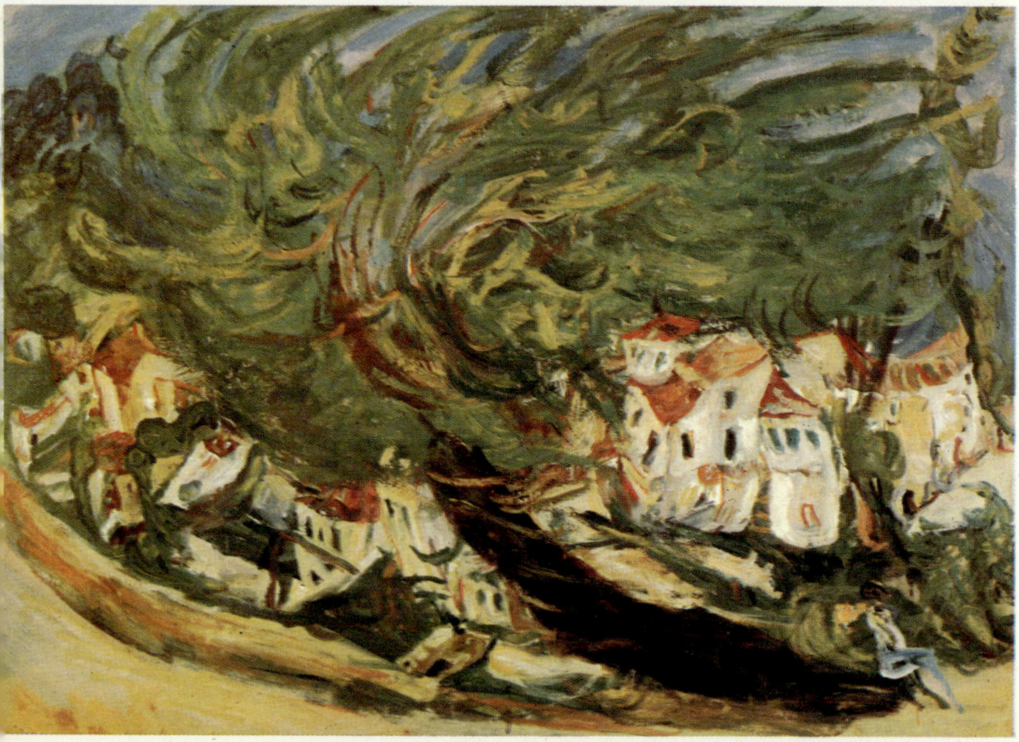

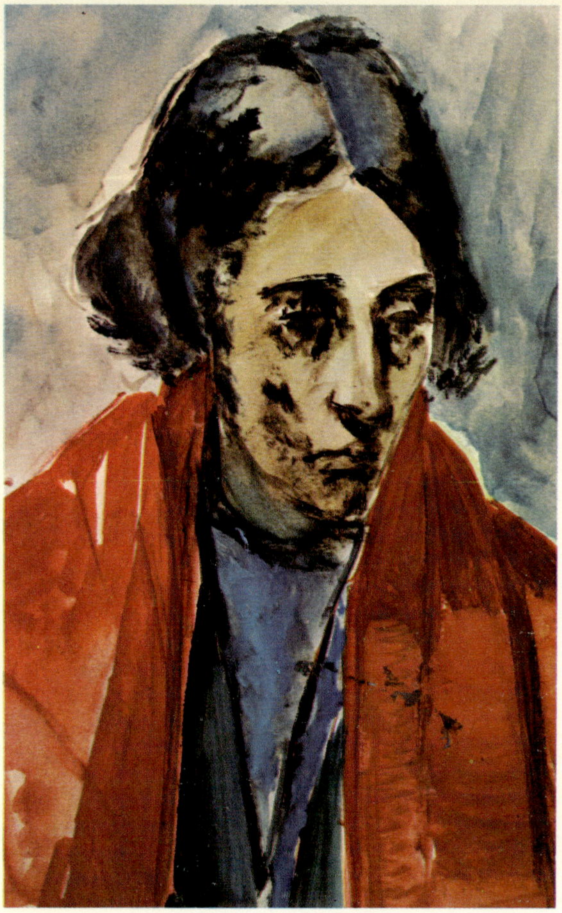

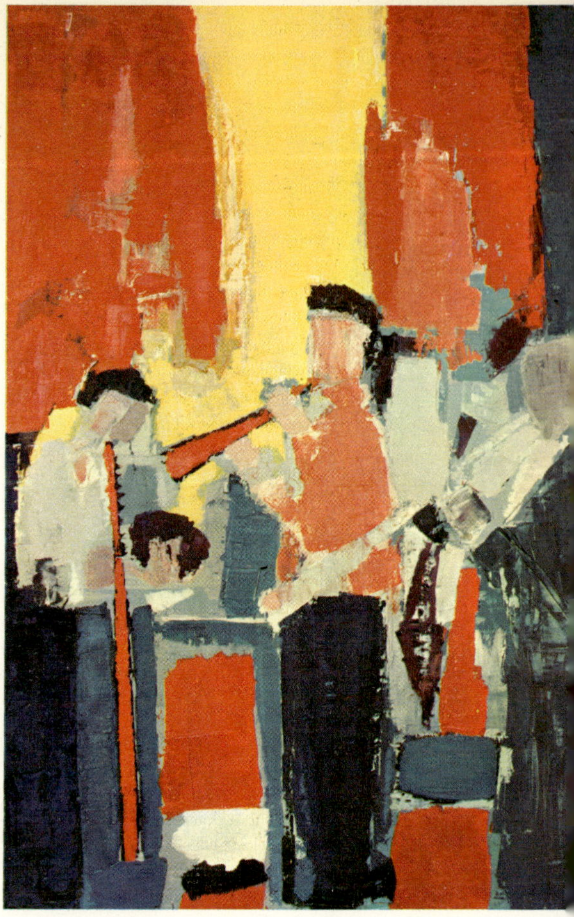

After that he went to Provence, but the Midi had scarcely any effect on him. When he stayed at Beauvallon as the guest of Paul Géraldy*, he hastened to black out the windows of his room so that he could paint in the half-light; he sent his models away after ripping his unfinished canvases; he revisited landscapes a hundred times before starting to paint, in the hope of finishing his canvas at a single sitting with the fervour which engendered his major works.

He preferred Touraine and Beauce to Provence. There is an unexpected grace in his landscapes of these provinces. Of all his works, *Chartres Cathedral*, painted in 1933, is probably his most complete and finished picture.

For a long time he had been suffering from a stomach ulcer, and suffering was certainly not calculated to improve a man who believed in neither happiness nor talent.

Grave though the risks which his Jewish origin incurred were, he accepted the events of 1940 with fatalism, and did not try to get out of France. He lay low in Touraine and painted strangely serene landscapes. Perhaps the French climate had some effect on him in the long run. Perhaps, as he grew older, he found calm as Utrillo finally did. But his health was in such danger that in 1943 he had to be moved to a Parisian clinic, where he died after an operation.

The striking thing about his work considered as a whole is that there is no evidence of logical development. No "styles", no "periods" as with Picasso, Braque and Utrillo. *Houses*, one of his earliest works, already shows the delirium of Expressionism—in form at least, for his colours, later stimulated to frenzy by the Midi, were still dull.

Nicolas de Staël
St Petersburg 1914-Antibes 1955
Portrait of Jeannine
Oils on canvas
Private collection, Seure

Nicolas de Staël
The Musicians (Souvenir of Sidney Bechet)
Oils on canvas
Private collection, Paris

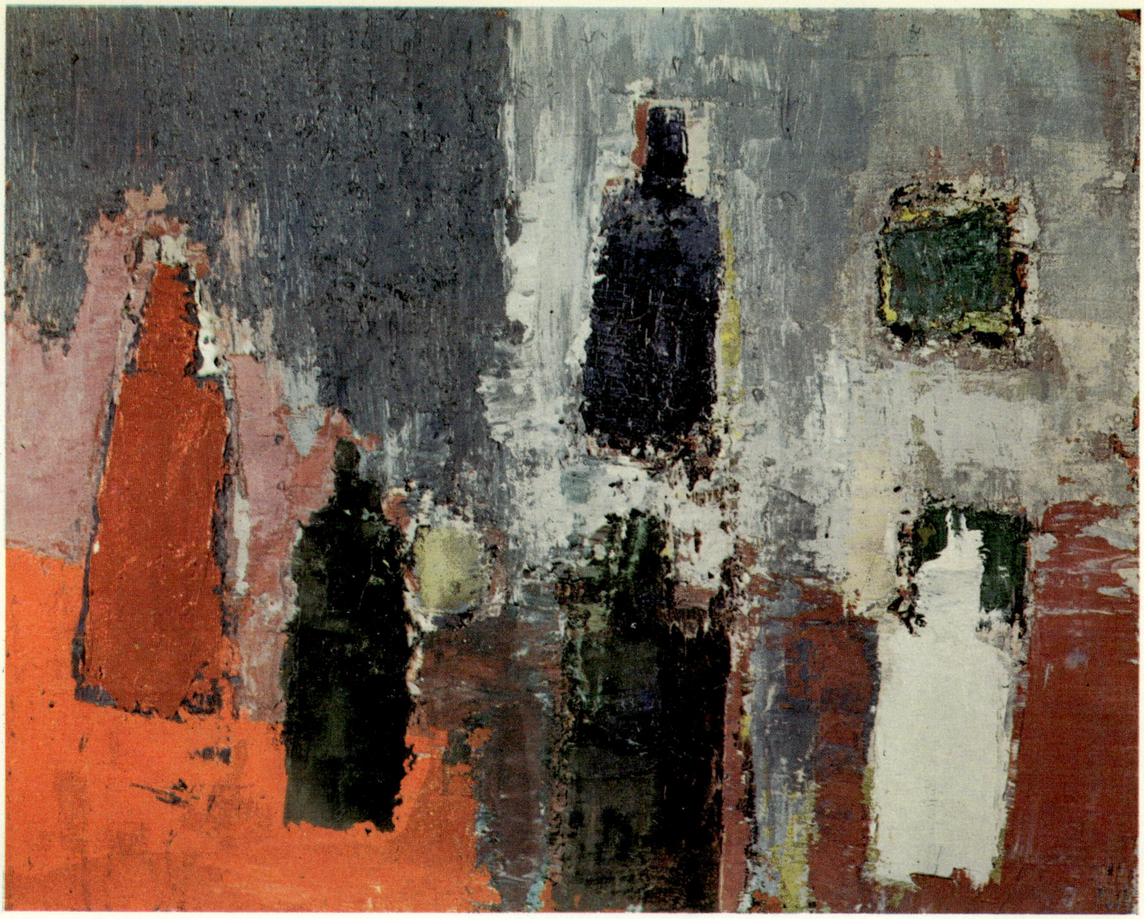

But from 1919 onwards nothing could temper his ardour; he painted everything in the throes of violent emotion, to the extent that he left the choice of his models to chance in order to feel the first shock of contact more sharply. Except for Van Gogh, probably no painter has worked more rapidly. He was well aware that this haste, indispensable for recording the sensation at the moment he experienced it, could detract from the solidity of his painting, so he attached great importance to the preparation of his canvas.

When a subject struck him, he constantly tried to recapture his first impression: there exist, for instance, four versions of *Tree at Vence*, one from 1926, three from 1929. About this time, attending a service in a Provence church, he was struck by the red and white outfits of the choir-boys, and arranged for them to go and pose for him. This was the origin in particular of the masterpiece in the Walter Collection, far less of a caricature than many other portraits where the models' features are no longer human. Exaggerating and distorting shapes, he imposed the same pinched-waist, elbows-out pose on a best man, a boot-boy or a page at Maxim's.

His obsessions often led him to paint dead animals. His series on the subject of *The Flayed Ox* bear witness to that admiration for Rembrandt which induced him to make the journey to Holland several times. In Rembrandt's *Flayed Ox* in the Louvre, however, there is a smile, that of the young woman emerging from the shadows; but Soutine's versions are grimly bloody; he concentrated on his subjects until, sometimes, the stench drove him out of his studio. No less disturbing are his flayed rabbits and the poultry—chickens, turkeys and ducks—that he painted indefatigably.

Nicolas de Staël
The Bottles
Oils on canvas 25″ × 30″
M. Buichard Collection, Berne

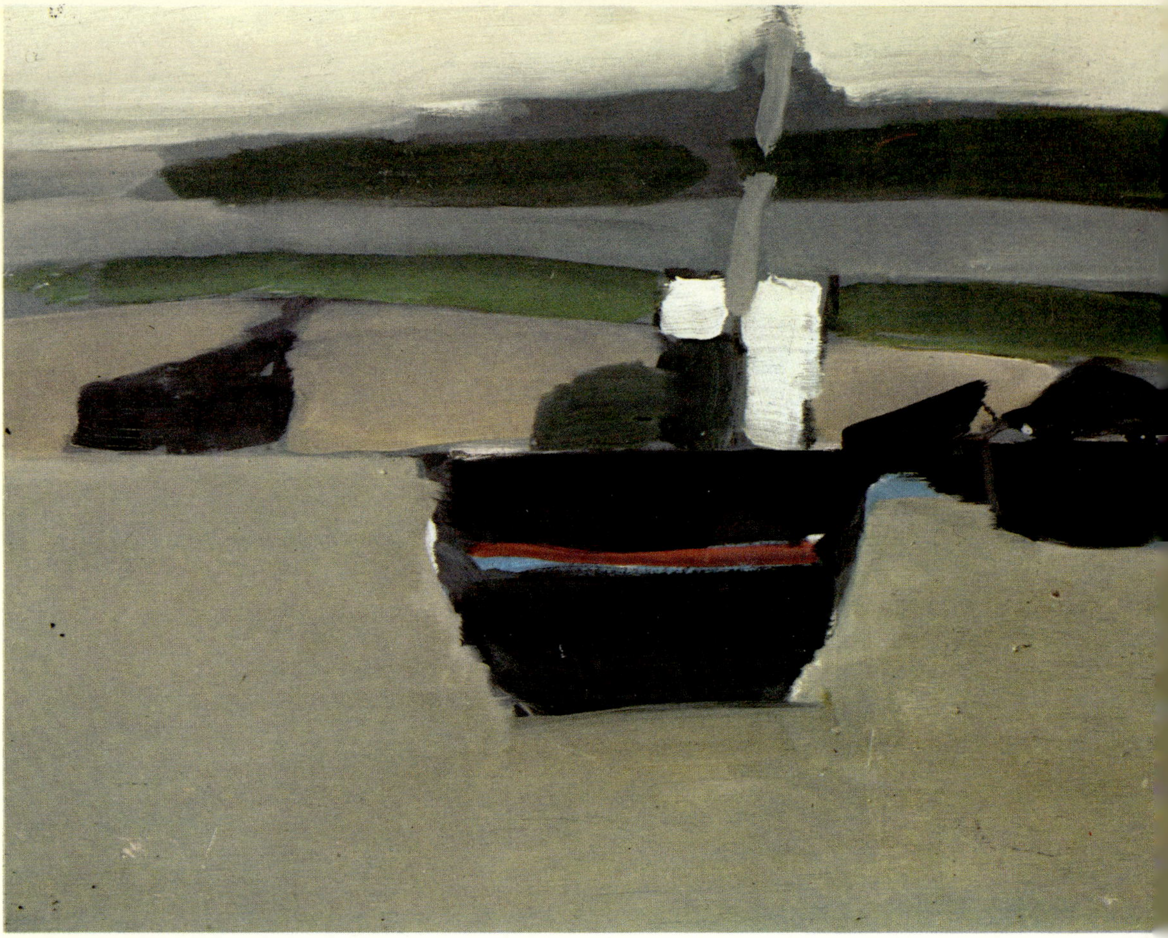

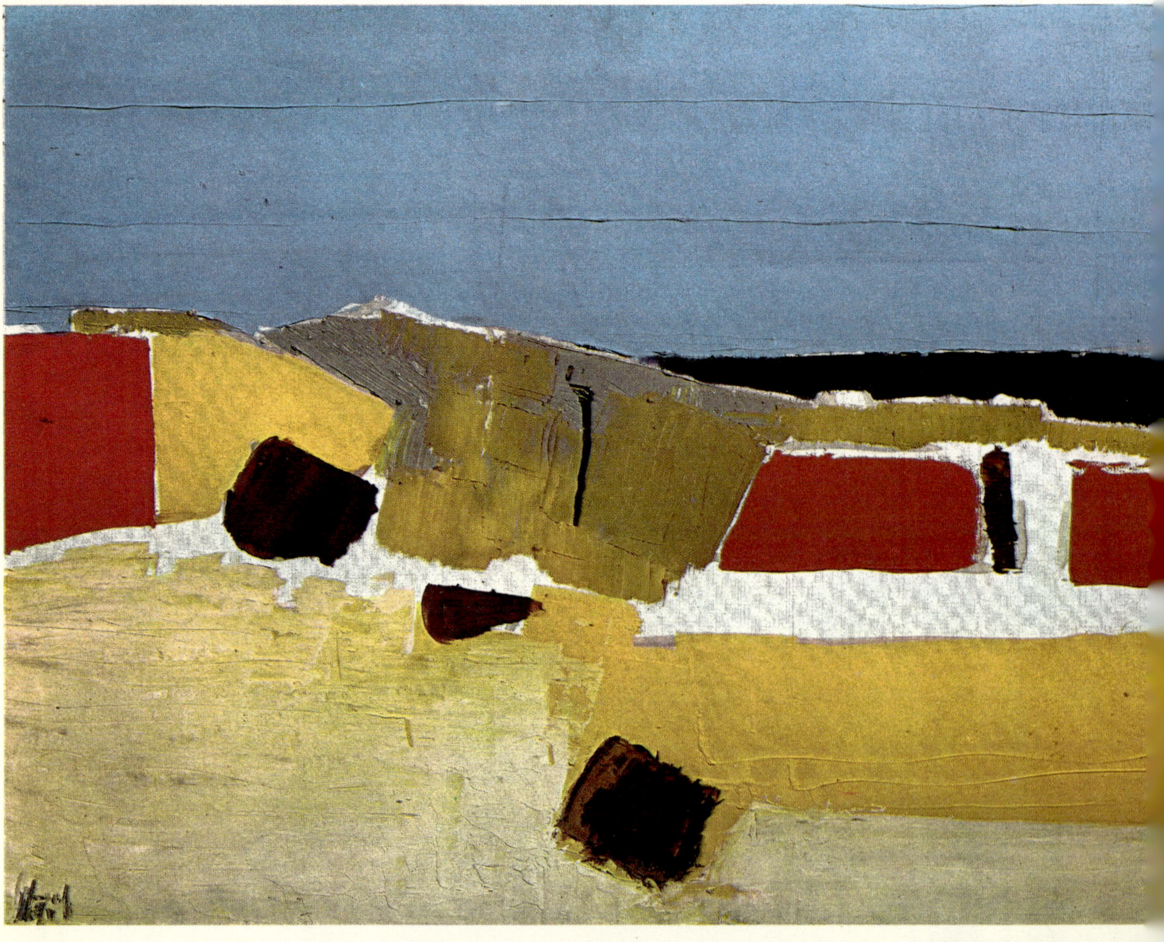

Nicolas de Staël
Low Tide, 1954
Oils on canvas 18″ × 24″
Bayeler Gallery, Basle

Nicolas de Staël
Agrigento, 1953
Oils on canvas 21″ × 29″
Sonia Henie Collection, Oslo
▼

However violent these canvases, the landscapes are more so, convulsed as though the ground were about to gape and swallow up the chaotic houses and the spinning trees streaked with furious thick slashing brush-strokes. But these "state-of-mind" landscapes were not mere pegs; they had to stir the painter in the first place, and he came back to them until he had exhausted their substance.

Nicolas de Staël

With an instinctive desire to escape a dangerous period, a whole section of French art fled into the realms of imagination during the second world war. Artists like Manessier* and Bazaine again took up the experiments in form previously adumbrated by the Cubists. Nevertheless, it was primarily two artists of Russian origin, André Lanskoy* and Nicolas de Staël, who established Abstract Art in France.

Although in de Staël's earliest non-figurative works there are easily recognisable reminiscences of French painters of the turn of the century, as soon as the frontiers were opened his style drew nearer to that practised abroad. From 1948 onwards he abandoned the earthy tones he had mainly used until then in favour of brilliant colours.

At the time when he was already considered one of the leading Abstract painters of the Paris school, he rejected this classification with such conviction that his subsequent evolution comes as no surprise; his later style reveals that he had resolved to consider nature no longer merely as a repertoire of shapes, but to interpret it directly.

It is possible that, had he lived, de Staël would have been the only contemporary painter capable of reconciling a refusal to break with the known world and an attitude which considered painting as an end in itself and sought nothing in nature but impressions and starting-points.

His "return to the object" in his ultimate works is so marked that he can be considered the creator of a kind of figurative abstraction: at the time when he died, he was intent on expressing Mediterranean lyricism with the blue of sky and sea and the white cubes of the houses actually *represented.*

De Staël always affirmed that he worked from reality, but his long-standing relationship with the world was so subjective that he must be left to explain it himself, as one of his biographers, Gindertael, quotes: "I cannot start from nothing. When there is no nature before me, the picture is always bad." He thought this right from the start, and it should be borne in mind by those who have concluded, from the ultimate phases of his work, that he repented, or was finally converted to, figurative art. When asked, "What about nature?" he replied: "When one feels cold in winter, one is uncomfortable; too hot in summer, ditto. We are constantly invaded by nature." Nature, for de Staël himself, was primarily the surroundings that he could "experience"; and for his subsequent painting it was a point of reference. "I want my picture or drawing," he explained, "to be like a tree or a forest. One progresses from a line or a thin mark to a point or a blot, as one progresses from a twig to a trunk. But everything must hold fast, everything must be in place." In the most incongruous things he discovered "a basic principle of unity".

He seems to have adopted simple forms for his painting out of a need for order, in reaction against a world at whose mercy he had for so long been tossed about.

He was born on 5 January 1913 in St Petersburg. Belonging to the famous Baltic family of Staël-Holstein, he emigrated with the Russian aristocracy and went to live in Brussels at the age of twelve.

There he was educated and entered the Royal Academy of Fine Arts in the class of the teacher Van Haelen. Then began that wandering life which led him to Holland, Spain, North Africa and Italy.

In 1937 he settled in Paris and worked at the Académie Moderne, directed by Fernand Léger. When war broke out he joined the Foreign Legion and fought in the Tunisian campaign.

After demobilisation he settled in Nice, and his works dating from 1941 and 1942 are either strictly representational, as in *Portrait of Jeannine* and *Still-life*, or totally lacking in reference to reality like *Composition* and *The Young Fate*. He hesitated between two worlds, two conceptions of painting. Then he decided for Abstract art and his works follow the curve of his life.

Until then he had been fairly prosperous, but he suddenly seems to have found himself in more or less total penury. He gave up working with a palette-knife, which used up an enormous amount of paint, and turned to a style more measured, not in shapes, but in use of material. In 1947 the American market opened to him, and he was able to return to his colour orgies, now using a trowel instead of a palette-knife.

Gradually he stopped seeking inspiration in periodicals devoted to Abstract art, and consented to look at nature.

He held his first exhibition in Paris in 1945, then married a French girl and obtained his naturalisation.

The year 1952 was crucial for the young painter. His *Flowers* shows him as a violent colourist, like so many other Russians. *Footballers*, painted in broad applications, indicates that he was leading up to his rupture with non-figurative art. For some time the Mediterranean had a softening effect on him. He wandered from Provence to Sicily, then settled in Antibes and took a studio on the ramparts. It was there that he committed suicide, on 16 March 1955, just before a fresh exhibition in Paris.

During the last four years of his life his lyricism exploded violently, but he could also handle subtle modulations in works such as *Standing Nude*, of 1953. In contrast, *Corner of the Studio* is composed in a dazzling key of white and blue.

This work, in his last style, appeals to us by the mystery surrounding it. Was Jean Cocteau right when he decided that de Staël's suicide was the result of a terrible inner debate? Had he lived, would he have returned to abstraction? Would he have definitely chosen figuration? Of course, no one can tell.

Evidence and Documents

Fernand Léger

. . . I have been severely criticised for having (in 1918) approached the machine part as an artistic possibility. I am anxious to discuss this question.

Although I am the first to have produced pictorial effects from this modern element, I have not the slightest intention of shouting from the house-tops that " this is the only thing ".

The machine part, like everything else, is only a *means*, *not an end.*

But if one wishes to create a work of strength, firmness and artistic intensity, if one wants to create an organic work, if one wants to create and obtain the equivalent of the " thing of beauty " which modern industry sometimes produces, it is tempting to make use of those materials as basic matter.

A picture, arranged and orchestrated like a score, has the same geometrical needs as any other objective human creation (industrial or commercial).

There are the weights of the volumes, the relationships of the lines, the balance of the colours. All things which necessitate absolute order. All those qualities are strongly present in actual commercial objects—sometimes (rarely) in artistic products. In this case, there is nothing to do but fold one's arms and admire. But most of the time, these qualities are sparse, as in a landscape or a still-life. So the painter's contribution comes into play and he organises, or imposes his order on disorder. He creates, he achieves balance.

The situation at the present time is fairly disastrous. Art is " rivalled " by the useful object, which is sometimes beautiful. Or more or less disturbing. We must do as well or better. It is absolutely undeniable that geometric relationships, volumes, lines and coloured surfaces (aeroplanes, cars, agricultural machines, all commercial articles, etc.) *can* be beautiful.

If they *always* were, the role of the artist would no longer serve any useful purpose. There are some modern window displays and arrangements which are absolutely perfect and impossible to use; they are no longer separate raw materials; they have become a factual entity. The question becomes one of quantity, for if the production of these things satisfied public demand, there would be nothing left for the artist to do. A need would be supplied and art would be the loser.

I repeat, the artist's position in the face of these objects is often disturbing.

I personally hope to extricate myself by seeking a state of intensive organisation.

To do this, I apply the law of artistic contrasts, which, I believe, has never been applied until today. I group opposing values: flat surfaces against modelled surfaces, three-dimensional people against flat house-fronts, shapely volumes of smoke against the bright surfaces of architecture, pure flat tones against modelled grey tones or vice versa.

Between these two relationships, which have eternally been the subjects of painting, I seek one relationship of never hitherto realised intensity.

Disturbance of the subject to be rendered has always embarrassed earlier artists. Many have had a dim sense of the value of plastic contrasts. None has been able to dominate his subject sufficiently to apply them integrally, that is to say, to deform the subject, if necessary, for the sake of the artistic result.

It follows from this principle that I personally can make a picture concrete and representational, or distorted and even abstract, with the same result of intensity and force.

From this fact I obtain *a state of intensive organisation*, and I am certainly above most commercial phenomena (industrial products). It is infinitely rare for useful items to associate in a relationship, in the same way that they enter into concord, in a state of beauty, with my deliberate organisation by contrast. These realisations rely on observation of modern life. That we live in a *geometrical world* is undeniable, and also that we live in a *state of frequent contrasts*. The most striking example is the advertisement hoarding—hard, fixed, local and violent, carving into the gentle and harmonious landscape. Similarly a present-day formal social event throws into contrast the black suits of the men, hard and abrupt, with the feminine dresses, more pretty and subtle. Period of contrasts.

An 18th-century occasion was simply tone on tone, similar costumes. Period of melody.

I am therefore in step with my period, and in the long run it is the result which counts. The end justifies the means.

The first painters began perhaps by painting sky, then clouds, then trees, then houses, then the design for the first road, then the telegraph pole and the car on that road. Why should anyone, at a moment of human evolution, wish to cry halt to a man who uses machine parts? Why? What justification? It is absurd. Art is subjective, that goes without saying, but the subjectivity is controlled, and applied to objective raw material.

A work of art is the *interaction* of these two qualities. To arrive at the fixed state—a state of durability, not too far to the right, not too far to the left, but in the middle—is extremely difficult. There has to be perfect equilibrium between instinct and control. The romantic tends to the left—towards excessive subjectivity (a warm state). The other tends to the right—towards excessive objectivity (a cold state).

Fernand Léger
Fonctions de la Peinture
Editions Gonthier, Paris 1965

Henri Matisse

What I pursue above all is expression. Sometimes I have been credited with a certain skill, while being accused of an ambition that was limited and did not go beyond the purely visual satisfaction which the sight of a picture can provide. But a painter's thought should not be considered apart from his abilities, for it is valid only in so far as it is served by abilities which must be the more complete (and by complete I do not mean complicated) as his thought is more profound. I cannot distinguish between the feeling I have about life and the manner in which I interpret it.

Expression, for me, does not reside in the emotion which erupts on a face or shows in a violent movement; it is in the whole disposition of my picture; the space occupied by bodies, the spaces around them, the proportions, all have a part in it. Composition is the art of arranging in a decorative manner the various elements the painter draws on to express his feelings. In a picture, each portion should be visible and should play the part, principal or supporting, accorded to it. Likewise everything which has no use in the picture is a hindrance. A work requires a total harmony: every superfluous detail will assume, in the mind of the spectator, the place of another essential detail.

The composition, which should aim at expression, is modified according to the surface to be covered. If I take a sheet of paper of given dimensions, I will trace on it a design which bears an obligatory relationship to the format. I will not repeat this same design on another sheet of different proportions, for instance, oblong instead of square. I will not be content simply to enlarge it if I have to work on a sheet of similar shape, but ten times the size. The design must have a power of expansion which animates the things surrounding it. The artist who wishes to copy a composition from one canvas on to a larger canvas must, in order to preserve the expression, conceive it afresh and modify its appearance, not simply square it up.

By making use of toning or contrast of colours, it is possible to achieve extremely agreeable effects. Often when I set to work at a first sitting I note down fresh, superficial sensations. A few years ago, I was sometimes satisfied with the results. If I were content with them today, now that I think I can see further, the picture would remain vague; I should have registered the fugitive sensation of a moment, which would not have done me justice, and which I would scarcely recognise tomorrow. I want to arrive at that state of sensory condensation which makes a picture. I could be contented with a first shot at a work, but it would soon bore me, and I prefer to retouch it so that I can recognise it later as a representation of my mind. At one time I couldn't leave my canvases hanging on the wall because they reminded me of moments of hyper-excitement, and I didn't like seeing them when I was calm. These days, I try to put calm into them, and I go back to them until they are finished.

Raymond Escholier
Henri Matisse
Floury éditeur, Paris
Text reproduced in
De la Palette à l'Ecritoire
Anthology published by André Lhote
Editions Corrêa, Paris 1946

Pablo Picasso

Act VI. (*The scene takes place in the drainage-room-cum-bed-sitter and bathroom of the Anguishes' villa.*)

Thin Anguish

The burning of my unhealthy passions inflames the wound of the chilblains enamoured of the prism which has set up house on the gilded curve of the rainbow and pours it out like confetti. I am merely the frozen spirit pressed against the fire's window-panes. I beat my head against my reflection and cry the merchandise of my sorrow to the windows closed against all compassion. My shirt, torn to shreds by the rigid fans of my tears, bites with the nitric acid of its blows the seaweed of my arms, dragging the robe of my feet and my cries from door to door. The little bag of sugared almonds I bought yesterday for Big Foot for 40 centimes burns my hands. A suppurating ulcer in my heart, love plays marbles between the feathers of its wings. The old sewing machine which rotates the horses and lions of the roundabout dishevelled by my desires minces my flesh into sausages and presents it living to the frozen hands of the still-born stars beating their wolfish hunger and oceanic thirst against the panes of my window. Enormous piles of logs resignedly await their fate. Let us make the soup. (*Reading from a cookery book*) Half a quart of Spanish melon, palm oil, lemon, beans, salt, vinegar, a little bread; place to cook over a slow fire; from time to time delicately fish out a soul in pain of purgatory; chill; print a thousand copies on Japanese serge and let the weather-glass take it and give it to the octopuses. (*Shouting through the drainage-hole of their bed*) Sister! Sister! Come here! Come and help me lay the table and fold the dirty linen soiled with blood and excrement! Hurry up, sister, the soup is already cold and is bursting at the bottom of the mirror in the ice-box. The entire afternoon I have been embroidering a thousand tales with this soup, which it will recount to you secretly in your ear, if you will keep until last the architecture of the skeleton's bunch of violets.

Pablo Picasso
Desire caught by the Tail

Pablo Picasso

I am talking about what helps me to live, what is good. I am not one of those people who try to get lost, to forget themselves, loving nothing, cutting down their needs, their tastes, their desires, and conducting their lives, in other words life, to the repugnant conclusion of their death. I do not strive to conquer the world solely by the abstract power of intelligence; I want everything to be palpable, real and useful to me, for only starting from here can I envisage my existence. Man cannot exist except in his own reality. He must therefore be aware of it. If not, he exists for other people only as a dead man, a stone or a heap of rubbish.

Of all the men who have best proved their life, and of whom no one could say they passed through the world without ever knowing they were there, Pablo Picasso is among the greatest. After having conquered the world, he had the courage to turn it against himself, sure that he would not be vanquished but revealed in his true stature. "When I have no blue, I use red," he said. Instead of a single straight line or a curve, he scatters a thousand lines which find their unity and truth within him. Despising accepted notions of objective reality, he has re-established contact between the object and the person looking at it, and consequently thinking of it, and has restored to us, in the most daring and sublime manner, infallible proof of the existence of men and the world.

Paul Eluard

Donner à voir

Georges Braque

Art is made to disturb. Science reassures.

There is trickery in all science. Any problem can be resolved if it is posed cleverly enough.

Art flies overhead; science supplies crutches.

In art there is only one valid quality: that which is inexplicable.

The painter knows things by sight, the writer knows their names: he benefits from favourable prejudice. For this reason criticism is easy.

The artist must not be asked for more than he can give; nor the critic for more than he can see.

Where talent is relied on, it is because imagination is lacking.

There can be no *effect* without twisting the truth.

Shock is creative.

A glowing hearth creates shadows around it. By contrast, both gain in intensity.

Comparison leads only to metaphor. It does not create.

The *guardian* may well conduct a whole flock: a single bull, no.

The lone pessimist tests his resistance to an idea; he is really seeking all that thwarts him.

The artist who no longer meets resistance touches perfection. But it is only technical perfection.

The *universal* is born of opposites. I discern this between Ingres and Corot. Not between Corot and Trouillebert.

Every lake has its shores.

Colours intensify each other when they are contrasted.

A vase gives shape to a void, as music does to silence.

A boat gains support from the pressure of the water; all that man has been able to determine is the level of buoyancy.

Jean Paulhan
Georges Braque
Text reproduced in
De la Palette à l'Ecritoire
Anthology published by André Lhote
Editions Corrêa, Paris 1946

Maurice Utrillo

. . . As I write these lines I have in front of me a canvas by Utrillo depicting the humble bistro of Saint-Bernard where the artist stayed for several years around 1934. It is a work of " climate ", if I may say so, and of delectation. It exudes such great charm that it induces that sensation remarked by Claudel in the presence of a Vermeer composition: " We do not look at it; not for a moment do we contemplate it with superior narrowed gaze: we are immediately inside it; we inhabit it. We are captured. We soak up this atmosphere it contains. Indeed, the house we are in has a soul. It is brimming with *the silence of the present time*" (my italics). Utrillo's art could not be better defined than by this last phrase. In this picture in particular " the silence of the present time " can be felt with such happiness, exactitude and penetrating intimacy, that one becomes both the accomplice and the compliant and overwhelmed victim.

Beneath the trees in the little square, over the cropped and dusty grass, circulate people like marionettes, with furtive, sleepwalking tread, as in all Utrillo's canvases. All sorts are depicted here: the man in a shirt with his pitiful female companion, the half-wit talking to herself, the red-stockinged gossip, and, everlastingly, haunting in her black dress and mourning *bibi* (hat), shiny high-heeled shoes and starched ruffles, the opulent figure of the " Rouquine ", the sexual vision which Utrillo cannot dispel. She bears a name in his memory. Her presence is almost equivalent to a confession, which, however painful, returns every time a suburban scene recalls a distant amorous and comic adventure for which the artist paid the price. It can thus be imagined of what " silence " the atmosphere of this canvas is composed. As for " the present time ",

A bitter time that brings
A poet only bane
Carried on anxious wings
Of chaos and of pain . . .,

perhaps it is that shown by an old chiming clock with a disjointed spring, which has been sitting on the counter for months between a chromolithograph framed in black and gold, and a legal notice about the suppression of public drunkenness. It is always this time in Utrillo's work, and he could not explain it himself except by eventually insinuating, when pressed for an answer, that it was invariably drinking time, given permission.

It is, in fact, recounted that, in the beautiful country of Saint-Bernard, having drained several tankards of Beaujolais in the bistro which occupies the right foreground of this picture, Utrillo decided to buy the château. I saw Maurice at Saint-Bernard. As in Montmartre, he led a strange existence there, divided between his painting and the exclusive cult he dedicated to Joan of Arc. A nurse-chauffeur drove the painter's car. Utrillo, famed in the village for his drunkenness, never went out alone. Failing the chauffeur, he was accompanied by his mother, Suzanne Valadon. A wine merchant who supplied the château suggested trading his wine against pictures, and although Utrillo was not allowed an extra ration, Utter, who could drink as much as he liked, took hogsheads in exchange for works by Suzanne, himself and Maurice, resulting in that shrewd vintner now possessing a collection which is the talk of the country.

On the Butte, Utrillo had already made the fortunes of numerous drink traders. As far as I know, however, he had never painted any picture comparable with this one of Saint-Bernard, with more naïve and fervent ingenuity. How many times he must have contemplated this tavern's white façade from his window! Each detail seems graven on his memory. Everything, down to the green of a table among the stands, helps to maintain the unlucky man's thirst by preserving the view from the terrace where the nurse-chauffeur perhaps allowed him to sit one morning. Indeed, no one is more scrupulous than Maurice over the accurate, evocative detail. Whether depicting venetian shutters whose slats can be counted, graffiti on the peeling walls, railings round parks or hospitals, seats in squares, or street lamps, he gives his pictures a precise and hauntingly authentic documentary quality.

Having once allowed me to state in a book that he drank absinthe, Utrillo showed me just how far he pursued his concern for accuracy by crossing out this passage in Daragnes' copy and writing in his tall spidery hand: "Wine! . . . The author is a villain, though my friend." And the word "wine" is underlined three times in red crayon.

The whole drama of his life, the whole power and strangeness of his talent, resides in this affirmation. Perhaps we should make this allowance for him as we do for Verlaine or Edgar Allan Poe. Heart-rending drama! But certain mornings-after allowed him to paint some of his best pictures: he expiated in them his shame and self-disgust, the humiliations publicly inflicted on him by a girl or an urchin, and his poignant wish to forget, to efface such lowness and ignominy by work. The whites—"his" whites—tend to be sorrowful. For a fairly long period they constituted the base or key of his work, all the resonances being formed through their intensity. Utrillo uses few shades, but contrasts and comparisons of tone which result in giving his canvases both strength and subtlety. At about the time of his hardest drinking, he used only the colour white, sometimes mixing it with plaster to obtain the more unusual effects. The dirty brown of an enclosure, a bar front or a fence, and the dark green of foliage play only secondary, supporting roles in these compositions, but so perfectly conceived and orchestrated are they that they impart to the whole a flavour, a vigour, and an unalterable touch of magic.

Francis Carco
L'Ami des Peintres
Editions du Milieu du Monde, Geneva 1944

s	Political Events	Arts	Intellectual Life	Theatre, Music, etc.
	League of Nations founded, without the USA. Congress of Tours. Birth of the French Communist party. Gandhi launches his civil disobedience campaign in India. Prohibition in the USA.	Ozenfant and Le Corbusier found the review *L'Esprit nouveau.* First exhibitions of La Patellière, Gromaire and Goerg. Realist manifesto published in Moscow by Pevsner and Gabo. Matisse: "Odalisques" series. Braque: *The Sugar-basin.* Picasso: *Pulcinella,* décor for Diaghilev. Duchamp: *L.H.O.O.Q.*	Valéry: *Le Cimetière Marin.* Breton and Soupault: *Magnetic Fields.* Claudel: *Le Père Humilié.* Bergson: *L'Energie Spirituelle.* Keynes: *The Economic Consequences of the Peace.*	Wiene: *The Cabinet of Dr Caligari.* Sjöström: *The Phantom Carriage.* Stravinsky: *The Song of the Nightingale.*
	Ireland achieves independence. Chinese Communist party founded.	Kandinsky founds the Academy of Arts and Sciences in Moscow. Picasso: *The Three Musicians.* Gris: *The Grapes.* Matisse: *Interior at Nice.* La Fresnaye illustrates Gide's *Paludes.* Léger: *Man with Dog.*	Gide: *Si le Grain ne meurt.* Pirandello: *Six Characters in Search of an Author.* Rilke: *Sonnets to Orpheus.* Max Jacob: *The Central Laboratory.* Kafka: *Introduction to the "Gestalttheorie".*	Dullin founds the Workshop Company. Prokofiev: *The Love of Three Oranges.* Cocteau and Les Six: *Les Mariés de la Tour Eiffel.* Niblo: *The Mark of Zorro.*
	Russia becomes the Union of Soviet Socialist Republics (USSR). Treaty of Rapallo. Mussolini comes to power. End of the English protectorate in Egypt.	Dada international exhibition. Picasso: *Two Women Running on a Beach.* Van Dongen: *Portrait of the Artist as Neptune.* Soutine: *The Little Pastrycook.*	James Joyce: *Ulysses.* O. V. de L. Milosz: *The Confession of Lemuel.* T. S. Eliot: *The Waste Land.* Pirandello: *Henry IV.* Roger Martin du Gard begins the Thibault series. Death of Proust. Banting and Best discover insulin.	Murnau: *Nosferatu.* Fritz Lang: *Dr Mabuse.* Flaherty: *Nanouk of the North.* Von Stroheim: *Foolish Wives.*

Dates	Political Events	Arts	Intellectual Life	Theatre, Music, etc.
1923	Defeat of the Hitler *putsch* at Munich. Poincaré orders the occupation of the Ruhr. *Coup d'état* by Primo de Rivera in Spain. Lenin relinquishes power. Stalin becomes head of the Soviet Politburo. Kemal Attaturk becomes president of the Turkish Republic.	Chagall begins the illustration of Gogol's *Dead Souls.* Duchamp: *The Bride Stripped Bare by her Bachelors, Even* (1915-1923) Picasso: *Seated Harlequin.* La Fresnaye: *Portrait of Guynemer.* First Tuileries Salon.	Rilke: *Duino Elegies.* Cocteau: *Thomas the Impostor.* Larbaud: *Lovers, Happy Lovers.* Mauss: *Essai sur le Don, Forme archaïque de l'Echange.* Lukacs: *Geschichte und Klassenbewusstsein* De Broglie: First principles of the *Mécanique ondulatoire.* Anti-tuberculosis vaccine: Bacillus Calmette-Guérin. Death of Barrès.	Honegger: *Pacific 2.* Opening of the Arcu School formed by th disciples of Eric Sati Stravinsky: *Les Noc* Milhaud, Cendrars Léger: *La Création Monde.* Von Stroheim: *Gree*
1924	Death of Lenin. Abolition of the Turkish Califate.	Masson: automatic designs. Derain: *Harlequin and Pierrot.*	First Surrealist Manifesto and foundation of the review *The Surrealist Revolution.* Saint-John Perse: *Anabase.* Reverdy: *Les Epaves du Ciel.* Thomas Mann: *The Magic Mountain.* Hitler: *Mein Kampf.* Deaths of Kafka and Conrad. Heisenberg lays down the principle of indetermination in physics.	René Clair: *Entr'ac* Léger: *Ballet Mécan* Fritz Lang: *Die Nibelungen.* Murnau: *The Last Laugh.* Death of Fauré.
1925	Stalin removes Trotsky from power. Chiang Kai-shek made leader of the Kuomintang. Hindenburg becomes President of Germany.	First Surrealist Exhibition at the Galerie Pierre. Exhibition of decorative arts in Paris. Braque: *Still-life on a Marble Table.*	Gide: *Les Faux-Monnayeurs.* Montherlant: *Les Olympiques.* Dos Passos: *Manhattan Transfer.*	Pirandello founds t Arts Theatre in Ro Alban Berg: *Wozze* Ravel: *L'Enfant et Sortilèges.*

Political Events	Arts	Intellectual Life	Theatre, Music, etc.
	Soutine: *Flayed Ox* (several versions). Gromaire: *War; The Tramp.* Death of La Fresnaye.	Millikan discovers cosmic rays. Pauli: Principle of Exclusion.	Prokofiev: *Romeo and Juliet.* Pabst: *Joyless Street.* Chaplin: *The Gold Rush.* Eisenstein: *The Battleship Potemkin.* Death of Satie.
Germany joins the League of Nations. Hirohito, Emperor of Japan.	Paul Klee's first personal exhibition in Paris. Opening of the Galerie Surréaliste. Zervos founds the review: *Les Cahiers d'Art.* Delaunay: *The Runners.* Braque: *Seated Nude with a Basket of Fruit.* Monet dies.	Eluard: *Capitale de la Douleur.* Roussel: *Poussière de Soleils.* Aragon: *Le Paysan de Paris.* Bernanos: *Sous le Soleil de Satan.* T. E. Lawrence: *Seven Pillars of Wisdom.* Rilke dies. H. Busch makes the first electronic lens.	Josephine Baker in *The Black Revue.* Prokofiev: *Pas d'Acier.* Lang: *Metropolis.* Pudovkin: *Mother.*
End of the military control of Germany. Defeat of the Socialist uprising in Vienna. Break between the Kuomintang and the Chinese Communists.	Matisse awarded the Carnegie Prize. Michaux: Works describing imaginary travels. Chagall illustrates La Fontaine's *Fables.* Gris dies.	Heidegger: *Sein und Zeit.* Michaux: *Qui je fus.* Correspondence between d'Antonin Artaud and Jacques Rivière. Mauriac: *Thérèse Desqueyroux.* Publication of Proust's *Temps retrouvé*, last volume of *Temps Perdu.* Elie Faure: *L'Esprit des Formes.* G. Lemaître: Hypothesis of the expanding universe. Manufacture of synthetic rubber.	Disney's *Mickey Mouse.* Dreyer: *The Passion of Joan of Arc.* Epstein: *The Fall of the House of Usher.* Abel Gance: *Napoleon.* *The Jazz Singer*, first talkie. Stravinsky: *Œdipus Rex.* Schœnberg: *Variations for Orchestra.* Theatres of the Cartel (Dullin, Jouvet, Baty, Pitoëff). Lindbergh flies the Atlantic.

Dates	Political Events	Arts	Intellectual Life	Theatre, Music, etc.
1928	Kellogg Pact. Implementation of the first Soviet Fifteen-year Plan. Chiang Kai-shek, President of the Chinese Republic.	Miró: *Dutch Interiors.* Chagall: *The Married Couple with the Eiffel Tower.* Derain receives the Carnegie Award.	D. H. Lawrence: *Lady Chatterley's Lover.* Malraux: *Les Conquérants.* Breton: *Nadja.* Aragon: *Treatise on Style.* Einstein formulates the theory of the unified field.	Brecht-Weil: *Threep* *Opera.* Sjöström: *The Wind.* Von Stroheim: *Quee* *Kelly.* Buñuel: *Un Chien Andalou.* Janaček dies.
1929	Lateran Agreement; creation of the Vatican City. Exile of Trotsky. Wall Street crash.	Brancusi: *Little Bird.* M. Ernst: *La Femme 100 Têtes.* Picasso: *Woman Seated by the Sea.*	Claudel: *Le Soulier de Satin.* Faulkner: *The Sound and the Fury.* Hemingway: *A Farewell to Arms.* Husserl: *Formale und transcendentale Logik.* Fleming discovers Penicillin.	Eisenstein: *The Gene* *Line.* Dziga-Vertov: *The* *with the Movie Cam* First European talki King Vidor: *Hallelu*
1930	Independence of Iraq. Collective farming in Russia. Final evacuation of Germany. Gandhi arrested.	Lipchitz: *Song of the Vowels.* Delaunay: *Circular Forms.* Dufresne: *The Raising of Lazarus.* Léger: *Still-life, Contrast of Objects.* Rouault illustrates *The Passion* and *The Circus* by Suarès. Picasso receives the Carnegie Award. Pascin dies.	Second Surrealist Manifesto. Musil: *Der Mann ohne Eigenschaften.* Malraux: *La Voie royale.* Pirandello: *Tonight we Improvise.* Suicide of Mayakovsky.	Messiaen: *Offrandes* *oubliées.* Stravinsky: *Sympho* *of Psalms.* A. Roussel: *Bacchus* *Ariane.* Ravel: *Concerto for* *Left Hand.* Sternberg: *The Blue* *Angel.* Buñuel: *L'Age d'Or* Cocteau: *Le Sang d* *Poète.*
1931	Proclamation of the Republic in Spain. The Japanese occupy Manchuria. Five million unemployed in Germany.	Chagall: *Synagogue in Safed.* Illustrations for Ovid's *Metamorphoses* and Balzac's *Chef-d'Œuvre inconnu* by Picasso.	P.-J. Jouve: *Noces.* Valéry: *Regards sur le Monde actuel.* Virginia Woolf: *The Waves.*	Lang: *M.* Pabst: *The Threepe* *Opera.* Chaplin: *City Light*

Political Events	Arts	Intellectual Life	Theatre, Music, etc.
	Le Corbusier: Swiss Pavilion for the Cité Universitaire.	Lorca: *Poema del Canto hondo.* *My Life*, Chagall's autobiography. Husserl: *Cartesianische Meditationen.* Building of the Empire State Building.	Murnau: *Tabou.* Whale: *Frankenstein.* Eisenstein: *Que Viva Mexico!* René Clair: *A Nous la Liberté.*
Salazar in power in Portugal. Franco-Soviet Pact. Britain abandons free trade.	Abstraction-Creation Group founded in Paris. Matisse illustrates Mallarmé's *Poésies.* Rouault: illustrations for Ambroise Vollard's *Réincarnations du Père Ubu.* Rouault: *Christ Mocked.*	Céline: *Journey to the End of the Night.* Faulkner: *Light in August.* Breton: *Les Vases communicants.* Mounier founds the review *Esprit.*	Howard Hawks: *Scarface.* Machaty: *Ecstasy.*
F. D. Roosevelt, President of the USA; the New Deal. Hitler, Chancellor of the Reich; first concentration camps in Germany.	Matisse: *The Dance.* Rouault: *The Holy Face.* The Nazis end the Bauhaus activities.	Malraux: *La Condition Humaine.* P.-J. Jouve: *Sueur de Sang.* Lorca: *Blood Wedding.* Joliot-Curie: artificial radio-activity. Electron microscope perfected in Germany. Foundation of the review *Minotaure.*	
Start of the Stavisky Scandal. Fascist riot in Paris of 6 February quelled. Hitler, Reichsführer. Assassination of Chancellor Dollfuss in Austria.	Picasso: *Tauromachia.* Salvador Dali illustrates Lautréamont's *Songs of Maldoror.* Masson: *Massacres.*	René Char: *Le Marteau sans Maître.* Leiris: *L'Afrique fantôme.* First congress of Soviet writers. Jdanov defines socialist realism. Chadwick discovers the neutron.	Hindemith: *Mathis der Maler.* Jean Vigo: *L'Atalante.*

Dates	Political Events	Arts	Intellectual Life	Theatre, Music, etc.
1935	Italy attacks Ethiopia. La Sarre returns to Germany. Anti-Semitic laws in Germany.	Dali: *Giraffe on Fire.* Grüber: *The Announcement of Winter.* Picasso: *The Muse.*	Giraudoux: *La Guerre de Troie n'aura pas lieu.* T. S. Eliot: *Murder in the Cathedral.* Fermi: atomic fission.	Claudel and Honeg *Joan of Arc at the S* Alban Berg: *Concer for violin and orches* Hitchcock: *The 39*
1936	Election of the Popular Front in France. Spanish Civil War. Anti-Comintern Nippon-German Pact. Hitler reoccupies the Rhineland.	Picasso appointed director of the Prado.	Céline: *Death on the Instalment Plan.* Bernanos: *Diary of a Country Priest.* Montherlant: *Les Jeunes Filles.* Gide: *Retour de l'URSS.* Pirandello dies. Lorca shot.	Chaplin: *Modern T* The Marx Brothers *Night at the Opera.* Jean Renoir: *The C of Monsieur Lange.* Bartók: *Music for strings, percussion a celeste.*
1937	Fall of the French Prime Minister Léon Blum. Italy joins the anti-Comintern pact. German destroyers shell Almería in Spain. The Japanese occupy Peking.	Universal exhibition in Paris: decorations by Delaunay, Léger, Lhote, Gromaire. In Germany, persecution of "degenerate" art. Picasso: *Guernica.* Braque: *The Duet.* Dufy: *La Fée Electricité.*	Malraux: *L'Espoir.* Reverdy: *Ferraille.* Breton: *L'Amour fou.* Gracq: *Au Château d'Argol.* Levine and Stetsor demonstrate the Rhesus factor.	Renoir: *The Great Illusion.* Alban Berg: *Lulu.* Ravel dies.
1938	Munich Agreement. Execution of Bukharin, Rykov and Jagoda in the USSR.	International Surrealist exhibition in Paris. Deaths of Kirchner, Dufresne.	Sartre: *La Nausée.* Bernanos: *Les Grands Cimetières sous la Lune.* Camus: *Noces.* Artaud: *Le Théâtre et son Double.* Husserl dies. Hahn: Uranium nucleus split.	Riefenstahl: *The O Games of 1936.* Donskoy: *The Childhood of Maxi Gorky.* Eisenstein: *Alexan Nevsky.*
1939	German-Soviet Pact. Hitler occupies Czechoslovakia and invades Poland. England, then France, declare war on Germany.	Chagall wins the Carnegie Award. Rouault: *Christ at the Praetorium* and *Christ on the Cross* (stained-glass windows).	Leiris: *L'Age d'Homme.* Gide: *Journal.* Brecht: *The Good Woman of Setzuan.*	John Ford: *Stagec* Renoir: *La Règle* Meyerhold arreste Pitoyev dies.

s	Political Events	Arts	Intellectual Life	Theatre, Music, etc.
		First Salon of the New Realities.	Sigmund Freud dies. First instalment of *Elements of Mathematics* by Bourbaki. Paul Müller: DDT.	
	Franco-German armistice. Pétain, French head of state. General de Gaulle's appeal to the French people. Trotsky assassinated. F. D. Roosevelt re-elected.	Matisse: *Woman Seated in an Armchair*. Villon: *Garden of Golgotha.* Paul Klee dies.	Blanchot: *Thomas l'Obscur*. Sartre: *L'Imaginaire*. Hemingway: *For Whom the Bell Tolls.* F. Scott Fitzgerald dies.	Chaplin: *The Great Dictator*. Webern: Cantata, Op. 29.

Artist	Town	Museum	Title	Date	Type	Dimensi (inches)
Braque, Georges (1882-1963)	Basle	Kunstmuseum	*Still-life*	1934	Canvas	
	Chicago	Art Institute	*Fruit and Guitar*	1938	Canvas	50 × 28
	London	Tate Gallery	*Still-life*	1925	Canvas on plywood	16 × 24
	London	Tate Gallery	*Guitar and Pitcher*	1927	Canvas	32 × 46
	New York	Museum of Modern Art	*The Small Table*	1926	Canvas	53 × 29
	New York	Museum of Modern Art	*The Clay Pipe*	1931	Canvas	11 × 14
	New York	Museum of Modern Art	*Woman with a Mandolin*	1937	Canvas	65 × 38
	Paris	Musée National d'Art Moderne	*Still-life on a Marble Table*	1925	Canvas	51 × 29
	Paris	Musée National d'Art Moderne	*Still-life with Pears*	1925	Canvas	8 × 18
	Paris	Musée National d'Art Moderne	*The Duet*	1937	Canvas	51 × 63
	Paris	Musée National d'Art Moderne	*The Carafe*	1941	Canvas	13 × 22
	Paris	Musée National d'Art Moderne	*The Black Fishes*	1942	Canvas	13 × 22
	Paris	Musée National d'Art Moderne	*The Green Carpet*	1943	Canvas	15 × 22
	Paris	Musée National d'Art Moderne	*The Salon*	1944	Canvas	47 × 59
	Paris	Musée National d'Art Moderne	*The Billiard Table*	1945	Canvas	59 × 76
	Paris	Louvre	*Brown Still-life*	1932	Canvas	52 × 76
	Paris	Louvre	*Vanitas*	1939	Canvas	15 × 22
	Paris	Louvre	*The Red Table*	1939-1952	Canvas	74 × 29
	Paris	Louvre	*The Loaf*	1941	Canvas	16 × 47
	Paris	Louvre	*Toilette by a Window*	1942	Canvas	51 × 39
	Paris	Louvre	*The Chair*	1948	Canvas	24 × 20
	Paris	Louvre	*The Bird and its Nest*	1956	Canvas	51 × 68
	Paris	Louvre	*In Full Flight*	1956-1961	Oil on canvas on plywood	45 × 67
	Paris	Louvre	*The Cliffs*	1961	Oil on hard-board	7 × 19

	Town	Museum	Title	Date	Type	Dimensions (inches)
	Paris	Louvre	*The Weeding Machine*	1961-1963	Canvas	47 × 69
	Washington	National Gallery	*Peonies*	1926	Wood	22 × 27
	Washington	National Gallery	*Seated Nude with a Basket of Fruit*	1926	Canvas	40 × 32
	Washington	National Gallery	*Still-life: The Table*	1928	Canvas	32 × 53
	Washington	National Gallery	*Still-life: Day*	1929	Canvas	45 × 58
ll, Marc 7)	Amsterdam	Rijksmuseum	*Portrait of the Artist with Seven Fingers*	1912	Canvas	51 × 42
	Amsterdam	Rijksmuseum	*Ida by the Window*	1924	Canvas	41 × 30
	Amsterdam	Rijksmuseum	*Synagogue at Safed*	1931	Canvas	29 × 36
	Amsterdam	Rijksmuseum	*The Equestrienne*	1931	Canvas	39 × 32
	Amsterdam	Rijksmuseum	*Bella in Green*	1934-1935	Canvas	40 × 31
	Amsterdam	Rijksmuseum	*The Madonna on a Sledge*	1947	Canvas	38 × 32
	Basle	Kunstmuseum	*Bella with Black Gloves*	1909	Canvas	35 × 25
	Basle	Kunstmuseum	*The Cattle Dealer*	1912	Canvas	38 × 79
	Basle	Kunstmuseum	*The Rabbi*	1923	Canvas	46 × 35
	Basle	Kunstmuseum	*The Yellow Calf*	1932-1933	Canvas	6 × 10
	Chicago	Art Institute	*The Birth*	1911	Canvas	44 × 77
	Chicago	Art Institute	*The Rabbi of Vitebsk*	1914	Canvas	46 × 36
	Chicago	Art Institute	*The White Crucifixion*	1938	Canvas	61 × 55
	Chicago	Art Institute	*The Juggler*	1943	Canvas	43 × 31
	Leningrad	Russian State Museum	*The Father*	1914	Oil on paper	20 × 15
	Leningrad	Russian State Museum	*The Mirror*	1914	Oil on hard-board	40 × 32
	Leningrad	Russian State Museum	*The Promenade*	1917-1918	Canvas	67 × 64
	London	Tate Gallery	*The Poet Reclining*	1915	Oil on hard-board	30 × 30
	London	Tate Gallery	*Bouquet with Lovers*	1947	Canvas	57 × 38
	Moscow	Tretyakov Gallery	*The Clock*	1914	Oil on hard-board	19 × 14

Artist	Town	Museum	Title	Date	Type	Dimens (inches)
	Moscow	Tretyakov Gallery	*Lovers over the City*	1915	Canvas	61 × 83
	Moscow	Tretyakov Gallery	*The Betrothal*	1917	Canvas	39 × 48
	Moscow	Tretyakov Gallery	*Love on the Stage*	1920-1921	Canvas	110 × 9
	Moscow	Tretyakov Gallery	*Music*	1920-1921	Canvas	83 × 41
	Moscow	Tretyakov Gallery	*The Dance*	1920-1921	Canvas	83 × 42
	Moscow	Tretyakov Gallery	*The Theatre*	1920-1921	Canvas	83 × 41
	Moscow	Tretyakov Gallery	*Literature*	1920-1921	Canvas	84 × 31
	Moscow	Tretyakov Gallery	*Introduction to the Jewish Theatre*	1920-1921	Canvas	158 × 4
	New York	Museum of Modern Art	*Me and the Village*	1911	Canvas	76 × 60
	New York	Museum of Modern Art	*Golgotha*	1912	Canvas	69 × 75
	New York	Museum of Modern Art	*Time is a River with no Banks*	1930-1939	Canvas	40 × 3
	New York	Guggenheim Foundation	*The Soldier Drinks*	1912	Canvas	43 × 3
	New York	Guggenheim Foundation	*The House is on Fire*	1913	Canvas	42 × 4
	New York	Guggenheim Foundation	*Paris Through the Window*	1913	Canvas	52 × 5
	New York	Guggenheim Foundation	*The Anniversary*	1915	Canvas	32 × 3
	New York	Guggenheim Foundation	*The Green Violinist*	1918	Canvas	77 × 4
	New York	Guggenheim Foundation	*Flowers in the Street*	1933	Canvas	38 × 4
	Paris	Musée National d'Art Moderne	*To Russia, to Asses and Others*	1911	Canvas	62 × 4
	Paris	Musée National d'Art Moderne	*Double Portrait with a Glass of Wine*	1917	Canvas	92 × 5
	Paris	Musée National d'Art Moderne	*Maternity*	1925	Gouache	20 × 2
	Paris	Musée National d'Art Moderne	*The Acrobat*	1930	Canvas	21 × 2
	Paris	Musée National d'Art Moderne	*To my Wife*	1933-1944	Canvas	51 × 7

	Town	Museum	Title	Date	Type	Dimensions (inches)
	Paris	Musée National d'Art Moderne	*War*	1943	Canvas	41 × 30
	Paris	Musée National d'Art Moderne	*Around Her*	1945	Canvas	52 × 43
	Paris	Musée National d'Art Moderne	*The Soul of the City*	1945	Canvas	42 × 32
	Paris	Musée National d'Art Moderne	*The White Cock*	1947	Canvas	
	Paris	Musée d'Art Moderne de la Ville de Paris	*The Dream*	1927	Canvas	32 × 40
	Philadelphia	Museum of Art	*The Poet or Half-past Three*	1911	Canvas	78 × 58
	Philadelphia	Museum of Art	*Dedicated to My Fiancée*	1911	Gouache on paper	24 × 17
	Philadelphia	Museum of Art	*Me and the Village*	1923	Canvas	20 × 18
n, André	Basle	Kunstmuseum	*The Vines in Spring*	1906	Canvas	35 × 46
-1954)	Basle	Kunstmuseum	*Forest at Martigues*	1909	Canvas	33 × 40
	Basle	Kunstmuseum	*Cadaqués, Spain*	1910	Canvas	24 × 29
	Basle	Kunstmuseum	*Calvary*	1912	Canvas	26 × 23
	Chicago	Art Institute	*The Last Supper*	1913	Canvas	90 × 113
	Chicago	Art Institute	*Flowers in a Vase*	1932	Canvas	30 × 38
	Chicago	Art Institute	*The Stag Hunt*	1938	Canvas	79 × 64
	Copenhagen	Royal Fine Arts Museum	*The Dancer*	1906	Canvas	40 × 32
	Copenhagen	Royal Fine Arts Museum	*The Two Sisters*	1914	Canvas	78 × 51
	Grenoble	Musée de Peinture et de Sculpture	*Cypresses at Cassis*	1907	Canvas	18 × 15
	Grenoble	Musée de Peinture et de Sculpture	*Portrait of Paul Poiret*	1915	Canvas	42 × 31
	Leningrad	Hermitage	*Man with a Newspaper*	1911	Canvas	64 × 39
	Leningrad	Hermitage	*Martigues*	1913	Canvas	56 × 36
	Leningrad	Hermitage	*The Green Trees*	1913	Canvas	46 × 32
	Paris	Musée National d'Art Moderne	*Nude by a Green Curtain*	1923	Canvas	36 × 29
	Paris	Musée National d'Art Moderne	*The Forest, Fontainebleau*	1927	Canvas	17 × 26
	Paris	Musée National d'Art Moderne	*The Blonde Girl*	1928	Canvas	15 × 13

Artist	Town	Museum	Title	Date	Type	Dimen (inches
	Paris	Musée National d'Art Moderne	*Woman's Face*	1929	Canvas	18 × 1
	Paris	Musée National d'Art Moderne	*View of Saint-Maximin*	1930	Canvas	24 × 2
	Paris	Musée National d'Art Moderne	*Still-life with Oranges*	1931	Canvas	36 × 4
	Paris	Musée National d'Art Moderne	*Gravelines*	1934	Canvas	26 × 3
	Paris	Musée National d'Art Moderne	*The Cup of Tea*	1935	Canvas	36 × 2
	Paris	Musée National d'Art Moderne	*Boats Grounded at Camaret*	1936	Canvas	24 × 2
	Paris	Musée d'Art Moderne de la Ville de Paris	*Three People Sitting on the Grass*	1906	Canvas	15 × 2
	Paris	Musée d'Art Moderne de la Ville de Paris	*Still-life on a Table*	1910	Canvas	36 × 2
	Paris	Musée d'Art Moderne de la Ville de Paris	*The River*	1911	Canvas	29 × 3
	Paris	Musée de l'Orangerie [1]	*Rustic Still-life*	1922	Canvas	23 × 4
	Paris	Musée de l'Orangerie	*The Kitchen Table*	1924	Canvas	47 × 4
	Paris	Musée de l'Orangerie	*Harlequin and Pierrot*	1924	Canvas	69 × 6
	Paris	Musée de l'Orangerie	*Nude with a Jug*	1924	Canvas	65 × 4
	Paris	Musée de l'Orangerie	*Still-life with Basket*	1926-1927	Canvas	23 × 2
	Paris	Musée de l'Orangerie	*Large Reclining Nude*	1928	Canvas	38 × 7
	Paris	Musée de l'Orangerie	*Portrait of Madame Guillaume in a Large Hat*	1929	Canvas	36 × 2
	Paris	Musée de l'Orangerie	*Pears and Jugs*	1930	Canvas	8 × 10
	Paris	Musée de l'Orangerie	*The Great Tree*	1930	Canvas	29 × 3
	Paris	Musée de l'Orangerie	*Provence Landscape*	1930	Canvas	13 × 1
	Paris	Musée de l'Orangerie	*Midi Landscape: Les Angles*	1931	Canvas	26 × 1
	Paris	Musée de l'Orangerie	*The Road*	1931	Canvas	26 × 2

[1] The canvases indicated as at the Musée de l'Orangerie constitute the gift of Paul Guillaume-André Walter to Fr
The whole of this collection has been the object of a provisional exhibition.

st	Town	Museum	Title	Date	Type	Dimensions (inches)
	Paris	Musée de l'Orangerie	*Landscape: Trees and Village*	1932-1933	Canvas	20 × 24
gen, Kees Van 877-1968)	Amsterdam	Rijksmuseum	*The Old Clown*	1910	Canvas	26 × 22
	Amsterdam	Rijksmuseum	*Portrait of Anna de Noailles*	1926	Canvas	78 × 53
	Chicago	Art Institute	*Woman by a White Window*	1910-1914	Canvas	51 × 31
	Chicago	Art Institute	*Rue de la Paix, Paris*	1910-1914	Canvas	39 × 32
	Chicago	Art Institute	*Tea in My Studio*	1910-1914	Canvas	36 × 28
	Paris	Musée National d'Art Moderne	*The Couple*	1920	Canvas	25 × 20
	Paris	Musée National d'Art Moderne	*Portrait of Madame Jasmy-Alvin*	1920-1925	Canvas	78 × 52
	Paris	Musée National d'Art Moderne	*Deauville, the Le Havre-Trouville Ferry*	*c.* 1920	Canvas	13 × 21
	Paris	Musée National d'Art Moderne	*Portrait of the Artist as Neptune*	1922	Canvas	67 × 47
	Paris	Musée National d'Art Moderne	*Portrait of Madame Jenny*	1926	Canvas	77 × 52
	Paris	Musée National d'Art Moderne	*Portrait of the Actress Paulette Pax*	1928	Canvas	51 × 43
	Paris	Musée d'Art Moderne de la Ville de Paris	*The Flowery Fountain-Basin*	*c.* 1925	Canvas	40 × 32
	Paris	Musée de l'Orangerie	*Portrait of Paul Guillaume*	1928	Canvas	40 × 29
	St-Tropez	Musée de l'Annonciade	*The Little Donkey on the Beach*	1930		
Raoul -1953)	Amsterdam	Rijksmuseum	*Regattas*	1938	Canvas	14 × 34
	Amsterdam	Rijksmuseum	*The Paddock*		Gouache	20 × 25
	Basle	Kunstmuseum	*View over Sainte-Adresse*	1924	Canvas	21 × 26
	Basle	Kunstmuseum	*Deauville*	1929	Canvas	24 × 29
	Chicago	Art Institute	*Open Window, Nice*	1928	Canvas	26 × 22
	Chicago	Art Institute	*Villerville*	1928	Canvas	32 × 40
	Chicago	Art Institute	*The Marne at Nogent*	1935	Canvas	32 × 40
	Copenhagen	Royal Fine Arts Museum	*Interior with Hindu Woman*	1930	Canvas	32 × 40
	Le Havre	Musée des Beaux-Arts	*The Blue Horses*	1925	Water-colour and gouache	20 × 26

Artist	Town	Museum	Title	Date	Type	Dimensio (inches)
	Le Havre	Musée des Beaux-Arts	*Bather, Cargo-boat, Sailing Ships and Butterflies*	1925-1927	Canvas	46 × 35
	Le Havre	Musée des Beaux-Arts	*The Veranda of Villerville*	1930-1935	Canvas	26 × 32
	Le Havre	Musée des Beaux-Arts	*Nogent, Pink Bridge and Railway*	1933	Canvas	29 × 40
	Le Havre	Musée des Beaux-Arts	*Standing Nude with Picture*	1943	Canvas	32 × 26
	Le Havre	Musée des Beaux-Arts	*Self-portrait*	1945	Canvas	18 × 14
	Le Havre	Musée des Beaux-Arts	*Gaston Dufy, Soldier*	1950	Canvas	25 × 21
	London	Tate Gallery	*Deauville, Drying Sails*	1933	Canvas	18 × 43
	London	Tate Gallery	*The Drying of Sails*	1933	Canvas	15 × 36
	Nice	Museum	*Vence*	1919-1920	Canvas	32 × 40
	Nice	Museum	*Homage to Claude Lorrain*	1927	Canvas	32 × 26
	Nice	Museum	*Portrait of Madame Raoul Dufy*	1930	Canvas	40 × 32
	Nice	Museum	*Nice in May*	1930-1933	Canvas	21 × 18
	Nice	Museum	*Evening in Harvest-time*	1935	Canvas	21 × 25
	Nice	Museum	*Firework, Casino de la Jetée*	1947	Canvas	26 × 22
	Nice	Museum	*Grand Concert*	1948	Canvas	26 × 32
	Nice	Museum	*Nude on a Patio*	1949	Canvas	39 × 39
	Nice	Museum	*Port of Marseilles*	1950	Canvas	29 × 36
	Nice	Museum	*Homage to Claude Debussy*	1952	Canvas	23 × 28
	Paris	Musée National d'Art Moderne	*Still-life with a White Tower*	1913-1947	Canvas	32 × 26
	Paris	Musée National d'Art Moderne	*Fisherman with a Net*	1914	Canvas	86 × 26
	Paris	Musée National d'Art Moderne	*The Three Bathers*	1919	Canvas	107 × 71
	Paris	Musée National d'Art Moderne	*Acrobats on a Circus Horse*	1923-1924	Canvas	26 × 32
	Paris	Musée National d'Art Moderne	*The Sea at Le Havre*	1924-1925	Water-colour and gouache	17 × 21
	Paris	Musée National d'Art Moderne	*The Paddock at Deauville*	*c.* 1930	Canvas	21 × 51
	Paris	Musée National d'Art Moderne	*The Riders under the Trees*	1931	Canvas	84 × 102

	Town	Museum	Title	Date	Type	Dimensions (inches)
	Paris	Musée National d'Art Moderne	*Apple Trees in Normandy*	1932	Canvas	20 × 26
	Paris	Musée National d'Art Moderne	*Amphitrite*	1935-1953	Canvas	95 × 22
	Paris	Musée National d'Art Moderne	*The Queen of England's Coach*	1936	Gouache on paper	20 × 26
	Paris	Musée National d'Art Moderne	*The Red Violin*	1948	Canvas	15 × 18
	Paris	Musée National d'Art Moderne	*The Stars*	1948	Canvas	32 × 26
	Paris	Musée National d'Art Moderne	*Still-life with Violin, Homage to Bach*	1952	Canvas	32 × 40
	Paris	Musée d'Art Moderne de la Ville de Paris	*Taormina*	1923	Canvas	18 × 22
	Paris	Musée d'Art Moderne de la Ville de Paris	*The Banks of the Marne*	1925	Canvas	24 × 29
	Paris	Musée d'Art Moderne de la Ville de Paris	*The Jetty at Honfleur*	1928	Canvas	26 × 32
	Paris	Musée d'Art Moderne de la Ville de Paris	*Nude on a Blue Ground*	1930	Gouache	26 × 19
	Paris	Musée d'Art Moderne de la Ville de Paris	*La Fée Electricité*	1937	Oil on panels	2,362 × 394
aire, Marcel	Basle	Kunstmuseum	*The Tramp*	1925	Canvas	40 × 32
2)	Paris	Musée National d'Art Moderne	*The Fairground Lottery*	1923	Canvas	51 × 63
	Paris	Musée National d'Art Moderne	*The Spring*	1929	Canvas	28 × 24
	Paris	Musée National d'Art Moderne	*The Lines of the Hand*	1935	Canvas	39 × 32
	Paris	Musée National d'Art Moderne	*The Forest*	1937	Canvas	39 × 51
	Paris	Musée National d'Art Moderne	*The Vagabond*	1939	Canvas	40 × 32
	Paris	Musée National d'Art Moderne	*Woman with Red Hair*	1945	Canvas	32 × 40
	Paris	Musée National d'Art Moderne	*Central Park, New York*	1951	Canvas	26 × 32
	Paris	Musée d'Art Moderne de la Ville de Paris	*The Street Musicians*	1919	Canvas	34 × 49

Artist	Town	Museum	Title	Date	Type	Dimens (inches
	Paris	Musée d'Art Moderne de la Ville de Paris	*The Woman from Martinique*	1921	Canvas	40 × 32
	Paris	Musée d'Art Moderne de la Ville de Paris	*Man in a Blue Smock*	1921	Canvas	32 × 26
	Paris	Musée d'Art Moderne de la Ville de Paris	*A Railway Station*	1922	Canvas	38 × 47
	Paris	Musée d'Art Moderne de la Ville de Paris	*The Boxer*	1922	Canvas	29 × 20
	Paris	Musée d'Art Moderne de la Ville de Paris	*Suburban Landscape*	1922	Canvas	32 × 40
	Paris	Musée d'Art Moderne de la Ville de Paris	*Reclining Nude on an Ochre Ground*	1923	Canvas	32 × 40
	Paris	Musée d'Art Moderne de la Ville de Paris	*The Street*	1923	Canvas	40 × 32
	Paris	Musée d'Art Moderne de la Ville de Paris	*Carriage on the Métro*	1923	Canvas	32 × 40
	Paris	Musée d'Art Moderne de la Ville de Paris	*Man with Bread*	1923	Canvas	32 × 26
	Paris	Musée d'Art Moderne de la Ville de Paris	*The Bargewoman*	1924	Canvas	40 × 32
	Paris	Musée d'Art Moderne de la Ville de Paris	*The Skittle Players*	1924	Canvas	40 × 32
	Paris	Musée d'Art Moderne de la Ville de Paris	*The School of Painting*	1924	Canvas	40 × 32
	Paris	Musée d'Art Moderne de la Ville de Paris	*The Beer Drinkers*	1924	Canvas	40 × 32
	Paris	Musée d'Art Moderne de la Ville de Paris	*The Flemish Reaper*	1924	Canvas	40 × 32
	Paris	Musée d'Art Moderne de la Ville de Paris	*War*	1925	Canvas	51 × 38
	Paris	Musée d'Art Moderne de la Ville de Paris	*Man with Dumb-bells*	1926	Canvas	32 × 40

t	Town	Museum	Title	Date	Type	Dimensions (inches)
	Paris	Musée d'Art Moderne de la Ville de Paris	*At the Piano*	1927	Canvas	40 × 32
	Paris	Musée d'Art Moderne de la Ville de Paris	*The Second-hand Dealer*	1927	Canvas	51 × 38
	Paris	Musée d'Art Moderne de la Ville de Paris	*The Navvies*	1927	Canvas	32 × 40
	Paris	Musée d'Art Moderne de la Ville de Paris	*The White Square*	1928	Canvas	51 × 38
	Paris	Musée d'Art Moderne de la Ville de Paris	*Woman with Bouquet*	1928	Canvas	39 × 32
	Paris	Musée d'Art Moderne de la Ville de Paris	*The Wheelbarrow*	1929	Canvas	32 × 26
	Paris	Musée d'Art Moderne de la Ville de Paris	*Nude with an Overcoat*	1929	Canvas	32 × 26
	Paris	Musée d'Art Moderne de la Ville de Paris	*The Sheaf of Corn*	1930	Canvas	32 × 26
	Paris	Musée d'Art Moderne de la Ville de Paris	*Peasant-woman with Basket*	1930	Canvas	32 × 26
	Paris	Musée d'Art Moderne de la Ville de Paris	*The Labours of the Soil*	1932	Canvas	65 × 51
	Paris	Musée d'Art Moderne de la Ville de Paris	*The Fairground Shooting Range*	1933	Canvas	40 × 32
	Paris	Musée d'Art Moderne de la Ville de Paris	*Pietà*	1933	Canvas	32 × 26
	Paris	Musée d'Art Moderne de la Ville de Paris	*Brooklyn Bridge*	1950	Canvas	21 × 26
, Fernand	Basle	Kunstmuseum	*Woman in Blue*	1912	Canvas	77 × 51
-1955)	Basle	Kunstmuseum	*Village in the Forest*	1914	Canvas	51 × 38
	Basle	Kunstmuseum	*Acrobats in a Circus*	1918	Canvas	38 × 46
	Basle	Kunstmuseum	*Mechanical Elements*	1918-1923	Canvas	83 × 67
	Basle	Kunstmuseum	*Woman and Child*	1922	Canvas	67 × 96

Artist	Town	Museum	Title	Date	Type	Dimensi (inches)
	Biot	Fernand Léger Museum	*My Mother's Garden*	1905	Canvas	18 × 15
	Biot	Fernand Léger Museum	*The Level-Crossing*	1912	Canvas	36 × 29
	Biot	Fernand Léger Museum	*Abstract Composition*	1919	Canvas	62 × 45
	Biot	Fernand Léger Museum	*Mural Composition*	1924	Canvas	71 × 32
	Biot	Fernand Léger Museum	*The Gioconda with the Keys*	1930	Canvas	36 × 29
	Biot	Fernand Léger Museum	*Multicoloured Divers*	1942-1946	Canvas	99 × 73
	Biot	Fernand Léger Museum	*The Tree in the Ladder*	1943-1944	Canvas	72 × 49
	Biot	Fernand Léger Museum	*The Builders*	1950	Canvas	118 × 86
	London	Tate Gallery	*Leaves and Shells*	1927	Canvas	38 × 51
	London	Tate Gallery	*Two Women Holding Flowers*	1954	Canvas	38 × 51
	New York	Museum of Modern Art	*The Screws*	1918	Canvas	32 × 26
	New York	Museum of Modern Art	*The Dinner*	1921	Canvas	72 × 99
	New York	Museum of Modern Art	*La Grande Julie*	1954	Canvas	44 × 50
	New York	Guggenheim Foundation	*Mural Painting*	1925	Canvas	70 × 31
	New York	Guggenheim Foundation	*Woman Filling a Vase*	1927	Canvas	58 × 38
	Paris	Musée National d'Art Moderne	*The Wedding*	1911	Canvas	62 × 42
	Paris	Musée National d'Art Moderne	*Contrast of Forms*	1913	Canvas	40 × 32
	Paris	Musée National d'Art Moderne	*Woman in Red and Green*	1914	Canvas	40 × 32
	Paris	Musée National d'Art Moderne	*Women in an Interior*	1922	Canvas	25 × 21
	Paris	Musée National d'Art Moderne	*Composition*	1929	Canvas	24 × 36
	Paris	Musée National d'Art Moderne	*Still-life with Keys*	1930	Canvas	58 × 38
	Paris	Musée National d'Art Moderne	*Still-life, Contrast of Objects*	1930	Canvas	38 × 51

	Town	Museum	Title	Date	Type	Dimensions (inches)
	Paris	Musée National d'Art Moderne	*The Blue Dancer*	1930	Canvas	58 × 46
	Paris	Musée National d'Art Moderne	*Composition with Three Figures*	1932	Canvas	72 × 111
	Paris	Musée National d'Art Moderne	*Composition with Parrots*	1935-1939	Canvas	155 × 189
	Paris	Musée National d'Art Moderne	*Adieu New York*	1946	Canvas	51 × 64
	Paris	Musée National d'Art Moderne	*The Leisures (Homage to Louis David)*	1948-1949	Canvas	61 × 73
	Paris	Musée d'Art Moderne de la Ville de Paris	*The Disks*	1918	Canvas	95 × 71
	Paris	Musée d'Art Moderne de la Ville de Paris	*Contrast of Forms*	1918	Canvas	16 × 10
	Paris	Musée d'Art Moderne de la Ville de Paris	*Woman with a Mirror*	1920	Canvas	14 × 11
	Paris	Musée d'Art Moderne de la Ville de Paris	*Still-life with Chandelier*	1922	Canvas	46 × 32
	Paris	Musée d'Art Moderne de la Ville de Paris	*Man with a Pipe*	1923	Canvas	36 × 26
se, Henri 1954)	Baltimore	Museum of Art	*Blue Nude. Souvenir of Biskra*	1907	Canvas	36 × 55
	Baltimore	Museum of Art	*The Pewter Pot*	1916-1917	Canvas	36 × 26
	Baltimore	Museum of Art	*Seated Dancer*	1927	Canvas	32 × 27
	Baltimore	Museum of Art	*Seated Odalisque*	1928	Canvas	22 × 15
	Baltimore	Museum of Art	*Pink Nude*	1935	Canvas	26 × 37
	Baltimore	Museum of Art	*Blue Eyes*	1935	Canvas	15 × 18
	Baltimore	Museum of Art	*Woman on a Red Chair*	1936	Canvas	14 × 9
	Basle	Kunstmuseum	*The Bank*	1907	Canvas	29 × 24
	Basle	Kunstmuseum	*Woman on a Sofa*	1922	Canvas	24 × 29
	Basle	Kunstmuseum	*Still-life with Oysters*	1940	Canvas	26 × 33
	Basle	Kunstmuseum	*Composition: Gouache Paper Cut-outs*	1947	Collage	20 × 86
	Chicago	Art Institute	*Women Bathing in a River*	1916-1917	Canvas	103 × 154
	Chicago	Art Institute	*The Green Sash*	1919	Canvas	19 × 17
	Chicago	Art Institute	*Woman by an Aquarium*	1921	Canvas	32 × 40

Artist	Town	Museum	Title	Date	Type	Dimens (inches)
	Chicago	Art Institute	*Woman on a Pink Sofa*	1921	Canvas	15 × 18
	Chicago	Art Institute	*Interior at Nice*	1921	Canvas	51 × 35
	Copenhagen	Statens Museum for Kunst	*Portrait with a Green Stripe*	1905	Canvas	16 × 13
	Copenhagen	Statens Museum for Kunst	*Luxe, Calme et Volupté*	1905	Canvas	83 × 54
	Copenhagen	Statens Museum for Kunst	*Interior at Nice*	1917	Canvas	46 × 35
	Copenhagen	Statens Museum for Kunst	*Interior with Violin*	1917-1918	Canvas	46 × 35
	Copenhagen	Statens Museum for Kunst	*Zulma*	1950	Gouache cut-out	93 × 57
	Merion, USA	Barnes Foundation	*The Joy of Life*	1906	Canvas	69 × 94
	Merion, USA	Barnes Foundation	Triptych: *The Three Sisters*	1916-1917	Canvas	38 × 77
	Merion, USA	Barnes Foundation	*The Music Lesson*	1917	Canvas	96 × 83
	Merion, USA	Barnes Foundation	*The French Window*	1919	Canvas	53 × 35
	Merion, USA	Barnes Foundation	*The Domino Players*	1921	Canvas	
	Merion, USA	Barnes Foundation	*Seated Moorish Woman*	1922	Canvas	18 × 15
	Merion, USA	Barnes Foundation	*Odalisque by a Screen*	1922	Canvas	23 × 36
	Merion, USA	Barnes Foundation	*The Dance* (II)	1932	Canvas	142 × 5
	Moscow	Pushkin Museum	*The Dance*	1910	Canvas	102 × 1
	Moscow	Pushkin Museum	*Music*	1910	Canvas	102 × 1
	Moscow	Pushkin Museum	*Moroccan in Green*	1913	Canvas	57 × 38
	Moscow	Pushkin Museum	*Madame Matisse*	1913	Canvas	58 × 38
	New York	Museum of Modern Art	*Moroccans on the Terrace*	1916	Canvas	70 × 11
	New York	Museum of Modern Art	*The Piano Lesson*	1916-1917	Canvas	97 × 84
	Paris	Musée National d'Art Moderne	*Luxury* (I)	1905	Canvas	83 × 54

Town	Museum	Title	Date	Type	Dimensions (inches)
Paris	Musée National d'Art Moderne	*The Painter and his Model*	1917	Canvas	58 × 38
Paris	Musée National d'Art Moderne	*Odalisque in Red Trousers*	1922	Canvas	27 × 33
Paris	Musée National d'Art Moderne	*Seated Nude on a Red Ground*	1925	Canvas	29 × 24
Paris	Musée National d'Art Moderne	*Decorative Figure on an Ornamental Ground*	1927	Canvas	51 × 39
Paris	Musée National d'Art Moderne	*The Green Sideboard*	1928	Canvas	33 × 41
Paris	Musée National d'Art Moderne	*Woman Reading on a Black Ground*	1939	Canvas	36 × 29
Paris	Musée National d'Art Moderne	*The Rumanian Blouse*	1940	Canvas	36 × 28
Paris	Musée National d'Art Moderne	*Still-life on a Marble Table*	1941	Canvas	18 × 15
Paris	Musée National d'Art Moderne	*The Two Friends*	1941	Canvas	24 × 20
Paris	Musée National d'Art Moderne	*Still-life with a Magnolia*	1941	Canvas	29 × 40
Paris	Musée National d'Art Moderne	*The Great Red Interior*	1948	Canvas	58 × 38
Paris	Musée National d'Art Moderne	*The Sadness of the King*	1952	Gouache cut-out	125 × 152
Paris	Musée d'Art Moderne de la Ville de Paris	*The Avenue of Olive Trees*	1919	Canvas	29 × 24
Paris	Musée d'Art Moderne de la Ville de Paris	*Odalisque in an Armchair*	1928	Canvas	24 × 29
Paris	Musée d'Art Moderne de la Ville de Paris	*The Dance* (I)	1931-1932	Canvas	142 × 505
Paris	Musée de l'Orangerie	*The Three Sisters*	1917	Canvas	36 × 26
Paris	Musée de l'Orangerie	*Nude in a Turban or the Young Girl and the Vase of Flowers*	1918-1921	Canvas	24 × 29
Paris	Musée de l'Orangerie	*Women on a Couch*, or *The Divan*	1918-1921	Canvas	36 × 29
Paris	Musée de l'Orangerie	*The Boudoir*	1921	Canvas	29 × 24
Paris	Musée de l'Orangerie	*Woman with a Mandolin*	1921	Canvas	19 × 16

Artist	Town	Museum	Title	Date	Type	Dime (inche
	Paris	Musée de l'Orangerie	*Odalisque*, or *The White Slave*	1921-1922	Canvas	32 × 2
	Paris	Musée de l'Orangerie	*Woman with a Violin*	1921-1923	Canvas	22 × 1
	Paris	Musée de l'Orangerie	*Draped Reclining Nude*	1923-1924	Canvas	15 × 2
	Paris	Musée de l'Orangerie	*Odalisque in Red Trousers*	1923-1925	Canvas	20 × 2
	Paris	Musée de l'Orangerie	*Odalisque in Grey Trousers*	1927	Canvas	21 × 2
Modigliani, Amedeo (1884-1920)	Buffalo	Albright-Knox Art Gallery	*The Servant*	1919	Canvas	60 × 2
	Buffalo	Albright-Knox Art Gallery	*Two Women*		Water-colour	15 × 1
	Chicago	Art Institute	*Madame Pompadour*	1915	Canvas	24 × 2
	Chicago	Art Institute	*Jacques Lipchitz and His Wife*	1916-1917	Canvas	32 × 2
	Chicago	Art Institute	*Woman in a Necklace*	1917	Canvas	36 × 2
	Copenhagen	Statens Museum for Kunst	*Self-portrait as Pierrot*	1915	Card-board	17 × 1
	Copenhagen	Statens Museum for Kunst	*Alice*	1916	Canvas	31 × 1
	London	Tate Gallery	*The Little Peasant*	1917	Canvas	40 × 2
	London	Tate Gallery	*Portrait of a Young Girl*	1917	Canvas	32 × 2
	London	Courtauld Institute	*Nude*	*c.* 1917	Canvas	36 × 2
	Merion, USA	Barnes Foundation	*Beatrice Hastings in a Hat*	1916	Gummed paper	
	Merion, USA	Barnes Foundation	*Young Girl Seated*	1918	Canvas	46 × 2
	Merion, USA	Barnes Foundation	*Hanka Zborowska*	1919	Canvas	36 × 2
	New York	Museum of Modern Art	*Seated Nude*	1914	Pencil and water-colour	21 × 1
	New York	Museum of Modern Art	*Bride and Groom*	1915	Canvas	22 ×
	New York	Museum of Modern Art	*Hanka Zborowska*	1917	Canvas	51 ×
	New York	Museum of Modern Art	*Woman Leaning on her Elbows*	1918	Pencil	20 ×

Town	Museum	Title	Date	Type	Dimensions (inches)
New York	Museum of Modern Art	*Large Nude*	1919	Canvas	28 × 46
New York	Museum of Modern Art	*Mario*	1919-1920	Pencil	19 × 12
New York	Guggenheim Foundation	*Nude*	1917	Canvas	28 × 45
New York	Guggenheim Foundation	*Portrait of a Student*	1917	Canvas	20 × 18
New York	Guggenheim Foundation	*Child in a Blue Jacket*	1918	Canvas	36 × 24
New York	Guggenheim Foundation	*Yellow Sweater*	1919	Canvas	39 × 25
Paris	Musée National d'Art Moderne	*Caryatid*	1914-1915	Oil on hard-board	24 × 21
Paris	Musée National d'Art Moderne	*Lolotte*	1917	Canvas	23 × 14
Paris	Musée National d'Art Moderne	*Portrait of Mme Haydn*		Canvas	36 × 24
Paris	Musée d'Art Moderne de la Ville de Paris	*Woman with Blue Eyes*		Canvas	32 × 21
Paris	Musée d'Art Moderne de la Ville de Paris	*Woman with Ear-rings*		Canvas	26 × 17
Paris	Musée d'Art Moderne de la Ville de Paris	*Lunia Czecowska with a Fan*	1919	Canvas	40 × 26
Paris	Musée de l'Orangerie	*Girl with Red Hair*	1915	Canvas	14 × 9
Paris	Musée de l'Orangerie	*Antonia*	1915	Canvas	32 × 18
Paris	Musée de l'Orangerie	*Woman with a Velvet Ribbon*	1915	Canvas	22 × 19
Paris	Musée de l'Orangerie	*Portrait of Paul Guillaume*	1915	Canvas	41 × 30
Paris	Musée de l'Orangerie	*The Young Apprentice*	1917-1918	Canvas	40 × 26
São Paulo	Museo de Arte	*Diego Rivera*	1914-1915	Canvas	40 × 32
São Paulo	Museo de Arte	*Portrait of Zborowski*	1917	Canvas	29 × 42
São Paulo	Museo de Arte	*Seated Woman*	1917	Canvas	36 × 26
São Paulo	Museo de Arte	*Renée*	1917	Canvas	24 × 15

Artist	Town	Museum	Title	Date	Type	Dimens (inches)
	Washington	National Gallery	*Adrienne*	1917	Canvas	22 × 15
	Washington	National Gallery	*Gipsy Woman with a Child*	1919	Canvas	45 × 29
	Zürich	Kunsthaus	*The Servant*	1916	Canvas	29 × 21
Picasso, Pablo (b. 1881)	Antibes	Musée Grimaldi	*Still-life with Fish and Jug*	1946	Canvas	47 × 99
	Antibes	Musée Grimaldi	*The She-goat*	1946	Canvas	47 × 59
	Antibes	Musée Grimaldi	*Pastoral, the Joy of Life*	1946	Canvas	47 × 99
	Barcelona	Museum of Modern Art	*Harlequin*	1917	Canvas	46 × 36
	Basle	Kunstmuseum	*Women on the Banks of the Seine*	1950	Oil on canvas on wood	39 × 79
	Cologne	Wallraf-Richartz Museum	*Head of Woman Reading*	1953	Wood	18 × 15
	London	Tate Gallery	*Seated Woman*	1923	Canvas	36 × 29
	London	Tate Gallery	*Goat's Skull, Bottle and Candle*	1952	Canvas	35 × 46
	New York	Museum of Modern Art	*Harlequin*	1915	Canvas	73 × 41
	New York	Museum of Modern Art	*Seated Pierrot*	1918	Canvas	36 × 29
	New York	Museum of Modern Art	*The Balcony*	1919	Canvas	14 × 1
	New York	Museum of Modern Art	*The Three Musicians*	1921	Canvas	79 × 9
	New York	Museum of Modern Art	*Still-life*	1924	Canvas	39 × 5
	New York	Museum of Modern Art	*Seated Women*	1926-1927	Canvas	51 × 3
	New York	Museum of Modern Art	*The Studio*	1927-1928	Canvas	59 × 9
	New York	Museum of Modern Art	*Woman Seated beside the Sea*	1929	Canvas	64 × 5
	New York	Museum of Modern Art	*Woman Before a Mirror*	1932	Canvas	64 × 5
	New York	Museum of Modern Art	*Guernica*	1937	Canvas	132 ×
	New York	Museum of Modern Art	*Night Fishing at Antibes*	1939	Canvas	81 × 1
	New York	Guggenheim Foundation	*Mandolin and Guitar*	1924	Canvas	56 × 7

Town	Museum	Title	Date	Type	Dimensions (inches)
Paris	Musée National d'Art Moderne	*Seated Woman Reading*	1920	Canvas	66 × 40
Paris	Musée National d'Art Moderne	*Still-life*	1922	Canvas	29 × 36
Paris	Musée National d'Art Moderne	*Female Torso*	1923	Canvas	40 × 32
Paris	Musée National d'Art Moderne	*Head of a Woman*	1924	Canvas	26 × 21
Paris	Musée National d'Art Moderne	*Still-life with Charlotte-Russe*	1924	Canvas	21 × 26
Paris	Musée National d'Art Moderne	*Still-life with Antique Head*	1925	Canvas	38 × 51
Paris	Musée National d'Art Moderne	*The Milliner's Workshop*	1925	Canvas	68 × 104
Paris	Musée National d'Art Moderne	*The Muse*	1935	Canvas	51 × 64
Paris	Musée National d'Art Moderne	*Still-life with Lemon and Oranges*	1936	Canvas	21 × 26
Paris	Musée National d'Art Moderne	*Portrait of a Woman*	1938	Canvas	39 × 30
Paris	Musée National d'Art Moderne	*Portrait of Mme Paul Eluard*	1941	Canvas	28 × 24
Paris	Musée National d'Art Moderne	*Aubade*	1942	Canvas	77 × 104
Paris	Musée National d'Art Moderne	*Still-life with Cherries*	1943	Canvas	21 × 32
Paris	Musée National d'Art Moderne	*The Rocking-Chair*	1943	Canvas	64 × 51
Paris	Musée National d'Art Moderne	*Woman in Blue*	1944	Canvas	51 × 38
Paris	Musée National d'Art Moderne	*The Enamelled Saucepan*	1945	Canvas	32 × 42
Paris	Musée de l'Orangerie	*Large Still-life*	1918	Canvas	34 × 44
Paris	Musée de l'Orangerie	*Three Women by a Fountain*	1921	Canvas	21 × 23
Paris	Musée de l'Orangerie	*Large Bather*	1921	Canvas	71 × 39
Paris	Musée de l'Orangerie	*Large Draped Nude*	1921	Canvas	61 × 38
Paris	Musée de l'Orangerie	*Large Woman with Tambourine*	1935	Canvas	38 × 52
Vallauris	Chapelle	*War*	1952	Fresco	197 × 394

Artist	Town	Museum	Title	Date	Type	Dimensi[ons] (inches)
	Vallauris	Chapelle	*Peace*	1952	Fresco	197 × 39[…]
	Washington	National Gallery	*Still-life*	1918	Canvas	38 × 51
	Washington	National Gallery	*The Lovers*	1923	Canvas	51 × 38
Rouault, Georges (1871-1958)	Avallon	Musée	*Stella Matutina*	1895	Canvas	106 × 51
	Avallon	Musée	*Stella Vespertina*	1895	Canvas	106 × 71
	Boston	Museum of Fine Arts	*Head of a Clown*	1948	Canvas	26 × 19
	Brussels	Musée Royal des Beaux-Arts	*Diplomat*	1938	Canvas	12 × 9
	Chicago	Art Institute	*The Academician*	1913-1915	Canvas	42 × 30
	Chicago	Art Institute	*The Italian*	1930	Canvas	18 × 12
	Chicago	Art Institute	*The Dwarf*	1936	Canvas	27 × 20
	Copenhagen	Statens Museum for Kunst	*Judges*	1908	Canvas	30 × 41
	London	Tate Gallery	*The Meal*	1900	Canvas	10 × 10
	London	Tate Gallery	*Aunt Sallys*	1907	Oil on paper pasted on canvas	30 × 41
	London	Tate Gallery	*The Three Judges*	1937-1938	Oil on hardboard	31 × 25
	Lyons	Musée des Beaux-Arts	*Carmencita*	1948	Canvas	21 × 15
	New York	Museum of Modern Art	*Three Judges*	1913	Gouache and oil on hardboard	30 × 41
	New York	Museum of Modern Art	*Christ Mocked*	1932	Canvas	36 × 28
	Paris	Musée National d'Art Moderne	*The Apprentice Worker*	1925-1926	Canvas	27 × 21
	Paris	Musée National d'Art Moderne	*The Holy Face*	1933	Canvas	36 × 26
	Paris	Musée National d'Art Moderne	*Christ at the Praetorium*	1939	Stained glass	42 × 31
	Paris	Musée National d'Art Moderne	*Homo Homini Lupus*	1944	Oil on paper mounted on canvas	25 × 18

Town	Museum	Title	Date	Type	Dimensions (inches)
Paris	Musée National d'Art Moderne	*De Profundis*	1946	Canvas	26 × 20
Paris	Musée National d'Art Moderne	*The Flight into Egypt*	1946	Canvas	16 × 20
Paris	Musée National d'Art Moderne	*The Dreamer*	1946	Canvas	14 × 10
Paris	Musée National d'Art Moderne	*Landscape with Tall Trees*	1946	Canvas	28 × 12
Paris	Musée National d'Art Moderne	*Fleurs de Convention*	1946	Canvas	24 × 21
Paris	Musée National d'Art Moderne	*The Little Sorceress*	1949	Canvas	35 × 28
Paris	Musée National d'Art Moderne	*Christian Nocturne*	1952	Canvas	38 × 21
Paris	Musée d'Art Moderne de la Ville de Paris	*Duet*	1904	Oil and pastel	9 × 5
Paris	Musée d'Art Moderne de la Ville de Paris	*Dressed as a Tabarin*	1905	Water-colour and pastel	28 × 21
Paris	Musée d'Art Moderne de la Ville de Paris	*Nude*	1906	Spirit	12 × 10
Paris	Musée d'Art Moderne de la Ville de Paris	*The Conference*	1908	Canvas	12 × 7
Paris	Musée d'Art Moderne de la Ville de Paris	*Christ Mocked*	1912	Canvas	17 × 12
Paris	Musée d'Art Moderne de la Ville de Paris	*Acrobat*	1913	Pen and wash	15 × 12
Paris	Musée d'Art Moderne de la Ville de Paris	*Landscape*	1913	Spirit	12 × 25
Paris	Musée d'Art Moderne de la Ville de Paris	*Vice Squad* (illustration for *Ubu Roi*)	1918	Brush drawing	13 × 9
Paris	Musée d'Art Moderne de la Ville de Paris	*Biblical Landscape*	1935-1936	Canvas	27 × 21
Paris	Musée d'Art Moderne de la Ville de Paris	*Christ and the Fishermen*	1937	Canvas	27 × 51
Paris	Musée d'Art Moderne de la Ville de Paris	*Pierrot*	1938	Canvas	29 × 21

Artist	Town	Museum	Title	Date	Type	Dimensi (inches)
	Paris	Musée d'Art Moderne de la Ville de Paris	*The Flight into Egypt*	1938	Canvas	16 × 11
	Paris	Musée d'Art Moderne de la Ville de Paris	*The Yellow Clown*	1938	Canvas	15 × 11
	Zürich	Kunsthaus	*By the Stream*	1948	Canvas	30 × 41
Soutine, Chaim (1894-1943)	Amsterdam	Rijksmuseum	*Flayed Ox*	1926	Canvas	65 × 45
	Avignon	Musée Calvet	*The Ray-fish*	1924	Canvas	32 × 19
	Avignon	Musée Calvet	*Decadence*	1924	Canvas	32 × 21
	Avignon	Musée Calvet	*The Village Idiot*	1924	Canvas	36 × 26
	Avignon	Musée Calvet	*View of Vence*		Canvas	26 × 22
	Chicago	Art Institute	*Landscape at Cagnes*	1923	Canvas	24 × 28
	Chicago	Art Institute	*Poultry*	1926	Canvas	39 × 25
	Chicago	Art Institute	*Little Village Square, Vence*	1929	Canvas	28 × 18
	Grenoble	Musée de Peinture et de Sculpture	*Flayed Ox*	1925-1926	Canvas	80 × 45
	Lucerne	Kunstmuseum	*Portrait of Lina*	1928-1929	Canvas	15 × 18
	Lucerne	Kunstmuseum	*The Housemaid*	1934-1935	Canvas	43 × 14
	New York	Museum of Modern Art	*Portrait of Madeleine Castaing*	1928	Canvas	40 × 29
	New York	Museum of Modern Art	*Portrait of Maria Lani*	1928-1929	Canvas	
	Paris	Musée National d'Art Moderne	*Poultry*	1925-1926	Oil on lined panel	50 × 32
	Paris	Musée National d'Art Moderne	*Pageboy*	*c.* 1927	Canvas	37 × 32
	Paris	Musée National d'Art Moderne	*Woman in a Blue Dress*		Canvas	32 × 24
	Paris	Musée d'Art Moderne de la Ville de Paris	*Grotesque*		Canvas	32 × 17
	Paris	Musée d'Art Moderne de la Ville de Paris	*Torso on a Blue Ground*		Canvas	17 × 20
	Paris	Musée d'Art Moderne de la Ville de Paris	*Woman in Red*	1922	Canvas	36 × 26

t	Town	Museum	Title	Date	Type	Dimensions (inches)
	Paris	Musée d'Art Moderne de la Ville de Paris	*The Pigs*	1941	Canvas	18 × 22
	Paris	Musée de l'Orangerie	*Gladioli*	1919	Canvas	25 × 17
	Paris	Musée de l'Orangerie	*The Houses*	1919-1922	Canvas	23 × 36
	Paris	Musée de l'Orangerie	*Landscape*	1919-1922	Canvas	36 × 26
	Paris	Musée de l'Orangerie	*The Little Baker*	1922	Canvas	28 × 17
	Paris	Musée de l'Orangerie	*The Fiancée*	1922	Canvas	32 × 18
	Paris	Musée de l'Orangerie	*Leaning Tree*	1922-1923	Canvas	24 × 32
	Paris	Musée de l'Orangerie	*The Table*	1922-1927	Canvas	39 × 32
	Paris	Musée de l'Orangerie	*The Village*	1923	Canvas	30 × 37
	Paris	Musée de l'Orangerie	*Beef and Calf's Head*	1925	Canvas	36 × 29
	Paris	Musée de l'Orangerie	*The Plucked Chicken*	1925	Canvas	26 × 18
	Paris	Musée de l'Orangerie	*The Rabbit*	1925	Canvas	30 × 14
	Paris	Musée de l'Orangerie	*Turkey and Tomatoes*	1925	Canvas	32 × 19
	Paris	Musée de l'Orangerie	*Still-life with Pheasant*	1925	Canvas	26 × 36
	Paris	Musée de l'Orangerie	*Portrait of a Man*	1925	Canvas	21 × 18
	Paris	Musée de l'Orangerie	*The Turkey*	1925-1926	Canvas	32 × 26
	Paris	Musée de l'Orangerie	*The Bell-boy*	1927-1929	Canvas	34 × 26
	Paris	Musée de l'Orangerie	*Young Englishwoman*	1928	Canvas	18 × 22
	Paris	Musée de l'Orangerie	*Choir-boy*	1928	Canvas	27 × 19
	Paris	Musée de l'Orangerie	*Pageboy*	1928	Canvas	40 × 32
	Paris	Musée de l'Orangerie	*The White House*	1932	Canvas	26 × 22

Artist	Town	Museum	Title	Date	Type	Dimensi (inches)
	Paris	Musée de l'Orangerie	*Landscape with Figure (The White Road)*	1932	Canvas	24 × 32
	Paris	Musée de l'Orangerie	*The Great Blue Tree*	1942	Canvas	32 × 13
	São Paulo	Museo de Arte	*The Great Tree*	1940	Canvas	39 × 30
	Washington	National Gallery	*Portrait of a Boy*	1928	Canvas	36 × 26
Staël, Nicolas de (1913-1955)	Antibes	Musée	*Still-life*	1955	Canvas	36 × 51
	Basle	Kunstmuseum	*Composition*	1952	Collage	73 × 52
	Boston	Museum of Fine Arts	*Rue Gauguet*	1949	Fibre panel	80 × 97
	London	Tate Gallery	*Marathon*	1948	Canvas	34 × 26
	New York	Museum of Modern Art	*Painting*	1947	Canvas	78 × 33
	Paris	Musée National d'Art Moderne	*Abstract Composition*	1946	Canvas	64 × 45
	Paris	Musée National d'Art Moderne	*The House-tops*	1952	Fibre panel	79 × 59
	Paris	Musée National d'Art Moderne	*Le Lavandou*	1952	Canvas	73 × 38
	Rotterdam	Boymans-Van Beuningen Museum	*The Bottles*	1952	Canvas	25 × 32
	Washington	Philips Memorial Art Gallery	*Painting*	1949	Canvas	11 × 16
	Zürich	Kunsthaus	*Composition*	1951	Canvas	63 × 30
Utrillo, Maurice (1883-1955)	Berne	Musée des Beaux-Arts	*Paris Suburb*	1910	Wood	24 × 18
	Berne	Musée des Beaux-Arts	*Rue Muller*	1912	Card-board	19 × 24
	London	Tate Gallery	*Saint-Martin Gate*	1911	Card-board	27 × 31
	London	Tate Gallery	*The Church of Saint-Hilaire*	1911	Canvas	21 × 24
	London	Tate Gallery	*Saint-Martin Gate*	1911	Canvas	30 × 36
	London	Tate Gallery	*Place du Tertre*	1911	Canvas	29 × 29
	Paris	Musée National d'Art Moderne	*The Roofs of Montmagny*	1906	Canvas	26 × 21
	Paris	Musée National d'Art Moderne	*The Garden of Montmagny*	1908	Card-board	30 × 21
	Paris	Musée National d'Art Moderne	*The Impasse Cottin*	1910	Card-board	25 × 18

Town	Museum	Title	Date	Type	Dimensions (inches)
Paris	Musée National d'Art Moderne	*View of Montmartre*	1910	Canvas	29 × 40
Paris	Musée National d'Art Moderne	*The "Lapin-Agile"*	1910	Canvas	20 × 24
Paris	Musée National d'Art Moderne	*The White Church*	1915	Canvas	20 × 25
Paris	Musée National d'Art Moderne	*The Rue du Mont-Cenis*	1915	Canvas	20 × 24
Paris	Musée National d'Art Moderne	*Suburban Church, the Steeple*	1917-1918	Canvas	24 × 32
Paris	Musée National d'Art Moderne	*The Quartier Saint-Romain, at Anse*	1925	Canvas	26 × 32
Paris	Musée National d'Art Moderne	*Rue Saint-Rustique, at Montmartre*	1926	Canvas	32 × 24
Paris	Musée d'Art Moderne de la Ville de Paris	*The Church of the White Friars*	1911	Canvas	32 × 24
Paris	Musée d'Art Moderne de la Ville de Paris	*Street at Corte*	1912	Canvas	26 × 32
Paris	Musée d'Art Moderne de la Ville de Paris	*La Fère-en-Tardenois*	1912	Canvas	32 × 24
Paris	Musée d'Art Moderne de la Ville de Paris	*Berlioz's House*	1915	Canvas	18 × 29
Paris	Musée d'Art Moderne de la Ville de Paris	*The Rue Seveste*	1923	Canvas	24 × 29
Paris	Musée de l'Orangerie	*Notre-Dame*	1910	Card-board	25 × 19
Paris	Musée de l'Orangerie	*Great Cathedral*	1910	Canvas	29 × 21
Paris	Musée de l'Orangerie	*Rue du Mont-Cenis*	1914	Wood	28 × 40
Paris	Musée de l'Orangerie	*Berlioz's House*	1914	Canvas	47 × 36
Paris	Musée de l'Orangerie	*Clignancourt Church*	1914	Canvas	29 × 39
Paris	Musée de l'Orangerie	*Saint-Pierre Church*	1914	Card-board	30 × 42
Paris	Musée de l'Orangerie	*Bernot's House*	1924	Canvas	39 × 57
Paris	Musée de l'Orangerie	*The Town Hall with Flags*	1924	Canvas	51 × 37

Artist	Town	Museum	Title	Date	Type	Dimensi (inches)
	Washington	National Gallery	*Saint-Séverin Church*	1912	Canvas	29 × 21
Villon, Jacques (1875-1963)	Lyons	Musée des Beaux-Arts	*The Horsewoman*	1951	Canvas	21 × 29
	New York	Guggenheim Foundation	*Perspective in Colour*	1921	Canvas	21 × 28
	New York	Guggenheim Foundation	*Portrait of the Artist's Father*	1924	Canvas	21 × 18
	Paris	Musée National d'Art Moderne	*Portrait of Raymond Duchamp-Villon*	1911	Wood	14 × 10
	Paris	Musée National d'Art Moderne	*Amro*	1931	Canvas	18 × 22
	Paris	Musée National d'Art Moderne	*The Adventure*	1935	Canvas	64 × 45
	Paris	Musée National d'Art Moderne	*Woman in Red*	1937	Canvas	36 × 26
	Paris	Musée National d'Art Moderne	*The Wrestlers*	1937	Canvas	37 × 33
	Paris	Musée National d'Art Moderne	*Portrait of Anne Dariel*	1940	Card-board	16 × 13
	Paris	Musée National d'Art Moderne	*Between Toulouse and Albi*	1941	Canvas	21 × 31
	Paris	Musée National d'Art Moderne	*The Writer*	1949	Canvas	36 × 29
	Paris	Musée d'Art Moderne de la Ville de Paris	*The Laugh*	*c.* 1930	Canvas	32 × 24
	Paris	Musée d'Art Moderne de la Ville de Paris	*The Scholar*	1933	Etching	10 × 8
	Paris	Musée d'Art Moderne de la Ville de Paris	*Great Composition*	1938	Canvas	195 × 1
	Paris	Musée d'Art Moderne de la Ville de Paris	*Vue de Dos*	1944	Canvas	32 × 26
	Paris	Musée d'Art Moderne de la Ville de Paris	*Along the Wood*	1958	Canvas	45 × 58
	Pittsburgh	Museum of Art	*Portrait of the Artist*	1949	Canvas	39 × 28
	St Louis	City Art Museum	*Norman Enclosure*	1953	Canvas	15 × 22
	Toledo, USA	Museum of Art	*Flowers*	1946	Canvas	36 × 29

Principal Exhibitions

Braque, Georges

1908 Paris: Exhibition at the Galerie Kahnweiler.

1914 Berlin, Dresden, Munich: Braque-Picasso Exhibitions.

1914 New York: 291 Gallery and the Secession Art Gallery.

1919 Paris, Galerie Léonce Rosenberg.

1922 Paris, Salon d'Automne: Full exhibition.

1929 Paris, Galerie Léonce Rosenberg.

1933 Basle, Musée des Beaux-Arts.

1936 Brussels, Palais des Beaux-Arts.

1943 Paris, Salon d'Automne: 26 pictures and 9 sculptures.

1945 Amsterdam, Rijksmuseum.

1946 London, Tate Gallery: Braque-Rouault exhibition.

1948 Hall at the Venice Biennale, where he received the Grand Prix for Painting.

1948-1949 New York, Museum of Modern Art; Cleveland, Cleveland Museum of Art: Retrospective exhibition.

1952 Exhibition in Japan.

1953 Berne, Zürich and Liège.

1956 Edinburgh and London: Retrospective exhibition.

1956 Cincinnati, Art Museum: Exhibition of sculpture.

1958 Rome, Barberini Palace.

1958 Participation in the Venice Biennale.

1958 Geneva, Galerie Rauch: Presentation of "l'œuvre graphique originale".

1961 Paris, Louvre: Exhibition: "The Studio of Georges Braque".

1963 Munich, Haus der Kunst.

1965 Paris, Louvre: Presentation of the Braque Donation.

Chagall, Marc

1914 Berlin, *Der Sturm*: First one-man exhibition.

1924 Paris, Galerie Barbazanges-Hodebert: First retrospective exhibition.

1926 New York: First one-man exhibition in that city.

1933 Basle, Musée: Retrospective exhibition.

1946 New York, Museum of Modern Art: Retrospective exhibition.

1947 Paris, Amsterdam, London: Retrospective exhibitions.

1951 Zürich, Berne: Retrospective exhibitions.

1952 Nice, Musée des Ponchettes.

1953 Turin: Retrospective exhibition.

1956 Basle, Berne, Brussels, Amsterdam: Retrospective exhibitions.

1959 Paris, Musée des Arts Décoratifs: Recapitulative exhibition.

1961 Paris, Musée des Arts Décoratifs: Exhibition of stained glass windows for Jerusalem.

1964 Lunéville, Musée: Engravings, 1922-1962.

1965 Tokyo: paintings and gouaches. Rouen: paintings and stained glass.

Derain, André

1906 Paris, Galerie Berthe Weill.

1908 Paris, Galerie Berthe Weill and Galerie Druet.

1914 Berlin, Dresden, Düsseldorf: One-man exhibitions.

1916 Paris, Galerie Paul Guillaume.

1922 Stockholm, Berlin, Frankfurt, Munich, New York: One-man exhibitions.

1928 Receives the Carnegie Award. Exhibits in London.

1929 Paris, Galerie Paul Guillaume; Berlin, Frankfurt, Düsseldorf.

1931 Paris, Galerie Paul Guillaume.

1931 Cincinnati, Art Museum.

1935 Berne, Kunsthalle: Retrospective exhibition.

1937 Paris, Petit-Palais: Derain participates in the great retrospective exhibition of the Indépendants.

1949 Paris, Galerie de Berri: "Homage to Derain".

1954-1955 Paris, Musée National d'Art Moderne: Retrospective exhibition.

1955 Paris, Galerie Charpentier: Retrospective exhibition.

Dongen, Kees Van

1904 Paris, Ambroise Vollard.

1908 Paris, Galerie D. H. Kahnweiler and Galerie Bernheim Jeune.

1908 Düsseldorf, Galerie Flechtheim.

1911 Paris, Galerie Bernheim Jeune: Two exhibitions.

1912 Brussels, Galerie Georges Giroux.

1913 Paris, Galerie Bernheim Jeune. The police take down a nude exhibited at the Salon d'Automne, judged indecent.

1917 Paris, Galerie d'Antin.

1921 Paris, Galerie Bernheim Jeune.

1927 Amsterdam, Rijksmuseum.

1937 Paris, Musée Galleria; Eindhoven, Stedelijk Van Abbemuseum, Amsterdam.

1938 Paris, Galerie Borghèse.

1942 Paris, Galerie Charpentier: Retrospective exhibition.

1943 Bordeaux, Musée des Beaux-Arts.

1949 Paris, Galerie Charpentier; Rotterdam, Van Boymans Museum: Retrospective exhibitions.

1952 Paris, Galerie Paul Pétridès.

1953 Paris, Galerie du Berri: Retrospective exhibition of the Fauve epoch.

1959 Geneva, Musée Rath; Nice, Galerie des Ponchettes: Retrospective exhibitions.

1960 Albi, Musée Toulouse-Lautrec: Exhibition of paintings, water-colours and designs.

1967-1968 Rotterdam, Van Boymans Museum: Retrospective exhibition.

Dufy, Raoul

1906 Paris, Galerie Berthe Weill: First exhibition. Also exhibited at the Salon d'Automne.

1923 Brussels, Galerie Le Centaure.

1930 Paris, Galerie Georges Petit.

1932 Paris, Galerie Bernheim Jeune.

1934 Brussels, Palais des Beaux-Arts.

1937 Paris, Petit-Palais: 34 paintings at the Exhibition of Masters of Independent Art.

1939 San Francisco, Museum of Art.

1941 Paris, Galerie Louis Carré.

1943 Brussels, Palais des Beaux-Arts.

1949 New York, Louis Carré Gallery.

1952 Grand Prix for Painting at the Venice Biennale.

1952 Geneva, Musée d'Art et d'Histoire: Retrospective exhibition.

1953 Copenhagen: Ny Carlsberg Glyptotek.

1953 Paris, Musée National d'Art Moderne: Retrospective exhibition.

1954 San Francisco, Museum of Art; Basle, Kunsthalle; London, Tate Gallery.

1960 Paris, Galerie Jacques Dubourg.

1963 Paris, Louvre, Galerie Mollien: Exhibition of the Dufy Donation.

1963 Paris, Galerie Louis Carré: Exhibition of tapestries.

Gromaire, Marcel

1921 Paris, Galerie La Licorne.

1923 Paris, Galerie La Licorne.

1925 Paris, Galerie Barbazanges.

1929 Paris, Galerie Pierre et Bernheim Jeune; Brussels, Galerie Le Centaure: Exhibition of water-colours.

1933 Basle, Kunsthalle: Important retrospective exhibition.

1942 Paris, Galerie Renou et Colle: Exhibition of water-colours and tapestries.

1947 Paris, Galerie Louis Carré.

1949 New York, Louis Carré Gallery.

1951 Paris, Galerie Louis Carré.

1954 Paris, Galerie Louis Carré.

1955-1956 Paris, Galerie Louis Carré: Exhibition of all his engraving work.

1955-1956 Besançon, Musée des Beaux-Arts: Full exhibition.

1957 Paris, Maison de la Pensée Française: exhibition of 70 paintings.

1960 Saint-Denis, Musée Municipal d'Histoire et d'Art.

1963 Paris, Musée National d'Art Moderne: Retrospective exhibition.

Léger, Fernand

1912 Paris, Galerie Kahnweiler: First one-man exhibition.

1919 Paris, Galerie de l'Effort Moderne (Léonce Rosenberg).

1925 New York, Anderson Galleries.

1926 Paris, Galerie des Quatre Chemins; New York, Brooklyn Museum.

1928 Berlin, A. Flechtheim Gallery.

1933 Zürich, Kunsthaus.

1934 Stockholm, Modern Gallery.

1935 New York, Museum of Modern Art; Chicago, Art Institute.

1937 Helsinki, Artek Gallery.

1942 New York, Paul Rosenberg Gallery.

1945 Cambridge, Fogg Art Museum.

1946 Paris, Galerie Louis Carré.

1948 New York, Sidney Janis Gallery: Large retrospective exhibition (1912-1948).

1949 Paris, Musée National d'Art Moderne: Retrospective exhibition.

1950 London, Tate Gallery.

1951 New York, Louis Carré Gallery: "70th Anniversary Exhibition".

1951 New York, Sidney Janis Gallery: "Early Léger (1911-1925)"

1952 Berne, Kunsthalle.

1953 New York, Museum of Modern Art.

1955 Lyons, Musée des Beaux-Arts.

1956 Paris, Musée des Arts Décoratifs: Retrospective exhibition.

1964 Foundation of the Léger Museum at Biot.

Matisse, Henri

1904 Paris, Ambroise Vollard: First exhibition.

1905 Paris: Participation in Salon d'Automne.

1906 Paris, Druet: Full exhibition.

1908 Berlin, Cassirer Gallery; New York, 291 Gallery; Moscow.

1910 Paris, Galerie Bernheim Jeune: First retrospective exhibition.

1915 New York, Montross Gallery.

1919 Paris, Galerie Bernheim Jeune: Full exhibition.

1924 Copenhagen, Ny Carlsberg Glyptotek: Retrospective exhibition.

1930 Berlin, Thannhauser Gallery: Retrospective exhibition.

1931 Paris, Galerie Georges Petit; New York, Museum of Modern Art: Retrospective exhibitions.

1936 Paris, Galerie Paul Rosenberg.

1938 Oslo, Copenhagen, Stockholm: Touring collective exhibition.

1945 Paris, Salon d'Automne: Important retrospective exhibition.

1945 London, Victoria and Albert Museum: Picasso-Matisse exhibition.

1948 Philadelphia, Museum of Art: Retrospective exhibition of paintings, drawings and sculptures.

1948 Paris, Salon de Mai: Cut-paper collages.

1949 Lucerne, Musée des Beaux-Arts: Retrospective exhibition.

1949 New York, Pierre Matisse Gallery.

1952 Inauguration of the Musée Henri-Matisse at Cateau-Cambrésis, France.

1956 Paris, Musée National d'Art Moderne: Retrospective exhibition.

1961 Paris, Musée des Arts Décoratifs: Presentation of the great cut-out gouaches.

1962 Paris, Galerie Dubourg: Exhibition of watercolours and drawings.

1963 Foundation of the Matisse Museum at Nice-Cimiez.

Modigliani, Amedeo

1915 Paris, 6 rue Huyghens: Exhibition in a private studio.

1918 Paris, Galerie Berthe Weill: Exhibition which was closed by the police.

1921 Paris, Galerie L'Evêque: First retrospective exhibition.

1926 Paris, Salon des Indépendants: Retrospective exhibition.

1926 Paris, Salon des Indépendants: Retrospective exhibition.

1930 Exhibition at the 18th Venice Biennale.

1933 Brussels, Palais des Beaux-Arts.

1934 Basle, Kunsthalle.

1944 New York, American-British Art Center: Exhibition of a private collection.

1946 Paris, Galerie de France.

1951 Cleveland, Museum of Art; New York, Museum of Modern Art.

1955 Vevey, Musée Jenisch: Utrillo-Valadon-Modigliani exhibition.

1955 Chicago, Art Institute: Exhibition of drawings.

1958 Paris, Galerie Charpentier: "One hundred paintings by Modigliani", recapitulative exhibition.

Picasso, Pablo

1897 Barcelona: First exhibition.

1901 Paris, Galerie Ambroise Vollard.

1909 Munich, Thannhauser Gallery.

1910 Paris, Galerie Ambroise Vollard.

1911 New York, Photo Secession Gallery.

1912 London, Stafford Gallery; Barcelona, Dalmau Gallery.

1913 Berlin, Neue Galerie.
From 1913 on, exhibited regularly in USA. (New York, Chicago), in Germany (Berlin, Cologne, Dresden, Munich), in Buenos Aires and Prague.

1919 Paris, Galerie Paul Rosenberg.

1932 Paris, Galerie Georges Petit; Berne, Kunsthaus: Retrospective exhibitions.

1936 Barcelona, Bilbao, Madrid: Travelling exhibition.

1939 New York, Museum of Modern Art: Retrospective exhibition.

1944 Mexico, Sociedad de Arte Moderno: Retrospective exhibition.

1944 Paris, Salon d'Automne.

1945 Paris, Galerie Louis Carré.

1945 London, Victoria and Albert Museum: Picasso-Matisse exhibition.

1949 Paris, Maison de la Pensée Française.

1950 Venice Biennale.

1953 Lyons, Rome, Milan, São Paulo: Retrospective exhibitions.

1955 Paris, Musée des Arts Décoratifs: Retrospective exhibition.

1955 Paris, Galerie Louis Carré.

1957 New York, Museum of Modern Art: Chicago, Art Institute: "75th Anniversary Exhibition".

1960 London, The Arts Council of Great Britain.

1962 New York, Saidenberg Gallery: "Picasso, An American Tribute".

1964 Tokyo: Retrospective exhibition.

Rouault, Georges

1910 Paris, Galerie Druet: First one-man exhibition.

1920 Paris, Galerie La Licorne.

1922 Paris, Galerie Barbazanges.

1924 Galerie Druet: Large retrospective exhibition.

1930 First exhibitions outside France: London, St George Gallery; Munich, Neumann Gallery; New York, Brummer Gallery; Chicago, Art Club.

1937 Paris, Petit-Palais: A room is devoted to him at L'Exposition de l'Art Indépendant (42 canvases).

1938 New York, Museum of Modern Art: Graphic works.

1940-1941 Boston, Washington, San Francisco.

1945 New York, Museum of Modern Art: Large retrospective exhibition.

1946 London, Tate Gallery: Exhibition with Braque.

1948 Venice Biennale.

1948 Zürich, Kunsthaus: Retrospective exhibition.

1952 Brussels, Palais des Beaux-Arts; Amsterdam, Rijksmuseum; Paris, Musée National d'Art Moderne: Retrospective exhibitions.

1953 Cleveland, Museum of Art; New York, Museum of Modern Art; Tokyo, National Museum: Retrospective exhibitions.

1954 Milan, Galleria d'Arte Moderna: Retrospective exhibition.

1956 Albi, Musée Toulouse-Lautrec.

1958 Tokyo, Mitzue: Homage to Rouault.

1960 Paris, Galerie Greuzevault; Marseille, Musée Cantini; New York, Perls Gallery.

1962 Basle, Beyeler Gallery; Paris, Galerie Charpentier.

Soutine, Chaim

1927 Paris, Galerie Bing.

1929 He refuses to participate in any exhibition.

1935 Chicago, Arts Club.

1937 London, Leicester Galleries; New York, Valentine Gallery and Mrs Cornelius J. Sullivan Gallery.

1940 New York, Carroll Carstairs Gallery.

1944 Paris: Retrospective exhibition at the Salon d'Automne.

1945 Paris, Galerie de France.

1945 Boston, Institute of Modern Art: Soutine and Chagall exhibition.

1947 Paris, Galerie Zak; London, Gimpel Fils

1950-1951 New York, Museum of Modern Art; Cleveland, Museum of Art.

1956 Paris, Maison de la Pensée Française.

1956 Paris, Galerie Charpentier: "One Hundred Paintings of Soutine".

1963 London.

Staël, Nicolas de

1944 Paris, Galerie L'Esquisse.

1945 Paris, Galerie Jeanne Bucher.

1950 Paris, Galerie Jacques Dubourg.

1951 New York, Theodore Schempp Gallery; Paris, Galerie Jacques Dubourg.

1952 London, Matthiesen Gallery.

1953 New York, Knoedler Gallery; Washington, The Philips Gallery.

1954 New York, Paul Rosenberg Gallery; Paris, Galerie Jacques Dubourg.

1955 Antibes, Musée Grimaldi: One-man exhibition.

1955 New York, Paul Rosenberg Gallery.

1956 Paris, Musée National d'Art Moderne (retrospective exhibition); London, Arthur Tooth & Sons; London, Whitechapel Art Gallery; Washington, The Philips Gallery; Edinburgh, Royal Scottish Academy.

1957 Paris, Galerie Jacques Dubourg; Berne, Kunsthalle.

1958 Paris, Galerie Jeanne Bucher; Arles, Musée Réattu; New York, Paul Rosenberg Gallery.

1959 Kassel: Homage to de Staël at the Biennale Documenta.

1960 Hanover, Kestner-Gesellschaft; Hamburg, Kunstverein; Turin, Galleria Civica d'Arte Moderna.

1961 New York, Stephen Hahn Gallery.

1963 Zürich, Gimpel und Hanover Galerie; London, Gimpel Fils Gallery; New York, Paul Rosenberg Gallery.

1964 Basle, Beyeler Gallery; Paris, Galerie Louis Carré.

1965 Rotterdam, Van Boymans Museum; Zürich, Kunsthaus.

1965-1966 Boston, Museum of Fine Arts; Chicago, Art Institute; New York, The Solomon R. Guggenheim Museum.

Utrillo, Maurice

1910 Paris, Galerie Libaude.

1913 Paris, Galerie Eugène Blot.

1919 Paris, Galerie Lepoutre.

1921 Paris, Galerie Berthe Weill: Maurice Utrillo-Suzanne Valadon exhibition.

1923 Paris, Galerie Bernheim Jeune.

1924 Basle, Kunsthalle.

1925 Paris, Galerie Fiquet, Galerie Barbazanges.

1929 Paris, Galerie Le Portique; Berne, Kunsthalle.

1934 Paris, Galerie André Schoeller.

1937 New York, G. Bignou Gallery.

1942 Basle, Kunsthalle.

1944 Paris, Galerie Pétridès.

1946 Innsbruck, Constance Gallery.

1949 Berne, Kunsthalle.

1953 Paris, Galerie Pétridès: Retrospective exhibition.

1956 Berlin, Fine Arts Academy.

1956 Valenciennes, Dijon, Besançon, Strasbourg, Rheims: Touring exhibition.

1957 New York, G. Wildenstein Gallery.

1959 Paris, Galerie Charpentier (100 paintings).

1963 Berne, Kunstmuseum.

Villon, Jacques

1905 Rouen: First exhibition with Duchamp-Villon.

1921 New York, Anonymous Society.

1928 New York, Brummer Gallery.

1933 Chicago, Arts Club.

1934 New York, Marie Harriman Gallery.

1942 Paris, Galerie de France.

1944 Paris, Galerie Louis Carré.

1949 Lugano: Grand Prix for Engraving at the International Exhibition.

1949 Boston, Institute of Contemporary Art.

1950 Venice: Special room at the Biennale.

1950 First Carnegie Award, International Exhibition at Pittsburgh.

1951 Paris, Musée National d'Art Moderne: Retrospective exhibition.

1955 Albi, Musée Toulouse-Lautrec.

1956 Venice: Grand Prix for painting at the Biennale.

1957 New York, The Solomon G. Guggenheim Museum: Jacques Villon, Raymond Duchamp-Villon, Marcel Duchamp exhibition.

1959 Paris, Bibliothèque Nationale: "Jacques Villon, Graphic works"

1960 Stockholm, Moderna Museet: Retrospective exhibition 1902-1959, paintings and engravings.

1961 Paris, Galerie Charpentier: "100 paintings of Jacques Villon".

Dictionary

A

Abstract

Abstract art is most properly described as non-figurative art. In both painting and sculpture, all work which does not depict perceptible or visible shapes from the world around us, the objective world, is abstract. This loss of artistic interest in figurative images is generally attributed to the invention of photography. As Matisse said, "The painter need no longer concern himself with paltry details. Photography does it much better and more quickly." In fact, the birth of non-figurative art corresponds to a general development in all 20th-century modes of artistic expression: namely, to dispense with the anecdote in order to attain the essence, or, in other words, to pass from the temporal reality of the world to the metaphysical realism of existence. To this end, colours and lines are no longer used to depict the outside world, either by copying or interpreting. Endowed with psychic values, they become both entities in themselves and symbols identified with the phenomena of awareness and perception. The origins of non-figurative art could also be associated with the primitive sources of art. Nevertheless, Cézanne is generally agreed to be the initiator of this raw use of pictorial language, though it was not deliberately applied until 1910. It was in 1910, in fact, that the Russian Kandinsky, then leading the "Blaue Reiter" (Blue Rider) movement in Munich, began to paint his first Abstract works. He accompanied them simultaneously with a significantly entitled theoretical book, *Concerning the Spiritual in Art*, which remains the Bible of Abstract Art. Almost at once, numerous other artists from all corners of Europe adopted this way of seeing, understanding and creating: the French Robert and Sonia Delaunay, the Czech Kupka (1912), the Russian Larionov, Gontcharova and Malevitch (1913), and the Dutch Mondrian (1913). Two tendencies, however, were instantly discernible. One was colourful, lyrical, musically inspired, and engendered various more or less ephemeral movements: Musicalism (Kupka), Orphism (Delaunay) and Rayonism (Larionov and Gontcharova). The other was geometrical, more metaphysical in character, more instinctive, and took the form of Suprematism (Malevitch), Constructivism (Tatlin) and Neo-plasticism (Mondrian). These approximate or arbitrary denominations are quoted only as points of reference; other movements have continually succeeded them, and all may be formally reduced to the two tendencies mentioned above. Non-figurative art lost its experimental interest and creative power just before the second world war, but received a second wind from the war itself, and from the present and future menaces threatening the individual. Since 1962, it seems to have become immersed in developing the formulas of the last half-century.

Académie Julian

In 1860, Rodolphe Julian opened an academy in the Passage des Panoramas, Paris, and it rapidly came to offer a training parallel to that of the Ecole des Beaux-Arts. In 1888, Bonnard, Sérusier,

M. Denis, Ranson, Ibels, Vuillard, Roussel and Piot, a group who at that time adopted the name of Les Nabis, attended the academy, now permanently settled at 31 rue du Dragon. Successively, Matisse, La Fresnaye, Lotiron, Segonzac, L.-A. Moreau, Boussingault, Derain, Léger and Marcel Duchamp spent a certain time there. Above all, the Académie Julian provided a fertile meeting-ground for a whole generation of painters dissatisfied with academic teaching.

Académie Ranson

In 1908 Paul Ranson founded an academy in order to establish the Nabis movement and to give teaching opportunities to Bonnard, Vuillard, M. Denis and Roussel. The determination to work out a new pictorial language, their refusal to perpetuate ossified formulas, and the freedom given to all, attracted numerous painters such as Vallotton, La Patellière, Kisling, Maillol, Christian Bérard, Gromaire, Le Moal and Manessier. Between 1930 and 1939, Bissière and Grüber taught there. The academy was closed during the second world war, but has been open again since 1951.

Anouilh, Jean (b. 1910)

French dramatist, born in Bordeaux. He is a prolific and bitterly pessimistic writer, and his plays, both in France and abroad, have had a lively success with the public. He himself divides his plays into four categories. *Pièces roses* (pink plays): *Le Bal des Voleurs* (1938), *Le Rendez-vous de Senlis* (1941); *pièces noires* (black plays): *L'Hermine* (1932), *Le Voyageur sans Bagage* (*Traveller without Luggage*) (1937), *La Sauvage* (1938), *Euridyce* (*Point of Departure*) (1942), *Antigone* (1944), *Jézabel* (1946), *Roméo et Jeannette* (1946), *Médée* (1953); *pièces brillantes* (brilliant plays): *L'Invitation au Château* (*Ring Round the Moon*) (1947), *La Répétition ou l'Amour puni* (1950), *Cécile ou l'Ecole des Pères* (1954); *pièces grinçantes* (bitter plays): *Ornifle* (1955), *Pauvre Bitos ou le Dîner de Têtes* (1956), *L'Hurluberlu ou le Réactionnaire amoureux* (1959), *L'Alouette* (1953), *Becket ou l'Honneur de Dieu* (1959).

Apollinaire, Guillaume (1880-1918)

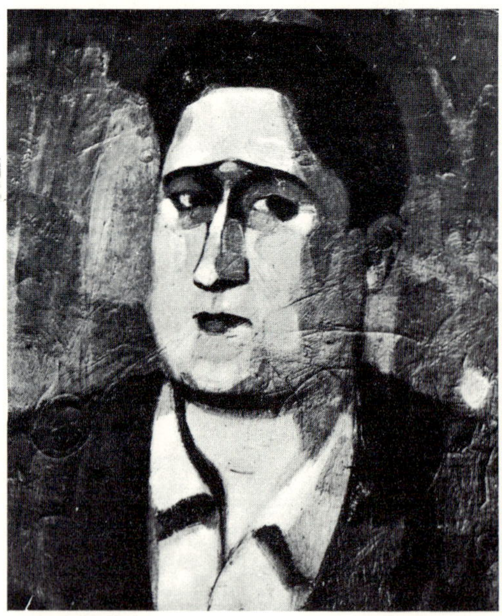

Jean Metzinger
Guillaume Apollinaire

His real name was Wilhelm Kostrowicki. French poet, born in Rome, died in Paris. The author of *Alcools* and *Calligrammes*, variously displaying relish, charm, vision or inventiveness, he was not solely one of the greatest French poets of the 20th century: his discoveries of young painters of his time and the support he gave them is greatly to his credit. He was twenty-two when he published his first articles on art in *L'Européen*. After that he was constantly associated with all the great movements at the start of this century. First came Fauvism in 1904, then Cubism, which he defended publicly well before his book, *Peintres Cubistes*, came out in 1913. Meanwhile he discovered Picasso: his first article on the Catalan painter is dated 16 May 1905. He was also friend and publicist to Robert Delaunay (for whose painting he invented the term Orphism), Giorgio de Chirico and the Italian Futurists. He was also in at the start of Surrealism. Apollinaire did not base his active and discriminating participation in the artistic life of his period on any sort of bias towards modernism or the *avant-garde*. He was simply one of those rare people who had the gift of turning his wide and deep culture not into a reassuring or nostalgic refuge, but into a rapture of creative originality and an inexhaustible appetite for the future.

Archipenko, Alexander (1887-1964)

Russian sculptor, born in Kiev. Before devoting himself to sculpture, he had a thorough training in painting in his native town, then in Moscow. In 1908 he moved to Paris and settled in La Ruche, where Laurens, Léger, Chagall, Lipchitz and Modigliani were his neighbours. The influence he received from these surroundings was counterbalanced by his own studies of Egyptian painting. He was one of the first to apply Cubist theories to sculpture, but in 1916 he turned towards a more traditional style. He taught in Berlin from 1920 to 1923, then in the United States, where he founded his own school of sculpture in New York, and where he spent the rest of his life.

Artigas, Josep Llorens (b. 1892)

Spanish potter, born in Barcelona. At the age of twenty-five, after studying at the Advanced School of Crafts in Barcelona, he obtained a grant which enabled him to go to Paris. He worked with Raoul Dufy from 1922 to 1932, then with Joan Miró and Georges Braque. He has used his talent to perfect purity of form and beauty of material in his high-temperature stoneware. His work is mostly valuable, however, for carrying out design by the great modern painters who are his friends.

Automne, Salon d'

In October 1903, Rambosson, Desvallières and Rouault, supported by Matisse, Marquet and Bonnard, decided to found the Salon d'Automne, in order to allow artists with common if not identical interests to exhibit their works together. Two years later, in fact, the Salon d'Automne welcomed Vlaminck, Derain, Matisse, Manguin, Marquet and Van Dongen for the first showing of Fauvism. Despite its president, the architect Franz Jourdain, who was violently opposed to Cubism, the Salon d'Automne played a most outstanding role until 1914.

Léon Bakst
Nijinsky in "La Péri"
Bibliothèque de l'Arsenal, Paris

B

Ballets Russes, Les

At the age of twenty-three, Sergei Diaghilev wrote: "I have found my vocation—to be a patron of the arts." And classic dance, which had not altered since the romantic era, gave birth to the new ballet, a synthesis of all the arts and techniques of the theatre: music, painting, architecture, dance and pantomime. Born in Novgorod on 19 March 1872, Sergei Diaghilev went to St Petersburg in 1890, and there made friends with the painter Alexandre Benois. He organised some large exhibitions: the salon for historical Russian painters in 1905 and the Russian section of the Paris Salon d'Automne in 1906, then presented five concerts of Russian music in Paris in 1907, also founded a periodical, *The World of Art*, and travelled across Europe. In 1907, Michel Fokine had mounted a ballet in Russia, and Diaghilev decided to present it in Paris. The first performance took place in Le Châtelet on 18 May 1909. The luxury of the décors by Léon Bakst, Benois and Korovine, and the extraordinary agility of the dancer Nijinsky, immediately aroused fantastic enthusiasm. The following year, the Ballets Russes returned with Stravinsky's *Firebird* and Rimsky-Korsakov's *Scheherazade* with a sumptuous décor by Bakst. Then came *Petrouchka* and *The Spectre of the Rose* in 1911. The 1912 season was tumultuous. Nijinsky's daring eroticism in his choreography for Claude Debussy's *L'Après-Midi d'un Faune* and the stylisation of Maurice Ravel's *Daphnis and Chloë* unleashed a furore. *Le Sacre du Printemps*, a new battle for *Hernani* and Rimsky-Korsakov's *Le Coq d'Or* completed this first period. The second and third periods of the Ballets Russes, lasting from 1917 until Diaghilev's death in Venice in 1929, saw the creation of more than forty ballets. Diaghilev gathered round himself musicians such as Sauguet, Satie, Milhaud, Poulenc, Manuel de Falla and Hindemith; he discovered Prokofiev;

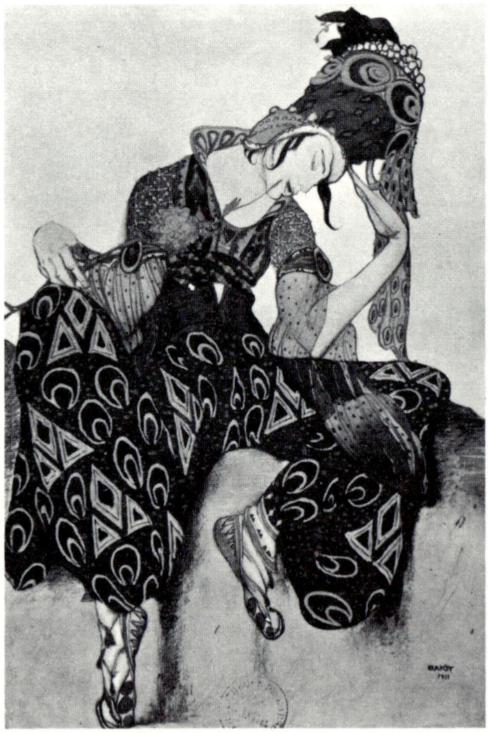

he approached Picasso, Braque, Derain, Matisse, Utrillo, Max Ernst and Miró, thus maintaining an incessant ferment of ideas and aesthetic curiosity. After *Parade* by Cocteau and Satie, with décor and costumes by Picasso, which caused a scandal, there followed *La Boutique Fantasque* (1919), Stravinsky's *The Song of the Nightingale* (1920) and *Les Noces* (1923), *Les Fâcheux* (1924), *La Tentation de la Bergère* (1926), *The Prodigal Son* with décor and costumes by Rouault and music by Prokofiev, and *Le Bal* with décor and costumes by de Chirico (1929). When Diaghilev died it was impossible to find a successor for him, and the company of the Ballets Russes was split by various rivalries and disbanded.

"Bateau-Lavoir"

Name meaning "Washing-Barge", given by the poet Max Jacob to a group of creaking buildings situated at the top of the steps ending at 13 rue Ravignan. They were originally inhabited by all sorts of members of the common people of Montmartre, but came to fame when Van Dongen, and later Picasso, settled there after 1905. Gradually other artists and writers moved in, including Max Jacob, Juan Gris, Pierre Reverdy and Mac Orlan. The very disparity of the group made it an extraordinary centre of attraction for a flood of visitors and people of interest: Cocteau, Dullin, Matisse, Vollard, Utrillo, Jarry, Kahnweiler, Salmon, Radiguet, Braque and Derain, to name but a few. Surely no other place in the world has ever, within so short a time, witnessed such an exchange of ideas and enthusiasms, nor been frequented by so many future celebrities. Cubism was born there in 1907, when Picasso painted *Les Demoiselles d'Avignon*. The story of the "Bateau-Lavoir" ends in 1914, when, one after another, its occupants and habitués were forced by the war, or their own fame or fortune, to leave Montmartre.

Bazaine, Jean (b. 1904)

French painter, born in Paris. He began by studying sculpture at the Ecole des Beaux-Arts, and did not devote himself entirely to painting until 1924. For a long time his style stayed midway between the figurative and the non-figurative, finally leaning towards the latter after the war. The best of his work is characterised by sumptuous colour, strict harmony of forms and values, and intense, subtle sensitivity. He carried out the stained glass in Assy Church, and the ceramic mural and stained glass in Audincourt Church. In 1948 he affirmed his authority by publishing a very valuable and reflective book: *Notes sur la Peinture d'aujourd'hui.*

Bazin, Germain (b. 1901)

French writer on art, born in Paris. Author of numerous monographs and critical studies: *Fra Angelico* (1941 and 1949), *Corot* (1942), *Le Mont Saint-Michel* (1933), *History of Italian Painting in the XIVth and XVth Centuries* (1937), *The Twilight of Images* (1946), *Great Dutch Masters* (1950), *History of Art* (1953), *Impressionist Treasures in the Louvre* (1958) and *A History of Contemporary Painting* (1934), written in collaboration with René Huyghe. He has been professor of museology at the Ecole du Louvre since

1941, and was head curator of paintings at the Musée du Louvre from 1951 to 1966.

Berenson, Bernard (1865-1959)

English-language art historian and critic, born near Vilna, Lithuania. He was brought up in Boston, and, after completing his education, lived for a long time in Italy. Besides numerous articles, published in both English and American magazines, his two principal books are *Italian Pictures of the Renaissance* (1932), a perspicacious general view of Venetian painting from the 15th to the 18th century, which has been of considerable import to modern criticism, and *Aesthetics and History* (1949).

Bernard, Emile (1868-1941)

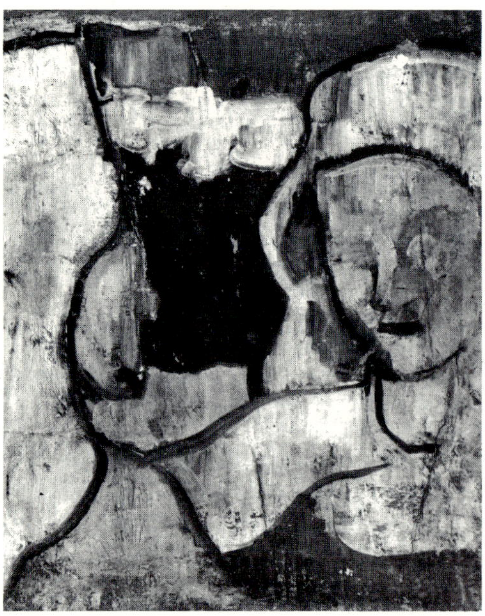

Emile Bernard
Three Breton Women
Maurice Denis Collection, Saint-Germain-en-Laye

Born in Lille in 1868, Emile Bernard showed an early interest in painting. He was barely sixteen when he entered Cormon's studio and there made the acquaintance of Toulouse-Lautrec. In 1886 he met Van Gogh and Gauguin. At Pont-Aven in Brittany, where they were in the habit of meeting, Gauguin and Emile Bernard elaborated Synthesism (Cloisonnism) after feverish discussions. In 1894 they went to Italy, then moved to Egypt, where they stayed for ten years. He was of enthusiastic mentality, devoted to theological discussion, and a tireless propagandist; he wrote numerous articles, founded a magazine, *La Rénovation esthétique*, and published his correspondence with Van Gogh, Gauguin and Redon, and his famous conversations with Cézanne. He died in Paris.

Bloy, Léon (1846-1917)

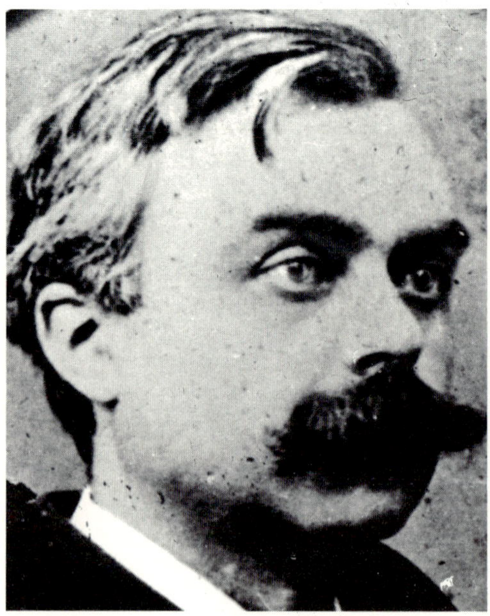

Léon Bloy
Viollet Collection

Constantin Brancusi
The Seal
Musée National d'Art Moderne, Paris

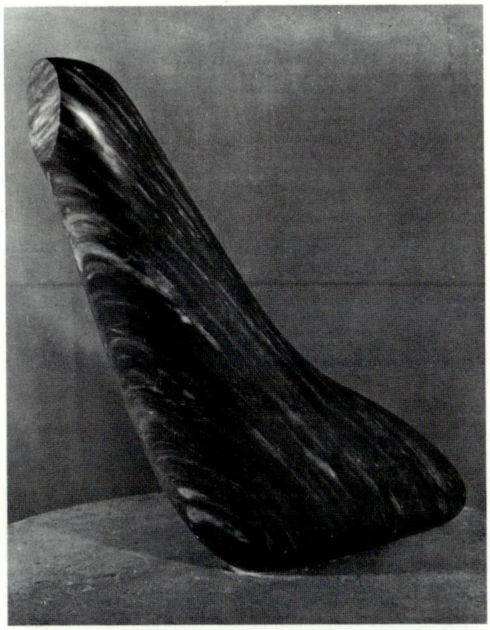

French writer, born in Périgueux, died in Bourg-La-Reine. He had an imprecatory style in which mysticism wrestled with provocation, and was a superb and scathing pamphleteer. His sorrowful, impetuous life was a long pilgrimage towards absolute perfection. His most significant work is probably *Journal*, a set of volumes with various titles in which he reveals his unhappiness and prophetic vision.

Bonnat, Léon (1833-1922)

French painter, born in Bayonne, died near Creil. He owes his lasting name less to his academic and religiously inspired painting (*Martyrdom of St Denis*, *Job*) than to his official portraits. From 1905 he took charge of the direction of the Ecole des Beaux-Arts, and he founded in Bayonne the museum which bears his name.

Bottini, Georges (1874-1917)

French painter and draughtsman, born in Paris. He lived in Montmartre, knew Toulouse-Lautrec, Steinlen and Galanis and specialised in illustrating books by light authors such as Jean Lorrain, Coquiot and Félicien Champsaur. He died mad, in the Villejuif asylum, after attempting to murder his mother.

Brancusi, Constantin (1876-1957)

Rumanian sculptor, born in Petishani Gorj, died in Paris. He studied at the Bucharest and Krakow Academies, then, in 1902, he decided to set out on foot for Paris, where he arrived in 1904. He refused to collaborate with anyone whatsoever (not even with Rodin, in whose studio he worked for some time) and lived quite alone from 1906 onwards, remaining unaffected by all fashions and methods. His sculpture, mostly non-figurative and totally non-anecdotal, was based for a long time on the form of the egg, which seemed perfect and essential to it. His most famous works include: *The New-Born* (1915), *Eve* (1921) and *Socrates* (1923). Until the very last he had an important influence on modern sculpture.

Buffet, Bernard (b. 1928)

French painter, born in Paris. Entered the Ecole des Beaux-Arts in 1944 but

Bernard Buffet
Nude Study of Seated Man
Droudan-David Collection, Paris

stayed only a short time. His limited colour-range, his Expressionism, which is either gloomy (emaciated people, empty or desolate landscapes) or terrifying (insects, giant birds, gaunt portraits), and his dry, acid style have secured him undiminished, world-wide fame since 1945.

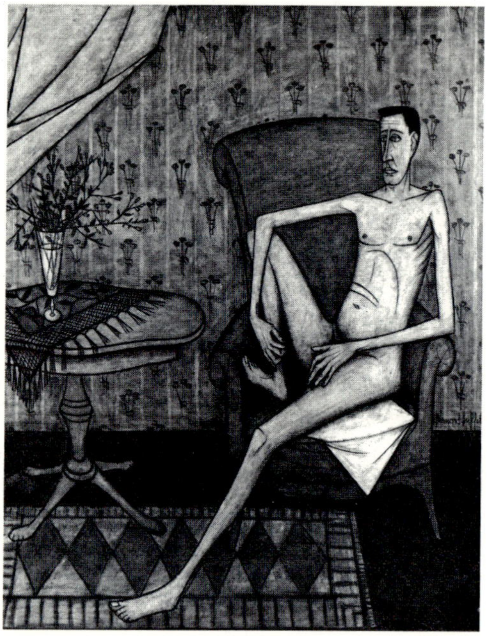

C

Camoin, Charles (1879-1965)

French painter, born in Marseilles. He was a fellow-pupil of Marquet in Gustave Moreau's studio at the Ecole des Beaux-Arts, Paris, and came mainly under the influence of Bonnard and Matisse. He has been erroneously classed alongside the Fauves because of his bright, simple colours, but he was really a prudent and moderate traditional painter.

Carco, Francis (1886-1958)

French poet and novelist, born in Nouméa. His real name was François Carcopino Tusoli. His best-known novel is *Jésus-la-Caille* (1914), which describes the bohemian life of Montmartre's twilight society. His subtly desolate poems were published as a collection in 1939. He was a friend of Modigliani and Utrillo, and owned important works by both these artists.

Castellane, Boniface de (known as Boni de Castellane) (1867-1932)

His marriage, in 1895, to Anna Gould, the daughter of an American millionaire, enabled him to lead a lavish existence and even to have a political career. As a deputy, he opposed the separation of the Church from the State. Divorce naturally ruined him, and he became an antique dealer. Van Dongen painted his portrait in 1928.

Boni de Castellane
at the time of his marriage to Anna Gould

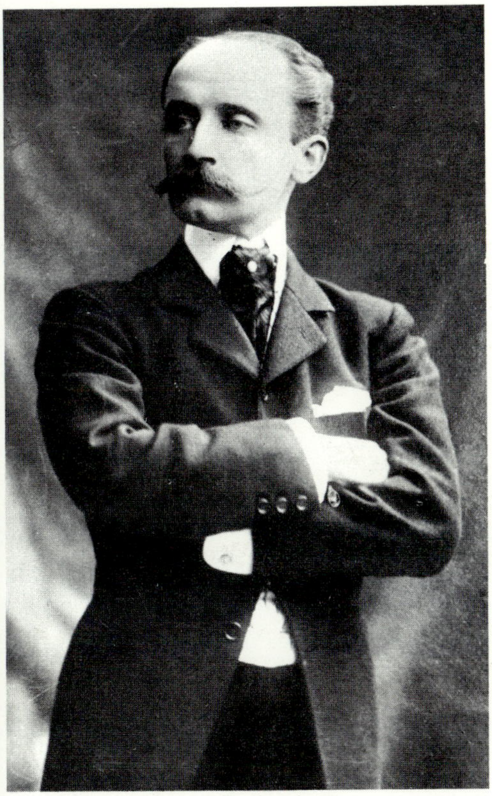

Cendrars, Blaise (1887-1961)

Frédéric-Louis Sauser, known as Blaise Cendrars, was born in Switzerland. At the age of seventeen, he ran away from his boarding school in Neuchâtel, crossed Europe and, in 1905, found himself in Manchuria working for a diamond trader when the Russo-Japanese War broke out. In 1912 he published *Les Pâques à New York*, a long poem of 205 lines which he composed in a single night, and, in the following year, the famous *Prose du Transsibérien et de la Petite Jehanne de France*, which was illustrated by Sonia Terk, the wife of Robert Delaunay. In 1914 he joined the Foreign Legion, was wounded and lost an arm. After the war he returned to prowling round the South while elaborating an important work. He was friendly with such *avant-garde* painters as Léger and Chagall, collaborated on Abel Gance's film *La Roue*, and published notably: *Dix-neuf Poèmes élastiques* (its experimental typography causing a great stir), *Du Monde entier* (1919), *Feuilles de Route* (1924) (memories of his travels in South America), *L'Or* (1925), *Moravagine* (1926) and *Rhum* (1930). In 1940 Cendrars retired to Aix-en-Provence and concentrated on recording some episodes of his eventful life. Using abrupt, vivid language with singular mastery, he wrote his last books: *L'Homme foudroyé* (1945) completed by *La Main Coupée* (1946), *Bourlinguer* (1948) and *Le Lotissement du Ciel* (1949). He died in Paris.

Cocteau, Jean (1891-1963)

French poet, born in Maisons-Laffitte, died in Milly-la-Forêt. In fact the term poet inadequately describes his artistic activities, which touched on all forms of expression: besides poetry itself (*Le Cap de Bonne-Espérance*, 1919; *Plain-Chant*, 1923), there were the fields of journalism (*Carte Blanche*, 1920), the novel (*Les Enfants terribles*, 1929), the essay (*Lettre à Jacques Maritain*, 1926), theatre (*Les Parents terribles*, 1938), cinema (*Le Sang d'un Poète*, 1932; *L'Eternel Retour*, 1934; *La Belle et la Bête*, 1946) and criticism (*Picasso*, 1923; *Le Greco*, 1944). In addition, he participated directly in the musical life of his time, for instance with the Ballets Russes (*Parade*, with music by Erik Satie and décor by Picasso), and as

Jean Cocteau

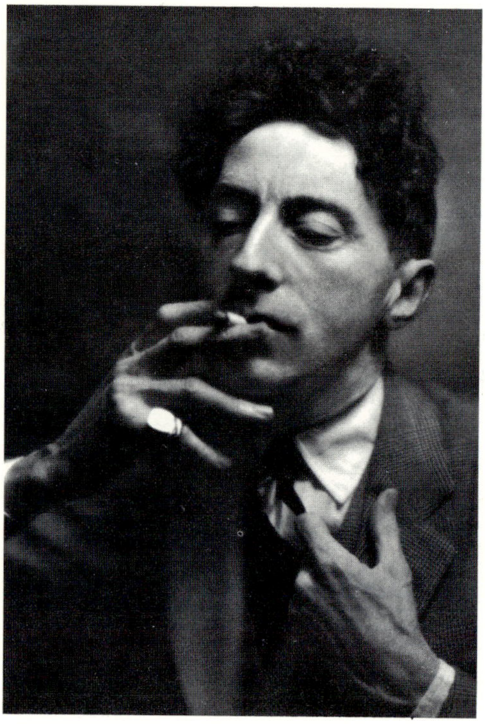

an extra-musical member of Les Six, which earned him the collaboration of Darius Milhaud (*Le Bœuf sur le Toit*), Francis Poulenc (*Les Biches*), Georges Auric (*Les Fâcheux*). He also published numerous albums of drawings (*Vingt-cinq Dessins d'un Dormeur*, 1929), illustrated his own works and decorated buildings (the Town Hall in Villefranche-sur-Mer and the chapel in Milly-la-Forêt). Cocteau's sharp, ready and concise intelligence, his dazzling wit and inexhaustible talent, inevitably suffered from the dispersion to which he submitted them. Their richness was a disadvantage rather than a help. It follows, therefore, that his work will probably endure only as an example of an extraordinary exercise in style.

Juan Gris
Guitar and Compote-dish, 1927

Cubism

An aesthetic movement born about 1907 from the encounter of two influences, Cézanne, with his structural and conceptual breakdown of colour and light, and the primitive arts with their instinctive breakdown of form and line. It was promoted by Picasso and Braque. The first-fruits of this new pictorial language are generally agreed to be the former's *Les Demoiselles d'Avignon*, 1907, and the latter's *Paysages de l'Estaque*, 1908. The movement was fully rounded out by Matisse and Derain, followed by Juan Gris and Léger. Cubism should also be regarded as a reaction against Impressionism and Fauvism, that is to say, against the excessive domination of colour alone. Cubism's contributions and methods include geometric configuration of the canvas, simultaneous depiction of the multiple facets of a solid shape which is thus deployed on the two-dimensional surface of the canvas, and emphasis on the architecture and essential rhythm of the things depicted. All at once objects became its subjects of choice in prefer-

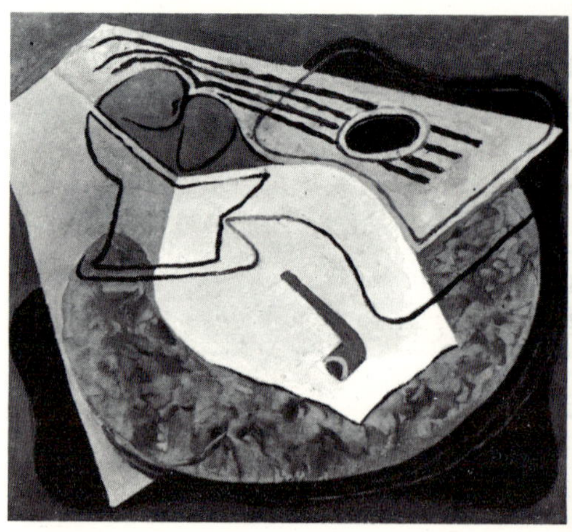

ence to landscape or human figures, still-life being the favourite genre. After a Cézanne period, Cubism went through two phases: analytical (1910-1912), then synthetical (1913-1914), the first being the province of Picasso and Braque, the second of Juan Gris and Léger. The first book devoted to Cubism was the work of its initiates, Gleizes and Metzinger.

D

Delaunay, Robert (1885-1941)

Born in Paris on 12 April 1885, Delaunay was first attracted towards theatre design, and this was the unusual way through which he came to painting. In 1904, when he was working in a studio in Belleville, he went to spend his holiday in Brittany, and there found memories of Gauguin and the school of Pont-Aven. Then he discovered Neo-Impressionism and became excited about Georges Seurat. He got to know Sonia Terk, who became his wife and whose career was to be always bound up with his own. Seurat had been discovered by the *avant-garde* shortly after Cézanne, and exercised a no less important influence on them; their interest was aroused both by his concern with construction and by his employment of colour according to laws which, far from being empirical, obeyed the optical theories elaborated by physicists. The Fauves were struck by his systematic use of pure tones, the Cubists by the discipline of his thought and his technique. Paradoxically, Robert Delaunay came more strongly under his influence than most: paradoxically, because there was no one more spontaneous or more in love with life than Delaunay, and there is nothing less doctrinaire than the notes he left. About 1912, he wrote, "I got the idea for a style of painting which would rely technically on nothing but colour—contrasts of colours, developing in time and gathering simultaneously at one stroke. I used Chevreul's scientific term: simultaneous contrasts. I played with colours as a musician would express him-

Robert Delaunay
The Joy of Life, 1931
Private collection, Paris

self through the fugue, with multi-coloured, fugal phrases." Apollinaire, when he invented the term "Orphism" for Delaunay's art, indicated how opposed his lyrical effusions were to the Jansenism of Picasso, Braque, Juan Gris and Metzinger. Delaunay's portrait of Metzinger, painted about 1906, reveals a certain kinship with the Fauves. Like them, he absorbed the influence of Cézanne, but, while in the "Bateau-Lavoir" and Villon's studio the talk was all of construction, Delaunay tended rather towards dissection. His variations on the Eiffel Tower and the ogival architecture of Saint-Séverin show him as being fairly near to Expressionism: he broke up the shapes the world offered to him so that he could remodel them in his own fashion.

In 1907 he went to Laon to do his military service, and there, painting the towers of the cathedral, he began to work out a personal style in which colour played an essential part. He was no more an orthodox Cubist than La Fresnaye; like him, he looked at the world and refused to limit his horizons to the guitar placed beside the folded newspaper. At that period there were certain similarities in their attempts, although Delaunay differed profoundly from the aristocrat La Fresnaye, being attracted by popular pleasures, as is shown in *Pig-Riding*, *Footballers* and *The Joy of Life*. At the same time he was obsessed by large monuments. He did many drawings of the nave of Saint-Séverin, studying the way the light broke on the pillars and the vault. Taking his sketches back to the studio, he set himself to invent a new perspective with its own dynamism. No painter of this time has shown more curiosity for all

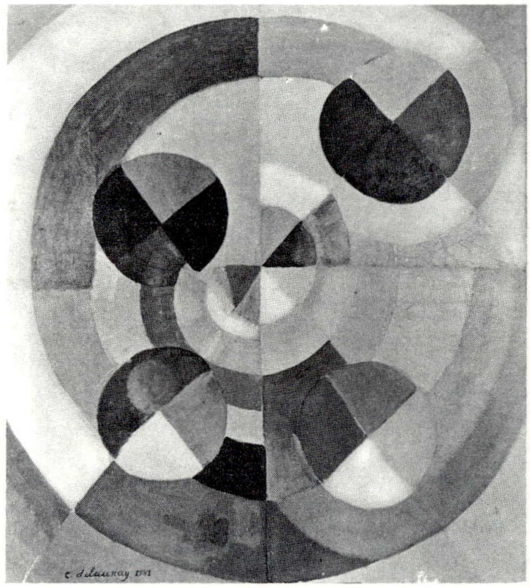

the problems that arose: colour, light, form and composition, he wanted to resolve them all. In this respect he stands as a precursor, not only of German Expressionists, but also of the Italian Futurists, not to mention the French Abstract artists who pillaged his experiments without making any acknowledgment to him. In 1911 Kandinsky invited him to take part in the "Blaue Reiter" exhibition in Munich, and his influence on German Abstract art was to be considerable.

The key year for him was 1912, when he painted his *Windows* which inspired Apollinaire to write probably his finest poem:

"From the red to the green all yellow dies..."

At the Indépendants he exhibited his large composition, *The City of Paris*, which remains his masterpiece. He took part in the Section d'Or exhibition in Paris, and Apollinaire presented a comprehensive showing of his work at "Der

Sturm" gallery in Berlin. From then on he exercised total freedom and could as readily raise the figure of a woman against the Paris sky as the Eiffel Tower; with reflecting surfaces or tattered shapes, his compositions always displayed a powerful temperament with lyricism taking precedent over deliberation. The war affected his experiments, as it did those of all painters of his generation. In 1914 he spent the summer in Spain. Having already been demobilised, he was in no way obliged to return to France, and so he stayed in Portugal, Madrid and Barcelona. He and Sonia were closely united, and influenced each other. Until then, Robert Delaunay had relied on the outside world, albeit by allusion, as in *Windows*, but from then on he adopted geometrical shapes and simplified his style. "Then," he said, "it occurred to me to eliminate the images seen in reality, objects which corrupted the order of the colours. I attacked the problem of formal colour." He experimented with materials, invented types of veneering, perfected a stone-lacquer, dreamed of monumental art, composed mosaics and designed plaster or bronze reliefs. Principally, this firm, precise draughtsman rejected all objective representation in order to devote himself to the study of light and violently coloured "rhythms". He had the chance to put his ideas into action at the Exhibition of Decorative Arts in 1925 and the International Exhibition in 1937, in which he composed ten large bas-reliefs in colour for the Railway Pavilion and the Air Pavilion. He launched into multiple experiments. He approached the Surrealists, though some way from them in temperament. He painted portraits of André Breton, Louis Aragon and Philippe Soupault. Then he concentrated on his series of *Rhythms* which, in 1930, heralded the post-war Abstract Art that he would never see. He retired to Auvergne in 1940, and died in Montpellier on 25 October 1941.

Divisionism

Also known as Pointillism, Divisionism was the method used by the Neo-Impressionists. Each brush-stroke is fragmented into tiny dots of pure colour. Its theorist, Signac, gave the following precise definition: "To divide is to secure all the benefits of luminosity, coloration and harmony: (1) by the optical blending of uniquely pure pigments (all the colours of the spectrum and all their tones); (2) by the separation of the various ingredients (local colour, reflected colour, and their interactions); (3) by the balance between these constituents and their proportions (according to the laws of contrast, gradation and irradiation); (4) by the choice of a stroke proportionate to the size of the picture." The head of the group was Seurat, and its principal adherents were Signac, Cross, Luce, Argand and Dubois-Pillet, all founder-members of the Salon des Indépendants.

Domergue, Jean-Gabriel (1889-1962)

French painter, born in Bordeaux. He attended the Académie Julian and won the Prix de Rome at the age of eighteen. Worldly and snobbish, he specialised in languid and sophisticated nudes of cur-

Jean-Gabriel Domergue
Portrait of a Woman
Private collection, Paris

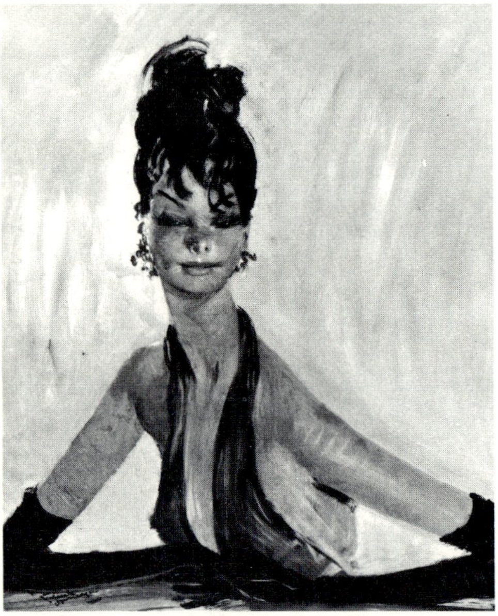

rent celebrities. In 1927 he settled in the famous Villa Fiesole in Cannes, and eventually bequeathed it to the town. He was a member of the Institute, and in 1955 he was appointed custodian of the Musée Jacquemart-André, where he organised some important exhibitions (Van Gogh, Lautrec, etc.).

Dorgelès, Roland (b. 1886)

French novelist, born in Amiens under the name of Lecavelé. Deeply affected by the first world war, he recorded his experiences in *Les Croix de Bois* (1919), which was illustrated by Dunoyer de Segonzac; the same year he published *Le Cabaret de la Belle-Femme*, a collection of short stories. These books earned him instant fame. Then followed *Saint Magloire* (1922) and *Le Réveil des Morts* (1923). He is a sensitive and lively writer and an attentive observer; like many writers of his generation, he has felt the lure of adventure. From his sojourn in Indo-China he produced *Ecrit sur la Route mandarine* (1925), and subsequently *Partir* (1926), *Ecrit entre Ciel et Eau* (1927) and *La Caravane sans Chameaux* (1928). Since 1929 he has been a member of the Académie Goncourt.

Duchamp, Marcel (1887-1968)

French painter, born in Blainville. Younger brother of Jacques Villon and Raymond Duchamp-Villon. He worked first as librarian in Paris. In 1911 he revealed himself in a surprising way, neither the teaching he received at the Académie Julian nor the early Fauve and Impressionist canvases predicting his sudden analytical style. Two years later he left Europe, which was too traditionalist for his liking. His contribution to the New York Armory Show with his sensational canvas *Nude Descending a Staircase* made him famous, but neither success nor the offers that beset him could deflect him from his path. He earned a living by giving French lessons. His meeting with Picabia and Man Ray in the United States was the origin of a movement which, in many ways, heralded Dadaism. This undoubtedly gave him the desire to go back to Europe where Dada was flourishing after the first world war. He also took part in the Surrealist movement until 1925. His work then falls into two categories: first, painting—a combination of Cubism, Futurism and Surrealism, its chief realisation being *The Bride Stripped Bare by her Bachelors Even* (1915-23); second, the "ready-

Jacques Duchamp-Villon
Seated Woman (bronze), 1914
Galerie Louis Carré, Paris

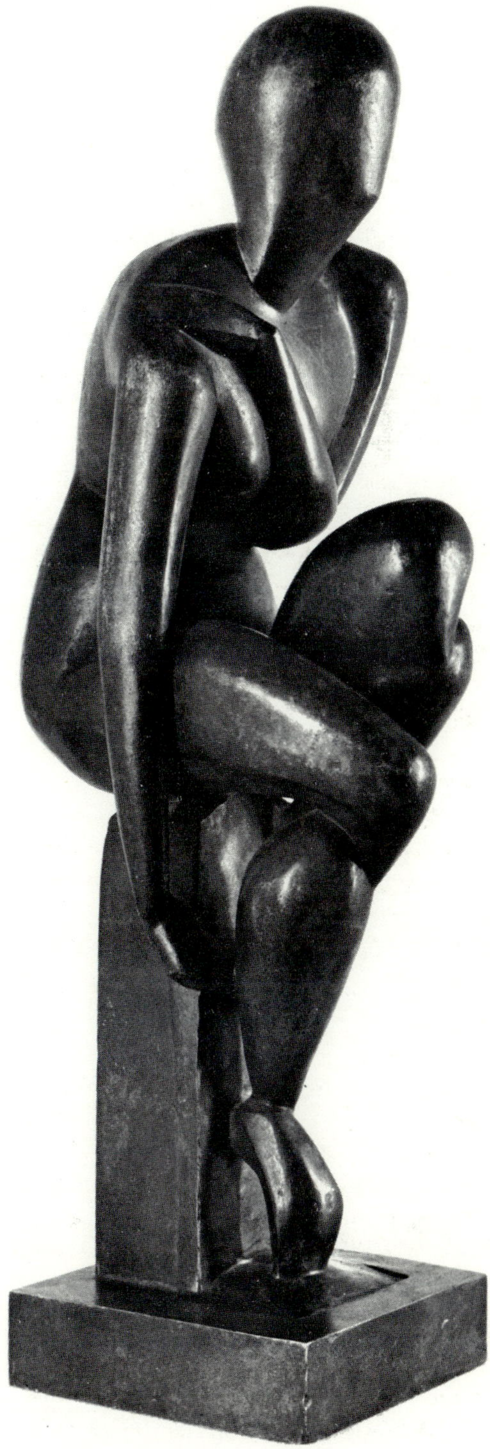

mades". As their name indicates, these were simply practical objects (a bottle-rack, a urinal) given the function of *objets d'art* by being exhibited as such, with occasional minimal alterations. This aspect of Marcel Duchamp's creative imagination did most to win him fame. He gave ceaseless inspiration to Europe an and American artists and was the uncontested father of Pop Art. Marcel Duchamp's singularity was, however, mainly of an ethical nature, for, determined not to be ensnared by his own inventions, he maintained his freedom by abandoning each as soon as begun. After 1938, the date of the Paris Surrealist exhibition, he dropped out of artistic life. He lived permanently in New York until his death on 1 October 1968.

Duchamp-Villon, Raymond (1876-1918)

French sculptor, born in Damville, died in Cannes. Brother of Jacques Villon and Marcel Duchamp. At the age of twenty-two he gave up his medical studies in favour of sculpture. For a long time he was under Rodin's influence, then his brothers' fascinating imaginations, not settling into his own style until he came into contact with the Cubists. His works, few in number but exceptionally disciplined and condensed, are not solely related to Cubism. In it he found solutions for the organisation of space and planes, and the essential expression of form, which opened the way, not only for Cubist, but for all modern sculpture. He carried out his most extreme experiments between 1912 and 1914, on one single theme, the horse.

Charles Dufresne
Self-portrait
Museum of Fine Arts, Algiers

Dufresne, Charles (1876-1938)

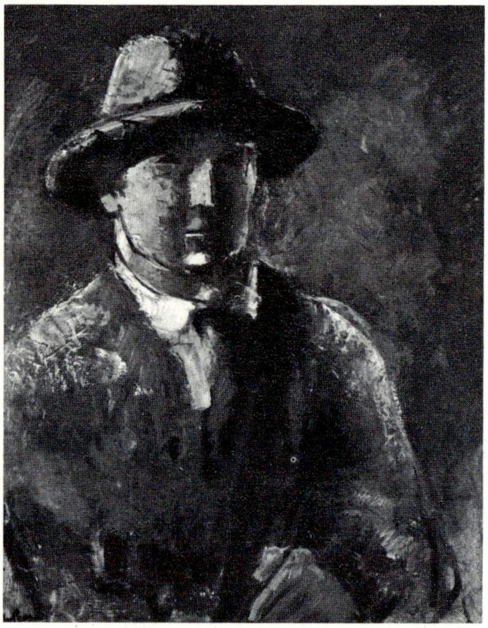

Charles Dufresne's present fame is not nearly as great as he deserves. The reason, perhaps, is that he refused to conform to nonconformity: he chose the unadventurous Salon de la Nationale to exhibit his compositions, which owed nothing to the fashionable movements. He was the only painter of our time who could claim a link with Delacroix, and like him he was not satisfied with the eternal still-life, the everlasting landscape; like him, he loved the East, and two years that he stayed in Algiers affected him deeply. Jean Cassou strongly indicates his unrealistic personality when he writes: "It should be unquestionable that the work of this great and generous artist will take its place in the prospect of history as it may later be written, when his exceptional personality has become familiar, and its qualities of mastery and imagination enjoyable without reserve." It is certain that a retrospective Dufresne exhibition today would be both a revelation and a rehabilitation.

Charles Dufresne remained on the fringe of all the movements to which more or less all of his contemporaries gravitated; born a year later than Jacques Villon and in the same year as Vlaminck, he was neither Fauve nor Cubist, although he did not ignore the two movements: his brilliant palette sometimes brought him close to Fauvism, while his interest in composition was akin to that of the Cubists, but he was deliberately meditative and did not care to launch into experiments. When he left for Algeria he was almost unknown, and it is only in the post-war salons that his works have been noticed. They are surprising less for their boldness than for their respect of tradition and their maturity. At a time when carefully defined categories are popular, this unclassifiable work is puzzling and difficult to place. When in 1920, however, he showed *The Water-Nymphs of the Marne*, no one doubted that the canvas constituted an event, but Dufresne was forty-four years old, and the myth of his youth was already established.

He was born at Millemont, near Paris, on 23 November 1876, and, like his friend the great sculptor Charles Despiau, he had the appearance of a peasant or a sailor; his father, in fact, was a fisherman at Granville. At the age of eleven he chose the profession of an engraver. After his apprenticeship he took a course in medallion engraving at the Ecole des Beaux-Arts and worked hard for his living in the studio of the sculptor Charpen-

Charles Dufresne
Woman in an Armchair
Demaeght Municipal Museum, Oran

tier, then with some sculptors of statues and some sellers of *objets d'art*. This difficult early time prevented him from concentrating on painting as he would have liked. In 1906, however, he was able to visit Italy. He could hardly ever escape his obscure tasks before nightfall, when he was able to go to the cafés and make numerous sketches heightened with water-colour. The bursary he received to go to the Villa Abd el-Tif in 1910 released him from this routine. During his stay in North Africa his imagination quickened and he escaped from the strict observation of reality which had limited his aims until then. He discovered exoticism without being seduced by its facile charm. His

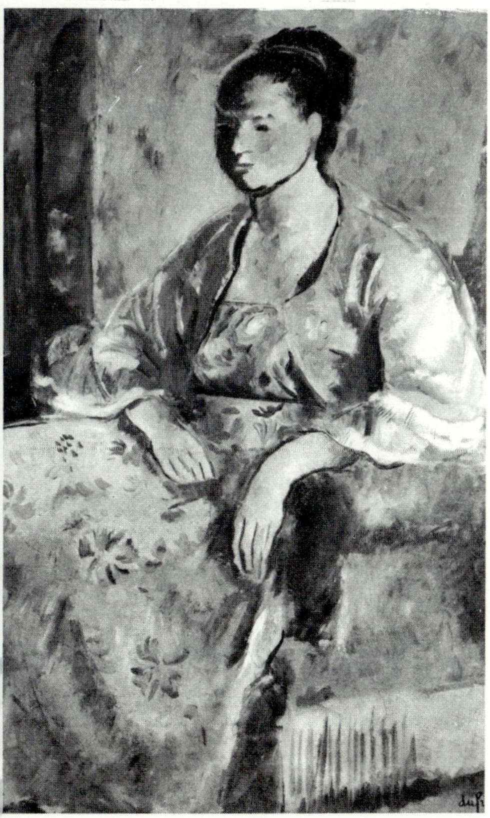

hunting series owes its inspiration to Africa and its technique to his preceding, long, obscure work. When he returned to Paris in 1912, he made the acquaintance of Dunoyer de Segonzac but did not join the group he formed with his friends Luc-Albert Moreau, Jean Marchand and Boussingault. He met Roger de La Fresnaye, but yielded less than he to the Cubist lure. He did not dismiss the *avant-garde*, however, and associated with Apollinaire, André Salmon and their friends. Too many ideas had sprung from his contact with the East and he turned to them rather than to the theories current at that time in the studios of Montmartre and Montparnasse. The pictures in his *African Hunt* series are dangerously unreal; they betray a desire to restore the tradition of the great composition, with blazing colours rigidly controlled; but their strict arrangement does not manage to bridle their fantasy.

He was far from the end of his experiments when he was called up on 2 April 1914. He waited in the trenches until 1916 when he was drafted to that camouflage unit whose history forms one of the most curious pages of the war. He was liaison officer to his friend Dunoyer de Segonzac, a duty which allowed him sufficient leisure to amass sketches from nature and imaginative compositions such as his water-colours of *The Taking of Noyen*. Demobilised, he resumed his experiments which led him to compositions less systematic than formerly. Without dropping his interest in construction, he followed the generosity of his own nature and the power of his imagination in *The Jungle*, *The Discovery of America* and *Orpheus*. With such unreal subjects

he was clever at avoiding both anecdote and the facilities of decorative art. Actually he was tempted by the latter and touched on theatre décor (*Antar* at the Opéra), mural painting, tapestry cartoon (*The Story of Paul and Virginia*, 1925) and engraving, which he had practised since adolescence.
His works are rarely seen, and he held only one important exhibition in Paris, at the Galerie Vilfrac, rue de Seine, in 1923. The same year he helped found the Salon des Tuileries and afterwards showed there regularly. His last works were mural compositions, those in the Ecole de Pharmacie and the Théâtre de Molière, and two large panels for the Palais de Chaillot in 1937. The following year he died in La Seyne-sur-Mer, just at the time when he had at last come to the notice of enlightened art-lovers.

E

Einstein, Albert (1879-1955)

German physicist, born in Ulm. His discovery of the theory of relativity revolutionised the world of physics. Nobel Prize 1921. He became a naturalised American in 1940.

Ensor, James (1860-1949)

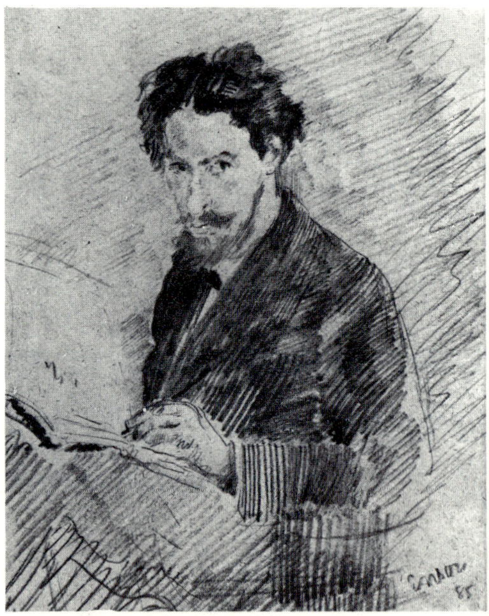

James Ensor
Portrait of the Artist, 1885
J. Boogaerts Collection, Brussels

Belgian painter, born and died in Ostend. He studied at the Académie des Beaux-Arts in Brussels. After an Impressionist period, first sombre, then dazzling and free, he ventured into a realm of fantasy and macabre vision where masks and skeletons in sinister celebration symbolise the passions and vices of men. In this respect he is the great precursor of Expressionism.

Maurice Estève
The Espalier, 1949
Private collection, Paris

Escholier, Raymond (b. 1882)

French poet and novelist, born in Paris. He is less known today for his literary works (*Le Sel de la Terre*, *Dansons la Trompeuse* and *Cantegril*, which earned the Prix Fémina in 1921) than for his art criticisms and essays, particularly some excellent studies on Daumier and Delacroix. He has been custodian of the Musée Victor Hugo and the Petit-Palais.

Estève, Maurice (b. 1904)

French painter, born in Culon, Cher. He studied painting at the Académie Colarossi and the Louvre, then, in 1923, settled in Barcelona as the director of a design studio in a fabric factory. His painting was at first figurative, Post-Impressionist, gentle and almost elegiac, then, about the time of the second world war, underwent a transformation, becoming resolutely non-figurative. He did not lose his taste for pure colours, but disciplined his composition and structure. He aimed principally to reconcile form, space and light. Although he has exhibited little, he has established himself on a level with Bazaine and Manessier as a master of Abstract art in the French tradition.

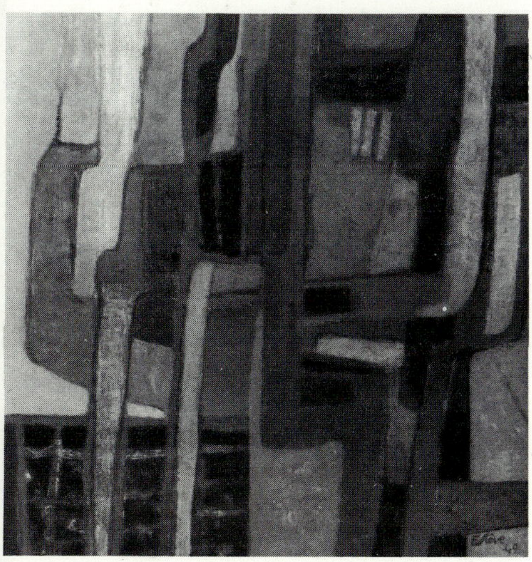

Expressionism

Expressionism does not exist in time and space; it belongs with the means, methods and manners of artistic creation and of man's whole history. In painting, it consists in externalising, sometimes exaggerating, psychic, emotional and subjective manifestations to which it is desired to give a dramatic or painful turn. In this sense, caricature, anecdotal distortion, the exaggeration of colour or design and the morbid or passionate romanticism of subjects naturally forms part of the method. In the modern period, the word Expressionism is always applied to a movement of German and Nordic origin and location. Its source springs from Van Gogh (and partly from Toulouse-Lautrec). Then came the Norwegian Edvard Munch and the Anglo-Flemish James Ensor. These were the artists who gave the revelation of their style and their universe to the German painters of the "*Brücke*" (Bridge) group which appeared in 1905. Nolde and Kirchner were its best representatives. To a certain extent, the "*Blaue Reiter*", which took over from "*Die Brücke*", also belonged to German Expressionism, but it evolved fairly quickly in a more intel-

Chaim Soutine
The Madwoman, 1920
Rokubin-Hayoshi Collection, Tokyo

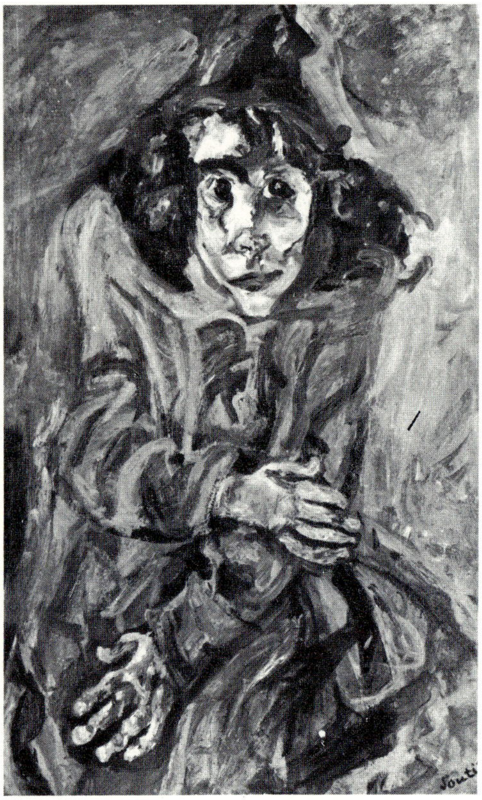

lectual direction. The Austrian Kokoschka and certain painters of the Paris school (Soutine, Chagall and Pascin) should also be linked with the Expressionism of that period and mood. The Latins have subscribed equally to the methods of Expressionism. Everything has invited them to do so in the world's permanent state of crisis, disturbance and danger since the first world war: in France, Rouault and, to a lesser degree, Gromaire and Picasso (notably in *Guernica*); in Mexico, Rivera, Orozco, Siquieros and Tamayo. The movement crossed the border-lines of the plastic arts and affected literature, theatre and cinema, notably in Germany in the 1920s.

F

Fauvism

French artistic movement, springing from the conjunction of two influences: that of Van Gogh (for pure, violent colour and the Expressionist style) and that of Cézanne (for structure, the value of balance and the cult of light). Both these influences overlapped in their separation of colour from anecdote—the subject of the picture. Georges Seurat and Paul Gauguin also have claims to the fatherhood of the movement. Fauvism was in gestation from 1900, but it was effectively and officially born at the Salon d'Automme, 1905. It was there, in fact, that the three founder-groups met for the first time: that of Matisse, coming from Gustave Moreau's studio (Marquet, Manguin and Camoin), that from Le Havre (Dufy, Friesz and, the following year, Braque), and finally the two friends from Chatou (Derain and Vlaminck). The names of Van Dongen and Rouault should also be added, as independent spirits who did their first true work with the same energy and the same love of pure colour. The ephemeral existence of Fauvism—it disintegrated after 1907—can be explained by the unusual state of tension and emotional involvement it demanded of its adherents. Derain defined it as an *auto-da-fé*. It was a trial in which French painting found its finest and most intense flame of passion, purity and daring. The emulation it provoked literally wrested their best works from several artists who could never again recapture the same fervour and brilliance: Marquet, Puy, Valtat, Camoin, Manguin, Chabaud,

Henri Matisse
Still-life with Fish, 1911
Pushkin Museum, Moscow

Kees Van Dongen
Portrait of Anatole France
Roudinesco Collection, Paris

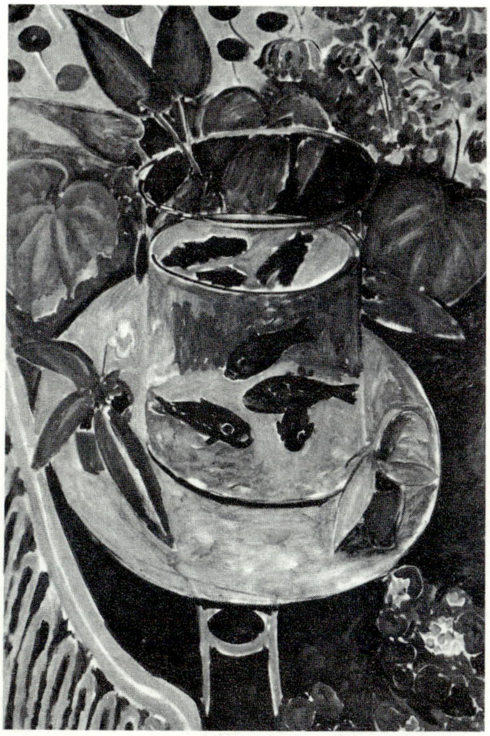

Friesz and, without doubt, Dufy and Vlaminck also.

Fénéon, Félix (1861-1944)

French writer and art critic, dealer associated with the Galerie Bernheim Jeune, perspicacious and informed defender of the Neo-Impressionists (Seurat in particular) and Les Nabis. His contribution to various Symbolist magazines and his pamphlet *Les Impressionnistes en 1886* made him as much a theorist as an advocate of the divisionist conceptions of painting.

Ferrier, Gabriel (1847-1914)

French painter, born in Nîmes, died in Paris. Prix de Rome 1872. Became a teacher at the Académie des Beaux-Arts in 1906. His work, thoroughly imbued with the period's conventional aesthetics, lacks vigour. Noteworthy, however, are *Women Smoking Indian Hemp* and *The Martyrdom of St Agnes*, now in the Rouen Museum, and the ceiling decoration in the Nîmes theatre foyer.

France, Anatole (1844-1924)

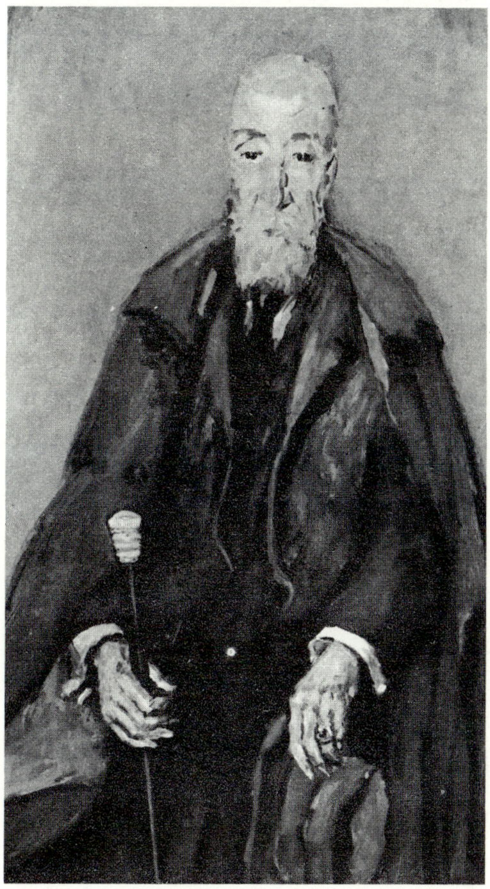

Othon Friesz
Still-life, 1941
R. Loyer Collection, Algiers

Anatole Thibault, who took the pseudonym of Anatole France, was born in Paris, the son of a bookseller on the Quai Malaquais. He was the enemy of all fanaticism (he sided with Dreyfus), an "honest man" devoted to liberty and social justice, and his work achieved unequalled success. In his limpid style, with its elegant and flexible irony, he wrote numerous novels, notably *Le Crime de Sylvestre Bonnard*, 1881, *Le Livre de mon Ami*, 1885, *Les Opinions de Jérôme Coignard*, 1893, *L'Ile des Pingouins*, 1908, *Les Dieux ont Soif*, 1912, and *Le Petit Pierre*, 1918. Nobel Prize 1921. Van Dongen painted a portrait of him which caused a furore.

Friesz, Othon (1879-1949)

French painter, born in Le Havre, died in Paris. His life falls neatly into three periods. Between 1898, when he arrived in Paris, and 1907, the young art student blossomed into a Fauve painter of vigour and liberality equal to the best. Between 1908 and 1914, violence disappeared from his work, but also the desire to experiment. Othon Friesz was already resting on his experience, and returned progressively to traditional painting. After the first world war, this return to facility became not only an artistic choice, but a moral one. He nevertheless exercised an influence over the group of young painters who studied in his studio.

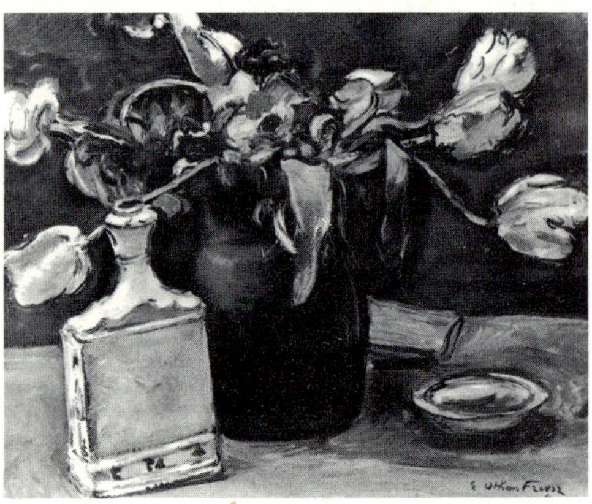

Futurism

Movement of Italian origin which attempted to introduce the mechanical, dynamic and energetic attributes of modern civilisation into painting, equating them with spiritual and artistic qualities. The birth of Futurism is dated from the manifesto by the poet F. T. Marinetti, published in *Le Figaro* of 20 February 1909. This manifesto, violently polemic, contained affirmations which have since become familiar sayings: "A racing-car is more beautiful than the *Victory of Samathrace*", or "Long live the action of killing", or "Art can be only violence, cruelty and injustice". In actual fact, Futurism was partly a reaction against the excessively static form within which Cubism confined painting, and partly against Italy's current state of social, political and intellectual stagnation. The first and principal members were Carrà, Boccioni, Russolo, Balla and Severini. Futurism's activities rapidly extended to theatre, poetry and music; but it had the brevity of its own violence. The death, in 1916, of its theorist and most talented creator, Boccioni, at the age of thirty-four, brought about its dispersal.

G

Galanis, Demetrius (1882-1966)

Painter-engraver, born in Athens. As the winner of a competition for humorous drawings with a visit to Paris as the prize, Galanis reached France when he was barely eighteen. Soon seduced by the Bohemian life of Montparnasse and the Butte, he became naturalised. *L'Assiette au Beurre*, *Gil Blas* and *Le Rire*, the main satirical papers of the time, secured him as a contributor. When war broke out in 1914, he enlisted, like Cendrars, in the Foreign Legion. When hostilities ceased, he remembered the teaching of Degas, who instructed him in engraving, and embarked on an important work consisting of illustrating no less than a hundred books, such as *Le Grand Meaulnes*, *Les Amours de Marie*, *Les Nourritures terrestres*, *Le Roi Candaule* and *Asmodée*, which made him one of the most conspicuous illustrators of the years around 1925.

Géraldy, Paul (b. 1885)

French poet and dramatist, born in Paris. The publication, in 1913, of *Toi et Moi*, an effusive poem of slightly affected delicacy, aroused lively enthusiasm from the public. He later dropped poetry, and wrote several brilliant, superficial comedies, including *Les Noces d'Argent* (1921) (produced in London as *Silver Wedding*), *Grands Garçons* (1922) and *Robert et Marianne* (1925).

Gérôme, Jean-Léon (1824-1904)

French painter and sculptor, born in Vesoul, Haute-Saône, died in Paris. Artist of no great originality and a discreetly pompous academism; the essential part of his work is a set of historical paintings celebrating ancient Greece.

Giacometti, Alberto (1901-1966)

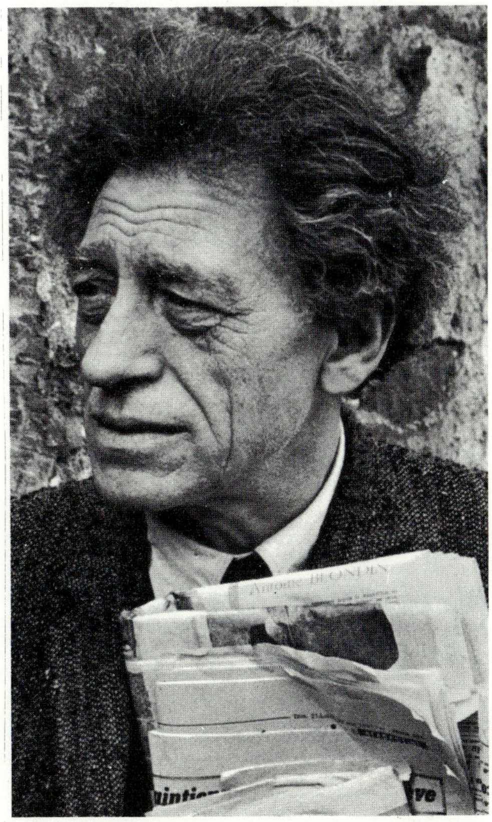

Swiss painter and sculptor, born in Stampa. He studied in Geneva, then Rome. From 1925 to 1928 he was interested in "object-sculpture". In 1930 he was attracted by the Surrealist movement,

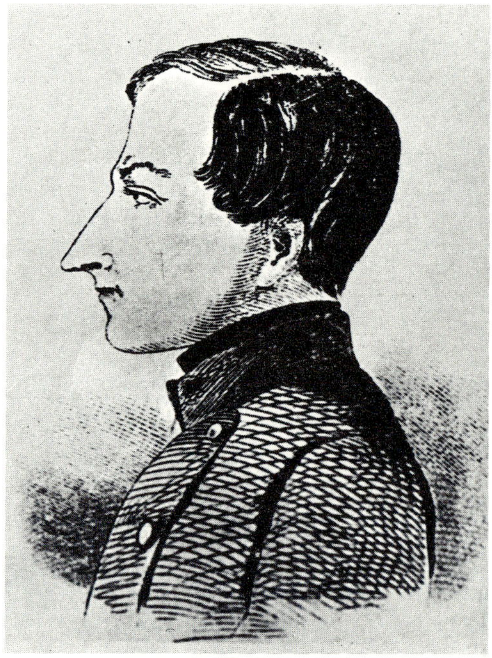

Gogol
Viollet Collection

but his independence and solitariness soon made him diverge. From 1935 onwards the human form absorbed all his attention and stimulated all his inspiration. He made numerous characters and portraits in an agonised, filiform, Expressionist style, animated by two major preoccupations: one, the suggestion of infinite space surrounding humanity's precarious presence; two, the expression of the terror inherent in all flesh and constantly revealing the primitive man within us.

Gleizes, Albert (1881-1953)

French painter, born in Paris, died in Avignon. His activities went considerably beyond the boundaries of creative art: linked by his works to the evolution of Cubism, he was equally involved in his role of theorist and propagandist. His book, *Du Cubisme*, written in collaboration with Metzinger, remains the definitive work on the movement. From 1917 onwards he was inclined towards religious preoccupation, but did not lose his early pictorial conceptions. On the contrary, he attempted to give them greater weight and freedom within his new awareness of himself. To this end he published *La Peinture et ses Lois* in 1923, *L'Homocentrisme ou Retour à l'Homme chrétien* and *La Forme et l'Histoire* in 1932.

Gogol, Nicolai Vasilyevich (1809-1852)

Russian novelist and dramatist, born in Sorotchintsy in the Ukraine, died in Moscow. When he was barely twenty-two, he published eight stories, lively and picturesque descriptions of the Russian countryside. In 1835 he wrote *Taras Bulba*, a highly coloured epic poem which won immediate success. In 1842 came *The Overcoat*, a story which prompted Dostoyevsky to describe him as being at the fountainhead of all modern Russian literature. The same year, Gogol published *Dead Souls*. Although unfinished—the author himself destroyed the third part—this "novel-poem", a passionate denunciation of serfdom, is undoubtedly Gogol's masterpiece. It was illustrated by Chagall with some striking etchings.

Grüber, Francis (1912-1948)

Since its beginning, French painting has gone through a series of pendulum movements which for a long time assured its

Francis Grüber
Job
Private collection

equilibrium. (Only in the last twenty years has the triumph of non-figurative art made a break with the tradition of each generation reacting against the one preceding.) Thus the Cubists' intellectual exercises and their constructive and decorative interests were opposed, about 1935, by a group of young artists devoted to the strict observation of reality. The most categorical of those united under the banner of "New Forces" were Robert Humblot, Georges Rohner and Henri Jannot, who were joined by Civet, Despierre, Tailleux and Vénard, and although Francis Grüber always remained fiercely independent, he worked along the same lines. René Huyghe wrote of Grüber's drawing that it was "abrupt, brittle, angular, jerky. He bristles with points like barbed wire and hacks indentations like sharp splinters of glass, drawing unprecedented in France. This aggressive, dislocated style, expressing an almost cruel tension, is found expanded in Germany in the crooks, jerks and scratches of Dürer, Wolf Hüber and Grünewald." He goes on to ask, "Under the impact of what moral shock, what obsessions, what upsetting of life, what monstrous circumstances, what surrounding cruelty, would French graphic art renounce its familiar inflexions and be carried away by this compelling fever?" To answer this question, it is necessary to go back to the perilous pre-war years and consider the actual life of Francis Grüber. He was born in Nancy on 15 March 1912; his mother came from Poland, and his father, a painter-glazier and Nancy schoolmaster, from Lorraine. He spent most of his life in Montparnasse, in the Passage d'Alésia, where his father, assisted by his brother, had his studio. In these surroundings the child began to draw very early. He suffered terrible bouts of asthma, so drawing became a diversion for him, and, being unable to attend school regularly, he frequented neighbouring studios, that of Braque and that of Bissière, who encouraged and advised him. In 1928 he entered the Académie Scandinave, where Waroquier, Dufresne and Friesz were teaching. Friesz had the greatest influence on him and at the end of his life Friesz's young pupils, Cortot in particular, recognised him as a master. Grüber's strong personality rapidly emerged. Made hypersensitive by illness, and becoming the master of a very firm technique, he interpreted in his works the anguished world about him. He revived Expressionism with an acute analysis of reality, concentrating particularly on the nude. He used emaciated models, posed in the glaucous light of his studio in the Passage d'Alésia.

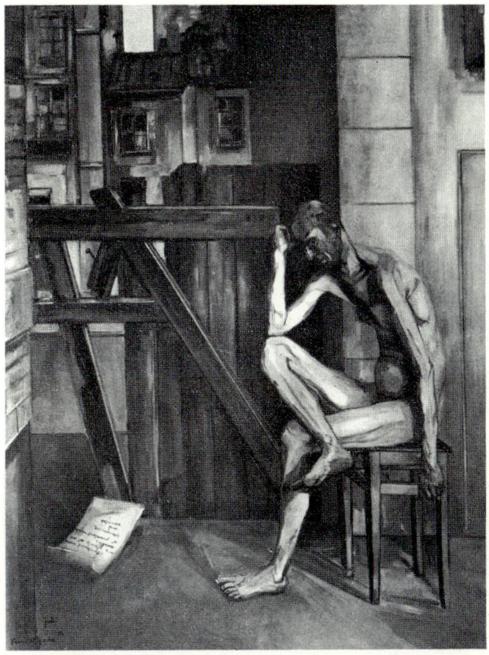

Francis Grüber
Art and Science
Musée d'Art et d'Industrie, Saint-Etienne

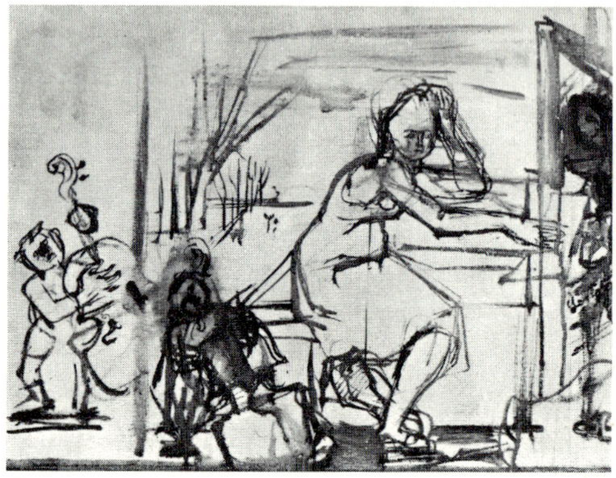

He was a very individual colourist, cleverly using touches of dramatic red to relieve his monochrome canvases dominated by grey and green. His ambition led him towards large-scale composition. He decorated the Lycée Lakanal and, at the height of the war, his *Homage to Jacques Callot* was at once a cry of love for Lorraine and a protest against the occupation of his country. The Germans were not blind: they would not authorise the picture to be shown until the painter had erased the blue-white-and-red flowers in the martyred woman's hand. When very young, Grüber went with his brother to Belgium, where he discovered Bosch and Brueghel and was particularly struck by the altar screen of *The Mystic Lamb* in Saint-Bavon's, Ghent. He was attracted by such German masters as Altdorfer, and realised the need for order and internal organisation of pictures; he profoundly admired Louis David. He rapidly became prominent with his intelligence, strong personality, sharp wit and culture which he owed solely to himself. At the age of eighteen, when his elders founded the Salon des Tuileries, he was one of their first guests. In 1942 he succeeded Bissière as a teacher at the Académie Ranson. Before the war his canvases had been rarely seen except in the modest galleries on the left bank, but during the Occupation art-lovers and critics no longer doubted that, at the age of thirty, he was the master of realistic fantasy. His large exhibition in 1945 established him firmly. But a highly active, irregular life increasingly aggravated his already deficient health, which soon interfered with his work. His style remained firm and his expression vigorous, but he could work for only a few hours a day; it was a poignant spectacle to see this still-young man climbing out of bed, irresistibly drawn towards the half-finished canvas. His style became more intense, more economical. He relinquished none of his ambitions, as witness his *Job* painted in 1944. He spent a long time over his pictures never hesitating to destroy any which did not entirely satisfy him, and his work remains the most striking testimony left to us by a terrible period. In 1947 he was ultimately rewarded with the Grand Prix National, but he died on 1 December 1948. So much for the curtailed work by a man whose premature death still leaves a painful gap in the development of French painting. (G. Ch.)

Guérin, Charles (1875-1939)

French painter and engraver, born in Sens, died in Paris. Pupil of Gustave Moreau. His nudes and still-lifes reveal a talent of discreet ability, always standing apart from the great movements of contemporary painting.

Amedeo Modigliani
Paul Guillaume
Viollet Collection

Guillaume, Paul (1893-1934)

French art critic and picture dealer, born and died in Paris. When very young he became enthusiastic about Negro sculpture, assembling with remarkable knowledge and flair an astonishing collection which eventually supplied its finest pieces to the famous Barnes Collection, the remainder being dispersed by auction in 1965. He founded the archaeological society for Negro art, and in 1915 published the first album of Negro sculptures in collaboration with Apollinaire. In this respect he has played an appreciable role in the history of modern art. Besides this, in 1915 he began to support Modigliani. The exhibitions he devoted to Picasso, Matisse, Utrillo, Derain, La Fresnaye, de Chirico and Vlaminck enabled him to assemble an important private collection. His widow, remarried to the architect Jean Walter, presented it to the State in 1960, and it was exhibited at the Paris Orangerie in 1966

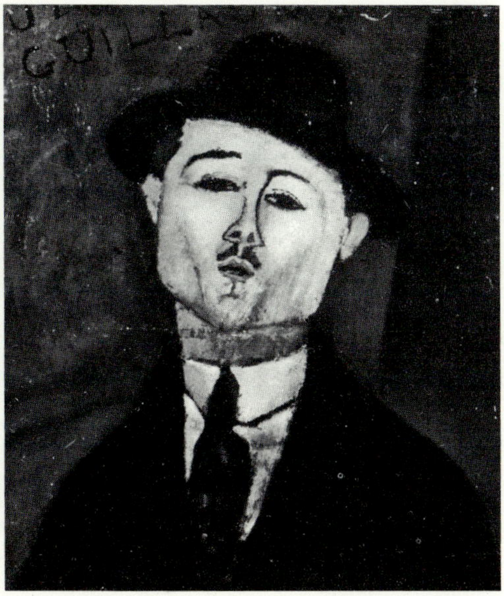

H

Huysmans, Joris-Karl (1848-1907)

French writer of Dutch origin, born in Paris. He was a disciple of Zola, first publishing naturalistic novels. With *A Rebours* (1884) he inaugurated his Symbolist period and attempted to work out a spiritual sensuality in a systematic way. " After such a book the author can only fire a pistol at himself or throw himself at the foot of the cross," wrote Barbey d'Aurevilly. Soon afterwards Huysmans was converted to Catholicism, as described in *En Route* (1895). He died in full mystic fervour.

Max Jacob
Portrait inscribed to René de Berval

Alfred Jarry
Beginning of *Ubu Roi*

J

Jacob, Max (1876-1944)

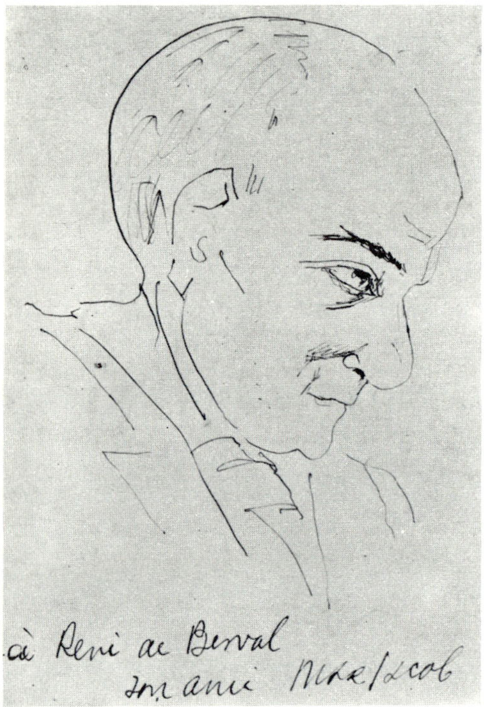

French poet, born in Quimper, died in the concentration camp at Drancy. He was a fantasist, but his fantasy proceeded from the purest and most penetrating humour; tormented, but with a delightful vivacity, his style has affected all modern poetry (*Le Cornet à Dés*, 1917; *Le Laboratoire central*, 1921). He was born a Jew, but his conversion to Catholicism in 1909 explains the nature of his poetry, which is full of mysticism, sometimes feigned or mocking, sometimes exalted or ecstatic. Sometime critic on the *Moniteur des Arts*, he was friendly with the " Bateau-Lavoir " painters, especially Picasso. In fact, even before Picasso's first exhibition at Vollard's, in 1901, Max Jacob was entirely devoted to the man and his work, even becoming, in a way, his impresario and manager. A few years before the second world war he retired to Saint-Benoît-sur-Loire, and it was there that the Germans arrested him before interning him at Drancy.

Jaloux, Edmond (1878-1949)

French writer, born in Marseilles, died in Lutry. He was sometimes lyrical, sometimes influenced by post-Symbolism, trying to build a romantic universe half-way between dream and reality, darkness and light. Nevertheless, he was a fine psychologist and a penetrating literary and artistic critic. His works include: *Les Amours perdues*, *Le Reste est Silence* and *L'Incertaine*.

Jarry, Alfred (1873-1907)

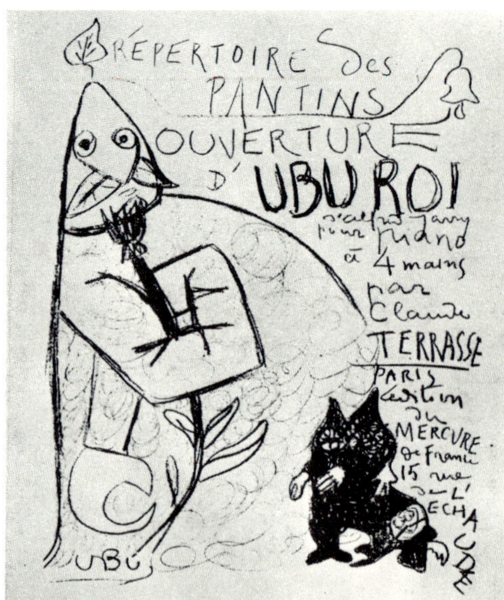

French writer, born in Laval. He had a short, brilliant life, writing the celebrated play *Ubu Roi* at the age of fifteen. Encouraged by the success of this masterpiece, he wrote two sequels, *Ubu enchaîné* then *Ubu cocu*, but the farcical tragedy had already lost its uninhibited bite. Although the absurd bore Ubu and this whole bombastic satire of satisfied stupidity were the true marks of his genius, Jarry also undertook less well-known work. His subsequent writings, *Les Minutes de Sable memorial* (1894), *César Antéchrist* (1895), *Les Jours et les Nuits* (1897) and *Le Surmâle* (1902), adequately show that an authentic disintegration of language had been put into practice, thus laying the ground for Surrealism. He died of tuberculosis.

K

Kahnweiler, Daniel-Henry (b. 1884)

Picture dealer, born in Mannheim, Germany. Through his enthusiasm for experimental painting, his material assistance and his writings, he wisely and generously helped first the Fauves, then the Cubists. The gallery he opened in Paris in 1907 became the meeting-place for Derain, Vlaminck, Van Dongen, Picasso, Braque, Juan Gris and Léger. At almost the same time he undertook the publication of art books (*L'Enchanteur pourrissant* by Apollinaire, illustrated by Derain; *Saint Martorel* by Max Jacob, illustrated by Picasso). He devoted himself so faithfully to this activity that today his works total about forty volumes illustrated by the most reputable names in modern painting. After the first world war the sculptors Manolo and Henri Laurens and the painters Beaudin and Masson joined his gallery. He has written monographs on Vlaminck, Derain and, in 1946, the most important, Juan Gris; he is, without doubt, the most fervent and informed of Gris' biographers. Since 1939 he has gradually relinquished his role as a discoverer of new talent and has entrusted the direction of his gallery to his sister-in-law, Louise Leiris.

Kokoschka, Oskar (b. 1886)

Austrian painter, born in Pöchlarn, Austria, on 1 March 1886. He went to Vienna and studied at the School of Arts and Crafts from 1905 to 1909, shortly afterwards being appointed a teacher there. Moving in artistic and literary circles in the

Imperial capital, he painted numerous portraits of actors and writers, developing a tormented and visionary Expressionist style, at the same time writing for the *avant-garde* Berlin magazine, *Der Sturm*. From 1910 to 1914 he divided his activities between Berlin and Vienna. His meeting with Alma Schindler, the widow of the composer Mahler, inspired him to one of his masterpieces, *The Bride of the Wind* (1912). In 1915 he was seriously wounded in the war and went to live in Dresden, where he taught at the Academy until 1924, at which time he started travelling about Europe, North Africa and the Near East. He returned to Vienna, but when Chancellor Dollfuss was assassinated he left again and went to Prague. In Germany, 427 of his canvases were confiscated as "degenerate art". After Munich, he reached London, and acquired British nationality in 1947. The war inspired him to paint combat pictures and political allegories against the Nazi horror. Since 1955 he has resided in Switzerland, continuing his pictorial experiments and giving remarkable teaching at the summer-school run by the Salzburg Academy of Fine Arts.

Kupka, Frantisek (1871-1957)

Czech painter, born in Opocno, Bohemia, died in Puteaux, France. Studied at the Academies of Prague and Vienna. He was a great traveller (Sweden, Norway, England and Germany), very interested in spiritualism and religion but equally attracted by French 18th-century philosophers and the Encyclopaedists, receiving his first great artistic jolt at an exhibition in Prague of French Impressionists. In 1895 he settled in Paris, where he was soon noticed for his talent as an illustrator of literary works, including Aeschylus' *Prometheus* and Leconte de Lisle's *Les Erinnyes*. He started as a figurative painter, but his figuration was very much interpreted, dominated by a concern with intellectual composition and the supremacy of pure colour; from 1910 onwards he developed firmly towards abstract painting. After the first world war Kupka extended his experiments to such a degree of purity and simplification that he was rarely understood. The declaration of his work that he set out at the Musée de Jeu de Paume in 1936 aroused more respect than enthusiasm. It was not until after the second world war that his role as innovator and uncompromising creator became finally recognised and almost world-famous. In 1946 Prague founded a museum named after him and devoted to his work.

L

La Fresnaye, Roger de (1885-1925)

A number of painters who fought in the first world war died prematurely, and among them was Roger de La Fresnaye; he never recovered from the tuberculosis he contracted in the army and spent his last years in Grasse, where he died on 27 November 1925. Both his origins and his tastes seemed to predestine him to join Dunoyer de Segonzac's group of friends. His intellectual curiosity led him to the Cubists. However, by the end of his all too short life he had developed a precise style which can be described as Mannerist. These fluctuations appear normal in an artist who was not averse to the movements of his period and wished to master them. His childhood drawings revealed a precocious ability and he met with no resistance when, in 1903, he decided to enrol at the Académie Julian. He was then eighteen, having been born in Mans on 11 July 1885. The Académie Julian has played a major role in the development of contemporary painting. At the time when Roger de La Fresnaye was emerging, one of the "massiers" (students in charge of funds) was Paul Sérusier, who had not yet received the revelation of the *Talisman*, painted by Sérusier with Gauguin's advice in 1888, but who was already exercising his influence over the young painters who were to become known as Les Nabis: Bonnard, Vuillard, Roussel, Maurice Denis, Redon and Vallotton were all pupils at the Académie. After these pioneers, a new generation of innovators preferred these independent studios to those of the Ecole des Beaux-Arts: Segonzac, Lotiron, Moreau, Boussingault, etc. These were La Fresnaye's first friends in the world of painters. The Julian spirit had also touched the Académie Ranson, where Maurice Denis was teaching; La Fresnaye enrolled at his studio and, during the years 1908-1909, came strongly under his influence. Like all the best of his generation, he was touched by Cézanne's grace, and *The Cuirassier*, which he exhibited at the Indépendants in 1911, shows how rapid his development had been. He was at first attracted to boldly simplified forms, but his Cubism soon diverged radically from that of Picasso, the Orphists or the Puteaux group. He employed an entirely personal style, solidly grafted on to reality. He and Delaunay and Léger alone were interested in their period: although he was not satisfied with the abstract solutions to the problem of composition these two artists suggested, he shared their liking for colour, and his large canvases are accented with some very bright touches. He was already in control of a firm technique; he owed his natural superiority to his upbringing in an aristocratic background and a refusal to be

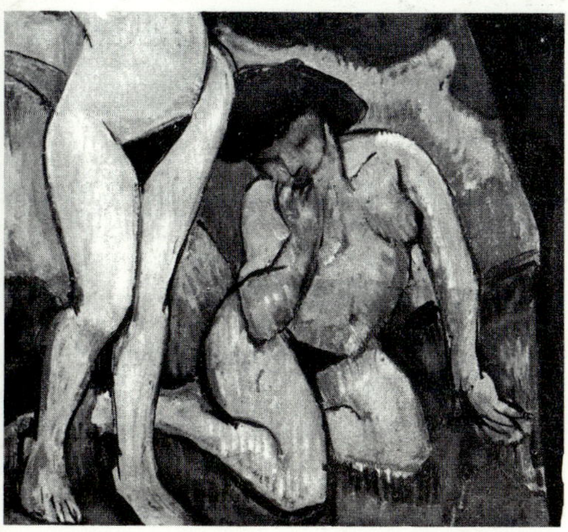

Roger de La Fresnaye
Nudes in a Landscape
Musée National d'Art Moderne, Paris

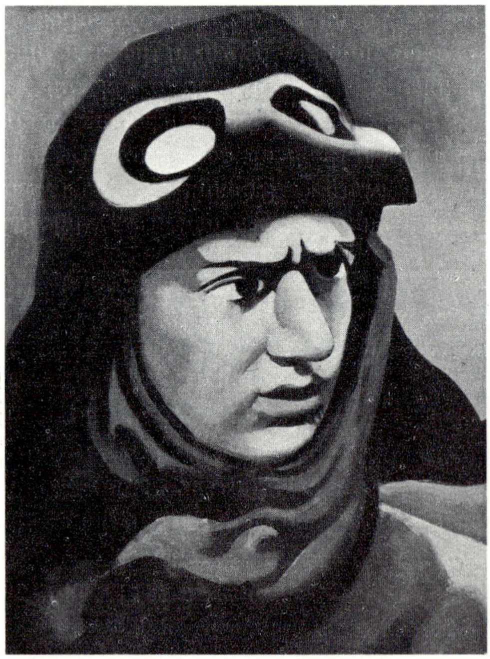

Roger de La Fresnaye
Portrait of Guynemer
Musée National d'Art Moderne, Paris

absorbed into any one of a number of movements which would gladly have welcomed him. He liked architectural shapes and striking, but not simplified, compositions, and in his intense output of the years 1911-1914 can be found the primers of many experiments attempted after the war by dissidents from Cubism. The visit he made to Germany in 1910 allowed him to escape from the theories then confronting each other in Paris studios and enabled him to take stock, which resulted in the austerity of his Meulan landscapes (*The Viaduct*, 1913) and in the discipline of his still-lifes, where the subjects are reduced to geometrical shapes as far from the aridity of certain too-faithful disciples of Cézanne as from the deliberate complexity displayed at that time by Braque and Picasso. Although he was a humanist Cubist, his sensitivity did not exclude a taste for grandeur and a certain heroic quality which strangely foreshadowed coming times: *The Conquest of the Air* (1913), now in the New York Museum of Modern Art, *The Fourteenth of July* and *The Artillery* (1913), and *Seated Man*, shown at the Indépendants in 1914, count among the rare monumental works of a period more concerned with analysis than vast synthesis. La Fresnaye had a natural instinct for balancing shapes. He did not reject the necessary disciplines, but did not let himself be imprisoned by them, and for this reason his compositions, dominated by large rectangular planes, are never devoid of life or movement. M. Jean Cassou, who has devoted some remarkably lucid pages to La Fresnaye, does not fail to remark that Cubism satisfied his taste for grandeur and his horror of eloquence: extreme sobriety, rigorous vigilance and scrupulous purity were inflexible conditions for him, and since he was himself an artist of the most refined sort, this operation of decanting nature to which he devoted himself was effected without clash or violence. The titles of the paintings and drawings he did after the war, while attempting a hopeless cure at Grasse, tell enough about his physical and mental state: *The Suffering Man* (March 1922), *The Vanquished* and *Sick Young Man* (1924). Speaking in 1920 of the portrait of his friend Gampert, he wrote: " My whole time lately has been engrossed with a rather unfortunate undertaking: the portrait of Gampert in an old style, I mean recognisable and, as far as possible, like him. I worked very hard: drawings, oil sketches on canvas—it was all no good. Finally I came down to a sort of miniature and spent unlimited time on it. The result is quite interesting, but, all the same, does not justify all the trouble I have taken." From this period we have mainly drawings, water-colours and gouaches which he painted even when his advancing illness kept him in bed. Can they be considered a testament? La Fresnaye achieved mastery in 1911; from 1914 the war interrupted his work. When he resumed he had been so deeply affected that, after a brief return to the abstract in 1918, he embarked on an entirely different course. Constructional concern certainly continued to dominate during these attempts of his last period, but the appearance of things wooed him irresistibly, as though he were trying to hold on to the world he was about to leave. How his work would have developed had the war not intervened, no one can say. It is permissible to think, however, that the death of this strong, independent personality impaired the development of French painting as terribly as that of Francis Grüber was to do a quarter of a century later. (G. Ch.)

Lanskoy, André (b. 1902)

Painter of Russian origin, born in Moscow. He briefly studied painting in Kiev, then settled in Paris in 1921. He was first attracted to traditional painting (portraits, landscapes, still-lifes), but since 1937 he has concentrated on non-figuration. His fresh, charming style rests on solid black and white composition over which play sometimes pure colours, sometimes perfectly handled pastel tints.

Montmartre
The "Lapin-Agile" in 1900

"Lapin-Agile"

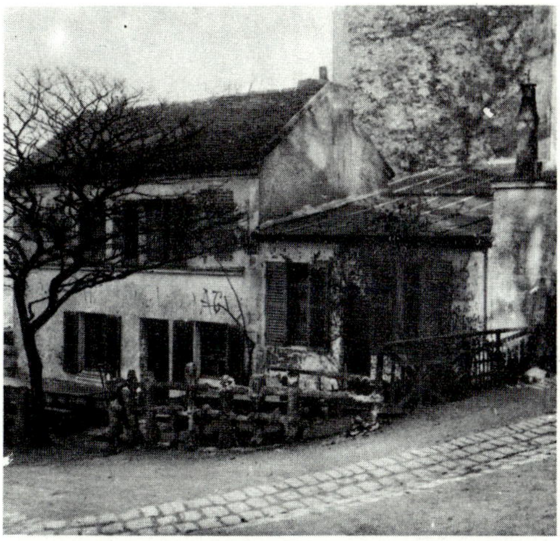

Bistro at the crossroads of the rue des Saules and the rue Saint-Vincent in Montmartre. It was run by Frédéric Gérard, a colourful character known to everyone as Frédé, whose daughter married Mac Orlan, and provided the setting for Mac Orlan's novel *Quai des Brumes.* It was a "literary" club, the haunt of scores of shady persons, rival of the "Bateau-Lavoir", frequented by numerous artists such as Modigliani and Francis Carco. Frédé's donkey went down in legend when Roland Dorgelès, making fun of the pictorial experiments of the time, let the animal swish its tail, duly loaded with paint, over a canvas he eventually entitled *Sunset over the Adriatic.* The picture was actually exhibited at the Salon des Indépendants, enabling the author of the trick to write a sensational article.

Laurens, Jean-Paul (1838-1921)

French painter, born in Fourquevaux,

Le Corbusier
Still-life, 1922
Musée National d'Art Moderne, Paris

Haute-Garonne, died in Paris. He used his very academic style to portray historical subjects of mainly religious inspiration. His works include: *The Pope and the Inquisitor*, *The Excommunication of Robert the Pious*, *The Death of St Geneviève*, etc.

Le Corbusier (1887-1965)

French painter and architect of Swiss origin, born in La Chaux-de-Fonds, died in Roquebrune-Cap-Martin. Real name, Charles-Edouard Jeanneret. Apart from being an architectural genius, universally recognised as the revolutionary inventor of new forms and possibilities in concrete, Le Corbusier played an equally considerable part in the realm of plastic arts. Before beginning to study architecture at the age of eighteen, he had taken a course at the Ecole des Beaux-Arts in La Chaux-de-Fonds and knew the art of engraving. He was very attracted by Cubism, but criticised it for debasing its principles; painting, for Le Corbusier, while remaining both the subject and the object of emotion, had to hold strictly to the essential lines and colours it borrowed from the surrounding world. These conceptions evolved into a theory by the name of Purism in the magazine *L'Esprit Nouveau*, founded by Le Corbusier, with Ozenfant, in 1920. Aware of the excessive geometric and artistic discipline of his pictorial experiments, Le Corbusier always claimed to be avoiding decorative effects. To this end, after 1929 he tried to introduce the human form into his painting, which, until then, had concentrated on still-life. But the very terms of his rules guided him ineluctably towards mural decoration, fresco and tapestry. It is

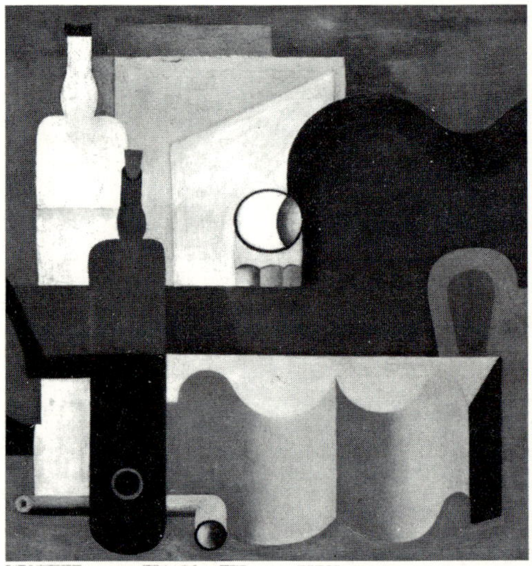

none the less evident that the liveliest humanism remained the constantly sought aim of his work both as a painter and as an architect.

Le Fauconnier, Henri (1881-1946)

French painter, born in Hesdin, Pas-de-Calais, died in Paris. At the age of twenty-five he entered the Académie Julian where he met Segonzac, Boussingault and La Fresnaye. In 1908 and 1909 he painted Breton landscapes already powerfully Cubist in construction. In fact, his meetings with the Cubists Gleizes, Metzinger and Picasso, and his contributions to the Salon d'Automne and the Salon des Indépendants in 1911, soon counted him among the masters of the new school. He also displayed a great talent for teaching, and became studio head of the Académie de la Palette in 1912. The following year, however, he abandoned Cubism for Expressionism. He was in Holland when the war broke out, and stayed there, developing his new style, until 1920. When he returned to France, his Expressionism evolved towards more austerity.

Lipchitz, Jacques (b. 1891)

Sculptor, born in Druskieniki, Lithuania. Intended for an engineering career, but interested in the plastic arts, he went to Paris in 1909. He took courses at the Ecole des Beaux-Arts and the Académie Julian. His meeting with Picasso, then Juan Gris, encouraged him in the Cubist style he had chosen. But the static appearance of Cubism did not satisfy him. He felt the appeal of shapes which were at once more subtle, complex and symbolic, his religious and humanitarian preoccupations mingling with erotic impulses. In 1940 he sought refuge in the United States, and in 1946 settled in Hastings-on-Hudson, near New York. His works include a *Madonna* in Assy Church.

Lorjou, Bernard (b. 1908)

French painter, born in Blois. Self-taught, deeply impressed by Spain and its painting—which he discovered in the course of a journey at the age of twenty-three—then by the northern Expressionists (Grosz and Permeke), he has kept to the fringe of present trends in art. His bright, imprecatory work, deliberately realistic if not popular, has benefited by his strong instinct for publicity and the support of numerous society patrons. He was one of the founders of the " L'Homme Témoin " movement which later discovered Buffet, Minaux and Couty.

M

Mac Orlan, Pierre (b. 1882)

French writer, born in Péronne; real name, Pierre Dumarchey. His main works are a romanticised account of his youth: *Le Petit Manuel du Parfait Aventurier* (1920), where he defines his conception of armchair adventure; *Quai des Brumes* (1927), the desolate atmosphere of which pleased Marcel Carné, who filmed it in 1938; *La Cavalière Elsa* and *Les Poésies documentaires complètes*, a complete collection of his poetry. Since 1950 he has been a member of the Académie Goncourt.

Maillol, Aristide (1861-1944)

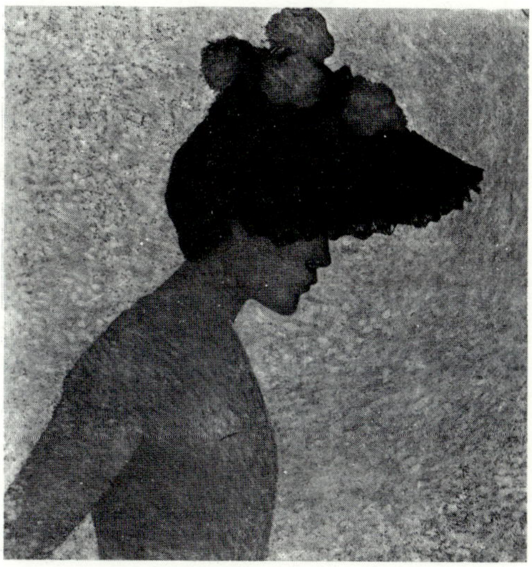

Aristide Maillol
Young Woman's Head seen in Profile
Perpignan Museum

French sculptor, born and died in Banyuls. His studies of painting and sculpture at the Paris Ecole des Beaux-Arts having left him very undecided about his vocation, he started as a painter and weaver, influenced by Gauguin and Denis. He did not devote himself to sculpture until 1901, when he was forty, and did not really establish his personality until he came back from a visit to Greece in 1906. His early works, however, already show his preoccupation with sensual masses set in a mould close to that of Ancient Greece. Serene and static, concerned only with beauty and healthy sensuality, he differs in this way from the tortured and dynamic style of Rodin, to whom he nevertheless owed a great deal. Nearly all his work is based on a single subject: the female body.

Manessier, Alfred (b. 1911)

French painter, born in Saint-Ouen, Somme, from a family of artisans (one grandfather being a rope-maker, the other a stone-cutter). After studying at the Lycée and the Art School in Amiens, he went to Paris and took a course in architecture at the Ecole des Beaux-Arts. He also frequented the Louvre and the academies in Montparnasse, notably the Académie Ranson, where he became a pupil of Bissière with Le Moal and Bertholle. His painting aimed to convey his inner experience, and although it used the reality of the visible world as a point of departure, this was transformed on the canvas into relationships of light, colour and shape. After his retreat to the Trappist monastery at Soligny in 1943, his works developed a mystic orientation. In this way he became a promoter of the convergence of non-figurative and religious art. Numerous stained-glass windows testify to his success in this field: the churches of Bresseux, Jura and All Saints', Basle. He won prizes at the São Paulo painting Biennale in 1953, and the Venice Biennale in 1962.

Manguin, Henri (1874-1943)

French painter, born in Paris, died in Saint-Tropez. At the age of twenty he entered Gustave Moreau's studio, was caught up in the whirlwind of Fauvism and participated in all the great developments of that movement. His reserve and liking for proportion and subtlety, however, prevented him from joining whole-heartedly in the violence and passionate commitment of his companions. Although he borrowed their style and their palette, he was mainly concerned to absorb them into traditional French paintings of nudes and landscapes.

Metzinger, Jean (1883-1957)

French painter, born in Nantes. Metzinger came very early to painting, was quickly disappointed in the various teachings he was offered, and thought at first that the work of the Neo-Impressionists and Fauves mirrored his own interest in liberating form and colour; but his intellectual and analytical love of purity led him ultimately to Cubism. From 1908 he joined Picasso and Braque as one of the artists completely involved in the success of the new school. In this connection, in 1911, he collaborated with Gleizes to produce the definitive exposé of the movement: *Du Cubisme*. From the same year he also attended meetings of the Puteaux Group at Jacques Villon's.

Gustave Moreau
Orpheus and the Muse

Moreau, Gustave (1826-1898)

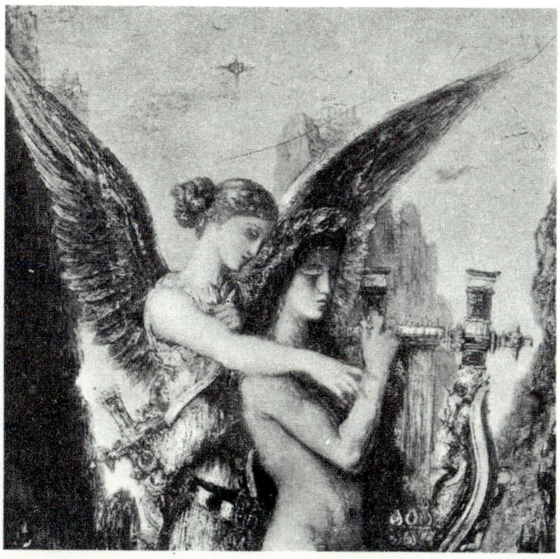

French painter, born in Paris. While he trained Matisse, Rouault, Marquet and Jean Puy at the Ecole des Beaux-Arts, and his generous and fertile teaching freely enabled each one of them to seek out his own individuality, he was at the same time a solitary painter of decadent romanticism. He was the contemporary of Villiers de l'Isle-Adam and Huysmans, and his art, which revived ancient pantheons in a dream-world of trivial fantasy, was, nevertheless, strangely prophetic. The Surrealists were making no mistake when they wanted to annex these haunted canvases where legendary figures—Sphinx, chimera, Salome—show off their androgynous anatomy amongst affected bric-à-brac sometimes gleaming with disturbing radiance.

N

Nabis, Les

This name, which means "prophets" in Hebrew, was adopted in 1888 by a group of young Parisian painters: Denis and Sérusier (who later emerged as the two theorists, the first writing *Théories* and *Nouvelles Théories* in 1913, the second *ABC de la Peinture* in 1921), Bonnard, Ranson, Ibels, Vuillard, Roussel and Piot. Fired by Gauguin's example, they set themselves up as the defenders of a new aesthetic. Reproaching the Impressionists for being too much the slaves of appearances, they tried, in their works of art, to interpret a synthetic and symbolic vision of the world. The lesson Gauguin taught them—simplicity of drawing, the use of pure colours broadly spread over flat surfaces devoid of modelling, linear perspective or depth, the practice of partitioning—led to the stylisation of forms. The adepts of this new art, soon joined by Vallotton, Verkade (who took holy orders in 1893) and the sculptor Maillol, turned deliberately to decorative techniques and revolutionised them. The group, which found its defenders in the *Revue Blanche* and at the Théâtre de l'Œuvre, organised its last exhibition in 1899 at Durand-Ruel's. Sérusier, the movement's promoter, alone remained faithful to the original ideology, the others all going their individual ways.

Noailles, Anna de (1876-1933)

French poetess, *née* Anna-Elisabeth Brancovan, born in Paris. Reacting against the Hermeticism of the Symbolist poets, her

Foujita
The Comtesse de Noailles

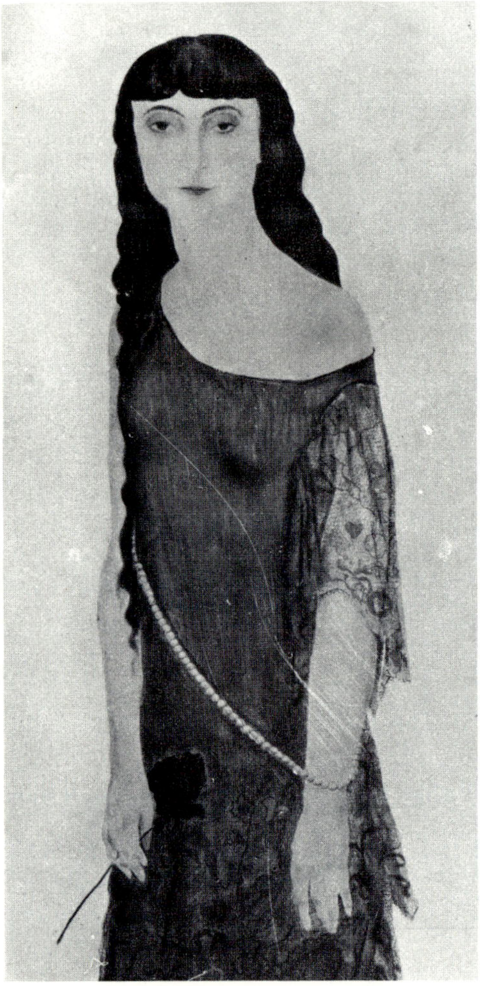

collections of poems, *Le Cœur innombrable* (1901) and *L'Ombre des Jours* (1902), celebrate the astonishment of the flesh before the world. The death of Maurice Barrès, to whom she was very attached, deepened her pantheistic lyricism, and her last collection, *L'Honneur de souffrir* (1927), is an unusually serious hymn to death. She was a member of the Belgian Royal Academy.

O

Olivier, Fernande

Her real name was Fernande Bellevallée; she was the daughter of Montmartre artisans, and married a sculptor, but was widowed very young; subsequently she earned her living by posing for the painters on the Butte. She was the companion of Picasso for a period of nine years; in fact, she was *La Belle Fernande* of the Spanish master's pink period and the model for the celebrated *Demoiselles d'Avignon* which started Cubism. This is her only claim to be included in the history of painting. She wrote a book of souvenirs, *Picasso et ses amis* (1933). She died in Neuilly in 1965.

Orphism

Name by which Guillaume Apollinaire chose, in 1912, to designate the painting of Robert Delaunay, Kupka and their followers, which involved the heightening of colours to the point of lyricism, but according to the laws of spectrum diffraction, complementary colour, and simultaneous contrast. Orphism was one of the two ways paved by Neo-Impressionism (the other being strict Cubism), the way which led, in fact, particularly in France, to non-figurative art.

Ozenfant, Amédée (1886-1966)

French painter, born in Saint-Quentin (Picardy). He studied classics in Spain, then art in his native town. It was in his magazine, *L'Elan*, in 1915, that he first drew attention to his experiments. There he set out the principles of Purism, though, properly speaking, the manifesto of Purism did not appear until 1918, under the title *Après le Cubisme*. Ozenfant wrote it in collaboration with Charles-Edouard Jeanneret whom he had met the preceding year, and who was to become famous under the name of Le Corbusier. Purism meant respecting the forms of the outside world, but in their essential architecture, without compliance or concession to the temptations of colour, feature or texture. Its excessive artistic stringency did not attract many followers, but the tenacity of Jeanneret and Ozenfant furthered and enlarged its creative impetus. Between 1920 and 1925, their magazine *L'Esprit nouveau* included, besides Purism, all the *avant-garde* experiments, and won a large readership. After 1925 Ozenfant extended his activities to a study of decorative and mural painting (*The Four Races* in the Paris Musée d'Art Moderne), publication (the two volumes of *Art* in 1928 and *Journey through Life*, a diary of the years 1931-1934) and teaching (he founded one school near Warwick Road in London, where he lived from 1935 to 1938, and another in New York, where he settled in 1938: the Ozenfant School of Fine Arts). He remained consistently faithful to the principles and theory of Purism. He died in hospital in Cannes at the age of eighty.

P

Pascin, Jules (Julius Pinkas, known as) (1885-1930)

Many painters of central European origin who were interested in Abstract art gravitated to Germany. France, however, attracted the most remarkable of them: Chagall, Soutine, Kisling and Pascin. Pascin was born in Vidin, Bulgaria, on 31 March 1885, but was in Munich, and barely fifteen, when his deft touch was noticed by Gustave Meyrink, writer of the novel *The Green Face*, who got him into *Simplicissmus*, the most famous of the satirical magazines in which several German painters made their débuts, just as *L'Assiette au Beurre* and *Le Rire* were helping artists like Villon and Van Dongen to make a living in France at the same period. Turning his back on his success as a caricaturist, Julius Pinkas, calling himself Pascin, went to try his luck in Paris. These early emigrations show his longing for new horizons, and are evidence of his deep dissatisfaction. Had he stayed in Germany, no doubt he would have become involved with Expressionism, to which he was drawn by temperament. In France he found a more balanced atmosphere which, without detriment to his versatile touch or rich imagination, allowed him to escape from the temptation of caricature, to which his friend the great artist George Grosz yielded, letting himself become absorbed by concerns foreign to painting. Pascin, by contrast, quickly discovered that inexhaustible subject, the female body. We are certainly indebted to him for admirable portraits of Pierre Falké, Mac Orlan, Salmon, Marcel Sauvage and Jean Oberlé, some extraordinarily fantastic compositions and innumerable sketches which are far superior to fleeting notes, but he remains the painter of woman, nude or slyly half-clothed.

At a time when the reign of pure painting was beginning, when the canvas was a surface covered with colours assembled in a certain order, he reverted to French 18th-century tradition. While Boucher's or Fragonard's coquettes, however, are limited to pleasing the fancy of the great lords of the time, Pascin's small, plump women are rather disturbing and, were there no mitigating humour, his eroticism could easily be oppressive. Looking at Pascin's life from the outside, it is all too easy to dwell on the appearance his journeys have of running away and on his death as a tragic melodrama. For those who knew him, he is remembered as a gentle, smiling man and a faithful friend whose only weakness was in leaving his choice of relationships to chance; as though frightened of being alone for a moment, he welcomed everyone who knocked on his door in the Boulevard de Clichy; painters, models, dealers and all sorts of spongers gathered round him every Saturday in some restaurant or other, and these companions were never presented with the bill.

His models were there, very young but well experienced. Pascin thought of them as "pensive cattle", and asked them only to stretch out on a divan or relax in an armchair with their slips raised enough to display their shapely bodies. He would take a large sheet of paper and draw on it in silver-point with single lines and no alterations. Then he would throw these sheets behind him, and they formed a large, untidy pile in a corner of the studio. Then he would take a canvas and rest it on his knees more often than on the easel. He dissolved a little pink and blue in benzene, and the flesh began to live. Or else he chose pastels, even more subtle, more apt for rendering all the flesh-tints of skin in half-light.

I am describing the years just before his death, when he appeared as a nonchalant

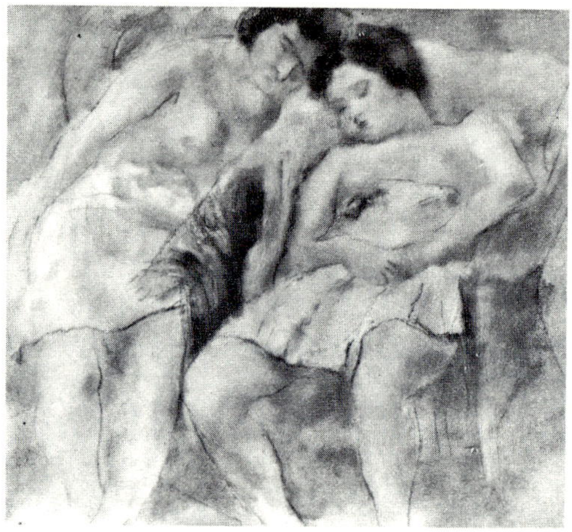

Jules Pascin
Two Women Asleep, 1929
Musée National d'Art Moderne, Paris

smiling sleep-walker, always available for parties and orgies. Nevertheless, these were the years when he accumulated canvases which seemed to swell miraculously in number. He was rarely seen to work, but when he died at the age of forty-five he left an enormous body of work which may be seen mostly at the Paris Musée de l'Art Moderne and the Grenoble Museum, to which his wife, Hermine David, and his friend, Lucy Krogh, made important gifts.

A great many experiments preceded that marvellous mastery he eventually attained. In 1907, in Berlin, he turned from caricature to complex compositions which already foreshadowed his future career. Then came France. Sure of himself though he could have been, he saw that he had still much to learn, and attended the Ranson and Grande Chaumière academies. In June 1914 he went to England with Hermine David. War broke out. In September he arrived in the United States. In 1916 and 1917 he spent a long time in Cuba doing many drawings and water-colours, then returned to the USA. He recorded his six years in the New World in innumerable sketches, not only of the Southern States, but also of New York, where he lived for a while in Brooklyn. Paul Morand tells us: "He visited Carolina, Louisiana and Havana, where the Creole languor exercised a definite influence on his work. Charleston, above all, engaged and intoxicated him, with its white, wooden, colonial-period houses buried in magnolias." Even more than the scene, however, it was the people who excited him. His water-colours of that period give the impression that America was populated entirely with coloured people, all of whom were his friends. However much entranced by his wandering life, he missed Paris, and by 1920 he was back. Still he travelled again. In 1923 he went to Perpignan, in 1924 to Tunis, and in 1927-1928 he paid another visit to the United States. Despite these absences, he was firmly anchored in Montmartre, not in the old village dear to Utrillo, but in the night-club quarter with the crooks, with whom he was not above taking a glass of wine, leaning on the counter in some Pigalle bar.

Piraeus was the nearest he ever again travelled to the East of his youth, but he loved the Mediterranean—Marseilles, of course, and Italy, Spain, Algeria and Tunisia. This was his own Orient, where the women lurked in dream-stirring shadows. After a last journey to Spain came his protracted suicide on 2 June 1930. Pascin the nomad? That is easily said. I prefer Pascin the hard worker, whose evident facility should not disguise from us how much expertise there was behind the draughtsman, engraver and painter; his parody-like compositions on the subjects of *The Prodigal Son*, *Suzanna and the Elders*, *Socrates and his Disciples mocked by the Courtesans* and *Dives and Lazarus* are works which owe nothing to fashionable trends but communicate with moments of our own awareness. Pascin's drawings and most of his engravings are rapid series of strokes, sometimes done without lifting the hand, so excellent was he at integrating the shapes of his subject in one perfect flowing line. I remember the first time I visited him. It was late in the morning, but he had not been in long. Climbing out of bed, he threw on an old overcoat which was lying about somewhere. I went into that studio which was piled with drawings, pastels and engravings. While we started to chat, he seized a large sheet of paper and began a composition, without ceasing to talk in his low, calm, slightly monotonous voice.

To tell the truth, this master, who so admirably understood the most troubled aspects of his period, hardly belonged to it at all, and this is probably why he chose to leave it so soon. He loved the night like Rétif de La Bretonne, and his strange behaviour is too reminiscent of the heroes of Hoffmann or Chamisso for one not to be tempted to identify him with the most extraordinary of them. (G. Ch.)

Poiret, Paul (1879-1944)

Famous couturier, born in Paris, who dealt

the 1900 outline a fatal blow by liberating women from the ornaments of padding and tight-lacing. Inspired by the Expressionist painters, the Ballets Russes, Les Nabis and the Fauves, he was the first to put bright colours together in appliqué and

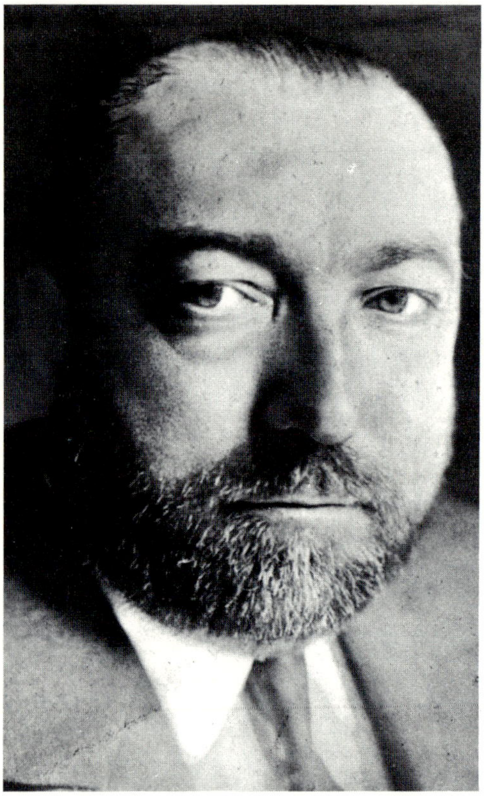

create a new style for which Iribe, Dufy and Vlaminck worked. Sophisticated and extravagant, he did not confine his activities to couture. He was in turn art patron, collector of paintings, editor, decorator and painter.

Princet, Maurice

Polytechnic student, then lawyer for the assurance company L'Abeille, friend of Picasso, Apollinaire and Braque, he was dubbed, probably inappropriately, "the mathematician of Cubism". In 1912 he wrote the introduction for Delaunay's exhibition at the Barbazanges gallery.

Maurice Ravel
Viollet Collection

R

Ravel, Maurice (1875-1937)

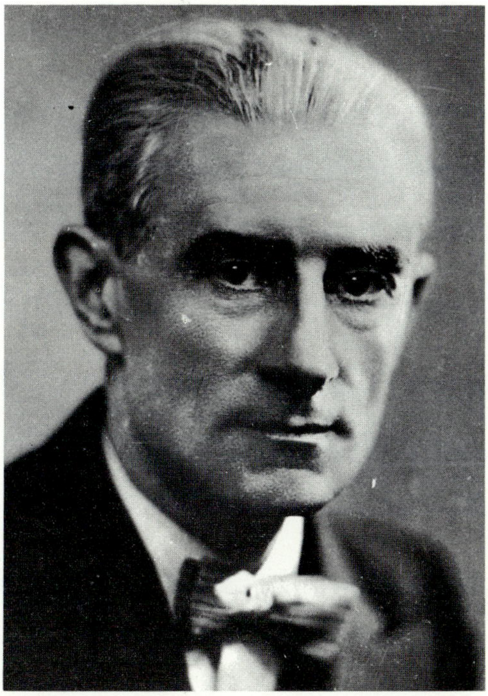

French composer, born in Ciboure, Lower Pyrenees, died in Paris. He was admitted to the Paris Conservatoire at the age of fourteen and won a second medal for piano two years later. In 1895 he produced his first work, the *Habanera*, and was twice rejected for the first Prix de Rome. He was a brilliant pupil of Gabriel Fauré, writing, between 1905 and 1908, *Miroirs*, *Histoires naturelles*, *Rhapsodie Espagnole*, *L'Heure Espagnole*, *Gaspard de la Nuit* and *Mother Goose*. His fame spreading, he composed a choreographic poem, *Daphnis and Chloë*, for Sergei Diaghilev's Ballets Russes. He was temporarily called up in 1917, and the same year composed a piano suite, *Le Tombeau de Couperin*. Then came *La Valse*, *L'Enfant et les Sortilèges*, an opera based on a libretto by Colette, and his famous *Boléro*, written in a fortnight for the dancer Ida Rubinstein. The two Piano Concertos written in 1930 completed his work. Ravel's style, with its magical enchantment, nervously delicate writing and transparent but strict melody, is without question one of the most refined of this century.

Reverdy, Pierre (1889-1960)

French poet, born in Narbonne, died in Solesmes. Although he never joined the Surrealists, he was hailed by them as the greatest living poet. He was austere, withdrawn, reticent and an early Catholic convert, his works all combining a certain descriptive realism with the most humble and restrained mysticism. He has explained it in *Gant de Crin* (1927) and *Le Livre de mon Bord* (1948). His best poems have been published in two collections, *Plupart du Temps* (1915-1922) and *Main d'Œuvre* (1913-1948). He was a friend of Max Jacob and Picasso, and dedicated a work to the latter in 1924.

Rivera, Diego (1886-1957)

Mexican painter, born in Guanajuato, died in Mexico City. His art training happened in two stages: first he studied at the Mexico School of Fine Arts, then he stayed in Paris and mixed with the painters of the Paris school and the "Bateau-Lavoir". He did not, however, adhere to either one of these teachings, the first sinning in his eyes through academism, the second by exces-

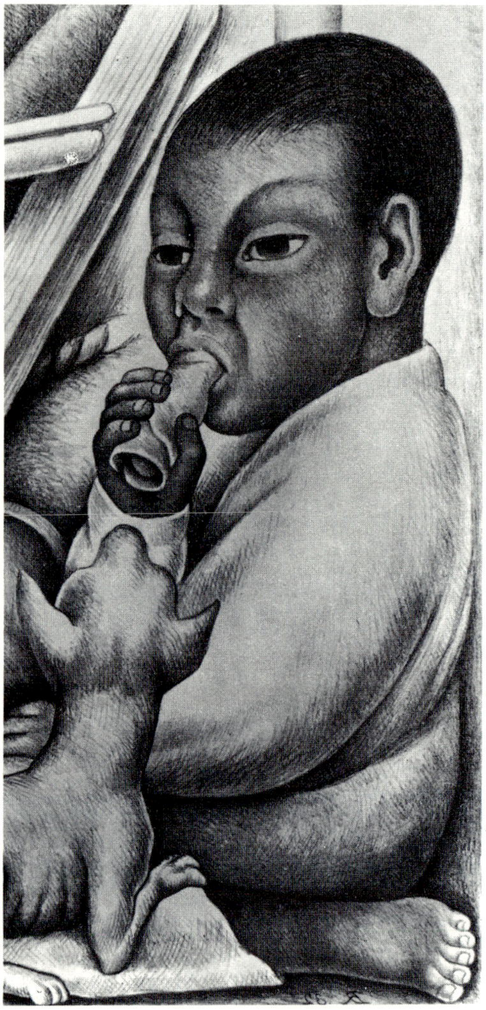

Diego Rivera
The "Taco", 1932

sive daring. On his return to Mexico he discovered his own way. Stimulated both by ancient Mayan and Aztec art and by his country's climate of revolution, he became the advocate of a national art with a folk spirit, with simplified drawing, violent colours and social or political subjects. With the aid of the responsible authorities, Diego Rivera obtained the commissions which best suited his style—frescoes for public buildings: the Bolivar amphitheatre of the University in 1922, the National School of Agriculture in Chapingo in 1927, the National Palace of Mexico from 1935 to 1944, etc. He revealed himself as one of the true founders, with Orozco, Siquieros and Tamayo, of that "heroic and monumental art after the example of the great traditions of America before the Spanish conquest" which he had dreamed of when in Paris.

Roy, Claude (b. 1915)

French essayist, novelist and poet; penetrating wit, theatre-lover, caustic and brilliant journalist of the extreme left. His writings, in their diversity, display an acute eclecticism: *Suite française*, *Lire Marivaux*, *Descriptions critiques*, *L'Homme en question*, *Anthologie de la Poésie chinoise*, and collections of poems: *L'Enfance de l'Art*, *Le Bestiaire des Amants* and *Le Poète mineur*.

Pablo Picasso
Portrait of the Poet Sabartès
Moscow Museum

S

Sabartès, Jaime (b. 1880)

Spanish painter and writer, born in Barcelona. In actual fact, he has never used his gifts on his own account, having very early bound himself in friendship to Picasso whom he knew when they were children in Barcelona. Having devoted himself to easing the material existence of the painter during his difficult early years in Paris, he became his secretary and, at the same time, his most informed, assiduous and accurate historiographer. (His publications include *Picasso, les Ménines et la Vie*, Cercle d'Art edition, and *Picasso, Portraits et Souvenirs*, Louis Carré.) His activity and important donations are responsible for the building and organisation of the Picasso Museum in Barcelona. Sabartès lives in Paris.

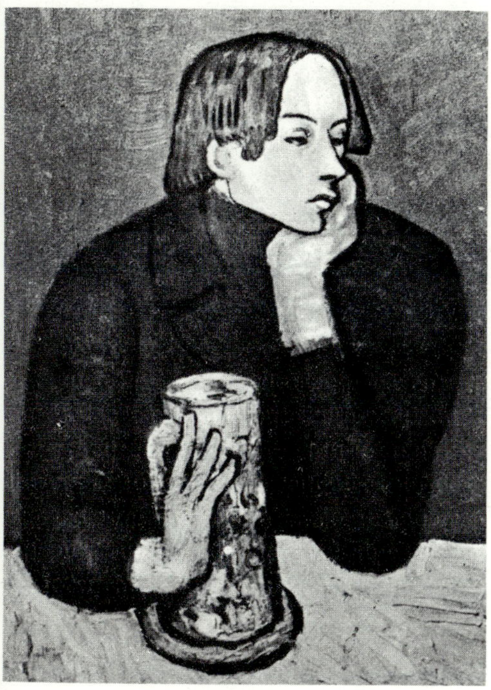

Salmon, André (1881-1969)

French poet and critic, born in Paris. Editor on *La Plume*, then on *Festin d'Esope*, a magazine run by Guillaume Apollinaire, he brought out his first book of poems in 1905, incorporating *Les Ames en peine*, *Corps sans Ame* and *Les Clefs ardentes*. He was friendly with Fauves and Cubists, the companion of Apollinaire, Mac Orlan and Max Jacob, defender of Dadaism and Surrealism, participating in all the great artistic movements of his time. In 1919, Picasso illustrated *Le Manuscrit trouvé dans un Chapeau*, and the following year Derain did *Le Calumet*. Then in 1921 came the novel *Tendres Canailles*, a picture of the anarchic society at the Buci crossroads, and *Créances*, 1926, another collection of attractively and acutely imaginative poetry. He recently published *Souvenirs sans Fin* in which he recounts his life. He died on 13 March 1969.

" Section d'Or "

The name, meaning " Golden Section ", borrowed from the treatise *Divine Proportion* written by the monk Luca Paciolo in 1509, under which the painter Jacques Villon chose to gather the adepts of Cubism, to signify their fidelity to Cézanne's teaching and their belief in geometric values and preordained ideal proportions. The idea came to him during the meetings he organised on Sunday afternoons in his studio at Puteaux. The " Section d'Or " was not a movement. The only group activity credited to them dates from October 1910 when they held an exhibition around the

Dunoyer de Segonzac
Illustration for *The Wooden Crosses* by Dorgelès
Bibliothèque Nationale, Paris

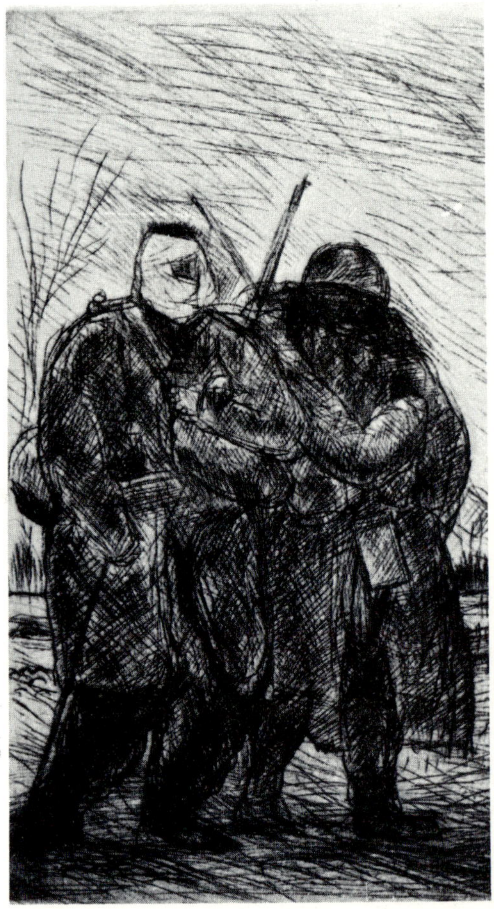

three brothers Jacques Villon, Marcel Duchamp and Raymond Duchamp-Villon, including works by Gleizes, Metzinger, Juan Gris, Léger, Lhote, La Fresnaye, Marcoussis, Dunoyer de Segonzac, Robert Delaunay, Herbin, Agero, Dumont, Jean Marchand and Luc-Albert Moreau. The only ones absent were Braque and Picasso, actually the two founders of Cubism. But Cubism was only a pretext. The affinities that brought these painters together covered interests both more general and more specific—that of Cartesian philosophy, for example, which they retained in common, though each soon went his own way. Brief though they were, the lessons of the "Section d'Or" nevertheless had the merit of inventive rivalry, and enjoyed great popularity among French and foreign collectors concerned with mathematically based creative art.

Segonzac, André Dunoyer de (b. 1884)

In the years leading up to 1914, it was difficult to foresee the direction painting was going to take. Chance turned in favour of the Cubists, not only because, thirty years later, the Abstracts appeared to take over from them, but also because the group of painters faithful to reality were literally wiped out: Jean-Louis Boussingault, André Marc, Roger de La Fresnaye and Luc-Albert Moreau all died prematurely as a result of the war. Segonzac, in the catalogue to his 1960 exhibition at the Galerie Charpentier, wrote, "From 1910 to 1914, two distinct schools were exhibiting at the same time in the different rooms at the Indépendants. One consisted of Fernand Léger, Le Fauconnier, Gleizes and Metzinger; the other room, immediately opposite, included La Fresnaye, Moreau, Marchand, Boussingault and myself. Until the war in 1914, these two parallel and neighbouring schools were maintained without hostility, each defending a different aesthetic although linked by a distant kinship." This kinship was a rejection of the academic formulas then popular.

André Dunoyer de Segonzac belonged to a family line which could be traced on one side to the original gentlemen of Le Quercy, and on the other to great bourgeois such as the Persil (caricatured by Daumier), who was keeper of the Seals under Louis-Philippe. Born at Boussy-Saint-Antoine in the Paris suburbs on 6 July 1884, Segonzac has always remained faithful to the Ile de France. He lives in Chaville, and it is the Morin valley which has inspired some of his most personal landscapes. Academic distinction at the Lycée Henri-IV did not foretell an artistic career, although he deliberately covered his exercise books with caricatures and attended the independent studio of the very official Luc-Olivier Merson. During his military service at La Flèche, he met Jean-Louis Boussingault just out of the Ecole des Arts Décoratifs, and this was a meeting as decisive as that of Vlaminck and Derain or Picasso and Braque. He soon formed a brotherly friendship with another young painter, Luc-Albert Moreau. They were both, without conviction, taking courses in Sudanese and Malagasy at the School of Oriental Languages, but they met mostly at Jean-Paul Laurens' studio, the Académie Julian and the Académie de la Palette where Desvallières and Charles Guérin had brought some of the spirit of Gustave Moreau's studio. After failing the entrance examination for the Ecole Nationale des Beaux-Arts, he rented a studio with Boussingault at 37 rue Saint-André-des-Arts. These young men thought that, beyond Impressionism (which all of that generation agreed to reject), they could link up with the tradition which went back to Gustave Courbet, and it was no mere chance that led Segonzac to acquire a masterpiece, *The Trout*, by the master from Ornans. They used a rather sombre style of great sobriety; their palette was based on earth colours and cold tones, and they determined to remain faithful to the objective observation of nature. Segonzac has never deviated from the way he embarked on then, from his 1906 study of a reclining man to his recent water-colours. No other body of work presents more unity; powerfully constructed, it refuses to make any sacrifice for effect, but its robustness is far from excluding poetry, as seen particularly in his etchings for the *Georgics*.

At the Salon des Indépendants in 1909, he exhibited a *Venus de' Medici* which can still surprise us today by the boldness of its simplified shapes and the sonorous power of its texture: "I worked on this painting for three months," he tells us, "going back all over it and working with full impasto and in depth; it was really a reaction against the Impressionist school."

One man identified with the Indépendants was the painter Paul Signac; he was one of its founders, and was elected president in 1908. He welcomed all experiment, and feeling sympathy for these young painters, leased them the country-house at Saint-Tropez he had just left to go to a newly built villa which, as an old sea-dog, he had named La Hune (The Crow's Nest). Segonzac has remained at Saint-Tropez, and the Maures landscapes hold an important place in his work. Perhaps today he regrets having pointed the way to this unknown little port for so many friends, starting with Colette, whose *La Treille muscate* he illustrated in the very surroundings where it was written. Like René Clair, he is obliged to migrate away from the summer crowds, but in winter he hastens back to paint numerous water-colours where the gulf gleams through the pines.

Like Dufy and Van Dongen, Segonzac had a society period in his life, but it has left

Dunoyer de Segonzac
Portrait of a Girl
Museum of Fine Arts, Algiers

little trace in his work: a few drawings done at the circus or the boxing-ring, his series of sketches of dancers, his illustrations for Paul Iribe's *Le Témoin* and Jacques Rouché's *La Grande Revue*, and the slim book he produced on the Ballets Russes in 1910. The society life of those pre-war years was dominated by two men, Sergey Diaghilev, who revived the art of ballet, and Paul Poiret, who made his couture house in the Faubourg Saint-Honoré one of the high spots of French art. Poiret designed the costumes for a production of *Nebuchadnezzar* mounted by Rouché at the Théâtre des Arts, and the sets were by Segonzac. It was Poiret again who paid 300 francs for his *Les Buveurs*, painted in the forest of Montmorency and exhibited at the 1910 Salon d'Automne. This is the earliest of the large compositions on show today in the room at the Musée National d'Art Moderne organised under the direction of the painter himself. But mixing in fashionable circles had no influence on his style which had never been more sober, more severe even, at least in his canvases, for at that time it could be said that it was the Parisian who drew, and the Quercy gentleman who painted. It was not until the war that these two aspects of his personality fused completely. After his mobilisation in the 353rd Infantry Regiment, he no longer drew Nijinsky, Fokine, Isadora Duncan and Ida Rubinstein, but soldiers in the trenches, soup fatigues at Bois-le-Prêtre, stretcher-bearers bringing in a wounded comrade. These are not merely documentary records, they have a lyrical lucidity; most of them are now assembled in the War Museum at Vincennes. From the trenches, Dunoyer de Segonzac passed to the camouflage section, with the rank of second-lieutenant. His *Notes from the Front*, published as an album, gave René Blum the idea of commissioning him to illustrate Roland Dorgelès' recently written *Wooden Crosses*. He hesitated. Until then his drawings, freely improvised on the subject, had been reproduced by photo-mechanical processes. Now he was being asked to engrave the etching-plates himself. He went and consulted his friend Laboureur, who taught him how to warm the sheet of copper and handle the acid; so a great engraver with very individual conceptions was born. In his preface to the exhibition of his engravings at the Biblio-

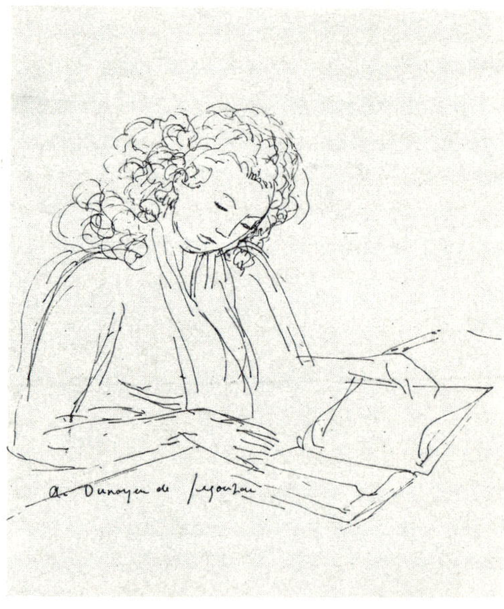

thèque Nationale he wrote: "I have always considered illustration to be a work parallel to that of the author, not a servile commentary on the text. The engraver must enter into the spirit of the book and, above all, create an atmosphere from it. In order to discover this, I have always lived

Pablo Picasso
Gertrude Stein
Metropolitan Museum, New York

the books I have illustrated." He is not only an admirable illustrator, but has also given us some evocative plates of landscapes, still-lifes, nudes, and the faces of Colette, Gide, Proust, Fargue and Henri Mondor. Vast as is his work as an engraver, it does not detract from that as a painter. Like the old Barbizon masters, with whom he has more than a little in common, he enjoys going in search of his subject. He sets out in the morning, his old car laden with canvases, palette and easel. When he has found a site he likes, he settles down and spends the happiest hours of his life in the depths of nature. For a long time he painted in the studio from sketches made on the spot. Then, as he became expert, he preferred water-colours of the subject; he treats these like oil paintings, not finishing them until after ten or twelve hours of uninterrupted work. Although Segonzac has always followed the same line, it is impossible not to notice a development in his technique and his spirit. Paradoxically, it was in his youth that he produced his dullest, most sombre works. Since, he has ceaselessly worked to gain his liberty, arriving at vividly coloured strokes which barely cover the canvas. He himself likes to point out his similarity to Cézanne, who at first used heavy impasto, while the fluidity of his later water-colours heralded the Tachists' experiments. His painting is solid in the resonant power of its texture, ambitious in the breadth of its subjects. He was twenty-five when he painted his *Drinkers*, and over the years he has embarked on large compositions which most of his contemporaries dare not attempt. His *Bathers* was a post-first world war event, with its robust and simplified shapes, and the boldly foreshortened female nude dominated by the standing man who has just come out of the water. Later, in 1936, he abandoned his gloomy colour-range when working on a similar composition, in the background of which is a *Mediterranean Beach* with its landscape of sea and mountain and the crowd of bathers. Thus, in full possession of his powers, he has tended to become more abandoned, rejecting the perhaps over-deliberate element in his youthful works. Segonzac is one of those artists who, far from suffering loss of ability with age, acquire, at the end of their lives, total mastery. (G. Ch.)

Stein, Gertrude (1874-1946)

American writer, born in Pittsburgh, Pennsylvania. A pupil of William James, she came to Europe and settled in Paris around 1900. Her private hotel at 27 rue de Fleurus

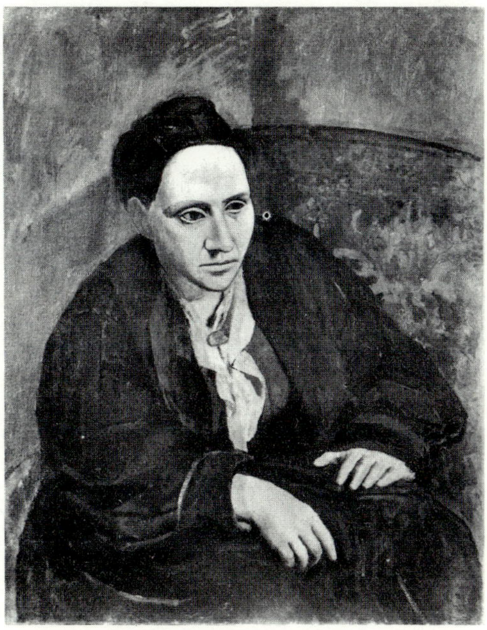

rapidly became a centre of attraction and meeting-place for French and Anglo-Saxon writers such as Sherwood Anderson and Ernest Hemingway, over whom she exercised a certain influence. She was a friend of Picasso, Braque, Gris, Matisse, Apollinaire and Marie Laurencin, and passionately defended Cubism, particularly commenting many times on the work of Juan Gris. Her *Autobiography of Alice B. Toklas*, published in 1933, recounts her memories of the painters she met—a trenchant and controversial evocation of the Cubist revolution.

Stravinsky, Igor Fedorovitch (b. 1882)

He was born in Oranienbaum, Russia. He was a pupil of Rimsky-Korsakov, but owes his musical training mainly to himself. At first he was influenced by the new French music of Ravel, Debussy, Dukas and Chabrier, but reacted violently against Impressionism and composed the boldly Expressionist *Firebird* (1910), *Petrouchka* (1911) and *The Rite of Spring* (1913) for Sergey Diaghilev's Ballets Russes; the latter work, with its dissonances and particular use of a vast orchestra, unleashed a furore. From 1914 to 1920, the composer reverted to a smaller orchestra, writing: *Renard*, " a burlesque story, sung and acted, designed for the stage "; *Les Noces*, a cantata for mixed choir and rich percussion involving no less than four pianos and thirteen percussion instruments; *The Soldier's Tale* to a text by Ramuz; and *Pulcinella*, a ballet using themes by Pergolesi, performed in Paris in 1919 with décor by Picasso. *Mavra* (1922), a comic opera, marked Stravinsky's new aesthetic orientation and his departure from his early luxuriance in favour of a more " classical " economy. In 1927 he composed a ballet, *Apollo Musagetes*, and during the next few years wrote his three most radical works: *Œdipus Rex* (1927), a Latin opera-oratorio with libretto by Jean Cocteau; *The Symphony of Psalms* (1930) for mixed choir and orchestra; and *Persephone* (1934), an opera-ballet to a text by André Gide. The same year he was naturalised French. Since 1940 he has lived in the United States and his latest works include Symphony in C (1940), *Danses Concertantes* (1941), *Scènes de Ballet*

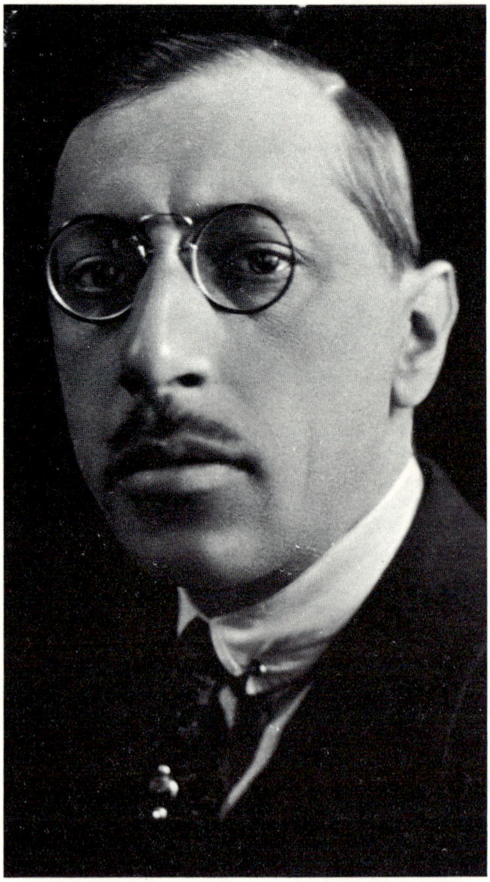

Albert Gleizes
Portrait of Stravinsky
Frigerio Collection, Paris

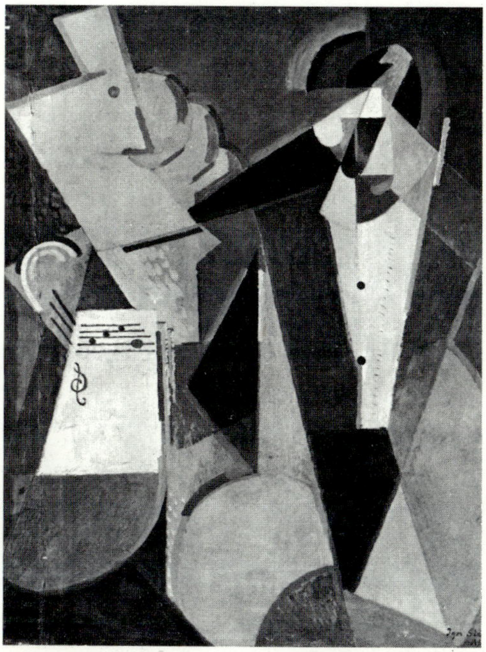

(1944), *Symphony in Three Movements* (1945), *Ebony Concerto* (1946), the ballets *Orpheus* (1948) and *Agon* (1957), a Mass (1948) and an opera *The Rake's Progress* (1951), with a libretto by W. H. Auden and Chester Kalman.

U

Utter, André (1886-1948)

French painter, born in Paris. Like many artists of his generation, he was part of the Bohemian life on the Butte Montmartre. He married the fiery Suzanne Valadon, which made him the step-father of Utrillo. He was self-taught, with a modest but quite vigorous talent; he illustrated Oscar Wilde's *Théâtre à Lire* and designed some décors for the Ballets Russes.

V

Vlaminck, Maurice de (1876-1958)

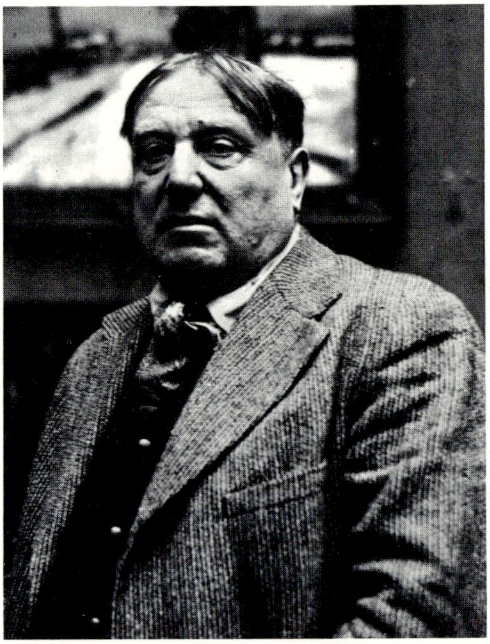

Although genius can never be reduced to logical explanation, there is nothing against searching in a man's life for the elements contributing to his personality as an artist. The ancestors of Maurice de Vlaminck—Maurice le Flamand—were Dutch mariners. His paternal grandfather, a master tailor by trade, had taught his craft to his son before leaving it to open a café in Lambrechies, near Lille. Vlaminck's father, then, was a tailor until being attracted to music. He taught piano in Paris, and there came to know a young pianist, a graduate from the Conservatoire, and their son Maurice was born on 4 April 1876, in the district of Les Halles, at 3 rue Pierre-Lescot. All his life he was torn between the domination of his father, from whom he inherited a powerful temperament and a love of liberty bordering on anarchy, and the puritan influence of his mother, a strictly orthodox Protestant. The severity of the judgments he passed on the world around him, his literary tastes, his rages against the decadence of our civilisation can only be explained by knowing that in his childhood he regularly frequented the Huguenot church of Saint-Germain-en-Laye. He was seven when his parents went to live in Le Vésinet, and he passed his whole childhood in that suburb of Paris. Already, however, he was establishing his independence, and reacted against the family background, partly by teaching himself to play the violin instead of pursuing regular studies, partly by becoming a cycling enthusiast. It was by giving violin lessons, playing in gipsy orchestras and winning bicycle races that he supported his family when he married and rapidly produced two daughters. "The four of us together," he said, "were only forty years old."

At his grandmother's he met a member of the Society of French Artists, M. Robichon, who talked painting to him, and his best biographer, Florent Fels,[1] pointed out a harness-maker in Le Vésinet, who drew strange portraits in the crude colours of his trade, and much impressed the young Vlaminck. So he tried painting, but he attached so little importance to this diversion that he always painted over the same canvas, and when he had finished a landscape he would rub it in the grass before going home. Still, he deliberately diverted his route to go along the rue Laffitte or the rue

[1] Art critic and historian (b. 1891); founder of *L'action* and *L'Art vivant.*

Le Peletier, past the windows of dealers showing Impressionists. It was there, in March 1901, that he received a decisive shock: at the Galerie Bernheim Jeune, he discovered Van Gogh. There is no doubt that in the Dutchman's energy he discovered the answer to the questions he had been asking himself when contemplating his own work. " On that day," he has said, " I loved Van Gogh more than my father." Another important event was his meeting with Derain. While Vlaminck led a fairly disorganised life, doing anything and everything to support his family, André Derain was the son of well-to-do tradesmen from Chatou, although the bourgeois life hardly satisfied him. He also was seeking some diversion in painting, and he quickly welcomed the influence of this slightly older man to whom he confided his feeling for this art. In his book, *Post-Mortem Portraits*, Vlaminck wrote: " Without this meeting the idea would never have occurred to me to make painting my profession and live by it. It is equally certain that Derain owes it to the same circumstances that he did not pursue the studies that would have led him to Centrale and made an engineer of him." The lives of both of them settled down in the 1900s. They together rented a studio on the Ile de Chatou where they painted all day long, the employment Vlaminck found as a second violin at the Théâtre du Château-d'Eau assuring his material well-being. Soon he became the painter of the melancholy suburbs, as Utrillo was the painter of old Montmartre. A little later, Ambroise Vollard put him and Derain under contract and sent them to London, but he was unable to accept this displacement; he wandered idly about until dusk, and Derain said to him, " Before you get down to painting, you're waiting for it to look like Chatou."

When Derain went off to do his military service, the two friends exchanged letters which Vlaminck published in 1956. Left alone, he continued to paint with complete spontaneity and even, apparently, with a certain spirit of fun, happily signing a landscape with the name of a very official painter sounding closely like his own: Flameng. In 1905, these years of apprenticeship came to an end. Derain was back, and side by side they exhibited at the 21st Salon d'Automne, the one the critic Vauxcelles dubbed the " *cage aux fauves* " (wild beasts' cage). Certainly Vlaminck was not the first painter of the Paris school to use pure colours " just as they came out of the tube ". Van Gogh had done it before him, so had the Neo-Impressionists, particularly Signac, who stubbornly rejected any mixing of tones. Matisse himself concentrated on parallel experiments. But Vlaminck's influence was none the less decisive in all fields. Was it not he who revealed to Picasso those Negro masks which inspired his *Demoiselles d'Avignon*? Was it not he who induced the Montmartre painters to adopt the clothing of boxers and cyclists: caps, velvet trousers and roll-necked sweaters? Like him, Derain and also Braque and Van Dongen were of Herculean stature, and when they went to visit an exhibition together, this group of stalwarts from the Butte was quite impressive. Vlaminck was the greatest of all the Fauves, the most individual, the most passionate, the most determined to overthrow all traditions. His extraordinarily daring landscapes, still-lifes and violently coloured figures are arresting for their deliberate

Maurice de Vlaminck
The Dancer from the "Rat-Mort", 1906
Private collection, Paris

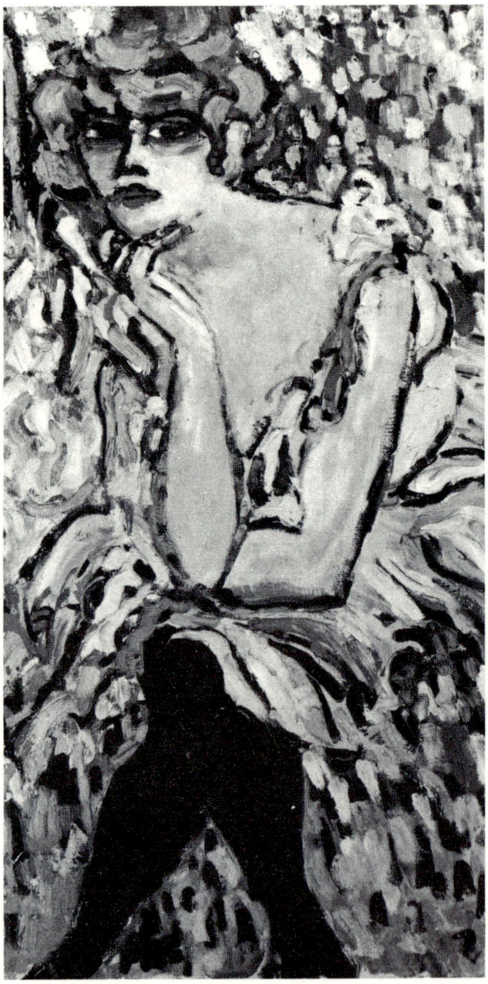

total simplification. The explosion was brief: *Apollinaire by the Seine*, *The Village* and *The Dancer at the "Rat-Mort"*, dating from 1906, are Vlaminck's last Fauve canvases.

Just as the retrospective Cézanne exhibition, following the death of the Impressionist master from Aix, influenced all the painters of that generation, and his *Puteaux Landscape* and *Still-life with Pitchers* could have been signed by Braque or Picasso, so the *Large Nude on a Divan* was a Matisse before Matisse. These years of fermentation reveal a certain confusion among the young artists who had decided to bring all the pictorial traditions into question. Vlaminck, who was the first to devote himself utterly to these experiments, was also the first to find his ultimate way. The year 1908 was critical in his development. He moved away from Cézanne and the simplifications which would have led him to Cubism; the landscape *Tugs and Sailers* shows him resolutely taking the path of expressive realism from which he never departed. The reproach that Vlaminck has inevitably incurred is that he never renewed himself. At the age of thirty he was at the height of his powers. Certainly he did not always exploit his prodigious gifts as extensively as could be wished. Landscape and still-life were the two subjects he treated almost exclusively. The *Portrait of M. Itasse*, known as *Dear Friend*, painted in 1924, was only an ironic diversion. The man himself, however, is not absent from his work: it is he who has built these houses and these roads and planted these trees; he reveals his presence in the smoke rising from the chimney, the food collected in the kitchen: the allusion is more eloquent than the real presence.

As soon as he had broken away from Paris, pointedly describing it as a modern Babylon, Vlaminck refused to paint anything else but the images he brought back from his cross-country drives: heavy snow, the road disappearing under the bonnet of the car, petrol stations set up at crossroads like red memorials, gaunt trees, skies and seas swept by the wind of romanticism. These momentarily glimpsed sights were transformed in the studio into brooding canvases as violent in their blacks and dark greens as were formerly his Fauve canvases splashed with blue, red and yellow. His still-lifes, on the other hand, were not painted from memory, but only after he had arranged on the table the side of beef, the bottles and the stone pitcher. Here this great lyricist deliberately bridled himself; he was content to observe, and asked the most humble objects, fruits and wild flowers to speak for him. The mastery recognisable in his most finished works he attained during the first world war which, although he did not leave Paris, was for him too the most moving event of his life. It led him to desert the capital, break with Derain and adopt a stubbornly pessimistic view of the world and life. He vacated his Montparnasse studio and settled in Valmondois, the country of Corot and Daumier, not far from Auvers, where Van Gogh committed suicide. But he was still too near the town, which he visited less and less often, and in 1925 he moved to the borders of La Beauce and Le Perche. There he discovered an old country house overlooking the gently rolling landscape. The immense horizon reminded him of his beloved Northern plains from where his family came. In the distance, as in Flanders, was a glorious belfry: from the bay-window of his studio, he enjoyed a wide view of the plain and could see the steeple of Verneuil-sur-Avre on the horizon. A sort of two-storey tower justified the name of La Tourillère. It was there that he died on 11 October 1958. (G. Ch.)

W

Walden, Herwarth (1878-1941)

German poet, musician, dramatist, essayist and editor, born in Berlin, assumed deceased after his emigration to Russia in 1941. His name is linked to all the movements which revolutionised German art at the beginning of this century, notably in the plastic arts (the " *Brücke* " and " *Blaue Reiter* " movements). His role as an originator and a catalyst for talents, his encyclopedic knowledge and his perspicacity were exercised mainly through the magazine *Der Sturm* between 1910 and 1928.

Weber, Max (1881-1961)

American painter, born in Bialystok, Russia, died in the United States. He was deeply influenced by his discovery of Cézanne and the Fauves when he lived in Paris between 1905 and 1908. When he returned to the United States he became the propagandist of the European *avant-garde*, notably organising the first Douanier Rousseau exhibition at the 291 Gallery in New York in 1910. His own work, influenced in turn by Expressionism, Cubism and Futurism, reveals a restless, anguished artist striving for an impossible synthesis.

Printed in Italy.

Bibliography

Apollinaire, G., *Méditations esthétiques, les Peintres cubistes*, Paris 1913.

Aragon, L., *Matisse*, Geneva 1946.

Barr, A., *Picasso*, New York 1946.

Basler, A., *Modigliani*, Paris 1931.

Berr de Turique, M., *Dufy*, Paris 1930.

Bloy, L., *L'Invendable*, Paris 1909.

Braque, G., *Le Jour et la Nuit*, Paris 1952.

Ceroni, A., *Modigliani*, Milan 1958.

Chagall, M., *Ma Vie*, Paris 1931.

Charbonnier, G., *Le Monologue du Peintre*, 2 vols., Paris 1960.

Charensol, G., *Rouault*, Paris 1925; *Utrillo*, Paris 1932.

Cocteau, J., *Modigliani*, Paris 1950.

Cogniat, R., *Dufy*, Paris, n.d.

Cooper, D., *Fernand Léger et le Nouvel Espace*, Geneva 1949.

Courrières Edition: *Van Dongen*, Paris 1925.

Courthion, P., *Matisse*, Paris 1934.

Courthion, P., *Dufy*, Geneva 1951.

Descargues, P., *Fernand Léger*, Paris 1955.

Diehl, G., *Henri Matisse*, Paris 1954.

Dorival, B., *Les Etapes de la Peinture française contemporaine*, 3 vols., Paris 1943, 1944, 1946.

Dorival, B., *Rouault*, Paris 1956.

Dethuit, G., *Nicolas de Staël*, Paris 1950.

Escholier, R., *Matisse*, Paris 1937.

Escholier, R., *Matisse, ce Vivant*, Paris 1956.

Fierens, P., *Van Dongen*, Paris 1927.

Francastel, P., *Art et Société*, Lyons 1951.

Garaudy, R., *Fernand Léger*, Paris 1965.

George, W., *Fernand Léger*, Paris 1929.

Gleizes, A., and Metzinger, J., *Du Cubisme*, Paris 1912.

Gundertaël, R. V., *De Staël*, Paris 1950.

Huyghe, R., *Les Contemporains*, Paris 1939.

Kahnweiler, D. H., *Derain*, Leipzig 1920.

Lassaigne, J., *Jacques Villon*, Paris 1950.

Lassaigne, J., *Dufy*, Geneva 1954.

Lassaigne, J., *Matisse*, Geneva 1959.

Lecuire, P., *Voir Nicolas de Staël*, Paris 1953.

Léger, F., *Fonctions de la Peinture*, Paris 1965.

Leymarie, J., *Derain ou le Retour à l'Ontologie*, Geneva 1948.

Lhote, A., *Ecrits sur la Peinture*, Paris-Brussels 1946.

"The Masters", series edited by Georges Besson: Monographs on *Braque*, *Gromaire*, *Matisse*, *Utrillo*, *Rouault*.

Michel, M. G., *Les Montparnos*, Paris 1929.

Nacenta, R., *L'Ecole de Paris*, Paris 1960.

Papazoff, G., *Derain mon Copain*, Paris 1960.

Paulhan, J., *Braque le Patron*, Geneva 1946.

Penrose, R., *Picasso, his Life and Work*, London 1958.

Raynal, M., *Georges Braque*, Valori Plastici 1921.

Raynal, M., *Picasso*, Paris 1922.

Raynal, M., *Anthologie de la Peinture en France de 1906 à nos Jours*, Paris 1927.

Reverdy, P., *Picasso*, Paris 1924.

Roy, C., *L'Amour de la Peinture*, Paris 1956.

Roy, C., *Modigliani*, Paris 1958.

Sabartès, J., and Boeck, W., *Pablo Picasso*, Paris 1955.

Salmon, A., *Modigliani, sa Vie, son Œuvre*, Paris 1926.

Salmon, A., *Derain*, Paris 1929.

Salmon, A., *La Vie passionnée de Modigliani*, Paris 1957.

Stein, G., *The Autobiography of Alice B. Toklas*, New York 1933.

Tallendier, Y., *Naissance de la Peinture contemporaine*, Paris 1963.

Tudal, A., *De Staël*, Paris 1958.

Vallentin, A., *Picasso*, Paris 1957.

Venturi, L., *How to look at a Picture from Giotto to Chagall*, New York 1945.

Zervos, C., *Histoire de l'Art contemporain*, Paris 1938.

List of Illustrations

Page

Henri Matisse
Cateau-Cambrésis (North) 1869-Nice 1951
The Rumanian Blouse, 1940
Musée National d'Art Moderne, Paris 3

Fernand Léger
Argentan (Orne) 1881–Gif-sur-Yvette 1955
Tree against a Red Background, 1954
Sonia Henie Collection, Oslo 6

Georges Braque
Argenteuil 1882-Paris 1963
The Chair, 1948
Musée National d'Art Moderne, Paris 10

Henri Matisse
Luxe, Calme et Volupté, 1904
Private collection, Paris 12

Henri Matisse
Interior with Aubergines
Grenoble Museum 13

Henri Matisse
Woman Reading against a Black Background, 1939
Musée National d'Art Moderne, Paris 14

Henri Matisse
Odalisque with Blue Armchair, 1925
Bayeler Gallery, Basle 14

Henri Matisse
Corn Poppies, 1953
Matisse Family 15

Georges Rouault
Paris 1871-1958
Clown, 1904
Bayeler Gallery, Basle 17

Georges Rouault
At the Mirror, 1906
Musée National d'Art Moderne, Paris 18

Georges Rouault
The Holy Face, 1933
Musée National d'Art Moderne, Paris 21

Georges Rouault
Pierrot
Sonia Henie Collection, Oslo 22

Georges Rouault
Biblical Landscape, 1956
Bayeler Gallery, Basle 22

Jacques Villon
Damville (Eure) 1875-Paris 1963
The Cedar, 1948
Sonia Henie Collection, Oslo 23

Jacques Villon
Portrait of the Engraver J.-P. Dubray, 1933
Musée Fabre, Montpellier 25

Page

Jacques Villon
Equestrienne, 1951
Musée des Beaux-Arts, Lyons 26

Jacques Villon
Athenian Women, 1955
Sonia Henie Collection, Oslo 27

Jacques Villon
The Little Town, 1944
Sonia Henie Collection, Oslo 27

Kees Van Dongen
Delfshaven 1877-Monte Carlo 1968
Moroccan Women at Cap Spartel, 1910
In the artist's possession 28

Kees Van Dongen
The Amazon, c. 1922
Private collection, Paris 33

Kees Van Dongen
Fernande, 1903
In the artist's possession 34

Kees Van Dongen
Back View of Seated Woman, 1905
In the artist's possession 34

Kees Van Dongen
Nude with Garter, 1910
In the artist's possession 35

Raoul Dufy
Le Havre 1877-Forcalquier (Lower Alps) 1953
Riders under the Trees, 1931
First version of the portrait of J. B. Auguste
Kessler and his family on horseback
Musée National d'Art Moderne, Paris 36

Raoul Dufy
Indian Woman, 1928
Galerie Louis Carré, Paris 36

Raoul Dufy
Concert in Orange, 1948
Louis Carré Collection, Paris 37

Raoul Dufy
Studio with Two Models, 1930
Mabille Collection, Brussels 37

Raoul Dufy
The Casino at Nice, 1928
Bayeler Gallery, Basle 38-39

André Derain
Chatou 1880-Garches 1954
Woman in a Shawl, 1908
Private collection, Paris 40

Page

André Derain
Mountain Landscape, 1908
Fernande Graindorge Collection 43

André Derain
L'Estaque, 1905
Private collection, Paris 44-45

André Derain
Villeneuve-Loubet (Fauve period), 1905
Pierre Lévy Collection, Paris 46

André Derain
Still-life with Young Woman
Georges Daelmans Collection, Brussels 46

Fernand Léger
The Tug-Boat, 1920
Municipal Museum, Grenoble 49

Fernand Léger
Three Musicians
Munich Museum 50

Fernand Léger
Still-life with Three Fruits, 1954
Sonia Henie Collection, Oslo 51

Fernand Léger
Dancers with Birds, 1953
Sonia Henie Collection, Oslo 52

Fernand Léger
The Leisures (Homage to Louis David), 1948-1949
Musée National d'Art Moderne, Paris 53

Pablo Picasso
Málaga 1881
Three Dutch Women, 1905
Musée National d'Art Moderne, Paris 55

Pablo Picasso
Head and Shoulders of a Woman, 1907
National Gallery, Prague 56

Pablo Picasso
Newspaper, Glass and Packet of Cigarettes
Private collection, Paris 57

Pablo Picasso
Women on the Banks of the Seine, 1950
Kunstmuseum, Basle 58

Pablo Picasso
Spring
Private collection, Paris 58

Georges Braque
The Port of Estaque, 1906
Musée National d'Art Moderne, Paris 61

Page

Georges Braque
Still-life, 1932
Musée National d'Art Moderne, Paris 61

Georges Braque
The Round Table
Musée National d'Art Moderne, Paris 61

Georges Braque
The Carafe, 1941
Musée National d'Art Moderne, Paris 62

Georges Braque
The Weeding Machine, 1961-1963
Louvre, Paris 62

Maurice Utrillo
Montmartre 1883-Le Vésinet 1955
The Artist's House in the Country, 1933
Musée Fabre, Montpellier 64

Maurice Utrillo
Rue Saint-Vincent, Montmartre, 1930
Private collection, Geneva 65

Maurice Utrillo
Sacré-Cœur, 1948
Museum of Art and History, Geneva 67

Maurice Utrillo
Rue des Poissonniers, 1930
Private collection, Paris 68

Maurice Utrillo
Le Moulin de la Galette, 1913-1915
Private collection, Villeret 69

Amedeo Modigliani
Leghorn 1884-Paris 1920
Madame Zborowska with Clasped Hands, c. 1917
Private collection, Roubaix 71

Amedeo Modigliani
Man from Nice, 1919
Masurel Collection, Paris 71

Amedeo Modigliani
Landscape
Mme Netter's collection, Paris 71

Amedeo Modigliani
Little Girl in Blue
Mme Netter's collection, Paris 71

Amedeo Modigliani
Seated Nude
National Museum, Antwerp 72

Marc Chagall
The Married Couple with the Eiffel Tower, 1928
Private collection, Paris 74

Page

Marc Chagall
The Feast of Tabernacles, 1907-1918
Dr h.c. J. B. Belmont, Binningen 74

Marc Chagall
Obsession, 1943
In the artist's possession 75

Marc Chagall
Double Portrait with a Glass of Wine, 1917
Musée National d'Art Moderne, Paris 76

Marc Chagall
War, 1943
Musée National d'Art Moderne, Paris 79

Marcel Gromaire
Noyelles-sur-Sambre (North) 1892
The Lines of the Hand, 1935
Musée National d'Art Moderne, Paris 80

Marcel Gromaire
The Reaper, 1924
Girardin Collection, Paris 83

Marcel Gromaire
The Card Party, 1928
Pierre Lévy Collection, Troyes 83

Marcel Gromaire
Woman with Red Hair
Musée National d'Art Moderne, Paris 84

Marcel Gromaire
Houses near a Lake, 1951
Jacques L'Huillier Collection, Geneva 85

Chaim Soutine
Smilovitch 1894-Paris 1943
Pageboy, *c.* 1927
Musée National d'Art Moderne, Paris 87

Chaim Soutine
Portrait of a Woman
Bayeler Gallery, Basle 87

Chaim Soutine
The Pastrycook, 1922
Private collection, Paris 88

Chaim Soutine
The Red Flight of Steps at Cagnes
G. Waechter Collection, Geneva 91

Chaim Soutine
Leaning Tree, 1922
Private collection, Paris 91

Nicolas de Staël
St Petersburg 1914-Antibes 1955
Portrait of Jeannine
Private collection, Seure 92

Page

Nicolas de Staël
The Musicians (Souvenir of Sidney Bechet)
Private collection, Paris 92

Nicolas de Staël
The Bottles
M. Buichard Collection, Berne 93

Nicolas de Staël
Low Tide, 1954
Bayeler Gallery, Basle 94

Nicolas de Staël
Agrigento, 1953
Sonia Henie Collection, Oslo 94

Dictionary

Jean Metzinger
Guillaume Apollinaire 148

Léon Bakst
Nijinsky in "La Péri"
Bibliothèque de l'Arsenal, Paris 150

Emile Bernard
Three Breton Women
Maurice Denis Collection,
Saint-Germain-en-Laye 152

Léon Bloy
Viollet Collection 152

Constantin Brancusi
The Seal
Musée National d'Art Moderne, Paris 153

Bernard Buffet
Nude Study of Seated Man
Droudan-David Collection, Paris 154

Boni de Castellane
at the time of his marriage to Anna Gould 155

Jean Cocteau 156

Juan Gris
Guitar and Compote-dish, 1927 156

Robert Delaunay
The Joy of Life, 1931
Private collection, Paris 158

Jean-Gabriel Domergue
Portrait of a Woman
Private collection, Paris 160

	Page
Jacques Duchamp-Villon *Seated Woman* (bronze), 1914 Galerie Louis Carré, Paris	161
Charles Dufresne *Self-portrait* Museum of Fine Arts, Algiers	162
Charles Dufresne *Woman in an Armchair* Demaeght Municipal Museum, Oran	163
James Ensor *Portrait of the Artist*, 1885 J. Boogaerts Collection, Brussels	164
Maurice Estève *The Espalier*, 1949 Private collection, Paris	165
Chaim Soutine *The Madwoman*, 1920 Rokubin-Hayoshi Collection, Tokyo	166
Henri Matisse *Still-life with Fish*, 1911 Pushkin Museum, Moscow	167
Kees Van Dongen *Portrait of Anatole France* Roudinesco Collection, Paris	167
Othon Friesz *Still-life*, 1941 R. Loyer Collection, Algiers	168
Giacometti	169
Gogol Viollet Collection	170
Francis Grüber *Job* Private collection	171
Francis Grüber *Art and Science* Musée d'Art et d'Industrie, Saint-Etienne	172
Amedeo Modigliani *Paul Guillaume* Viollet Collection	173
Max Jacob *Portrait* inscribed to René de Berval	174
Alfred Jarry Beginning of *Ubu Roi*	174
Roger de La Fresnaye *Nudes in a Landscape* Musée National d'Art Moderne, Paris	177

	Page
Roger de La Fresnaye *Portrait of Guynemer* Musée National d'Art Moderne, Paris	178
Montmartre The "Lapin-Agile" in 1900	179
Le Corbusier *Still-life*, 1922 Musée National d'Art Moderne, Paris	180
Aristide Maillol *Young Woman's Head Seen in Profile* Perpignan Museum	181
Gustave Moreau *Orpheus and the Muse*	183
Foujita *The Comtesse de Noailles*	184
Jules Pascin *Two Women Asleep*, 1929 Musée National d'Art Moderne, Paris	186
Poiret, the great couturier	188
Maurice Ravel Viollet Collection	189
Diego Rivera *The "Taco"*, 1932	190
Pablo Picasso *Portrait of the Poet Sabartès* Moscow Museum	191
Dunoyer de Segonzac Illustration for *The Wooden Crosses* by Dorgelès Bibliothèque Nationale, Paris	192
Dunoyer de Segonzac *Portrait of a Girl* Museum of Fine Arts, Algiers	194
Pablo Picasso *Gertrude Stein* Metropolitan Museum, New York	195
Stravinsky	196
Albert Gleizes *Portrait of Stravinsky* Frigerio Collection, Paris	197
Maurice de Vlaminck	198
Maurice de Vlaminck *The Dancer from the "Rat-Mort"*, 1906 Private collection, Paris	200

This volume in the series
History of Art was printed in offset
by Grafiche Editoriali Ambrosiane, Milano.

The text was composed in Times 10-point type;
the first and third parts were printed
on machine-coated paper and the second part on
blue cartridge paper.

The cover and lay-out of the inside pages
were designed by Jean-Marie Clerc.

Printed in Italy 13 045 20